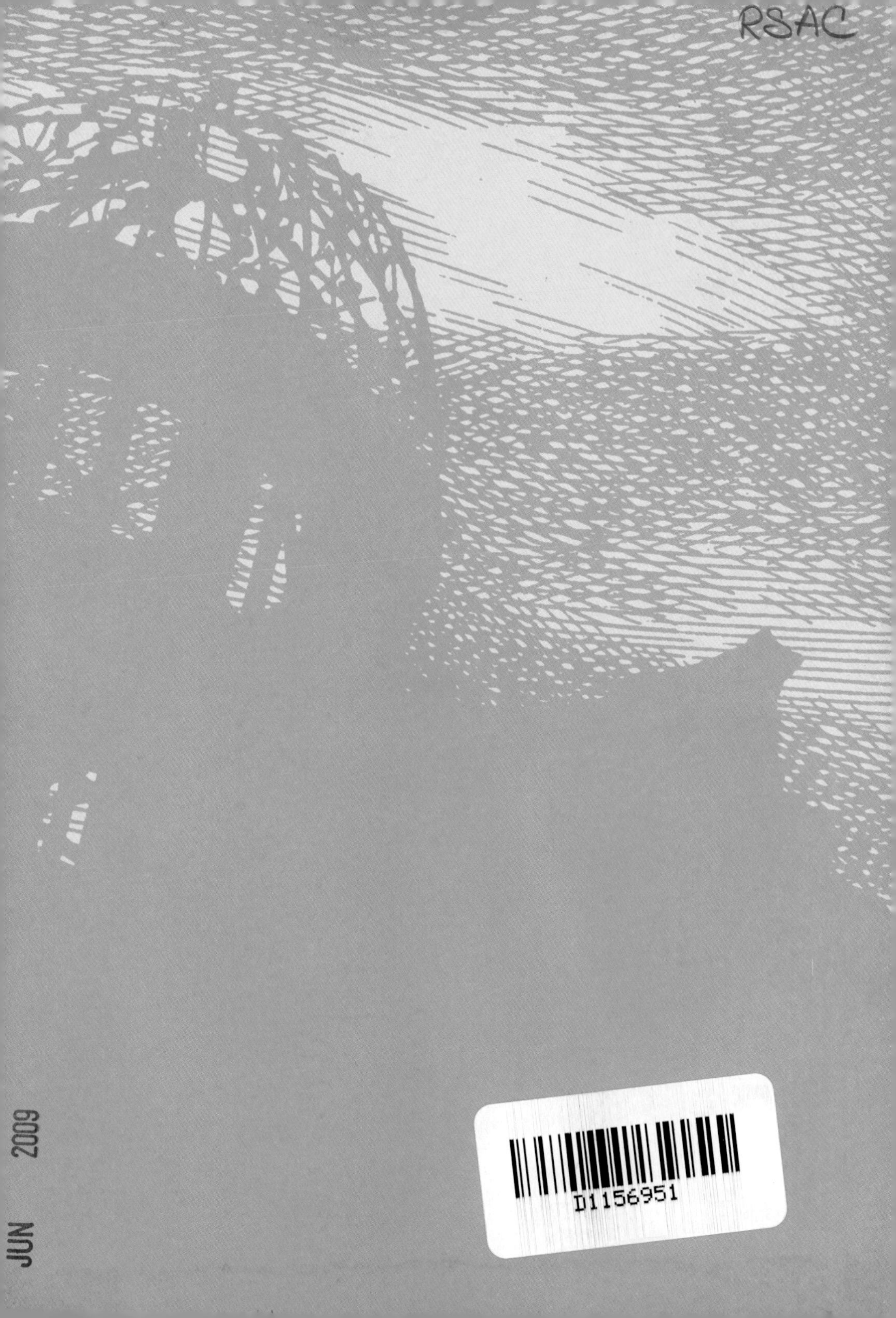

辰巳ヨシヒロ

ALSO BY YOSHIHIRO TATSUMI
The Push Man and Other Stories
Abandon the Old in Tokyo

All stories and art copyright © 1971, 1972, 2008 by Yoshihiro Tatsumi.
Introduction copyright © 2008 by Frederik L. Schodt.
This edition copyright © 2008 by Drawn & Quarterly. All rights reserved. No part of this book (except small portions for review purposes) may be reproduced in any form without written permission from the publisher.

Edited, designed, and lettered by Adrian Tomine.
Translated by Yuji Oniki.
Special thanks to Mitsuhiro Asakawa, John Kuramoto, Beatrice Marechal, Taro Nettleton, and Frederik L. Schodt.

Drawn & Quarterly
Post Office Box 48056
Montreal, Quebec
Canada H2V 4S8
www.drawnandquarterly.com

First hardcover edition: May 2008.
Printed in Singapore.
10 9 8 7 6 5 4 3 2 1

Library and Archives Canada Cataloguing in Publication
Tatsumi, Yoshihiro, 1935-
          Good-bye / Yoshihiro Tatsumi; editor: Adrian Tomine;
translator: Yuji Oniki.
ISBN 978-1-897299-37-1
          I. City and town life--Japan--Comic books, strips, etc.
I. Tomine, Adrian, 1974- II. Oniki, Yuji III. Title.
PN6790.J33T38 2008   741.5'952   C2007-907555-X

Distributed in the USA and abroad by:
Farrar, Straus and Giroux
19 Union Square West
New York, NY 10003
Orders: 888.330.8477

Distributed in Canada by:
Raincoast Books
9050 Shaughnessy Street
Vancouver, BC V6P 6E5
Orders: 800.663.5714

GOOD-BYE

INTRODUCTION

I have to confess. When I first agreed to write this introduction, I didn't know as much as I should have about Yoshihiro Tatsumi.

There is a reason for this, and it is important to be honest about it. I'm influenced by the current, highly commercialized world of *manga* in Japan, and it is cruel to many veteran artists. In truth, save for some connoisseurs, few *manga* readers in Japan today have probably heard of Tatsumi; as of New Year's Day, 2008, while there was an entry for Tatsumi on the English-language Wikipedia website, on the Japanese Wikipedia there was still none. To read Tatsumi's older work today is therefore to be reminded of how relentlessly obsessed readers are with something "new," how styles and pacing have changed, and how the whole world of male *manga* has been transformed by *shojo* and women's *manga*, a genre that barely existed when Tatsumi began drawing.

Yasukuni Shrine, Tokyo

Many Japanese people today probably find Tatsumi's work, with its focus on the underbelly of Japanese society, to be overly *kurai*, or "dark" and "pessimistic." And yet, if they would read his work carefully, they would find something often lacking in today's slick stories, something they need to know about. Tatsumi was a pioneer in the development of the *manga* medium (and especially *gekiga*) and he should be read for that reason

alone. But he is also a master of the short story format, in an era when long–form, serious *manga* are dominant. And he has a rare gift, shared by legendary *manga* artists such as Osamu Tezuka and Yoshiharu Tsuge, among others: he is absolutely original, and he is absolutely fearless in his willingness to examine what it means to be human.

The stories in this third volume of Tatsumi's work are collected from short pieces executed at the beginning of the 1970s. Not all the stories are set in that period, however, as the title work, "Good–Bye," presumably takes place during the U.S. occupation of Japan (1945—1952), when black markets still flourished and many women (derisively called "pan-pan") were forced to depend on American G.I.s. But all of the stories do share a loose timeframe, of what Japanese people might call the *sengo*, or "postwar" era, when Japan was still struggling to find a new way after the defeat of World War II. It had not yet become the prosperous manufacturing and technological giant (and provider of *manga*, *anime*, and "j–pop") that we know today.

To me, many of the physical settings are very real, and very nostalgic. I first went to Japan in 1965, and lived in Tokyo off and on during the period in which many of the stories are set. By

Hiroshima Peace Memorial (also known as the Atomic Bomb Dome), Hiroshima

then, one would never have guessed that Tokyo had been largely razed to the ground in the fire-bombing of World War II, for the city was in the midst of a building boom. The entire nation had entered a period of double-digit economic growth, and yet, compared to today, there was still a cheap, impoverished, and (especially in the winter) gloomy look to much of the city. Most houses were still made of wood and plaster, and often a bit shoddy. If I may generalize, the working class, in particular, was even more over-worked and socially exploited than it is today, and the media glorified submersion of the self in the group for the

Eisaku Sato, Prime Minister of Japan, 1964—1972

sake of a higher GNP, or gross national product. For many students, workers, and low-income families in Japan's cities of this era, the walls of apartments were thin, toilets were shared (and non-flush), and bathing was done only at the *sento*, or public baths. Tatsumi has got this mood down, even to the creaking sounds of the wooden stairways and sliding *fusuma* doors.

Even the music was different then. Today in Japan's cities, if there is an urban backbeat, it's likely to be rock or rap or techno-pop, with ads relentlessly encouraging everyone to smile. Then, nearly every bar and noodle shop played Japanese ballads written with three minor chords, almost always with a saxophone accompaniment. Few adults read *manga*. University campuses—and city streets, too—were often convulsed with riots, as baby boomers rejected the values of their parents and—taking quite literally the pacifist ideology bequeathed them by the United States at the end of World War II—opposed their government's

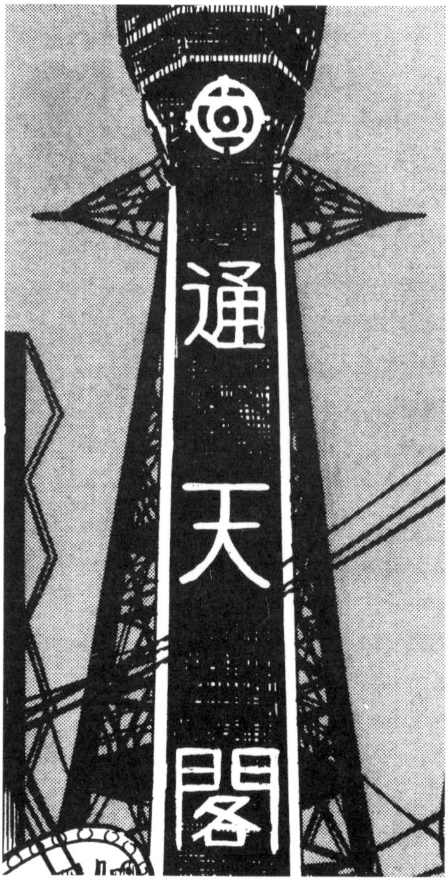
通天閣

Tsutenkaku Tower, Osaka

acquiescence and complicity in the U.S. invasion of Vietnam. It was a time when everything was open to question, and it was also a time—far more so than today—when many artists were inclined to take a serious look at society's problems.

For non-Japanese readers (and even many Japanese), the world Tatsumi depicts may seem quite alien. The social contracts that bind characters together are different. Even the visual symbols may be unfamiliar. Mushrooms are a stock *manga* symbol with erotic overtones. The Atomic Bomb Dome and the Memorial Cenotaph in Hiroshima evoke powerful historical memories in Japanese readers, as (to a far lesser extent) do references to Eisaku Sato, the prime minister from 1964—1972. Similarly, the Tsutenkaku Tower in the Shinsekai zone of Osaka immediately conjures up a mood of poverty, petty crime, and homelessness. But even non-Japanese readers may recognize the references to Tokyo's Yasukuni Shrine, where many of Japan's war dead are interred, for the same shrine is now the focus of complaints from China and Korea, where it is feared that Yasukuni also enshrines old-style nationalism and militarism.

And no matter what nationality, most readers will probably be able to relate to the emotions Tatsumi depicts. We may not like them, for some of them are ugly, and some of them are straight out of the collective human id. But we will probably recognize them, and we can probably learn from them. The collective nature of these emotions is also amplified by a limited set of character designs, for when similar faces appear on different characters over and over again, we soon realize that Tatsumi is not depicting specific individuals so much as an existential Everyman or Everywoman.

With Drawn and Quarterly's publication of this third volume of Yoshihiro Tatsumi's work, masterfully translated by Yuji Oniki, more and more English-language readers will be better able to appreciate Tatsumi's remarkable talents. I know I have. And I hope that more *manga* readers in Japan will, too.

FREDERIK L. SCHODT
San Francisco, California
January 2008

FREDERIK L. SCHODT has written extensively on the subject of Japanese cartooning. His books include *Manga! Manga! The World of Japanese Comics*, *Dreamland Japan*, and *The Astro Boy Essays*. As a translator, he has worked on English-language editions of titles such as *Barefoot Gen*, *Astro Boy*, *Phoenix*, *Ghost in the Shell*, and *The Four Immigrants Manga*.

YOSHIHIRO TATSUMI

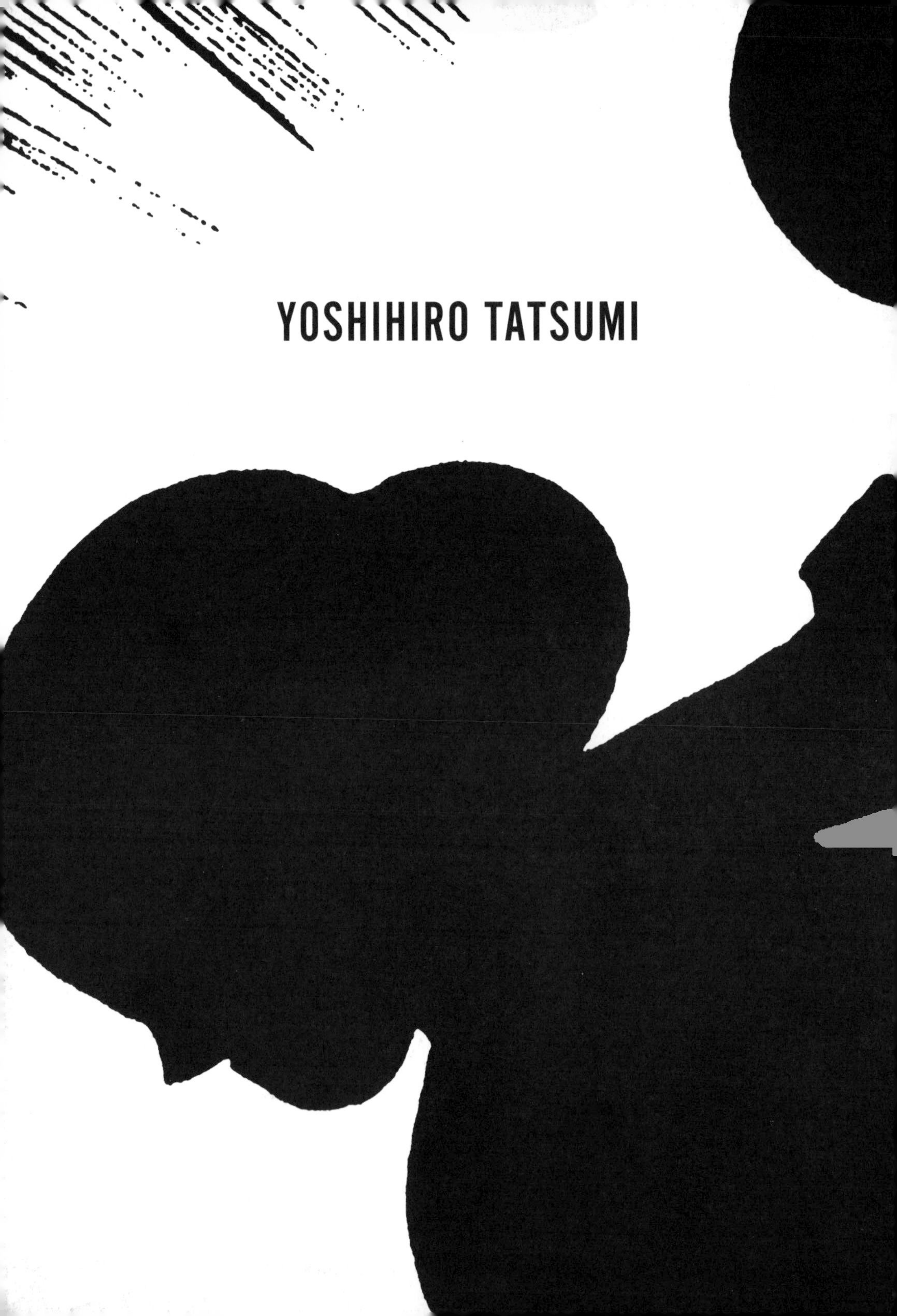

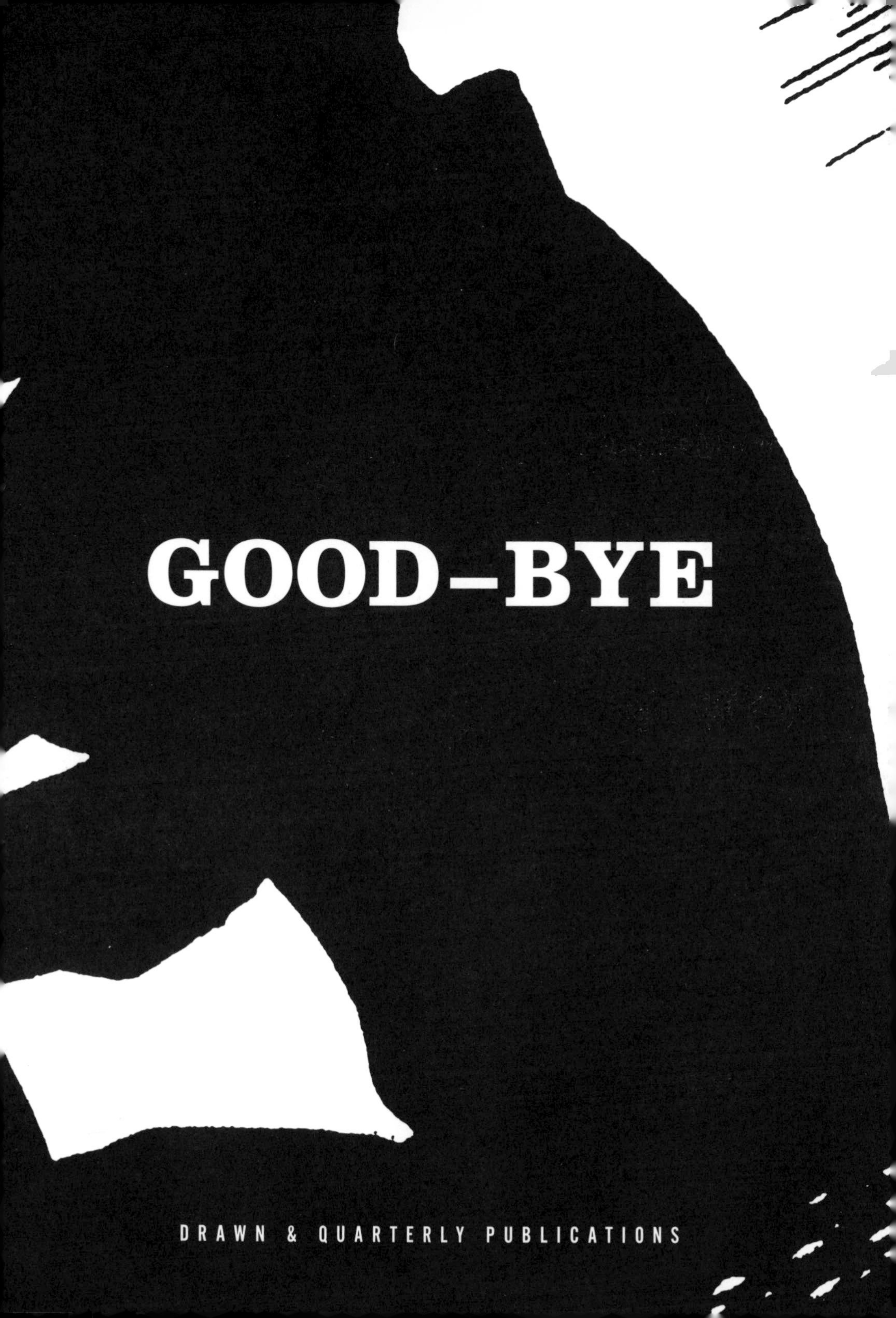

GOOD-BYE

DRAWN & QUARTERLY PUBLICATIONS

741.5 T1881g 2008
Tatsumi, Yoshihiro, 1935–
Good-bye

CONTENTS

Hell 13

Just a Man 43

Sky Burial 65

Rash 87

Woman in the Mirror 111

Night Falls Again 135

Life is So Sad 153

Click Click Click 167

Good–Bye 189

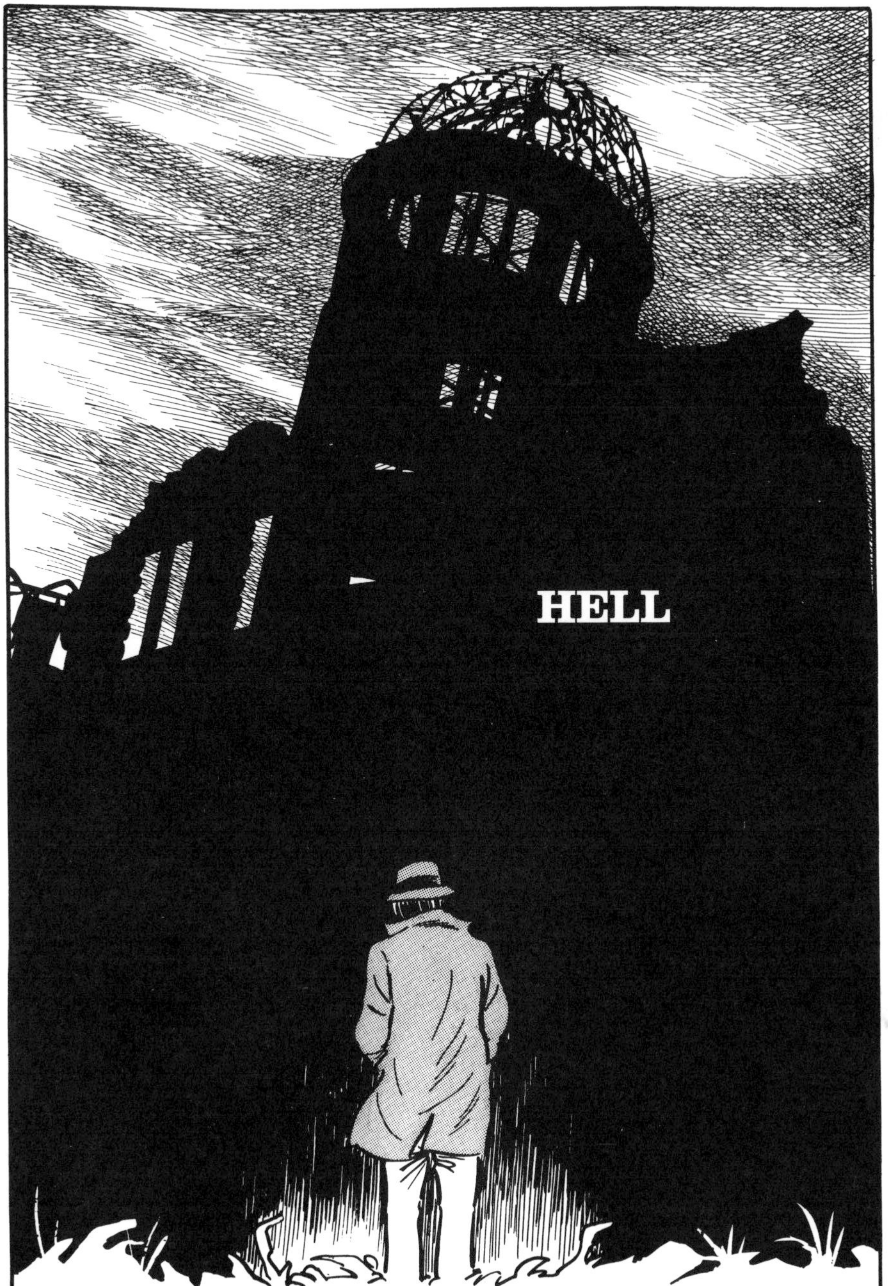
HELL

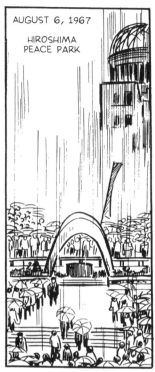

AUGUST 6, 1967

HIROSHIMA PEACE PARK

YOU DON'T DESERVE TO BE HERE, PRIME MINISTER SATO!

LET GO OF ME!

14

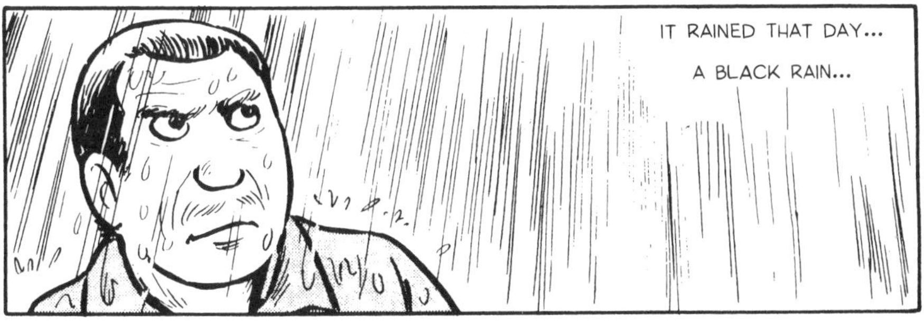
IT RAINED THAT DAY...
A BLACK RAIN...
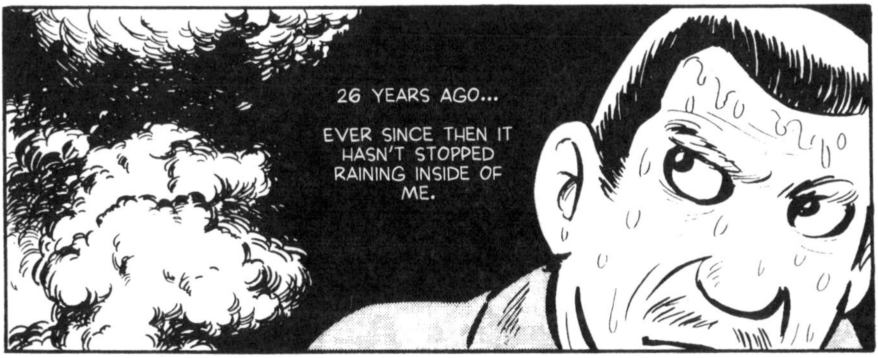
26 YEARS AGO...
EVER SINCE THEN IT HASN'T STOPPED RAINING INSIDE OF ME.
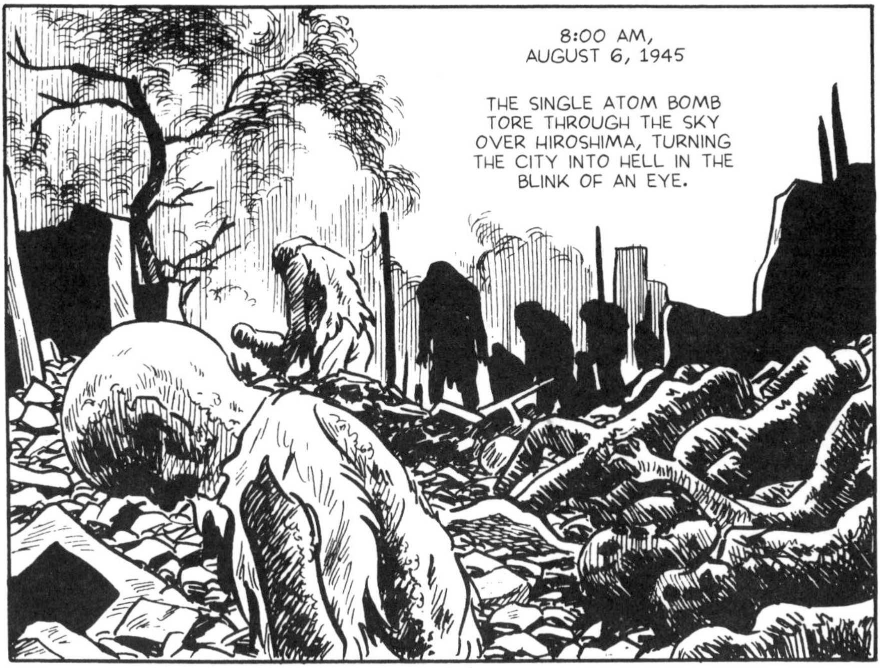
8:00 AM, AUGUST 6, 1945
THE SINGLE ATOM BOMB TORE THROUGH THE SKY OVER HIROSHIMA, TURNING THE CITY INTO HELL IN THE BLINK OF AN EYE.

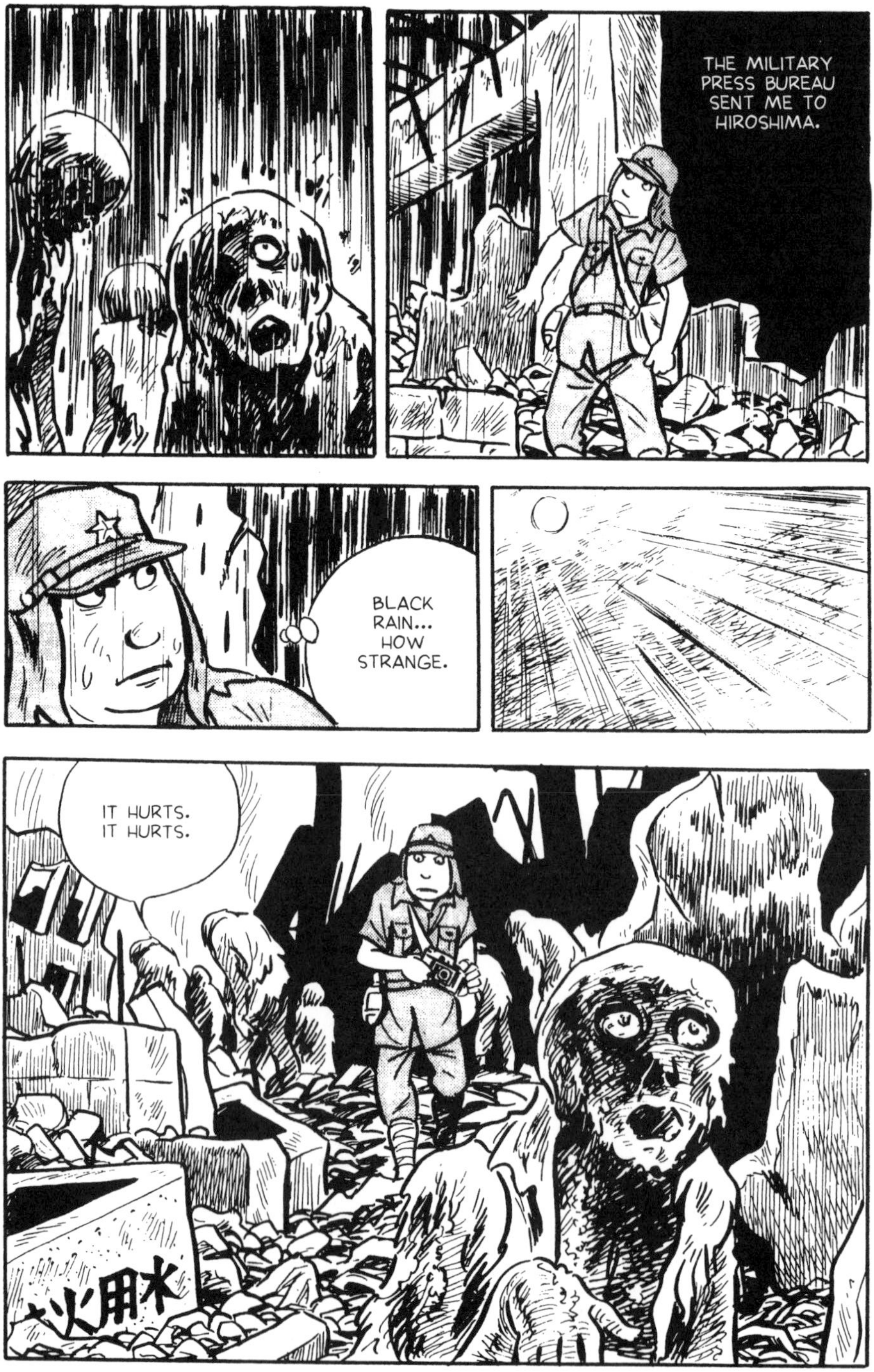
THE MILITARY PRESS BUREAU SENT ME TO HIROSHIMA.
BLACK RAIN... HOW STRANGE.
IT HURTS. IT HURTS.

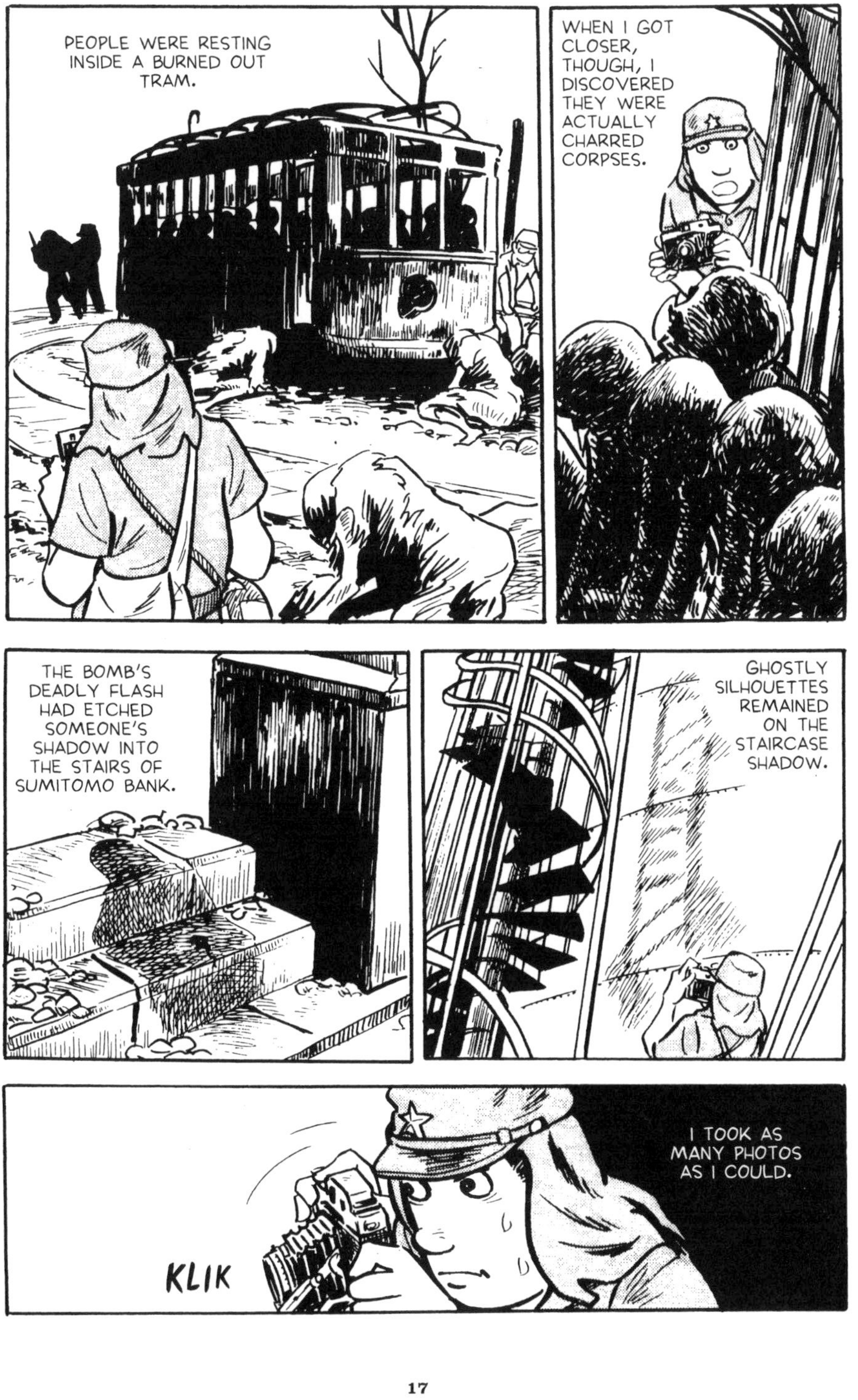
PEOPLE WERE RESTING INSIDE A BURNED OUT TRAM.
WHEN I GOT CLOSER, THOUGH, I DISCOVERED THEY WERE ACTUALLY CHARRED CORPSES.
THE BOMB'S DEADLY FLASH HAD ETCHED SOMEONE'S SHADOW INTO THE STAIRS OF SUMITOMO BANK.
GHOSTLY SILHOUETTES REMAINED ON THE STAIRCASE SHADOW.
I TOOK AS MANY PHOTOS AS I COULD.
KLIK

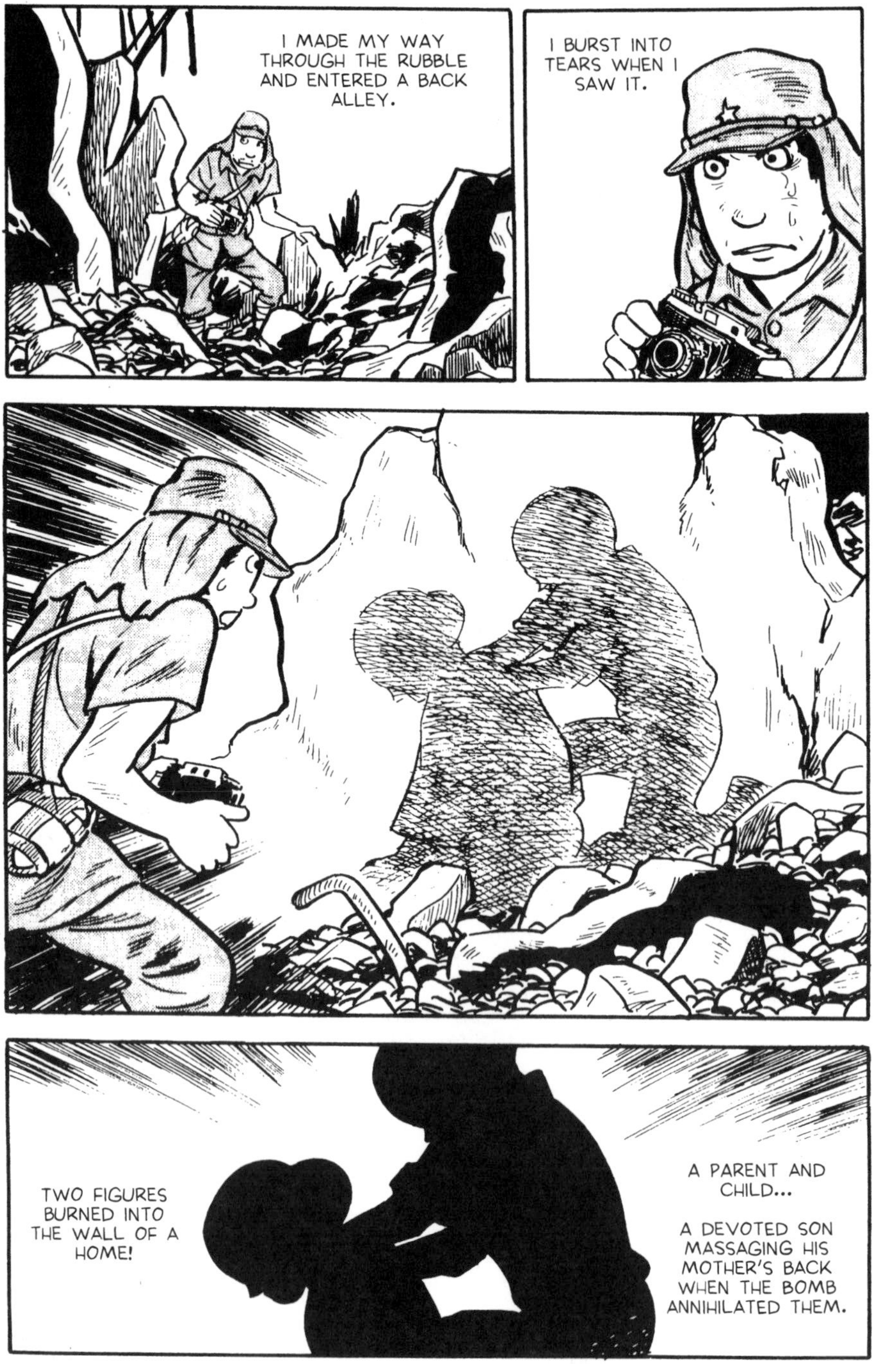
I MADE MY WAY THROUGH THE RUBBLE AND ENTERED A BACK ALLEY.
I BURST INTO TEARS WHEN I SAW IT.
TWO FIGURES BURNED INTO THE WALL OF A HOME!
A PARENT AND CHILD...
A DEVOTED SON MASSAGING HIS MOTHER'S BACK WHEN THE BOMB ANNIHILATED THEM.

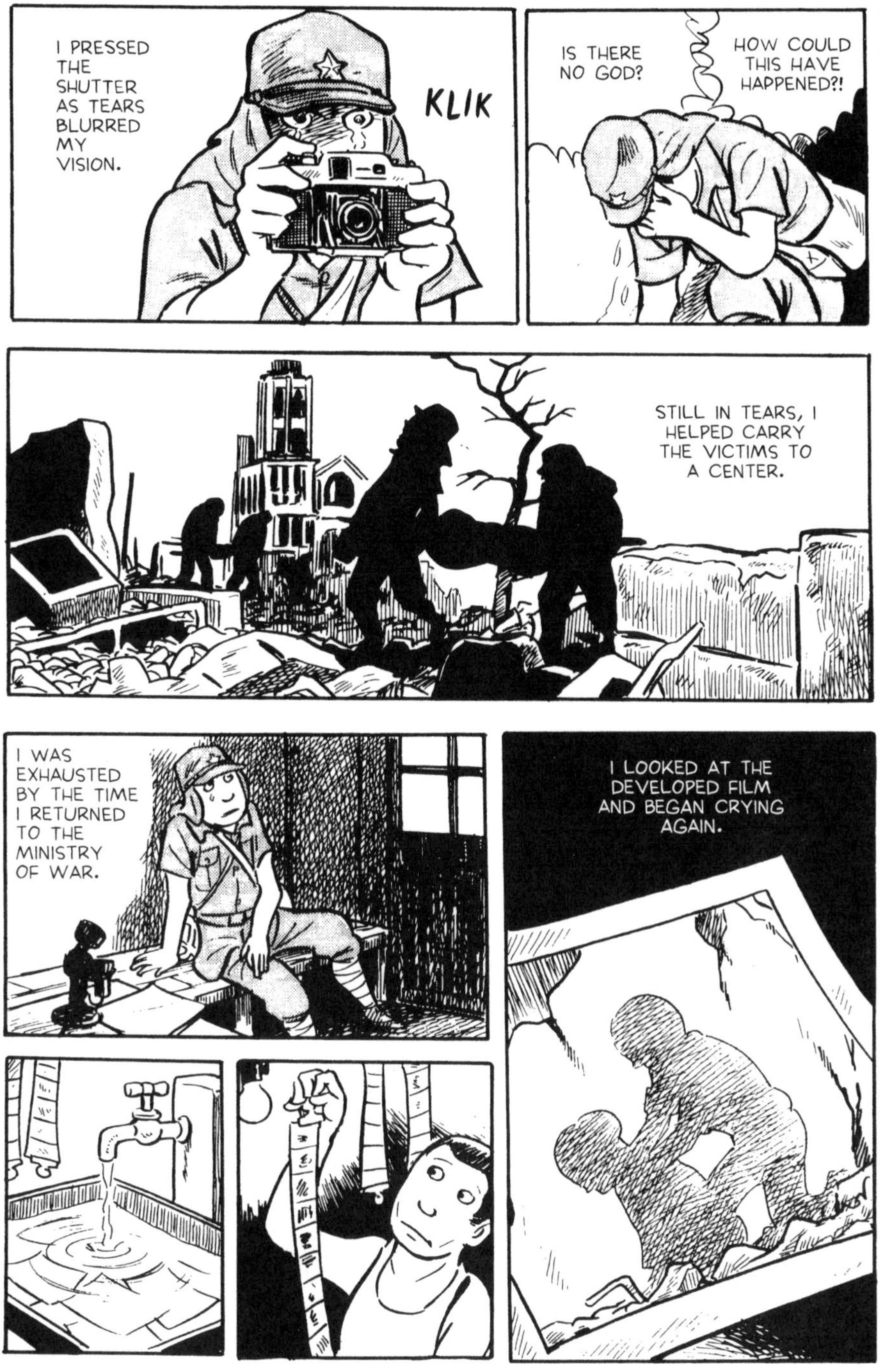
I PRESSED THE SHUTTER AS TEARS BLURRED MY VISION.
KLIK
IS THERE NO GOD?
HOW COULD THIS HAVE HAPPENED?!
STILL IN TEARS, I HELPED CARRY THE VICTIMS TO A CENTER.
I WAS EXHAUSTED BY THE TIME I RETURNED TO THE MINISTRY OF WAR.
I LOOKED AT THE DEVELOPED FILM AND BEGAN CRYING AGAIN.

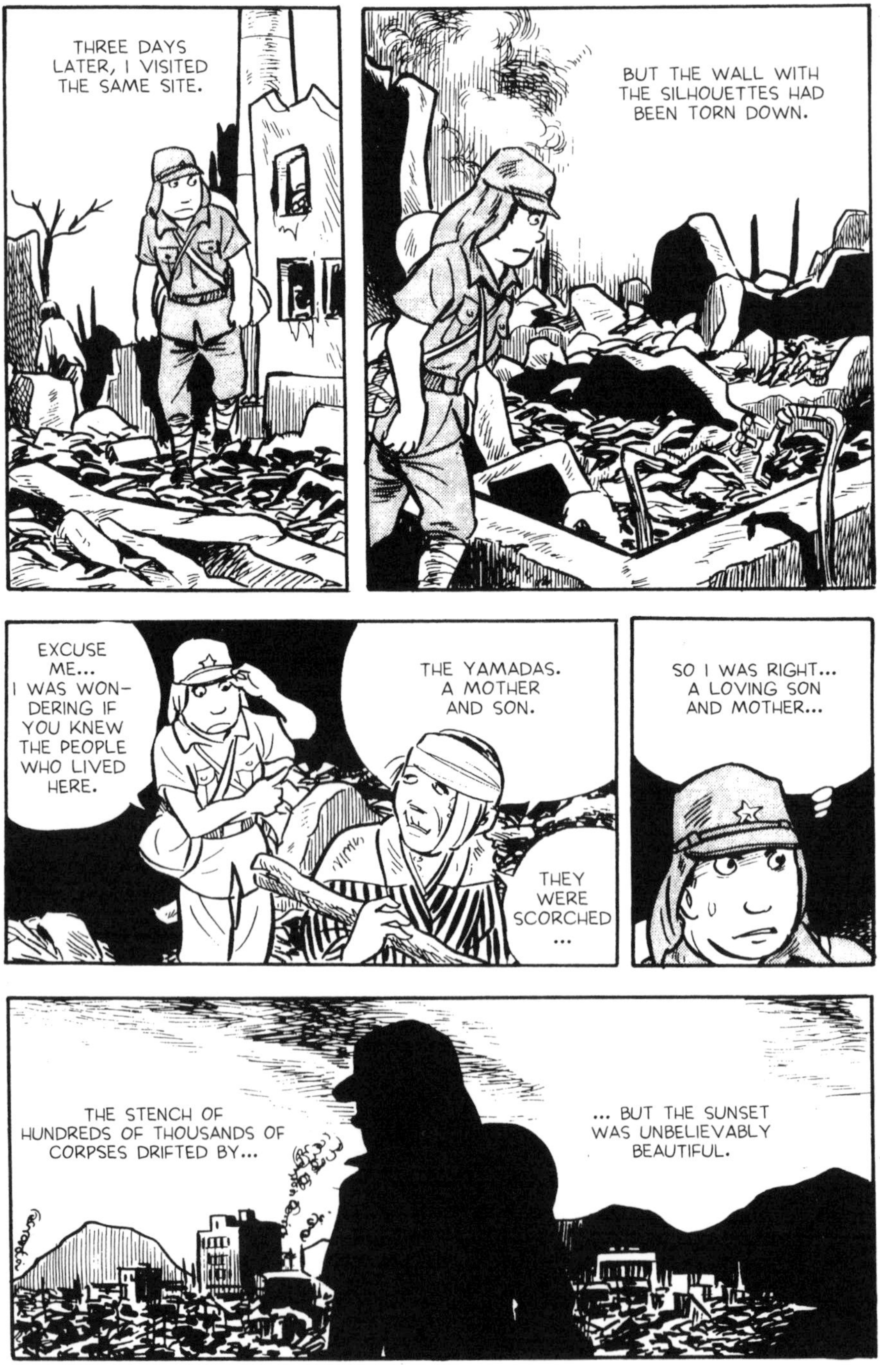
THREE DAYS LATER, I VISITED THE SAME SITE.
BUT THE WALL WITH THE SILHOUETTES HAD BEEN TORN DOWN.
EXCUSE ME... I WAS WON-DERING IF YOU KNEW THE PEOPLE WHO LIVED HERE.
THE YAMADAS. A MOTHER AND SON.
THEY WERE SCORCHED ...
SO I WAS RIGHT... A LOVING SON AND MOTHER...
THE STENCH OF HUNDREDS OF THOUSANDS OF CORPSES DRIFTED BY...
... BUT THE SUNSET WAS UNBELIEVABLY BEAUTIFUL.

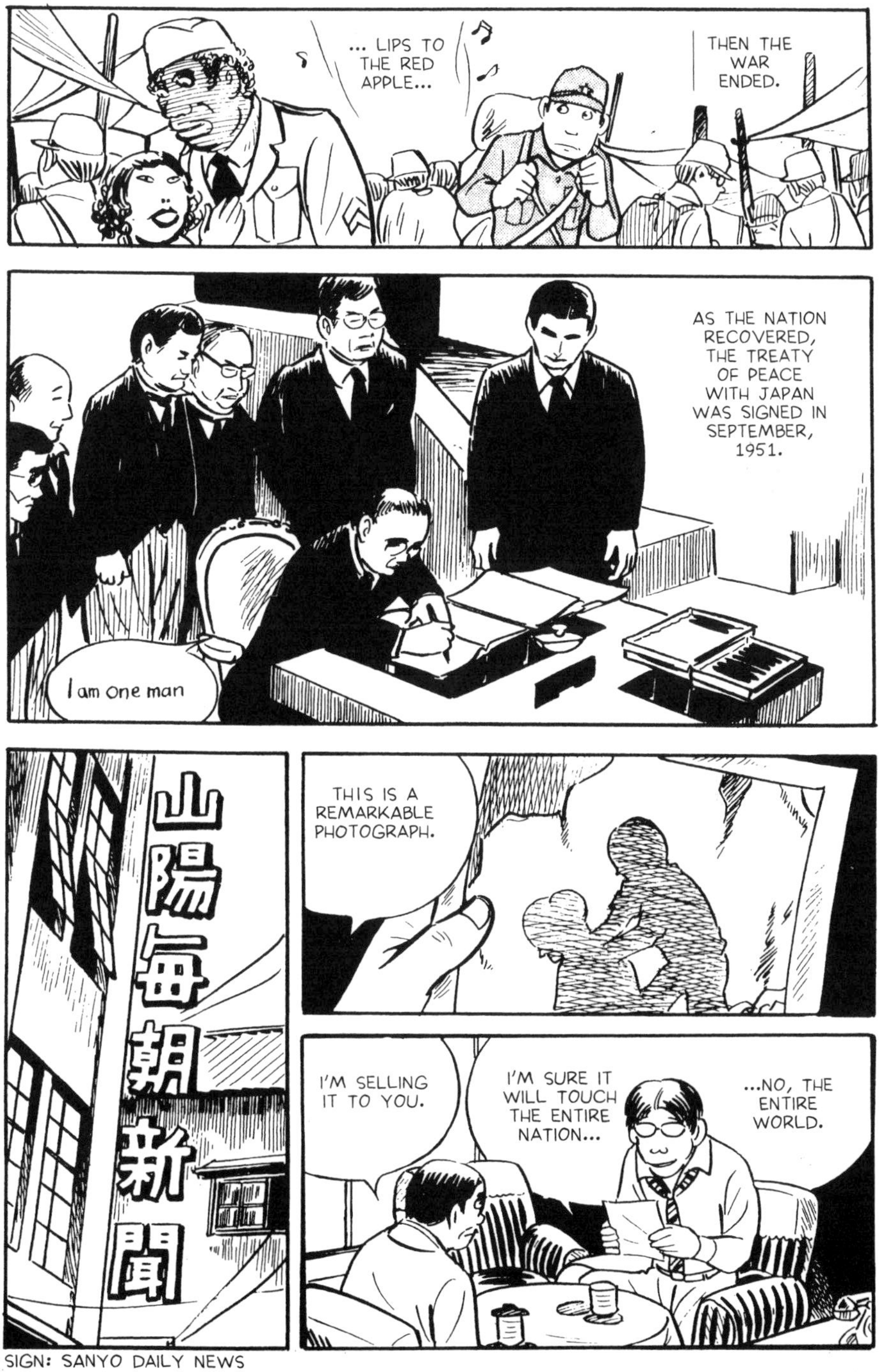
... LIPS TO THE RED APPLE...
THEN THE WAR ENDED.
AS THE NATION RECOVERED, THE TREATY OF PEACE WITH JAPAN WAS SIGNED IN SEPTEMBER, 1951.
I am one man
山陽毎朝新聞
THIS IS A REMARKABLE PHOTOGRAPH.
I'M SELLING IT TO YOU.
I'M SURE IT WILL TOUCH THE ENTIRE NATION...
...NO, THE ENTIRE WORLD.

SIGN: SANYO DAILY NEWS

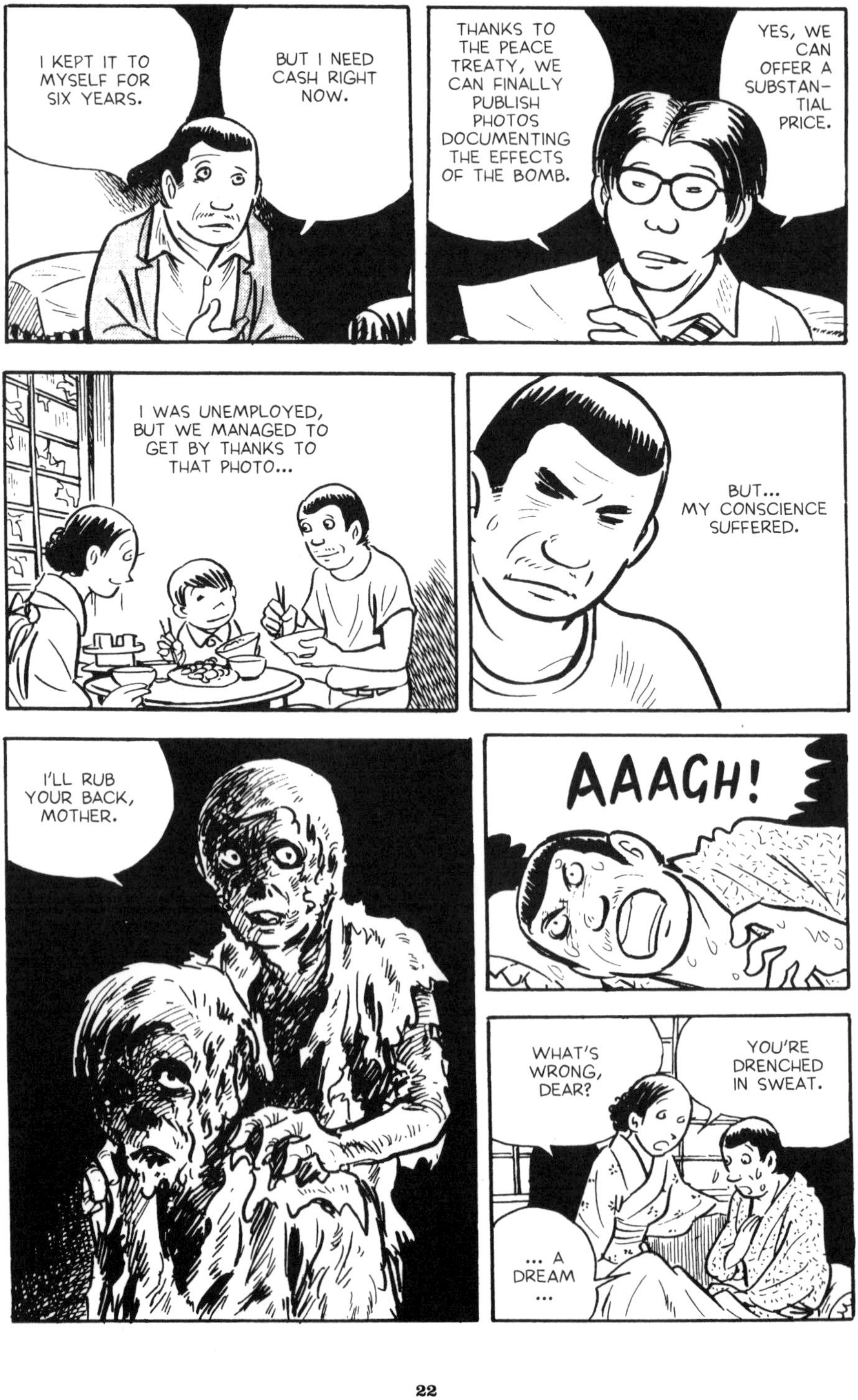
I KEPT IT TO MYSELF FOR SIX YEARS.
BUT I NEED CASH RIGHT NOW.
THANKS TO THE PEACE TREATY, WE CAN FINALLY PUBLISH PHOTOS DOCUMENTING THE EFFECTS OF THE BOMB.
YES, WE CAN OFFER A SUBSTAN-TIAL PRICE.
I WAS UNEMPLOYED, BUT WE MANAGED TO GET BY THANKS TO THAT PHOTO...
BUT... MY CONSCIENCE SUFFERED.
I'LL RUB YOUR BACK, MOTHER.
AAAGH!
WHAT'S WRONG, DEAR?
YOU'RE DRENCHED IN SWEAT.
... A DREAM ...

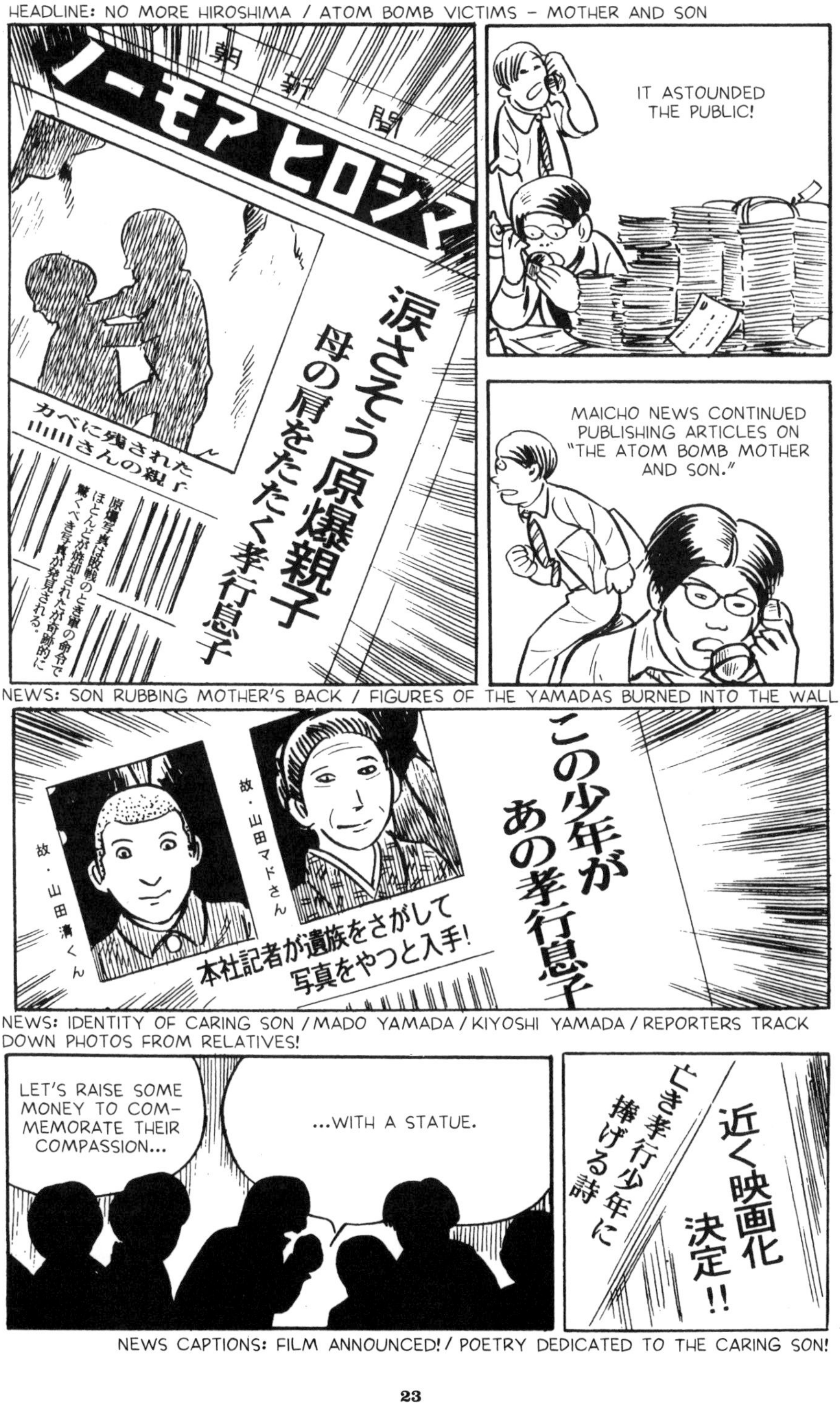
HEADLINE: NO MORE HIROSHIMA / ATOM BOMB VICTIMS – MOTHER AND SON
ノーモアヒロシマ
新聞
涙さそう原爆親子
母の肩をたたく孝行息子
カベに残された山田さんの親子
原爆写真は敗戦のとき軍の命令でほとんどが焼却されたが奇跡的に驚くべき写真が発見される。
IT ASTOUNDED THE PUBLIC!
MAICHO NEWS CONTINUED PUBLISHING ARTICLES ON "THE ATOM BOMB MOTHER AND SON."
NEWS: SON RUBBING MOTHER'S BACK / FIGURES OF THE YAMADAS BURNED INTO THE WALL
故・山田清くん
故・山田マドさん
本社記者が遺族をさがして写真をやつと入手!
この少年があの孝行息子
NEWS: IDENTITY OF CARING SON / MADO YAMADA / KIYOSHI YAMADA / REPORTERS TRACK DOWN PHOTOS FROM RELATIVES!
LET'S RAISE SOME MONEY TO COMMEMORATE THEIR COMPASSION...
...WITH A STATUE.
近く映画化決定!!
亡き孝行少年に捧げる詩
NEWS CAPTIONS: FILM ANNOUNCED! / POETRY DEDICATED TO THE CARING SON!

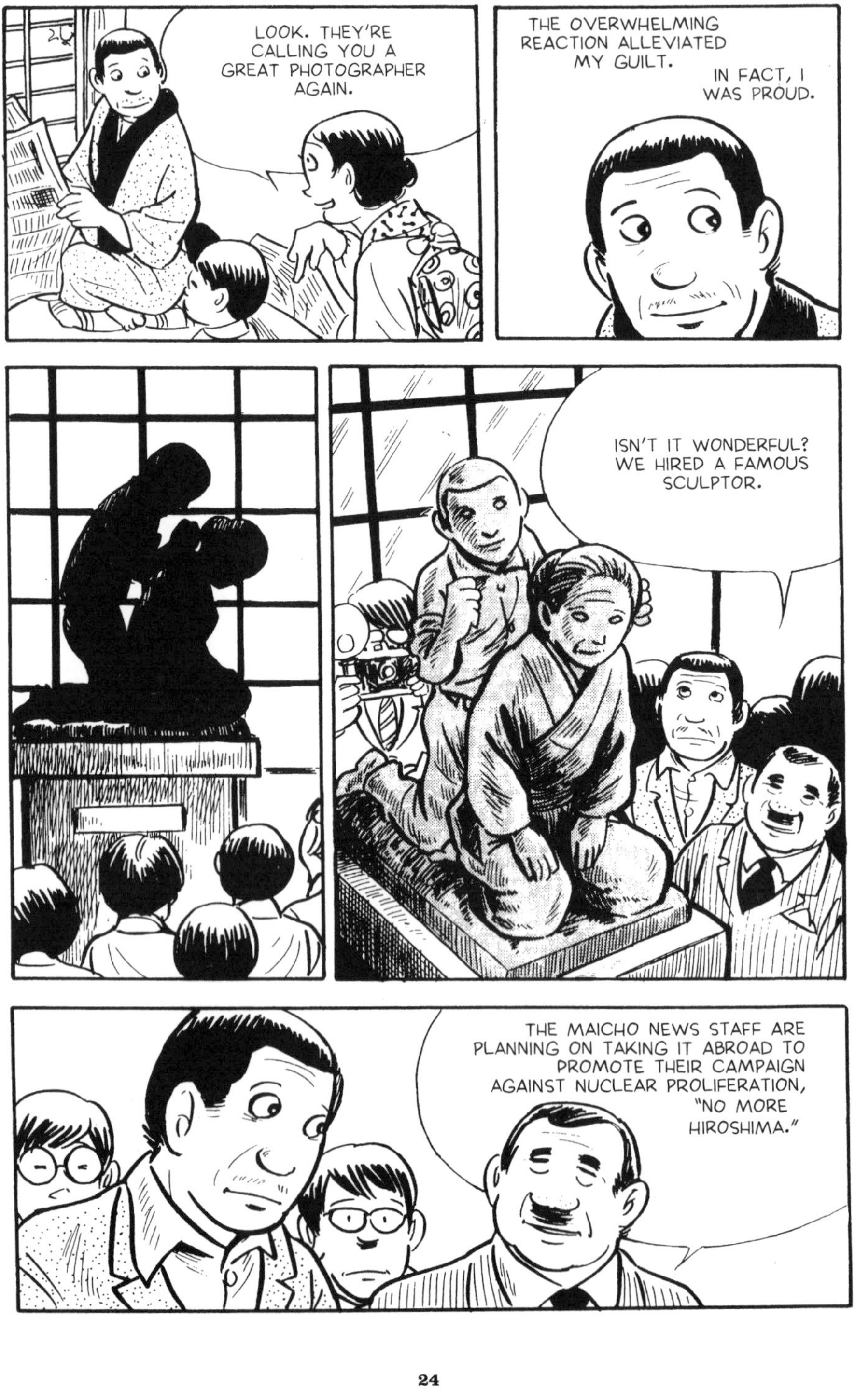
LOOK. THEY'RE CALLING YOU A GREAT PHOTOGRAPHER AGAIN.
THE OVERWHELMING REACTION ALLEVIATED MY GUILT.
IN FACT, I WAS PROUD.
ISN'T IT WONDERFUL? WE HIRED A FAMOUS SCULPTOR.
THE MAICHO NEWS STAFF ARE PLANNING ON TAKING IT ABROAD TO PROMOTE THEIR CAMPAIGN AGAINST NUCLEAR PROLIFERATION, "NO MORE HIROSHIMA."

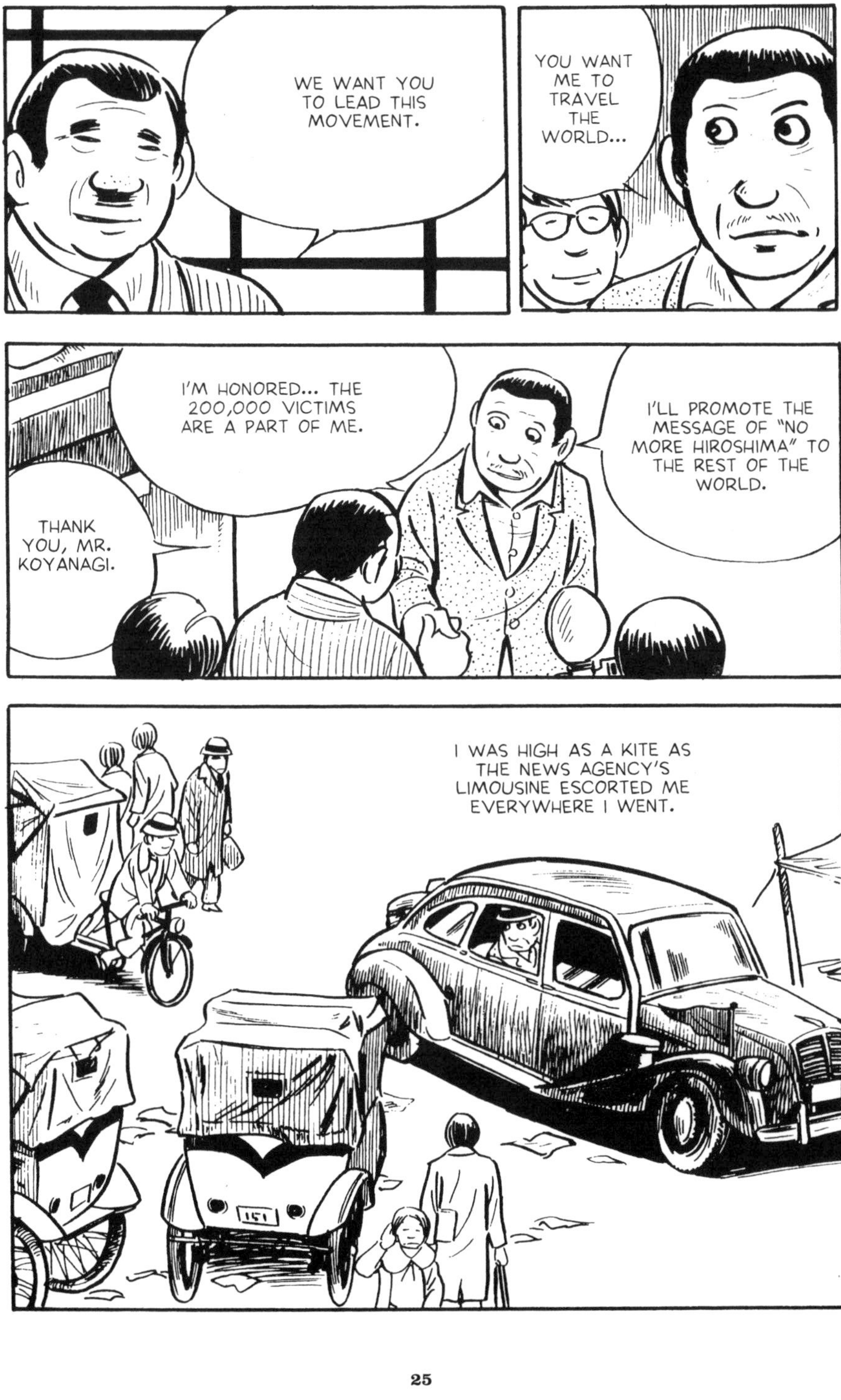
WE WANT YOU TO LEAD THIS MOVEMENT.
YOU WANT ME TO TRAVEL THE WORLD...
I'M HONORED... THE 200,000 VICTIMS ARE A PART OF ME.
I'LL PROMOTE THE MESSAGE OF "NO MORE HIROSHIMA" TO THE REST OF THE WORLD.
THANK YOU, MR. KOYANAGI.
I WAS HIGH AS A KITE AS THE NEWS AGENCY'S LIMOUSINE ESCORTED ME EVERYWHERE I WENT.
151

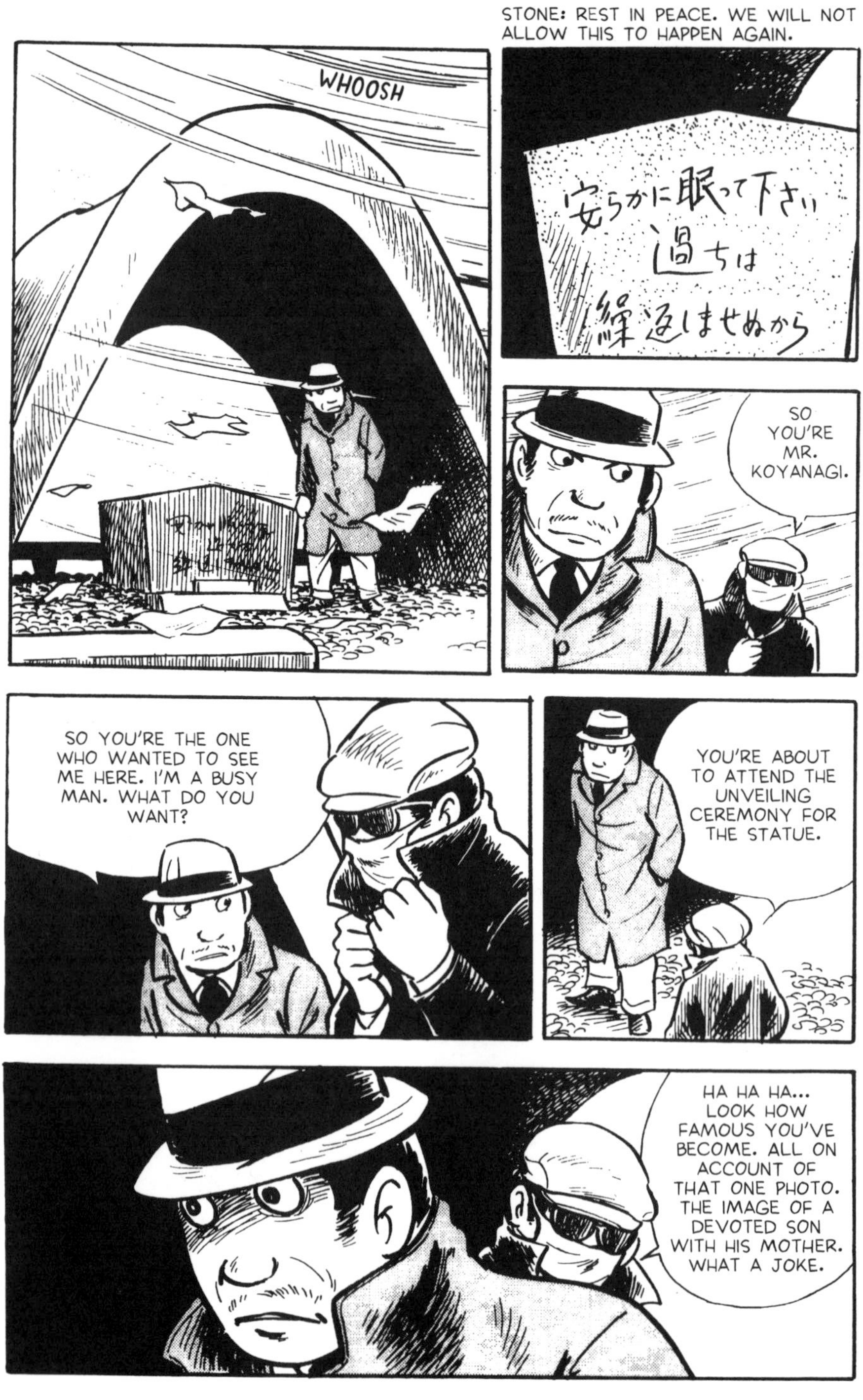
STONE: REST IN PEACE. WE WILL NOT ALLOW THIS TO HAPPEN AGAIN.
WHOOSH
安らかに眠って下さい
過ちは
繰返しませぬから
SO YOU'RE MR. KOYANAGI.
SO YOU'RE THE ONE WHO WANTED TO SEE ME HERE. I'M A BUSY MAN. WHAT DO YOU WANT?
YOU'RE ABOUT TO ATTEND THE UNVEILING CEREMONY FOR THE STATUE.
HA HA HA... LOOK HOW FAMOUS YOU'VE BECOME. ALL ON ACCOUNT OF THAT ONE PHOTO. THE IMAGE OF A DEVOTED SON WITH HIS MOTHER. WHAT A JOKE.

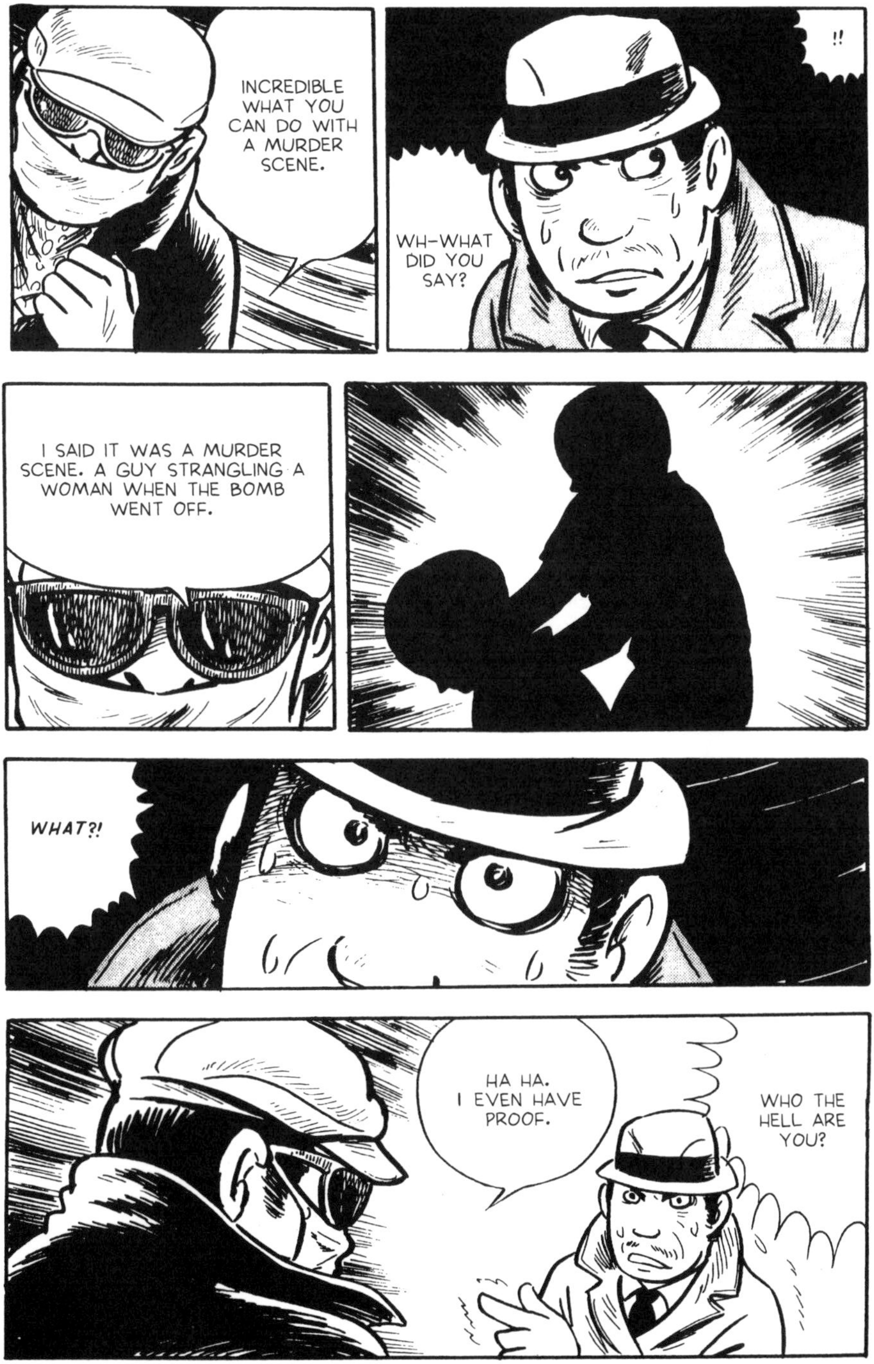
INCREDIBLE WHAT YOU CAN DO WITH A MURDER SCENE.
!!
WH-WHAT DID YOU SAY?
I SAID IT WAS A MURDER SCENE. A GUY STRANGLING A WOMAN WHEN THE BOMB WENT OFF.
WHAT?!
HA HA. I EVEN HAVE PROOF.
WHO THE HELL ARE YOU?

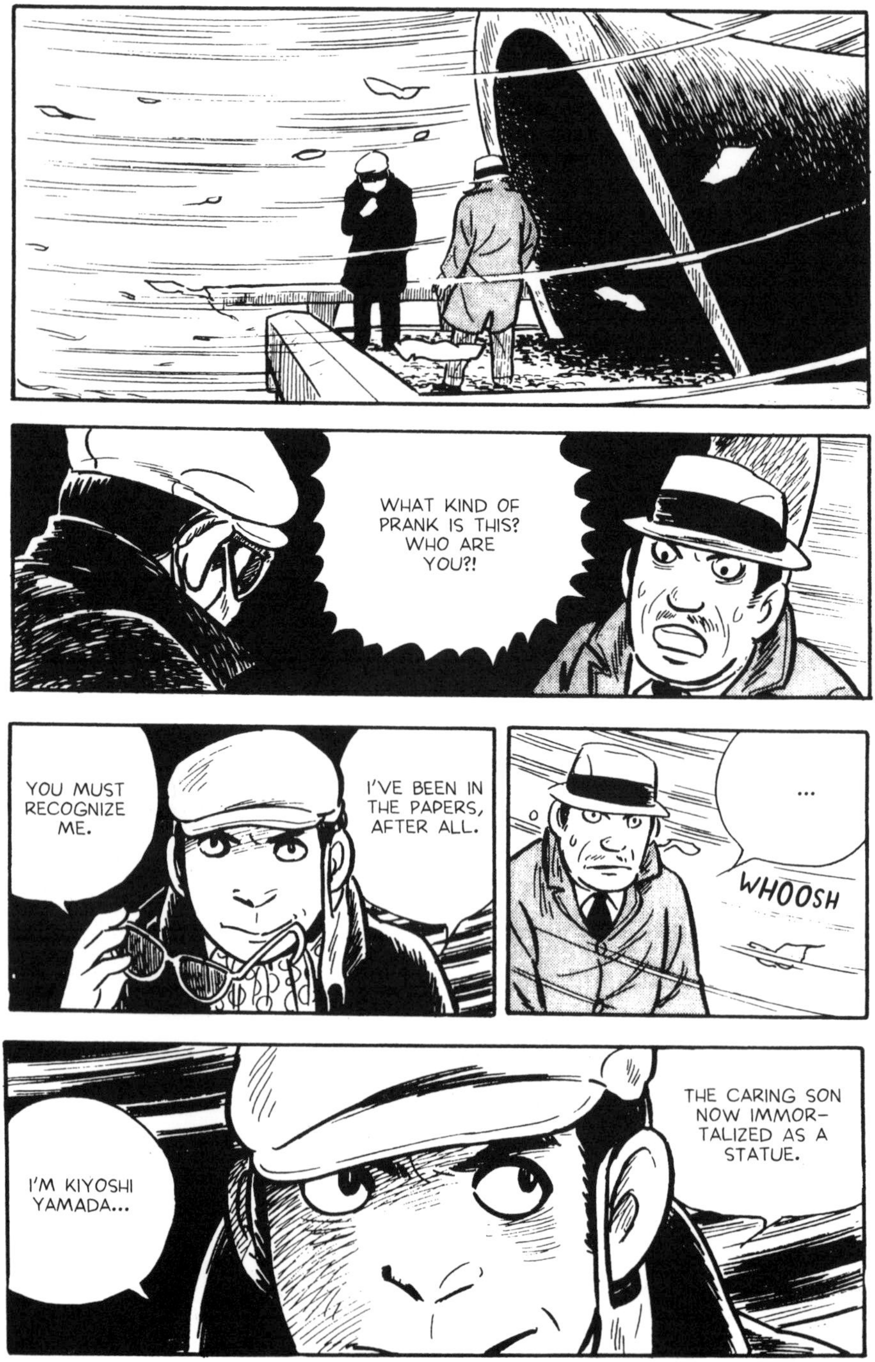
WHAT KIND OF PRANK IS THIS? WHO ARE YOU?!
YOU MUST RECOGNIZE ME.
I'VE BEEN IN THE PAPERS, AFTER ALL.
...
WHOOSH
I'M KIYOSHI YAMADA...
THE CARING SON NOW IMMOR-TALIZED AS A STATUE.

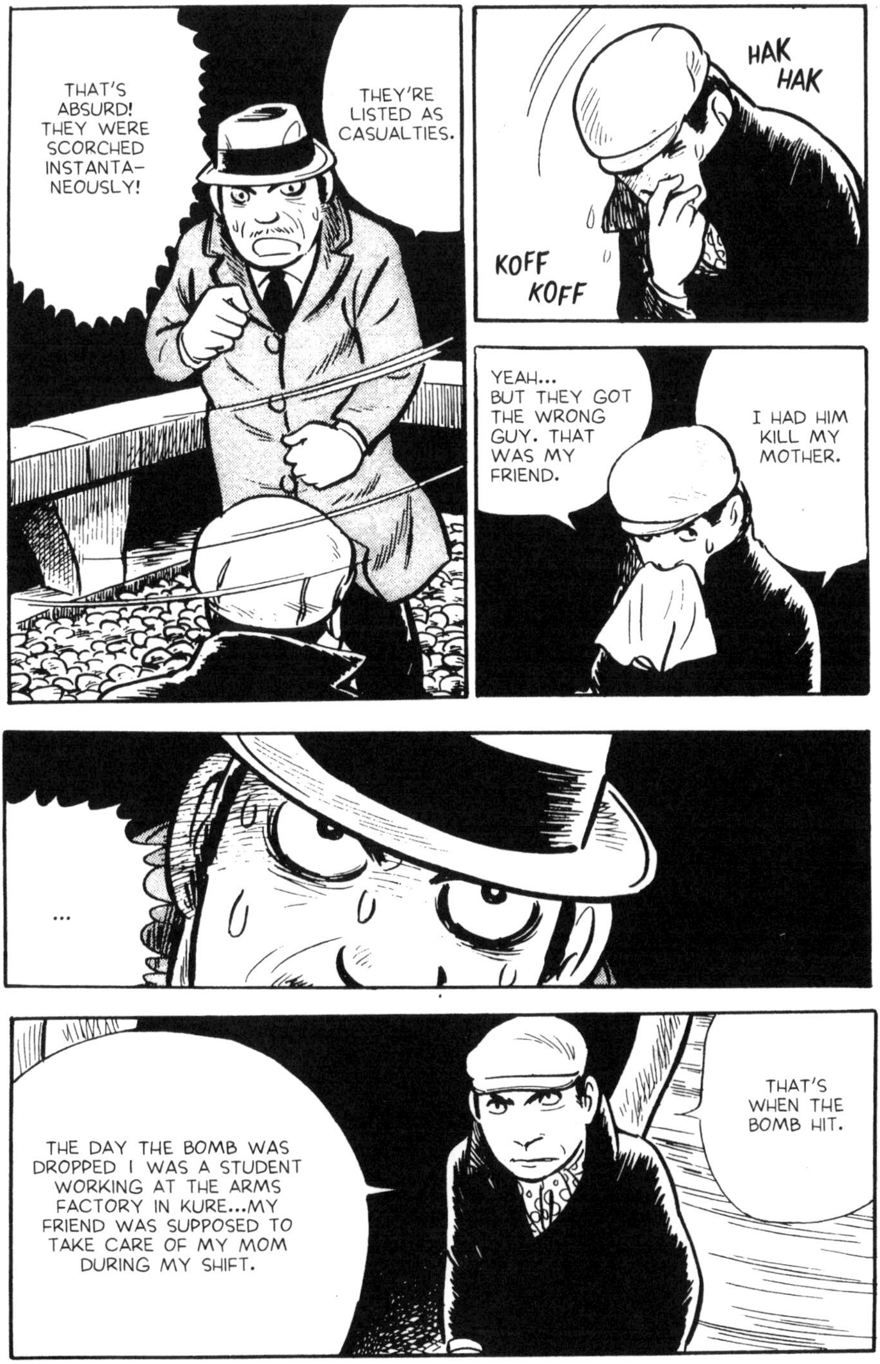
THAT'S ABSURD! THEY WERE SCORCHED INSTANTANEOUSLY!
THEY'RE LISTED AS CASUALTIES.
HAK HAK
KOFF KOFF
YEAH... BUT THEY GOT THE WRONG GUY. THAT WAS MY FRIEND.
I HAD HIM KILL MY MOTHER.
...
THE DAY THE BOMB WAS DROPPED I WAS A STUDENT WORKING AT THE ARMS FACTORY IN KURE...MY FRIEND WAS SUPPOSED TO TAKE CARE OF MY MOM DURING MY SHIFT.
THAT'S WHEN THE BOMB HIT.

I RETURNED TO HIROSHIMA IMMEDIATELY.

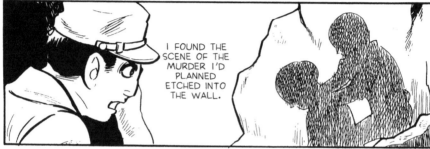

I FOUND THE SCENE OF THE MURDER I'D PLANNED ETCHED INTO THE WALL.

I PANICKED AND DESTROYED IT.

THE WALL...

... THAT'S RIGHT, IT WAS TORN DOWN.

I'M THE ONE WHO TORE IT DOWN. I THOUGHT I'D DESTROYED ALL THE EVIDENCE... BUT THEN ALL OF A SUDDEN EVERYONE'S STIRRED UP OVER THIS MOTHER AND SON STATUE... I COULDN'T BELIEVE IT.

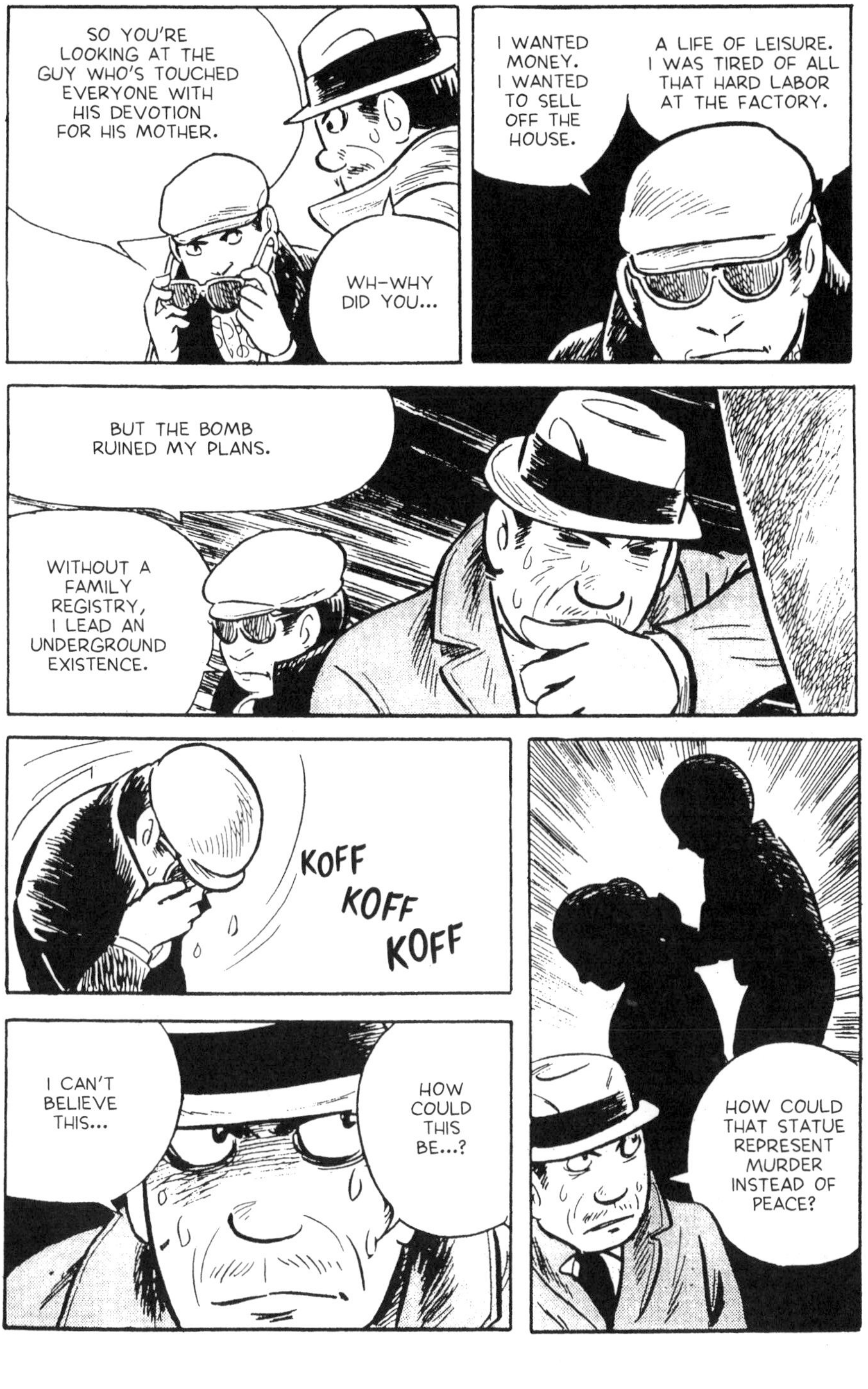
SO YOU'RE LOOKING AT THE GUY WHO'S TOUCHED EVERYONE WITH HIS DEVOTION FOR HIS MOTHER.
WH-WHY DID YOU...
I WANTED MONEY. I WANTED TO SELL OFF THE HOUSE.
A LIFE OF LEISURE. I WAS TIRED OF ALL THAT HARD LABOR AT THE FACTORY.
BUT THE BOMB RUINED MY PLANS.
WITHOUT A FAMILY REGISTRY, I LEAD AN UNDERGROUND EXISTENCE.
KOFF
KOFF
KOFF
I CAN'T BELIEVE THIS...
HOW COULD THIS BE...?
HOW COULD THAT STATUE REPRESENT MURDER INSTEAD OF PEACE?

SIGN: NO MORE HIROSHIMA/UNVEILING CEREMONY FOR THE HIROSHIMA MOTHER AND SON STATUE/SPONORED BY THE SANYO NEWS AGENCY

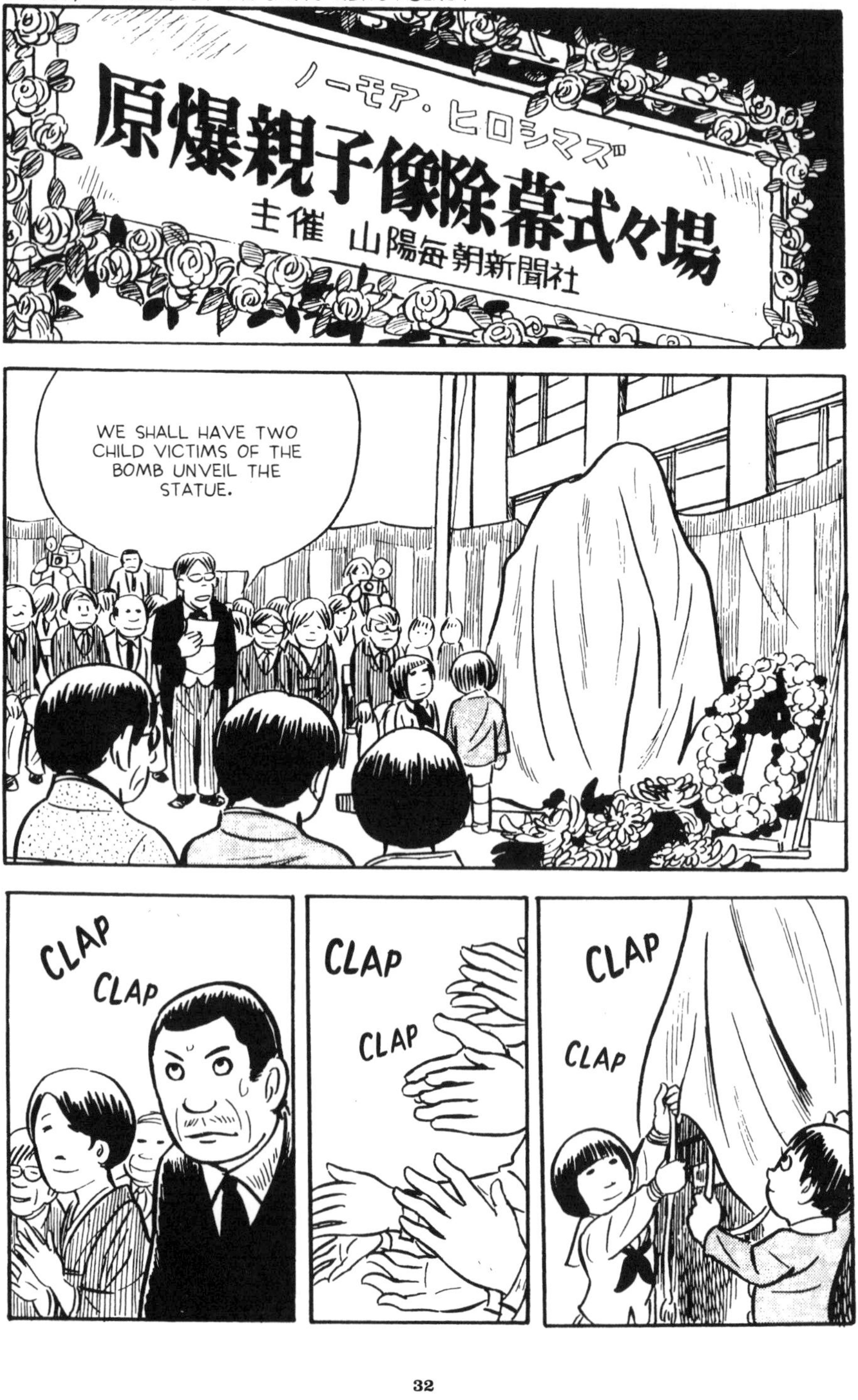
ノーモア・ヒロシマズ
原爆親子像除幕式々場
主催 山陽毎朝新聞社
WE SHALL HAVE TWO CHILD VICTIMS OF THE BOMB UNVEIL THE STATUE.
CLAP
CLAP
CLAP
CLAP
CLAP
CLAP

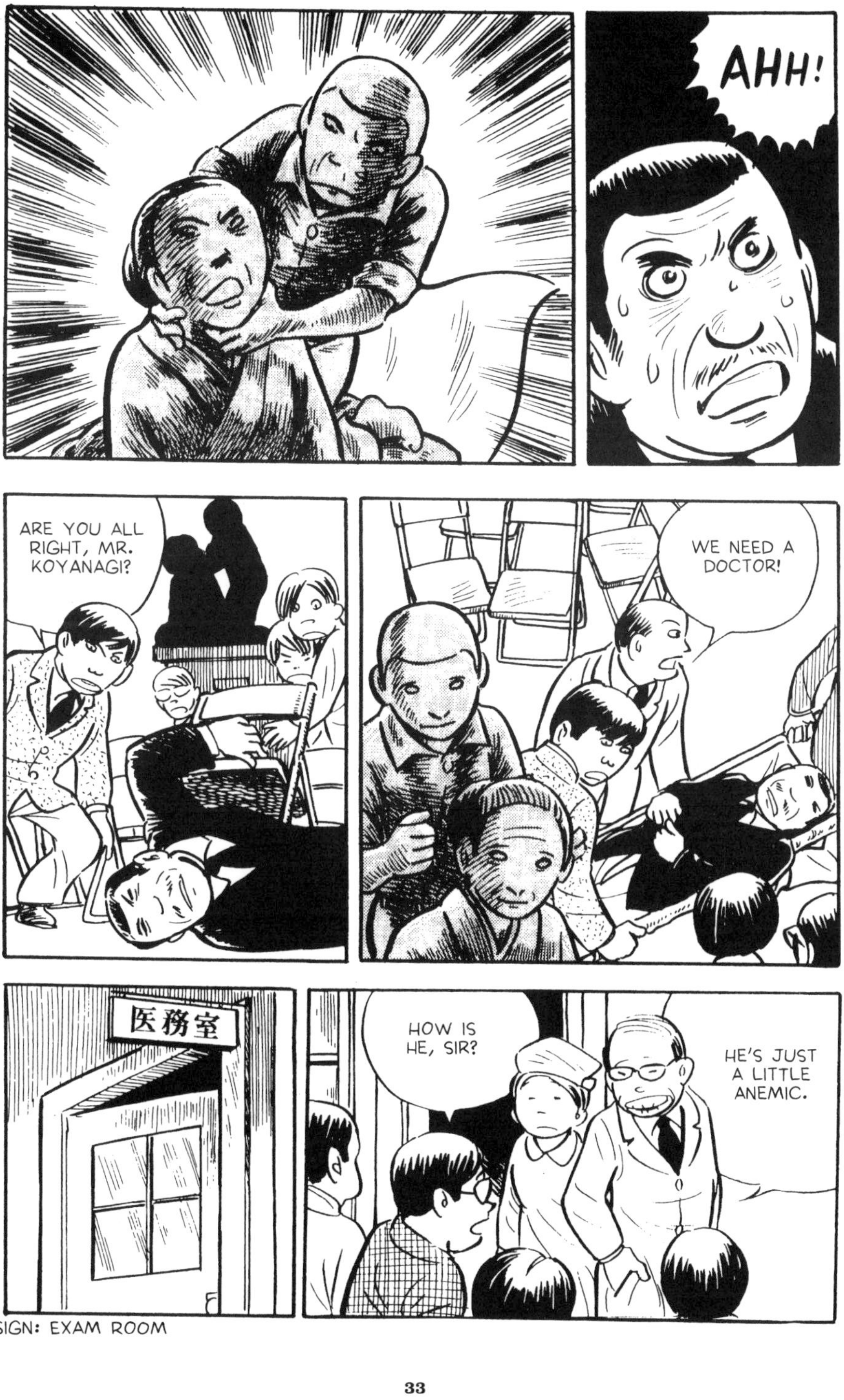
AHH!
ARE YOU ALL RIGHT, MR. KOYANAGI?
WE NEED A DOCTOR!
医務室
HOW IS HE, SIR?
HE'S JUST A LITTLE ANEMIC.
SIGN: EXAM ROOM

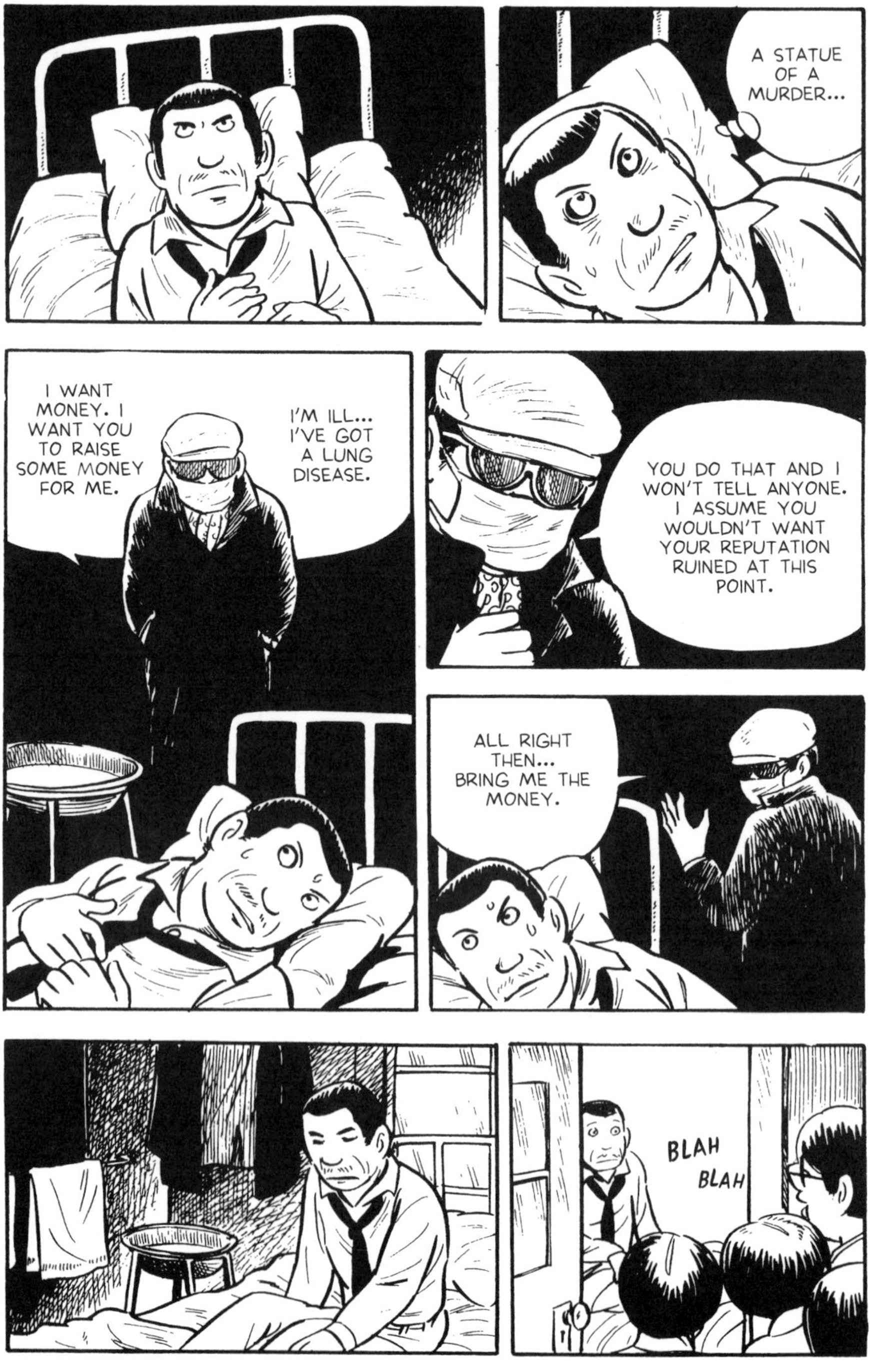
A STATUE OF A MURDER...
I WANT MONEY. I WANT YOU TO RAISE SOME MONEY FOR ME.
I'M ILL... I'VE GOT A LUNG DISEASE.
YOU DO THAT AND I WON'T TELL ANYONE. I ASSUME YOU WOULDN'T WANT YOUR REPUTATION RUINED AT THIS POINT.
ALL RIGHT THEN... BRING ME THE MONEY.
BLAH
BLAH

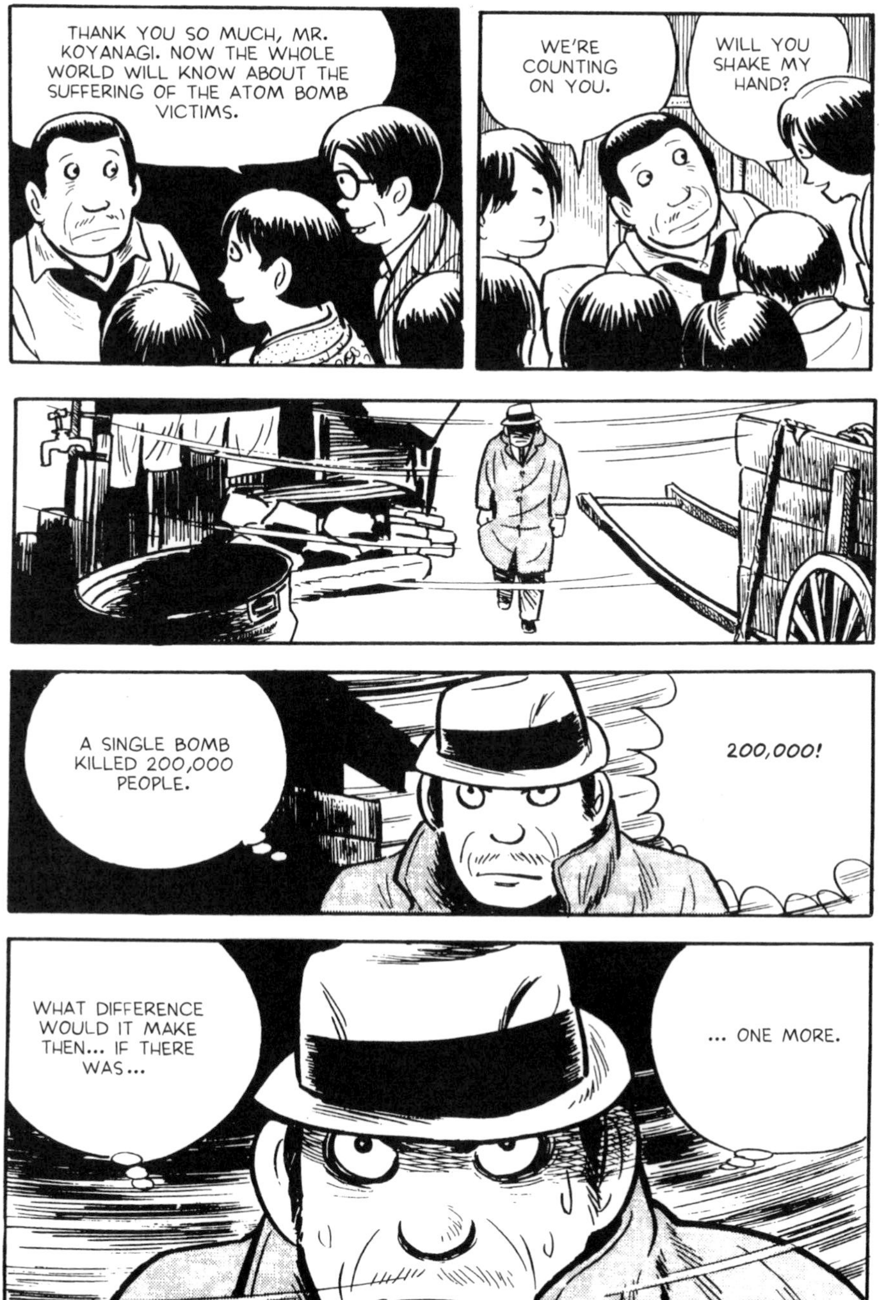
THANK YOU SO MUCH, MR. KOYANAGI. NOW THE WHOLE WORLD WILL KNOW ABOUT THE SUFFERING OF THE ATOM BOMB VICTIMS.
WE'RE COUNTING ON YOU.
WILL YOU SHAKE MY HAND?
A SINGLE BOMB KILLED 200,000 PEOPLE.
200,000!
WHAT DIFFERENCE WOULD IT MAKE THEN... IF THERE WAS...
... ONE MORE.

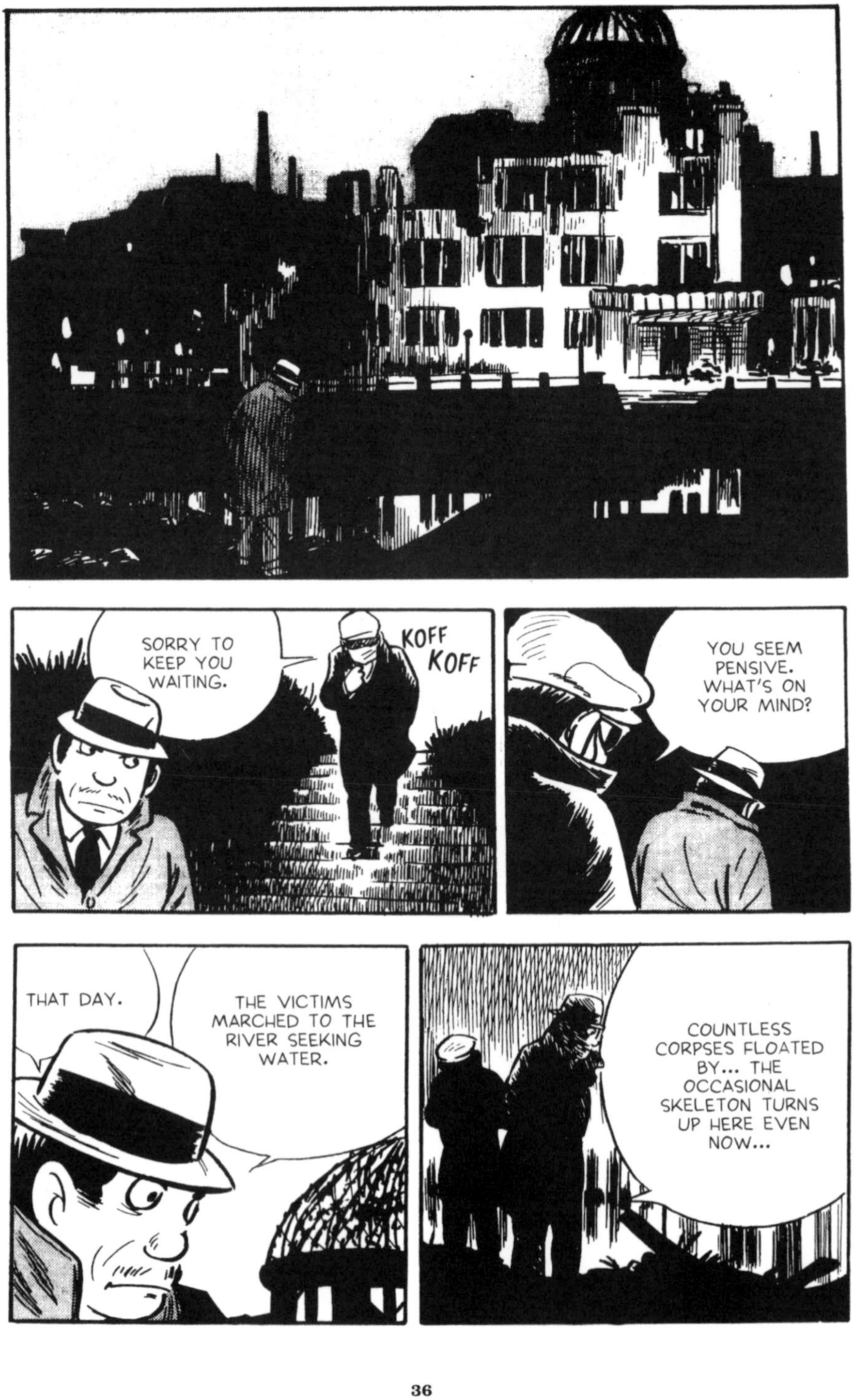
SORRY TO KEEP YOU WAITING.
KOFF KOFF
YOU SEEM PENSIVE. WHAT'S ON YOUR MIND?
THAT DAY.
THE VICTIMS MARCHED TO THE RIVER SEEKING WATER.
COUNTLESS CORPSES FLOATED BY... THE OCCASIONAL SKELETON TURNS UP HERE EVEN NOW...

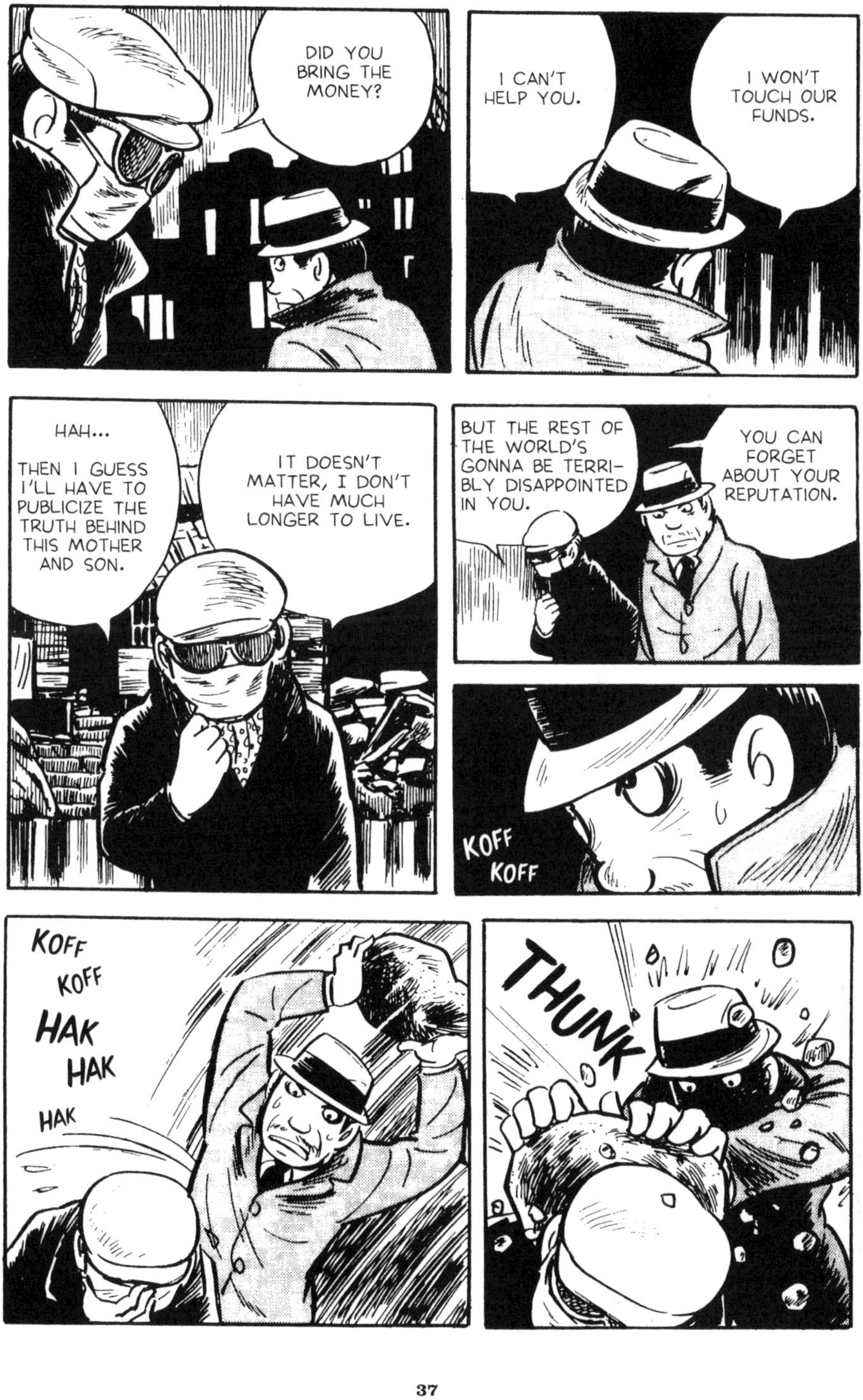
DID YOU BRING THE MONEY?
I CAN'T HELP YOU.
I WON'T TOUCH OUR FUNDS.
HAH...
THEN I GUESS I'LL HAVE TO PUBLICIZE THE TRUTH BEHIND THIS MOTHER AND SON.
IT DOESN'T MATTER, I DON'T HAVE MUCH LONGER TO LIVE.
BUT THE REST OF THE WORLD'S GONNA BE TERRIBLY DISAPPOINTED IN YOU.
YOU CAN FORGET ABOUT YOUR REPUTATION.
KOFF KOFF
KOFF KOFF HAK HAK HAK
THUNK

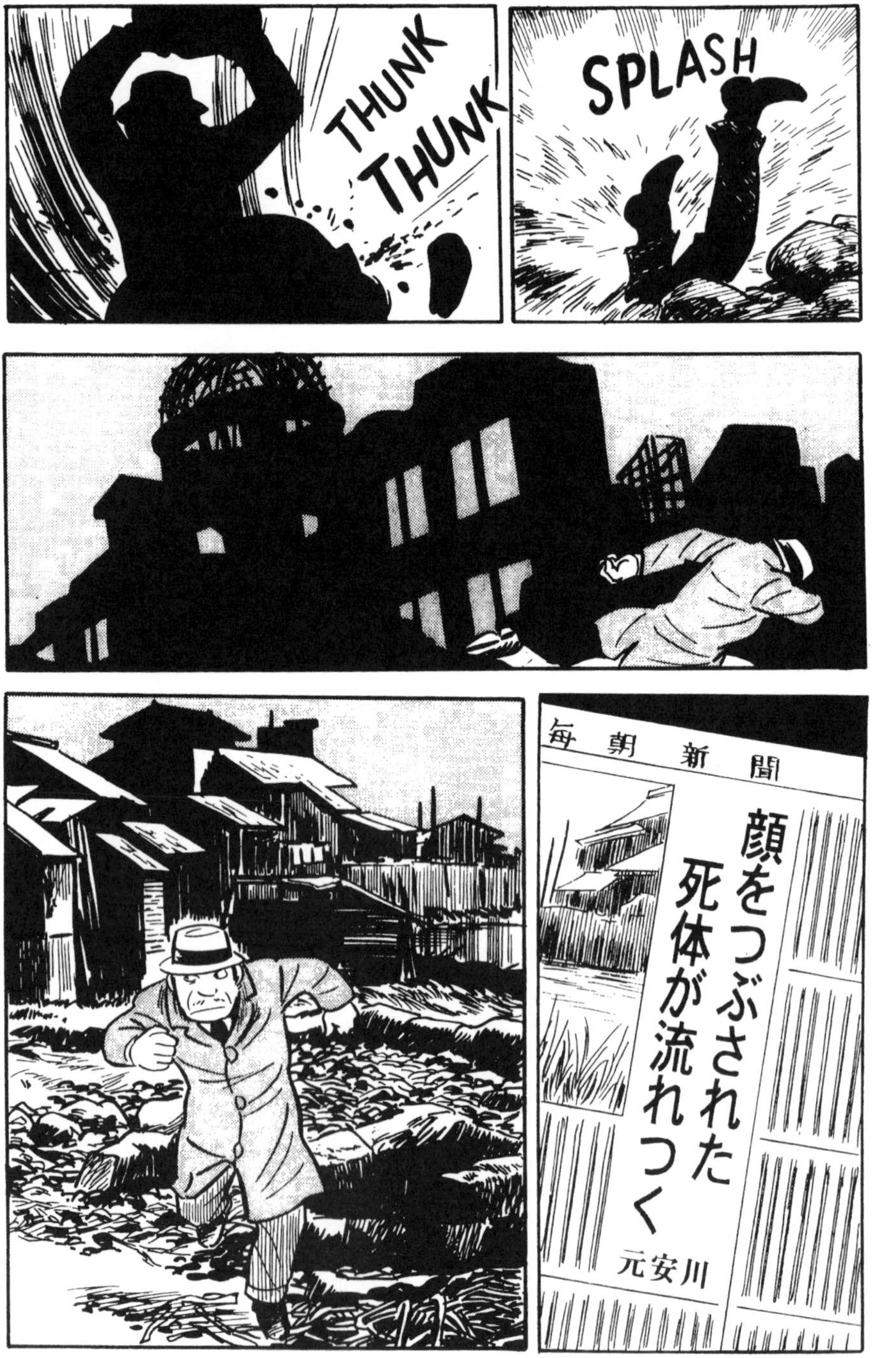
THUNK
THUNK
SPLASH
毎朝新聞
顔をつぶされた死体が流れつく
元安川

NEWSPAPER: MAICHO NEWS / UNIDENTIFIED CORPSE FOUND IN THE MOTOSAYU RIVER

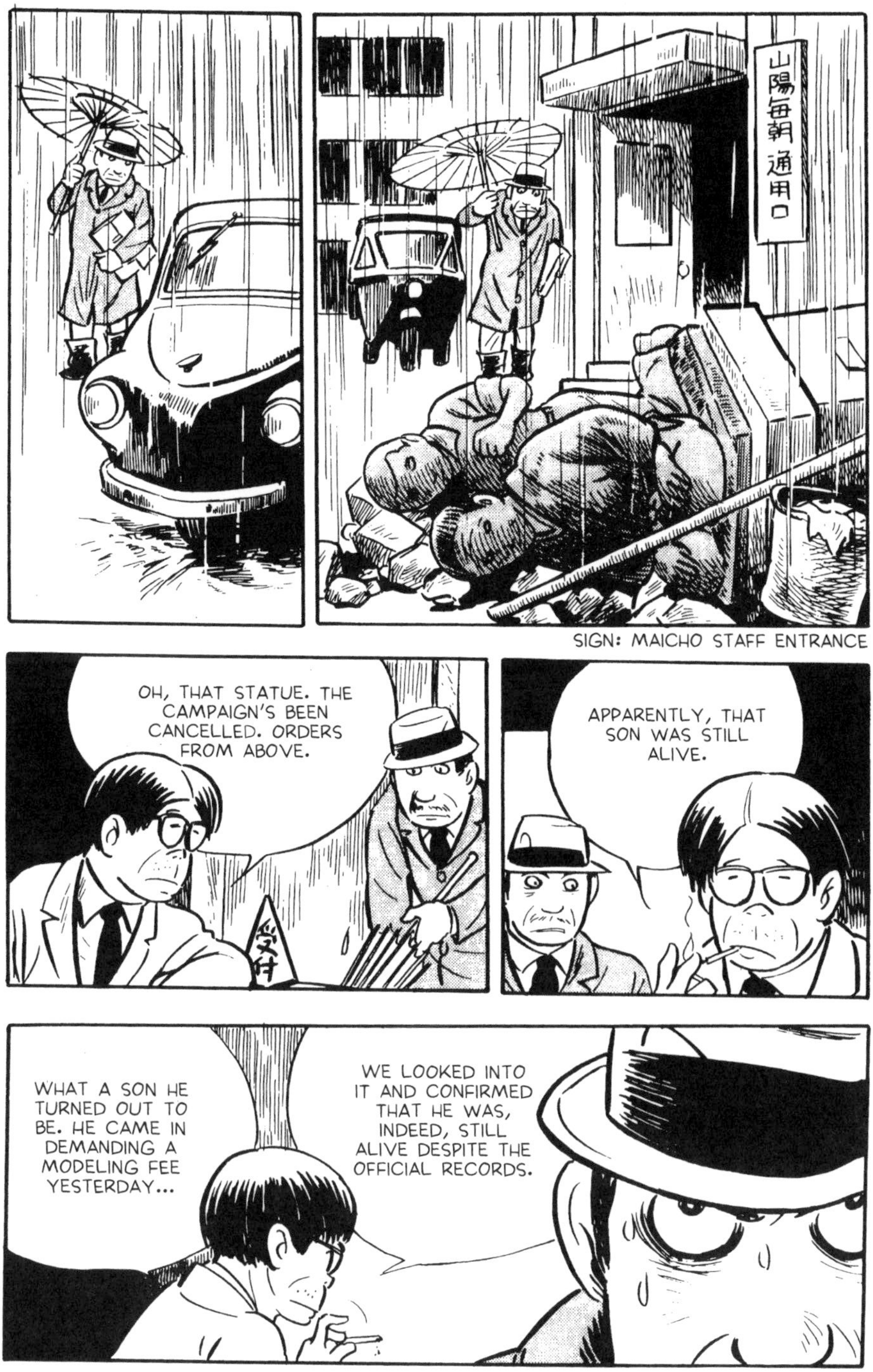
山陽毎朝 通用口
SIGN: MAICHO STAFF ENTRANCE
OH, THAT STATUE. THE CAMPAIGN'S BEEN CANCELLED. ORDERS FROM ABOVE.
受付
APPARENTLY, THAT SON WAS STILL ALIVE.
WHAT A SON HE TURNED OUT TO BE. HE CAME IN DEMANDING A MODELING FEE YESTERDAY...
WE LOOKED INTO IT AND CONFIRMED THAT HE WAS, INDEED, STILL ALIVE DESPITE THE OFFICIAL RECORDS.

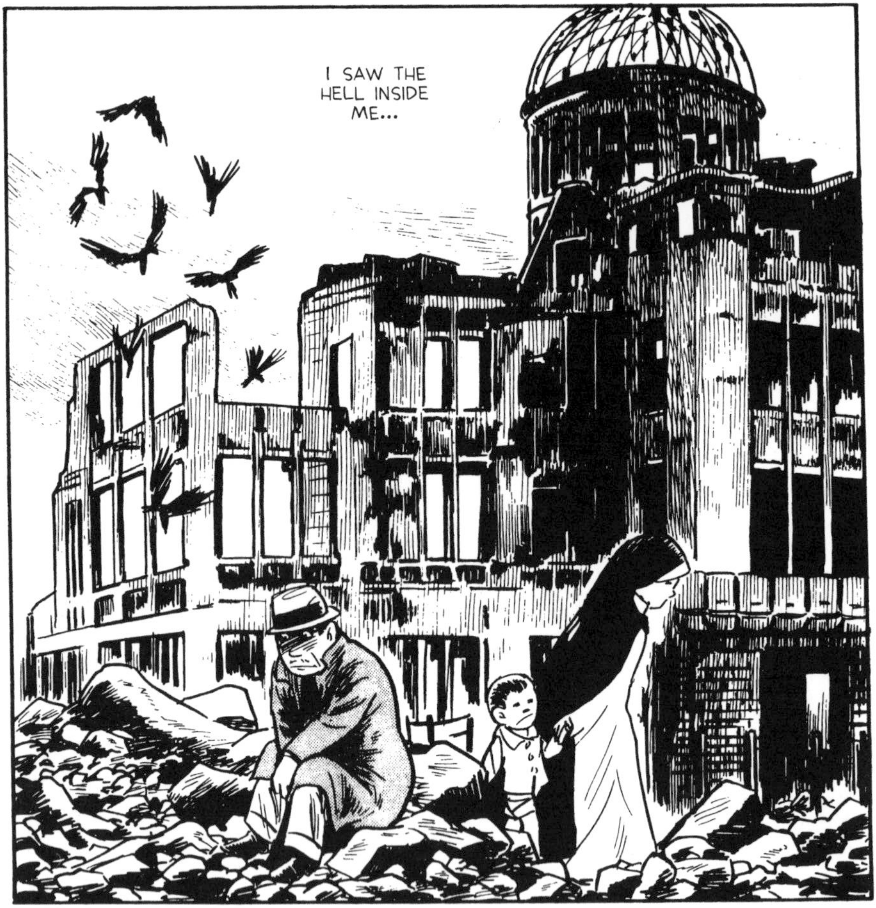
I SAW THE HELL INSIDE ME...

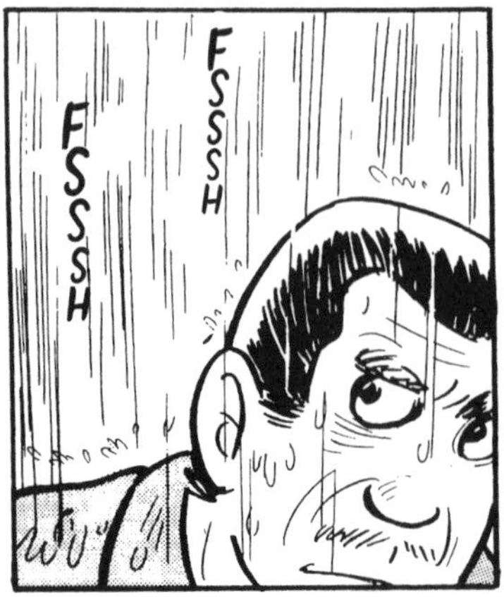
FSSSH
FSSSH

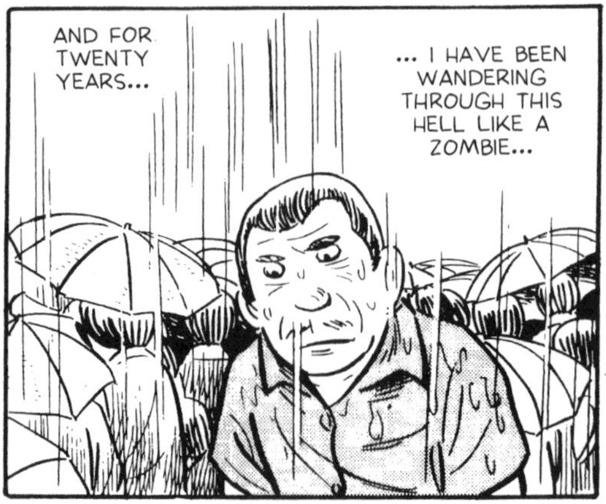
AND FOR TWENTY YEARS...
... I HAVE BEEN WANDERING THROUGH THIS HELL LIKE A ZOMBIE...

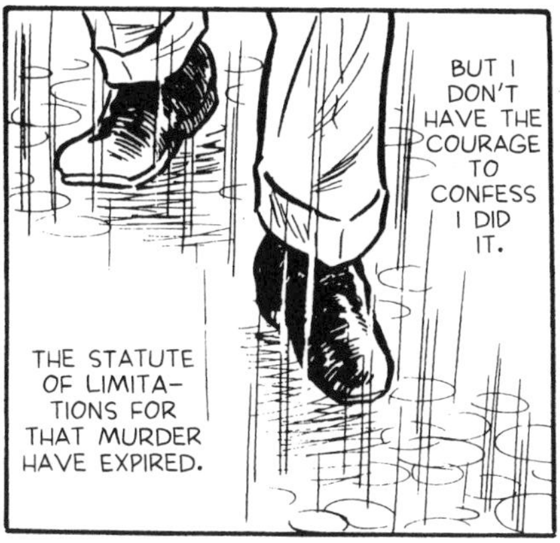
BUT I DON'T HAVE THE COURAGE TO CONFESS I DID IT.
THE STATUTE OF LIMITATIONS FOR THAT MURDER HAVE EXPIRED.

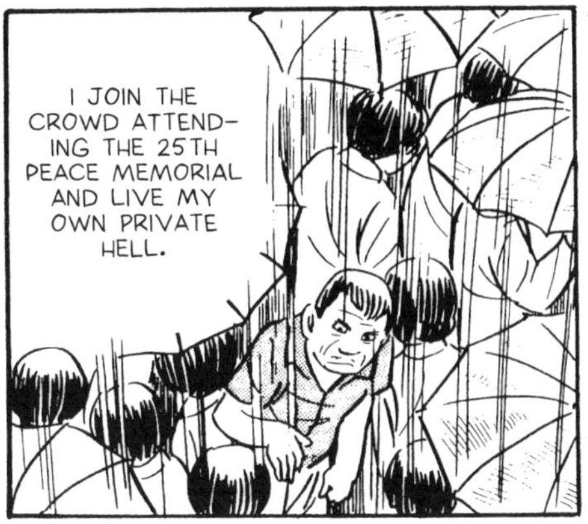
I JOIN THE CROWD ATTENDING THE 25TH PEACE MEMORIAL AND LIVE MY OWN PRIVATE HELL.

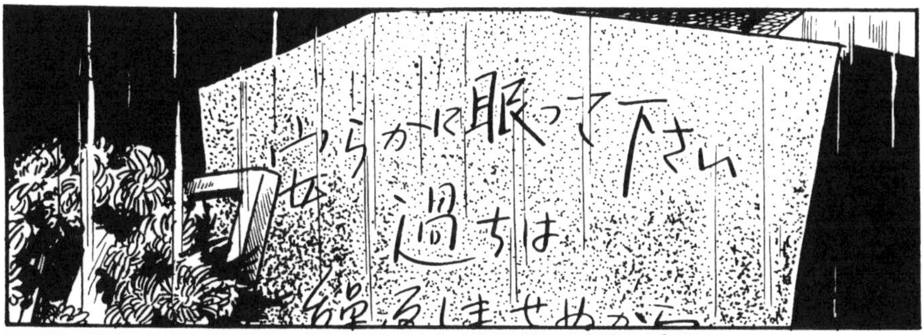
安らかに眠って下さい
過ちは

STONE: REST IN PEACE. WE WILL NOT ALLOW THIS TO HAPPEN AGAIN.

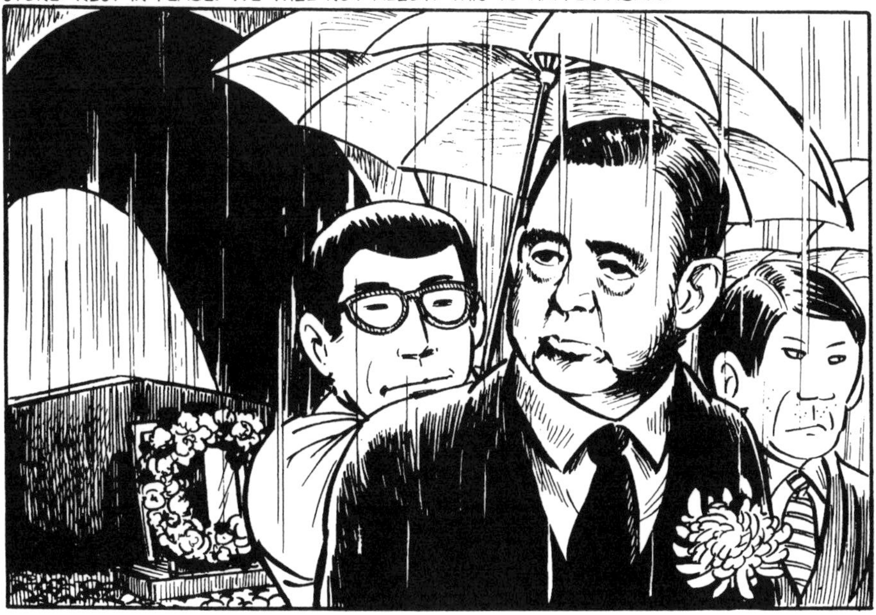

JUST A MAN

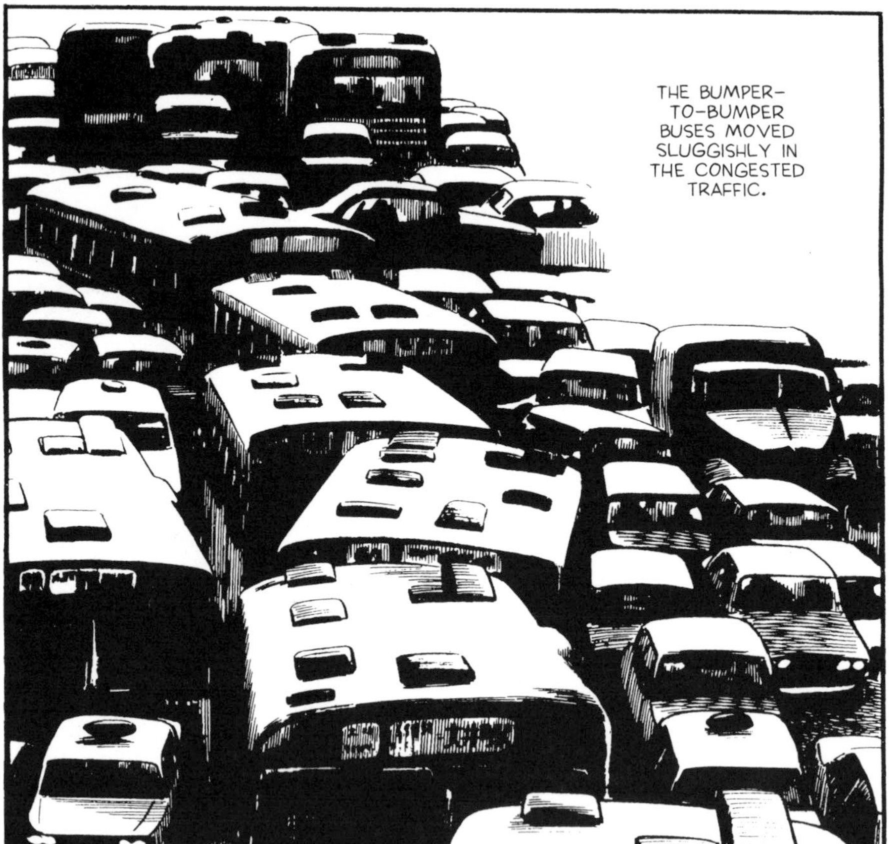
THE BUMPER-TO-BUMPER BUSES MOVED SLUGGISHLY IN THE CONGESTED TRAFFIC.

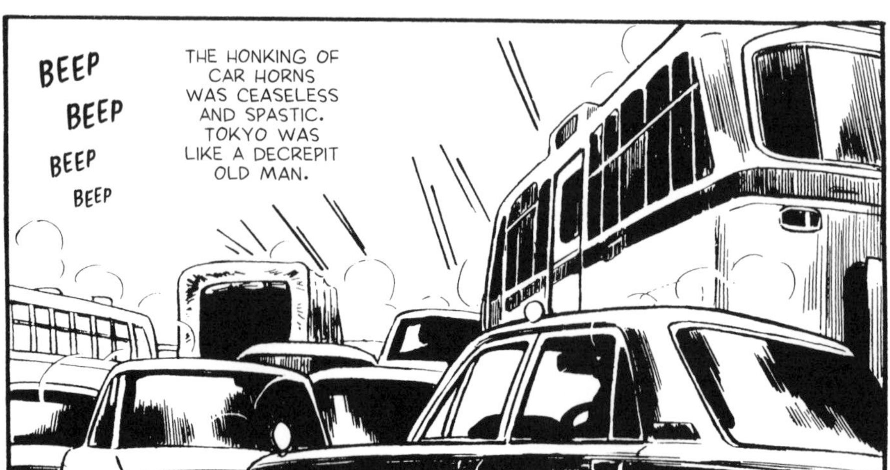
BEEP
BEEP
BEEP
BEEP
THE HONKING OF CAR HORNS WAS CEASELESS AND SPASTIC. TOKYO WAS LIKE A DECREPIT OLD MAN.

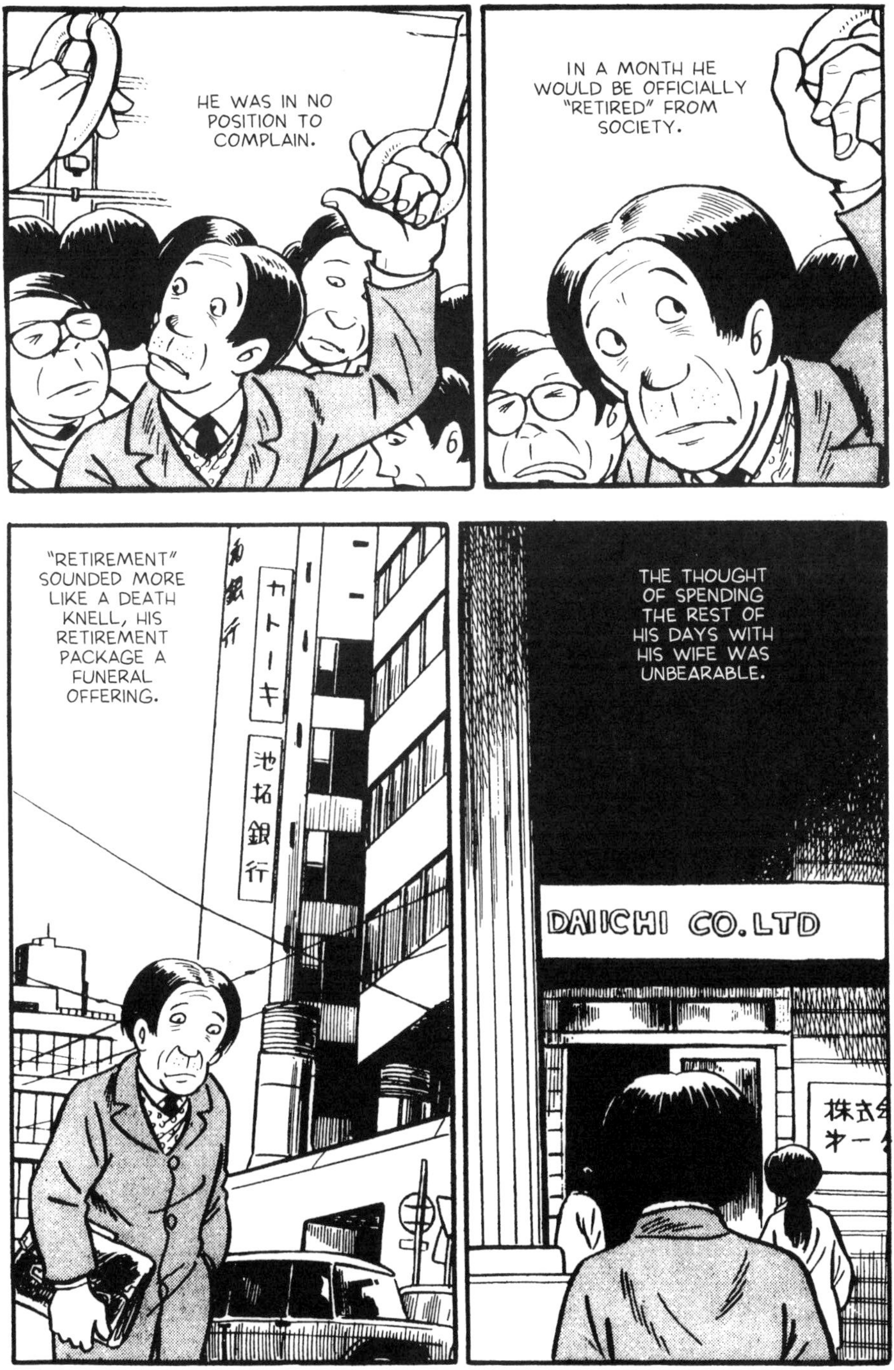
HE WAS IN NO POSITION TO COMPLAIN.
IN A MONTH HE WOULD BE OFFICIALLY "RETIRED" FROM SOCIETY.
"RETIREMENT" SOUNDED MORE LIKE A DEATH KNELL, HIS RETIREMENT PACKAGE A FUNERAL OFFERING.
カトーキ
池拓銀行
THE THOUGHT OF SPENDING THE REST OF HIS DAYS WITH HIS WIFE WAS UNBEARABLE.
DAIICHI CO.LTD

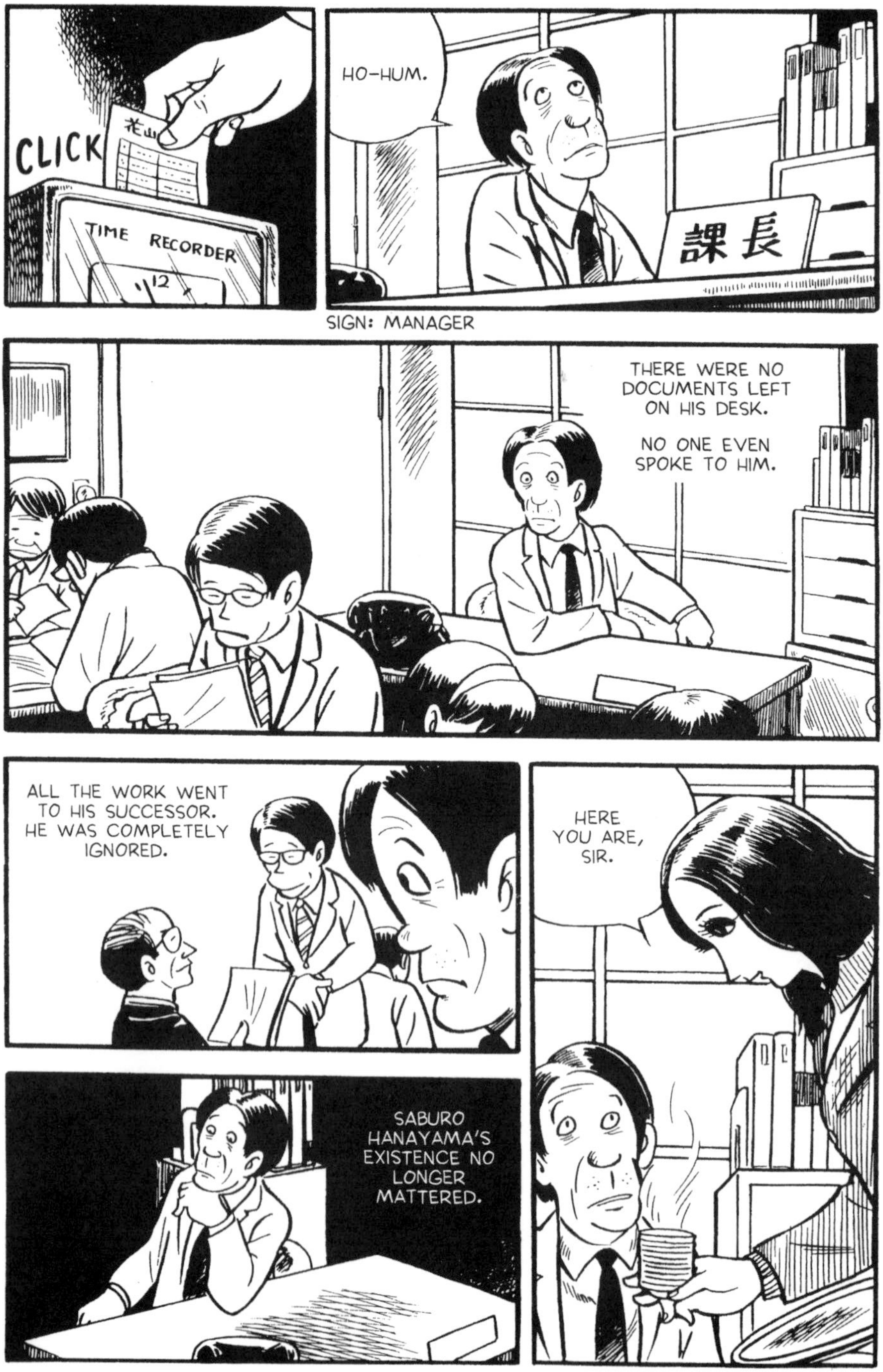
CLICK
花山
TIME RECORDER
12
HO-HUM.
課長
SIGN: MANAGER
THERE WERE NO DOCUMENTS LEFT ON HIS DESK.
NO ONE EVEN SPOKE TO HIM.
ALL THE WORK WENT TO HIS SUCCESSOR. HE WAS COMPLETELY IGNORED.
SABURO HANAYAMA'S EXISTENCE NO LONGER MATTERED.
HERE YOU ARE, SIR.

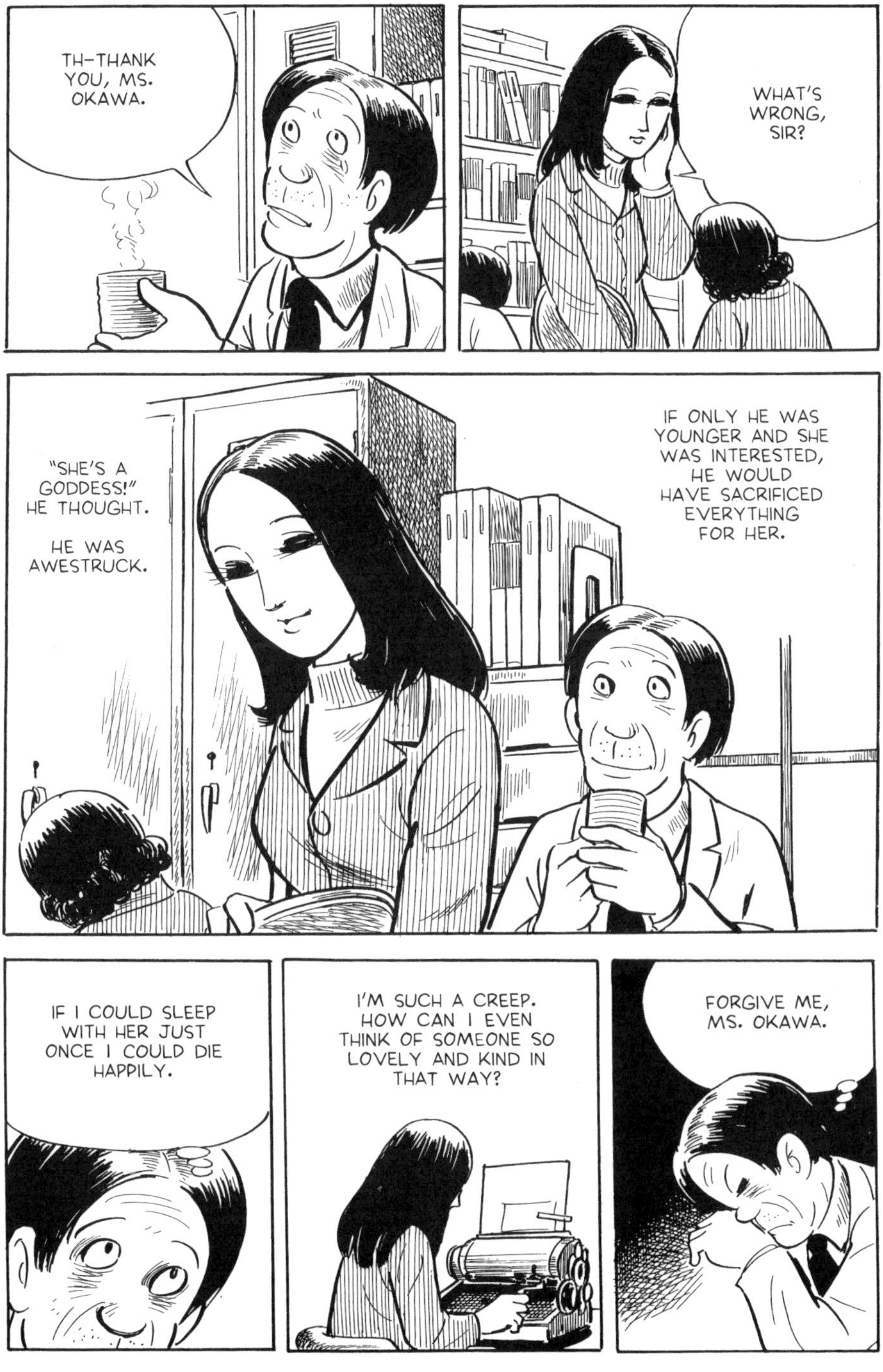
TH-THANK YOU, MS. OKAWA.
WHAT'S WRONG, SIR?
"SHE'S A GODDESS!" HE THOUGHT.
HE WAS AWESTRUCK.
IF ONLY HE WAS YOUNGER AND SHE WAS INTERESTED, HE WOULD HAVE SACRIFICED EVERYTHING FOR HER.
IF I COULD SLEEP WITH HER JUST ONCE I COULD DIE HAPPILY.
I'M SUCH A CREEP. HOW CAN I EVEN THINK OF SOMEONE SO LOVELY AND KIND IN THAT WAY?
FORGIVE ME, MS. OKAWA.

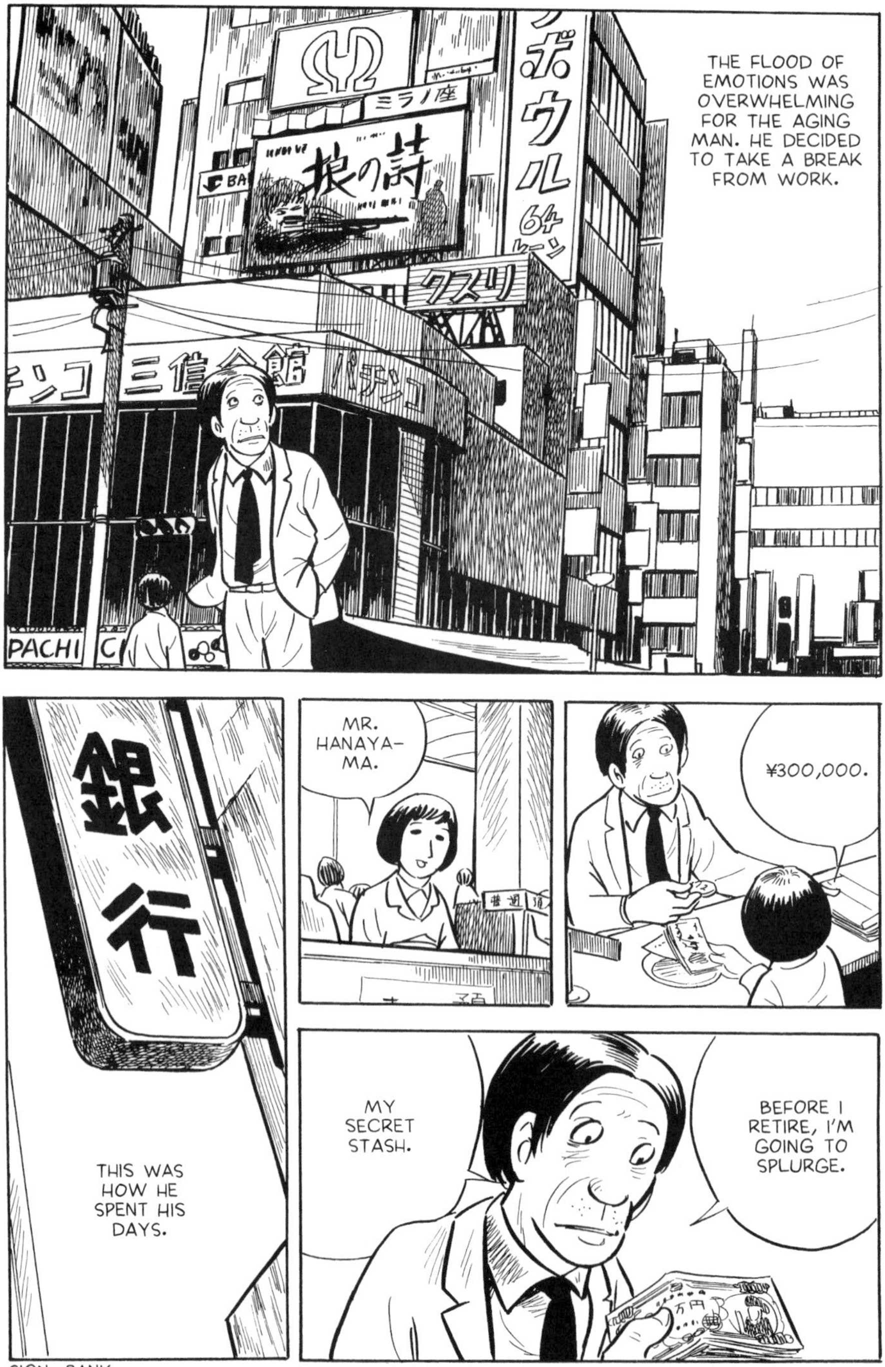
ミラノ座
狼の詩
クスリ
パチンコ
THE FLOOD OF EMOTIONS WAS OVERWHELMING FOR THE AGING MAN. HE DECIDED TO TAKE A BREAK FROM WORK.
銀行
THIS WAS HOW HE SPENT HIS DAYS.
MR. HANAYA-MA.
¥300,000.
MY SECRET STASH.
BEFORE I RETIRE, I'M GOING TO SPLURGE.
SIGN: BANK

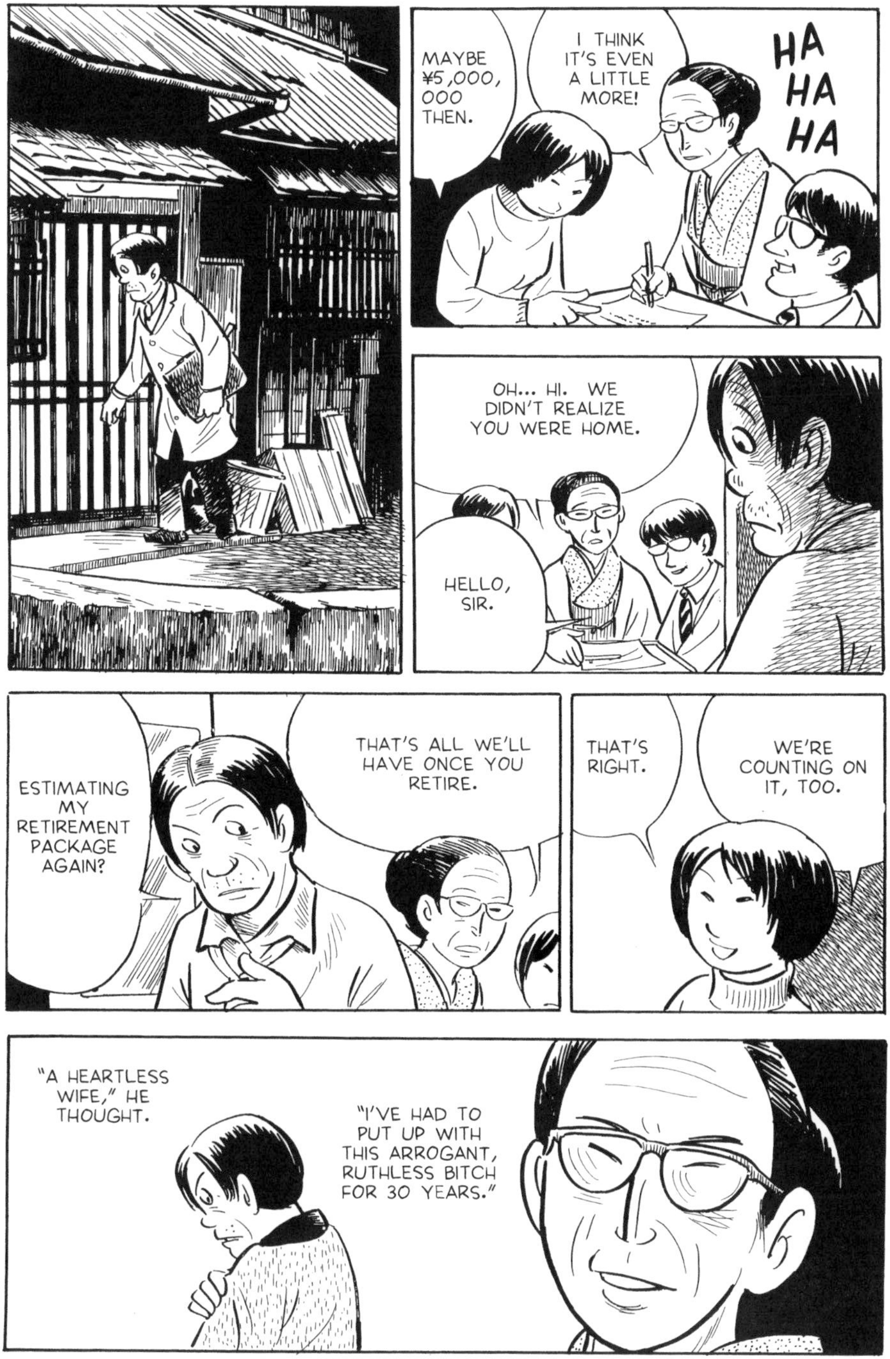
MAYBE ¥5,000,000 THEN.
I THINK IT'S EVEN A LITTLE MORE!
HA HA HA
OH... HI. WE DIDN'T REALIZE YOU WERE HOME.
HELLO, SIR.
ESTIMATING MY RETIREMENT PACKAGE AGAIN?
THAT'S ALL WE'LL HAVE ONCE YOU RETIRE.
THAT'S RIGHT.
WE'RE COUNTING ON IT, TOO.
"A HEARTLESS WIFE," HE THOUGHT.
"I'VE HAD TO PUT UP WITH THIS ARROGANT, RUTHLESS BITCH FOR 30 YEARS."

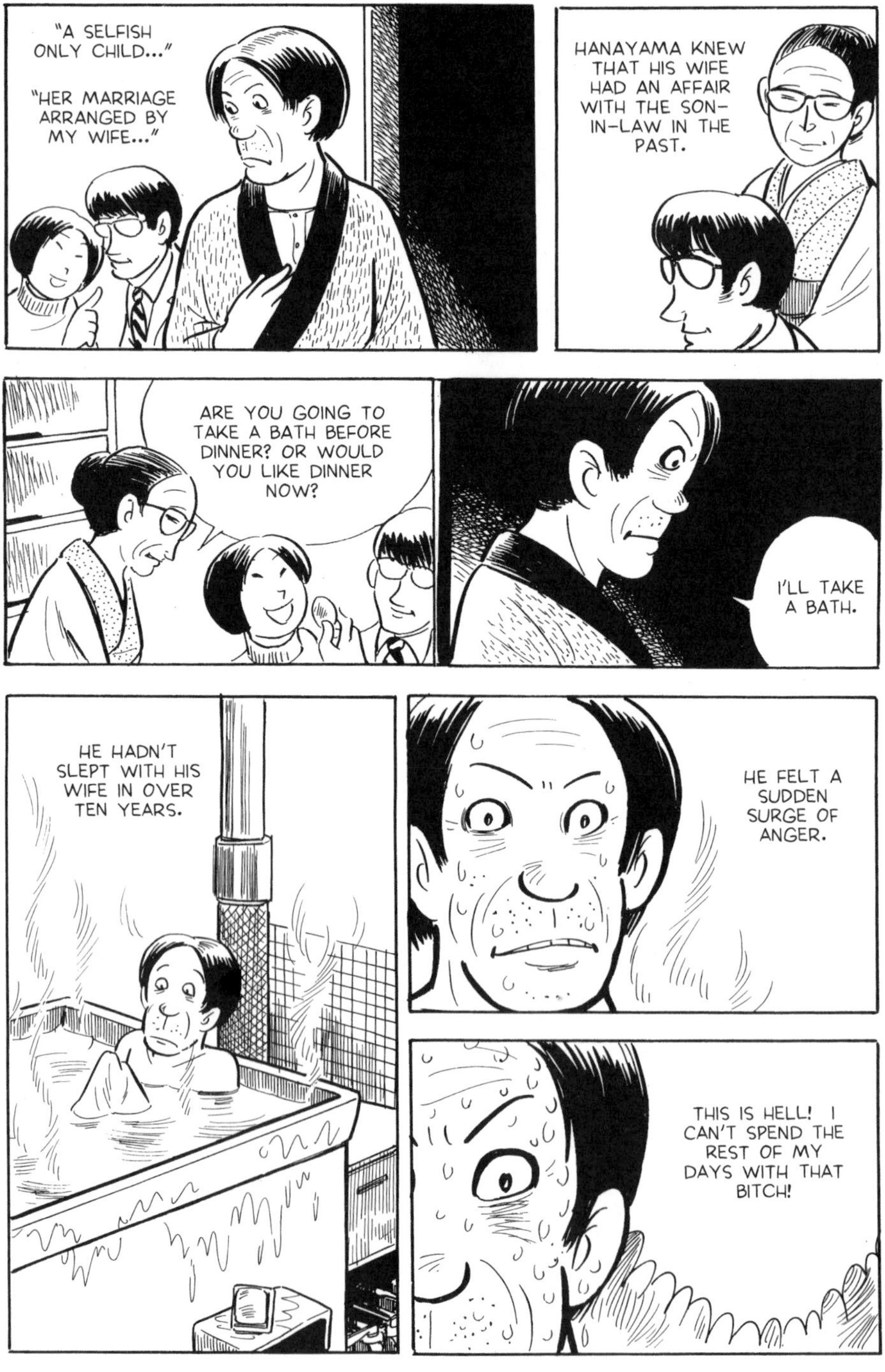
"A SELFISH ONLY CHILD..."
"HER MARRIAGE ARRANGED BY MY WIFE..."
HANAYAMA KNEW THAT HIS WIFE HAD AN AFFAIR WITH THE SON-IN-LAW IN THE PAST.
ARE YOU GOING TO TAKE A BATH BEFORE DINNER? OR WOULD YOU LIKE DINNER NOW?
I'LL TAKE A BATH.
HE HADN'T SLEPT WITH HIS WIFE IN OVER TEN YEARS.
HE FELT A SUDDEN SURGE OF ANGER.
THIS IS HELL! I CAN'T SPEND THE REST OF MY DAYS WITH THAT BITCH!

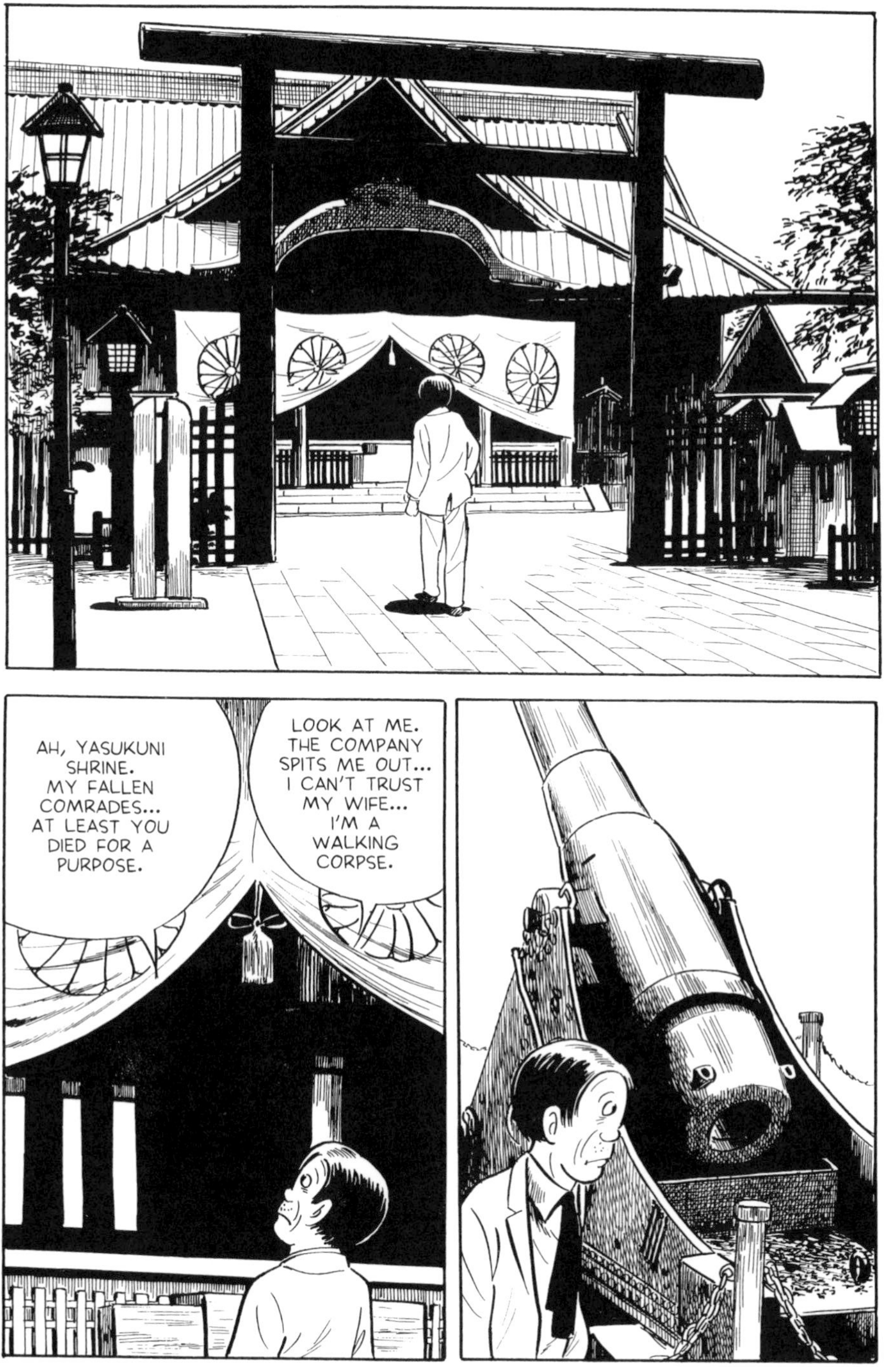
AH, YASUKUNI SHRINE. MY FALLEN COMRADES... AT LEAST YOU DIED FOR A PURPOSE.
LOOK AT ME. THE COMPANY SPITS ME OUT... I CAN'T TRUST MY WIFE... I'M A WALKING CORPSE.

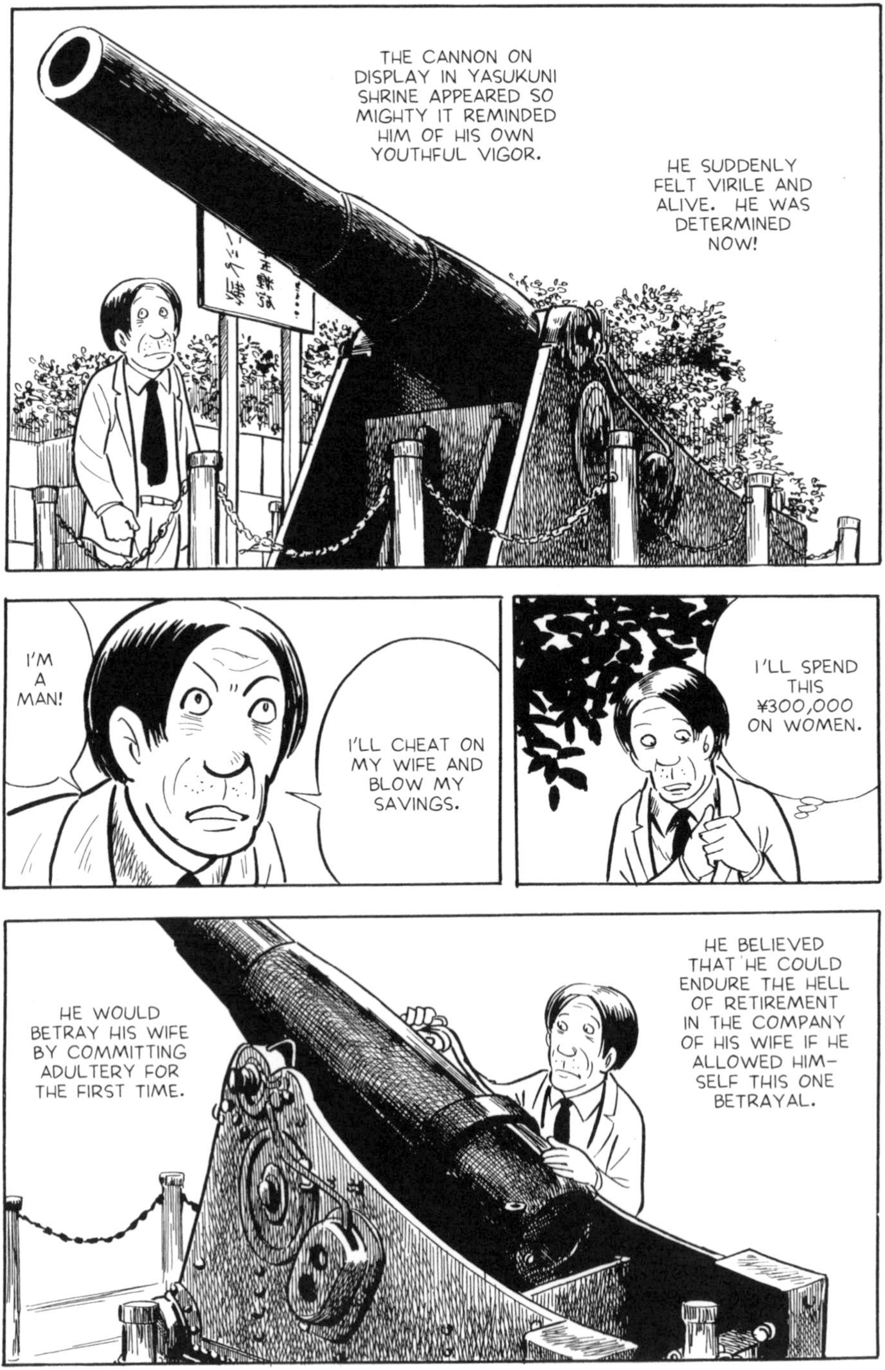
THE CANNON ON DISPLAY IN YASUKUNI SHRINE APPEARED SO MIGHTY IT REMINDED HIM OF HIS OWN YOUTHFUL VIGOR.
HE SUDDENLY FELT VIRILE AND ALIVE. HE WAS DETERMINED NOW!
I'M A MAN!
I'LL CHEAT ON MY WIFE AND BLOW MY SAVINGS.
I'LL SPEND THIS ¥300,000 ON WOMEN.
HE WOULD BETRAY HIS WIFE BY COMMITTING ADULTERY FOR THE FIRST TIME.
HE BELIEVED THAT HE COULD ENDURE THE HELL OF RETIREMENT IN THE COMPANY OF HIS WIFE IF HE ALLOWED HIM-SELF THIS ONE BETRAYAL.

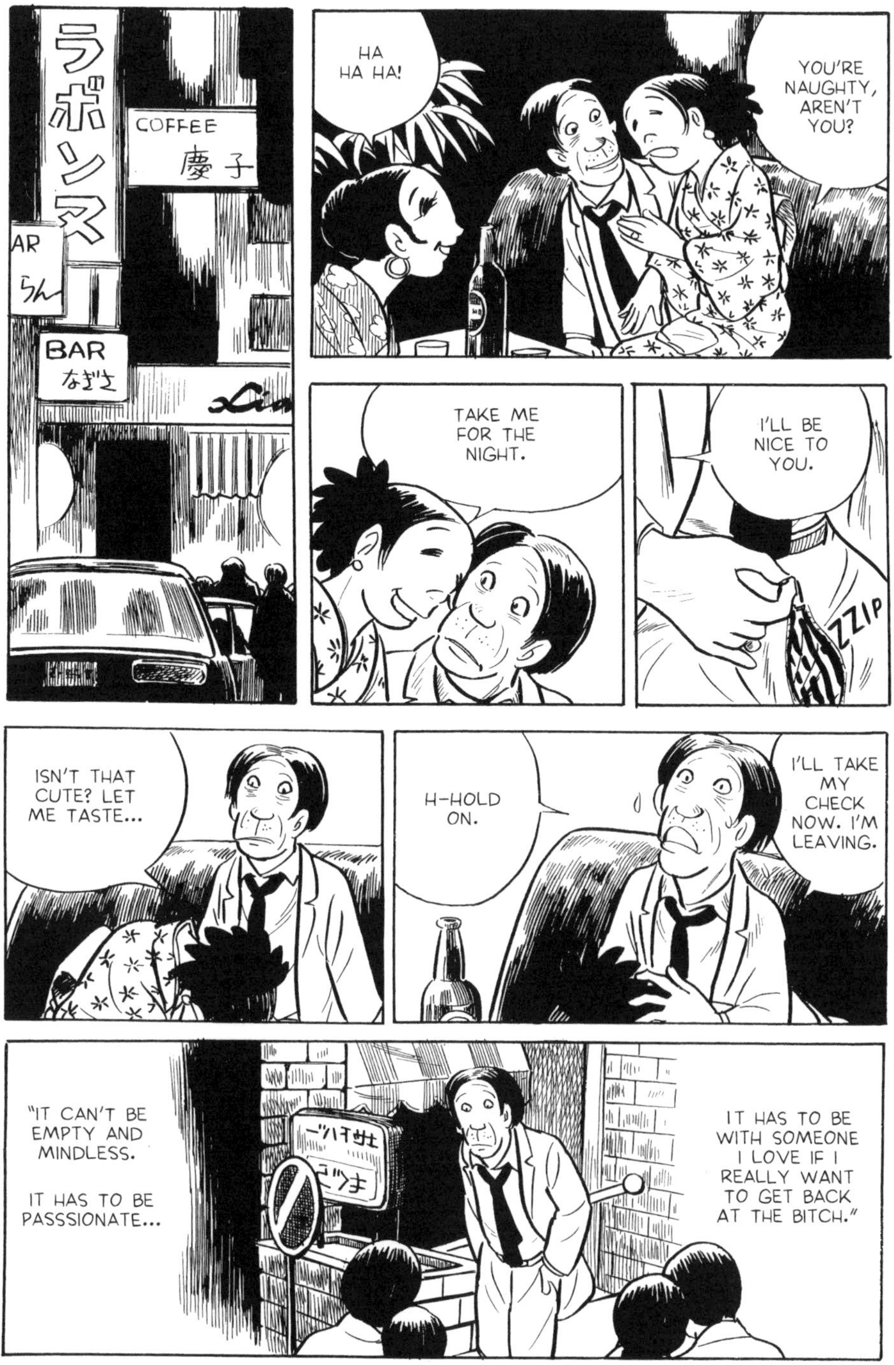
ラボンヌ
COFFEE
慶子
AR
らん
BAR
なぎさ
HA HA HA!
YOU'RE NAUGHTY, AREN'T YOU?
TAKE ME FOR THE NIGHT.
I'LL BE NICE TO YOU.
ZZIP
ISN'T THAT CUTE? LET ME TASTE...
H-HOLD ON.
I'LL TAKE MY CHECK NOW. I'M LEAVING.
"IT CAN'T BE EMPTY AND MINDLESS.
IT HAS TO BE PASSSIONATE...
IT HAS TO BE WITH SOMEONE I LOVE IF I REALLY WANT TO GET BACK AT THE BITCH."

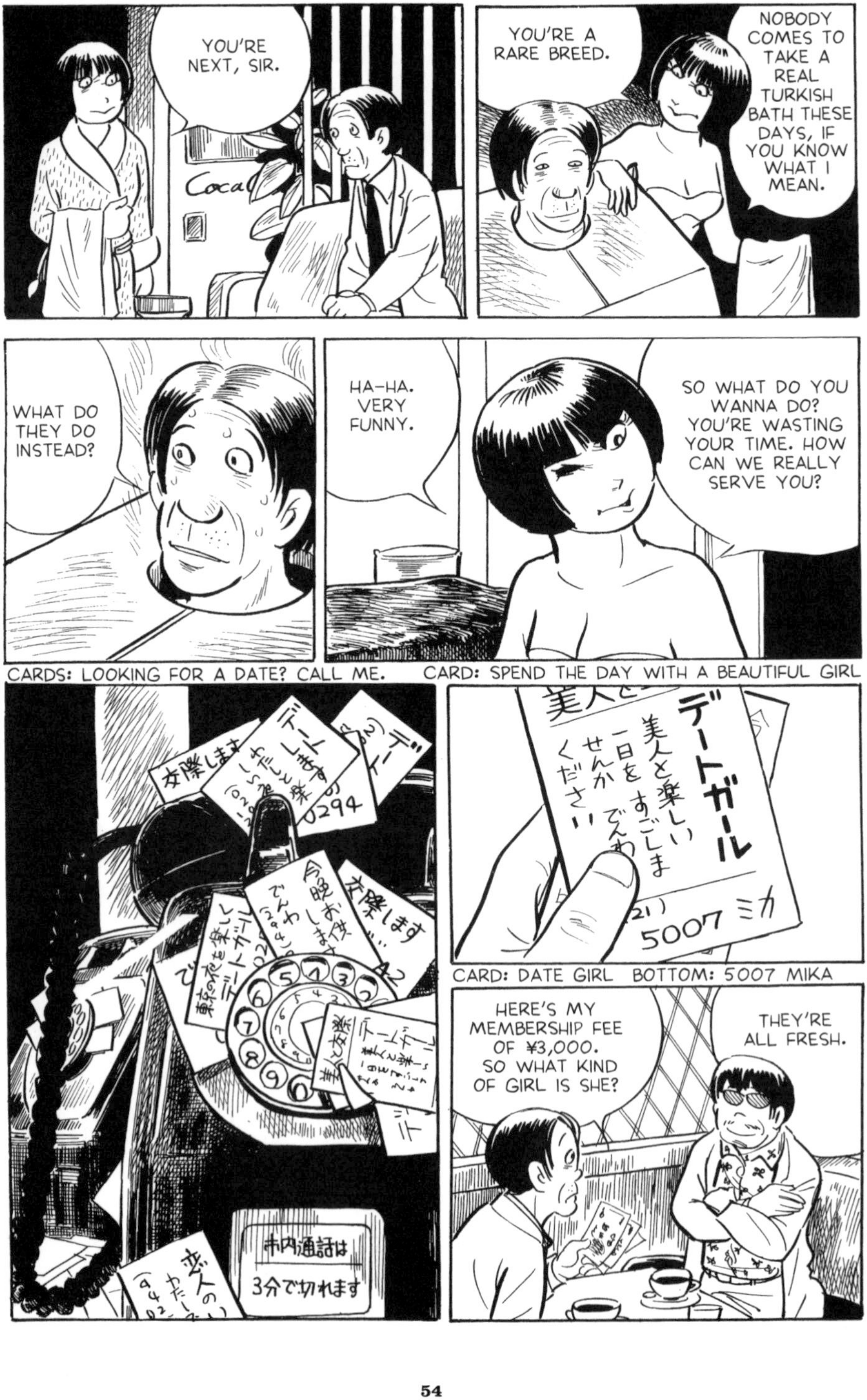
YOU'RE NEXT, SIR.
YOU'RE A RARE BREED.
NOBODY COMES TO TAKE A REAL TURKISH BATH THESE DAYS, IF YOU KNOW WHAT I MEAN.
WHAT DO THEY DO INSTEAD?
HA-HA. VERY FUNNY.
SO WHAT DO YOU WANNA DO? YOU'RE WASTING YOUR TIME. HOW CAN WE REALLY SERVE YOU?
CARDS: LOOKING FOR A DATE? CALL ME.
市内通話は
3分で切れます
CARD: SPEND THE DAY WITH A BEAUTIFUL GIRL
デートガール
5007 ミカ
CARD: DATE GIRL BOTTOM: 5007 MIKA
HERE'S MY MEMBERSHIP FEE OF ¥3,000. SO WHAT KIND OF GIRL IS SHE?
THEY'RE ALL FRESH.

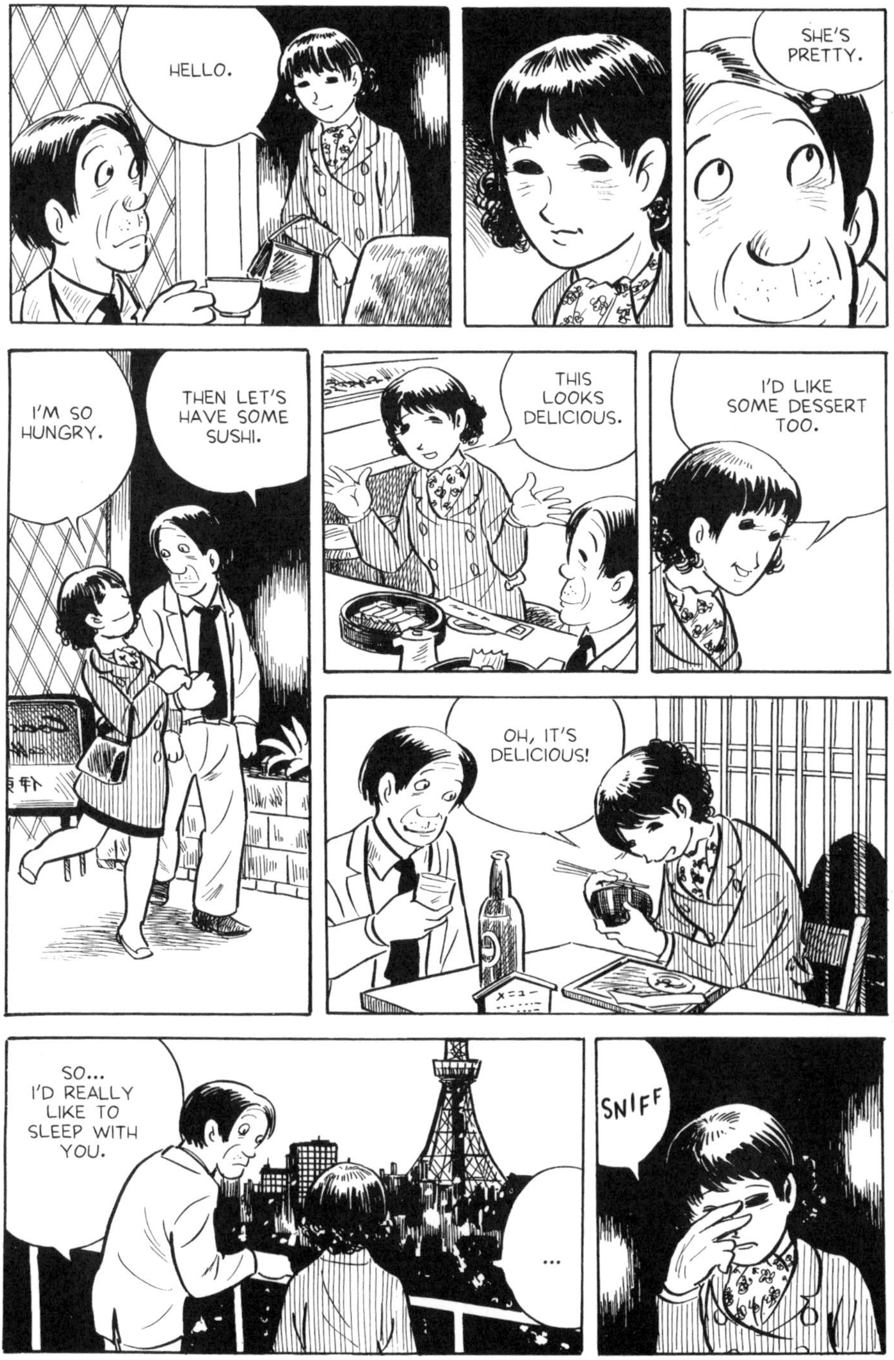
HELLO.
SHE'S PRETTY.
I'M SO HUNGRY.
THEN LET'S HAVE SOME SUSHI.
THIS LOOKS DELICIOUS.
I'D LIKE SOME DESSERT TOO.
OH, IT'S DELICIOUS!
SO... I'D REALLY LIKE TO SLEEP WITH YOU.
...
SNIFF

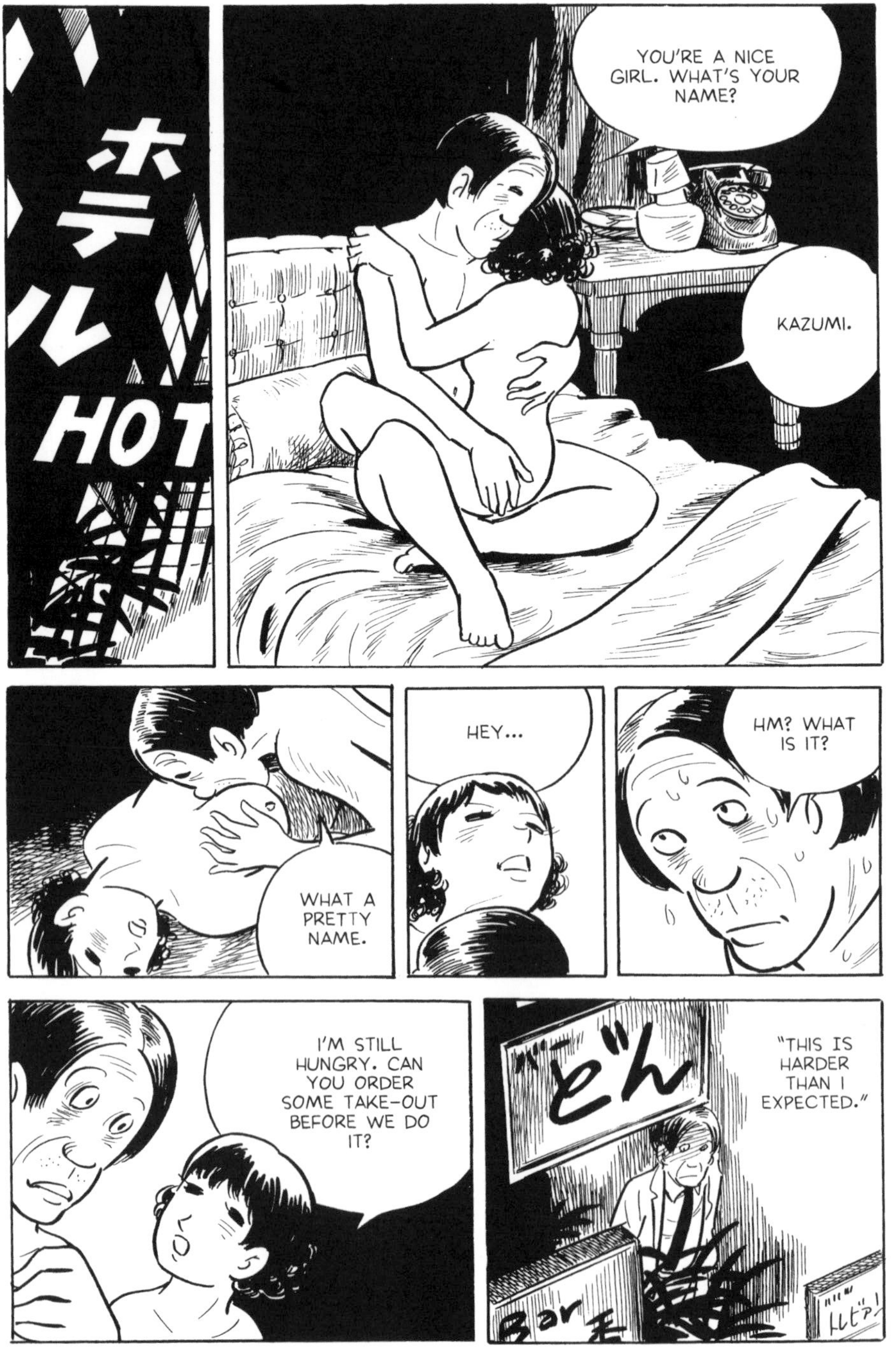
ホテル
HOT
YOU'RE A NICE GIRL. WHAT'S YOUR NAME?
KAZUMI.
WHAT A PRETTY NAME.
HEY...
HM? WHAT IS IT?
I'M STILL HUNGRY. CAN YOU ORDER SOME TAKE-OUT BEFORE WE DO IT?
バー どん
"THIS IS HARDER THAN I EXPECTED."

RAHH

RAHH

HE TRIED GAMBLING ON HORSES, SOMETHING HE'D NEVER DONE BEFORE.

BEFORE HE KNEW IT, HIS ENTIRE SAVINGS WAS GONE.

HE TOOK OUT A LOAN AGAINST HIS RETIREMENT PACKAGE AND GAMBLED MORE.

IT DIDN'T REALLY THRILL HIM. STILL...

... IT WAS ANOTHER WAY TO BETRAY HIS WIFE.

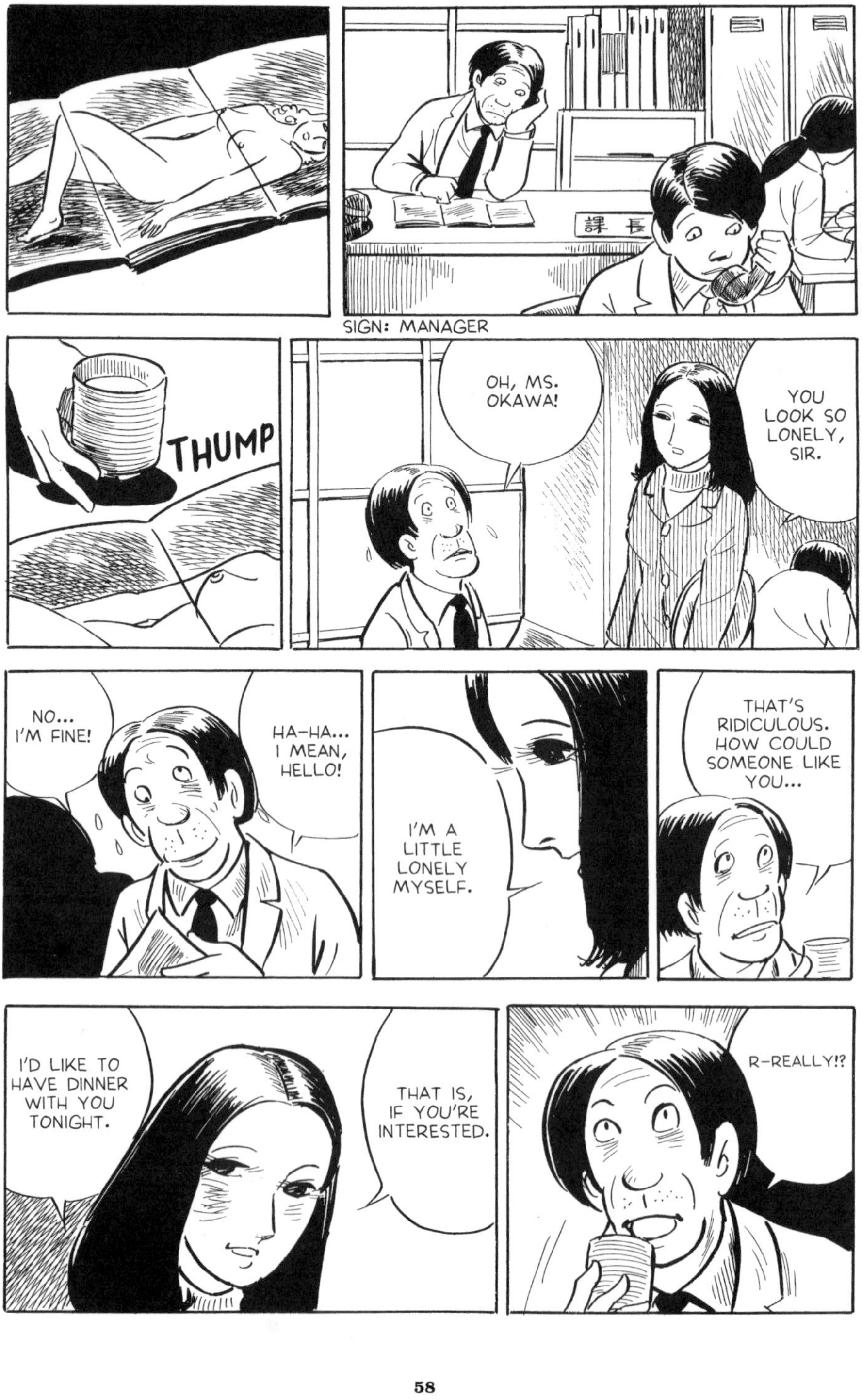
課長
SIGN: MANAGER
THUMP
OH, MS. OKAWA!
YOU LOOK SO LONELY, SIR.
NO... I'M FINE!
HA-HA... I MEAN, HELLO!
I'M A LITTLE LONELY MYSELF.
THAT'S RIDICULOUS. HOW COULD SOMEONE LIKE YOU...
I'D LIKE TO HAVE DINNER WITH YOU TONIGHT.
THAT IS, IF YOU'RE INTERESTED.
R-REALLY!?

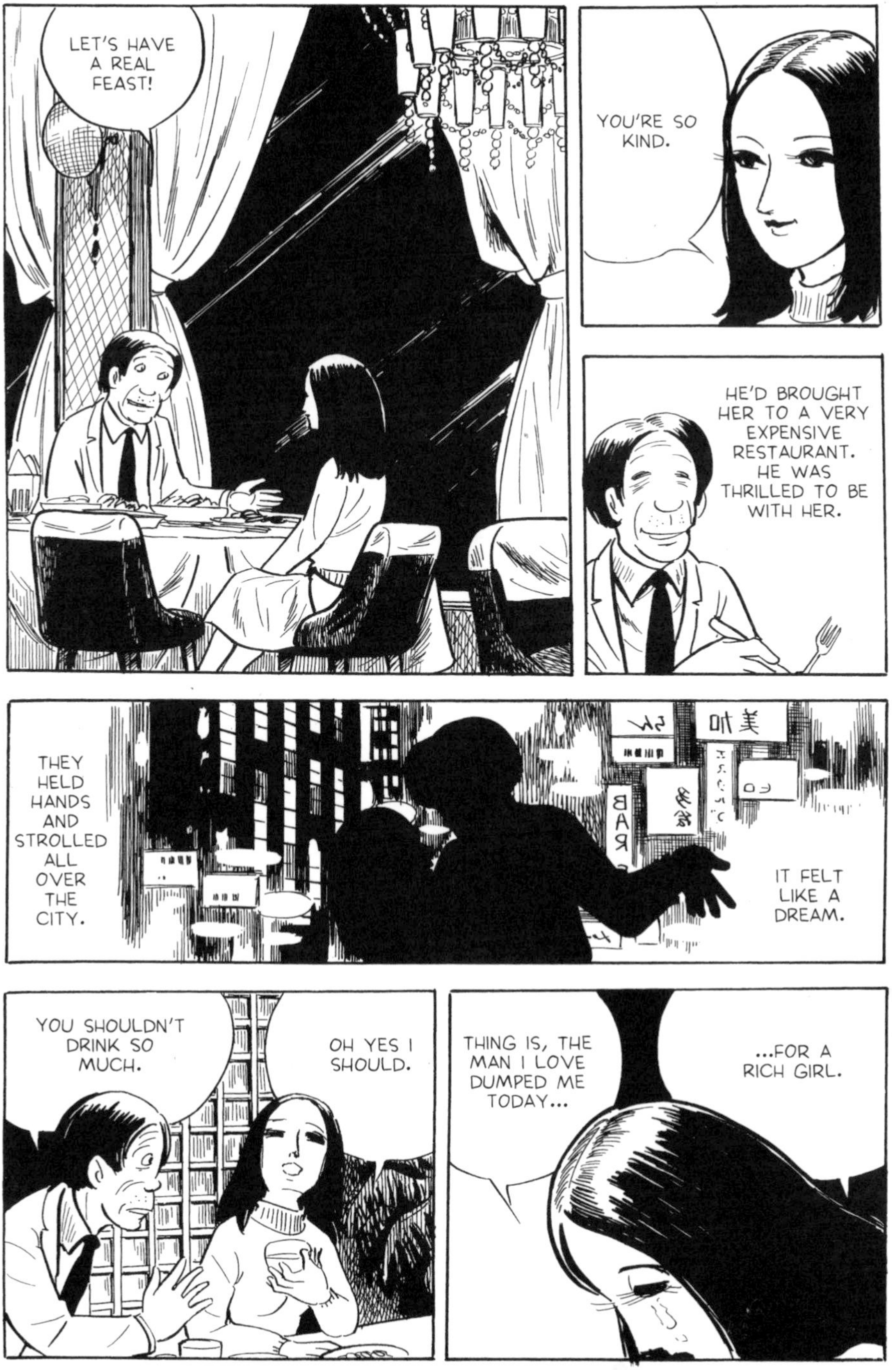
LET'S HAVE A REAL FEAST!
YOU'RE SO KIND.
HE'D BROUGHT HER TO A VERY EXPENSIVE RESTAURANT. HE WAS THRILLED TO BE WITH HER.
THEY HELD HANDS AND STROLLED ALL OVER THE CITY.
BAR
IT FELT LIKE A DREAM.
YOU SHOULDN'T DRINK SO MUCH.
OH YES I SHOULD.
THING IS, THE MAN I LOVE DUMPED ME TODAY...
...FOR A RICH GIRL.

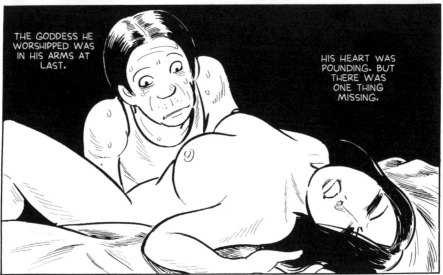

THE GODDESS HE WORSHIPPED WAS IN HIS ARMS AT LAST.

HIS HEART WAS POUNDING. BUT THERE WAS ONE THING MISSING.

THIS CAN'T BE HAPPENING.

HE PANICKED.

WHAT'S WRONG, SIR?

THEY BOTH WEPT. THE AFFAIR DID NOTHING TO EASE THE PAIN...

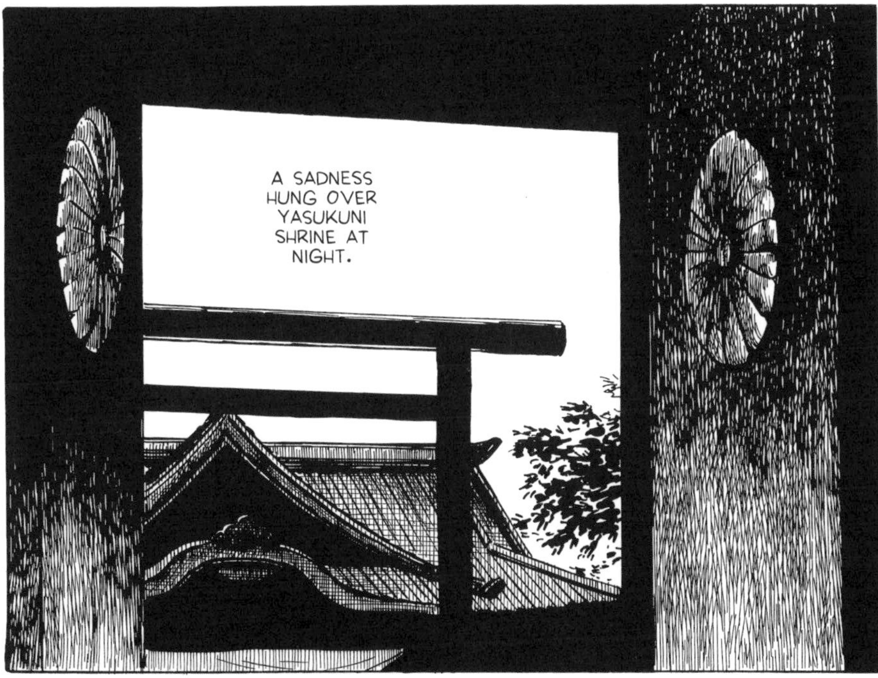
A SADNESS HUNG OVER YASUKUNI SHRINE AT NIGHT.

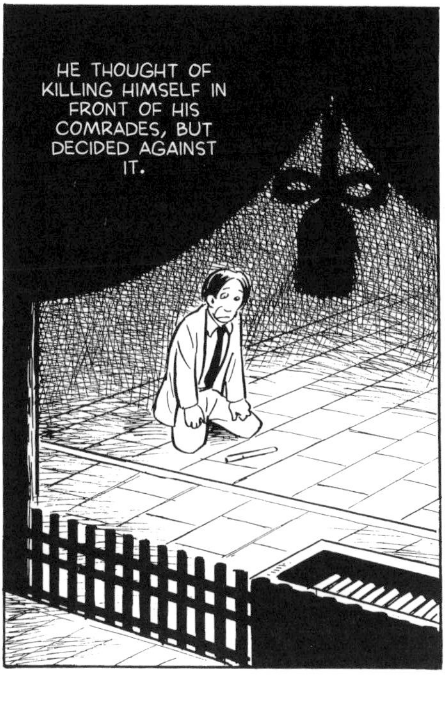
HE THOUGHT OF KILLING HIMSELF IN FRONT OF HIS COMRADES, BUT DECIDED AGAINST IT.

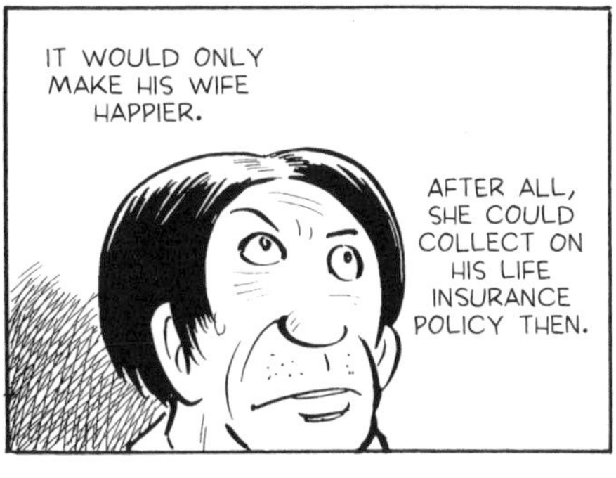
IT WOULD ONLY MAKE HIS WIFE HAPPIER.
AFTER ALL, SHE COULD COLLECT ON HIS LIFE INSURANCE POLICY THEN.

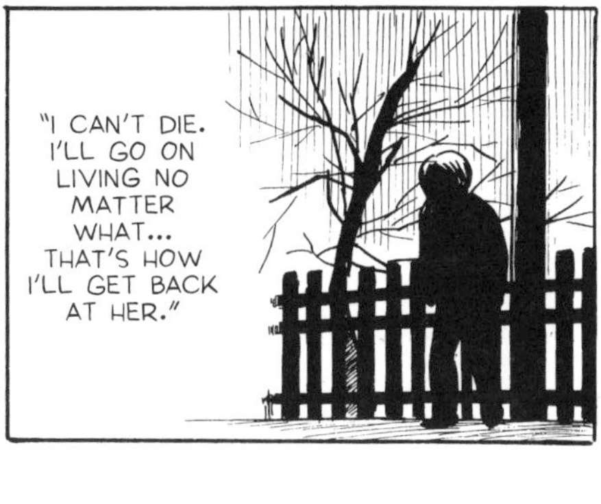
"I CAN'T DIE. I'LL GO ON LIVING NO MATTER WHAT... THAT'S HOW I'LL GET BACK AT HER."

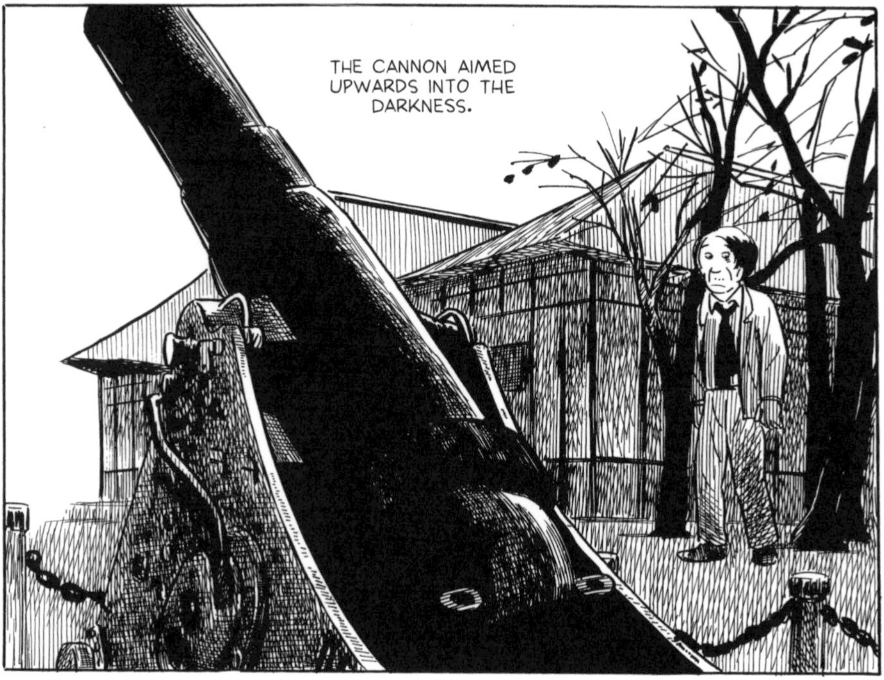
THE CANNON AIMED UPWARDS INTO THE DARKNESS.

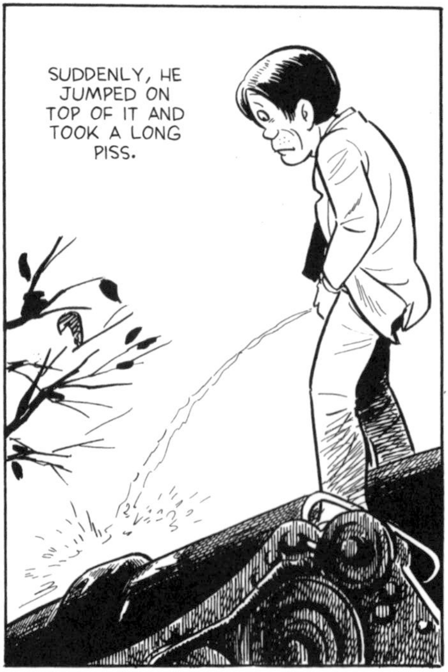
SUDDENLY, HE JUMPED ON TOP OF IT AND TOOK A LONG PISS.

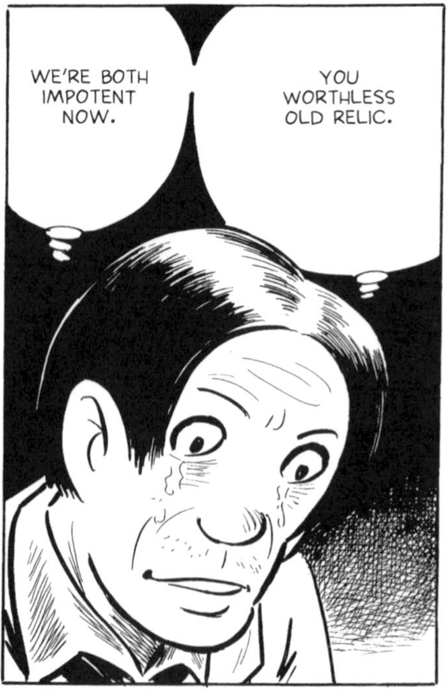
WE'RE BOTH IMPOTENT NOW.
YOU WORTHLESS OLD RELIC.

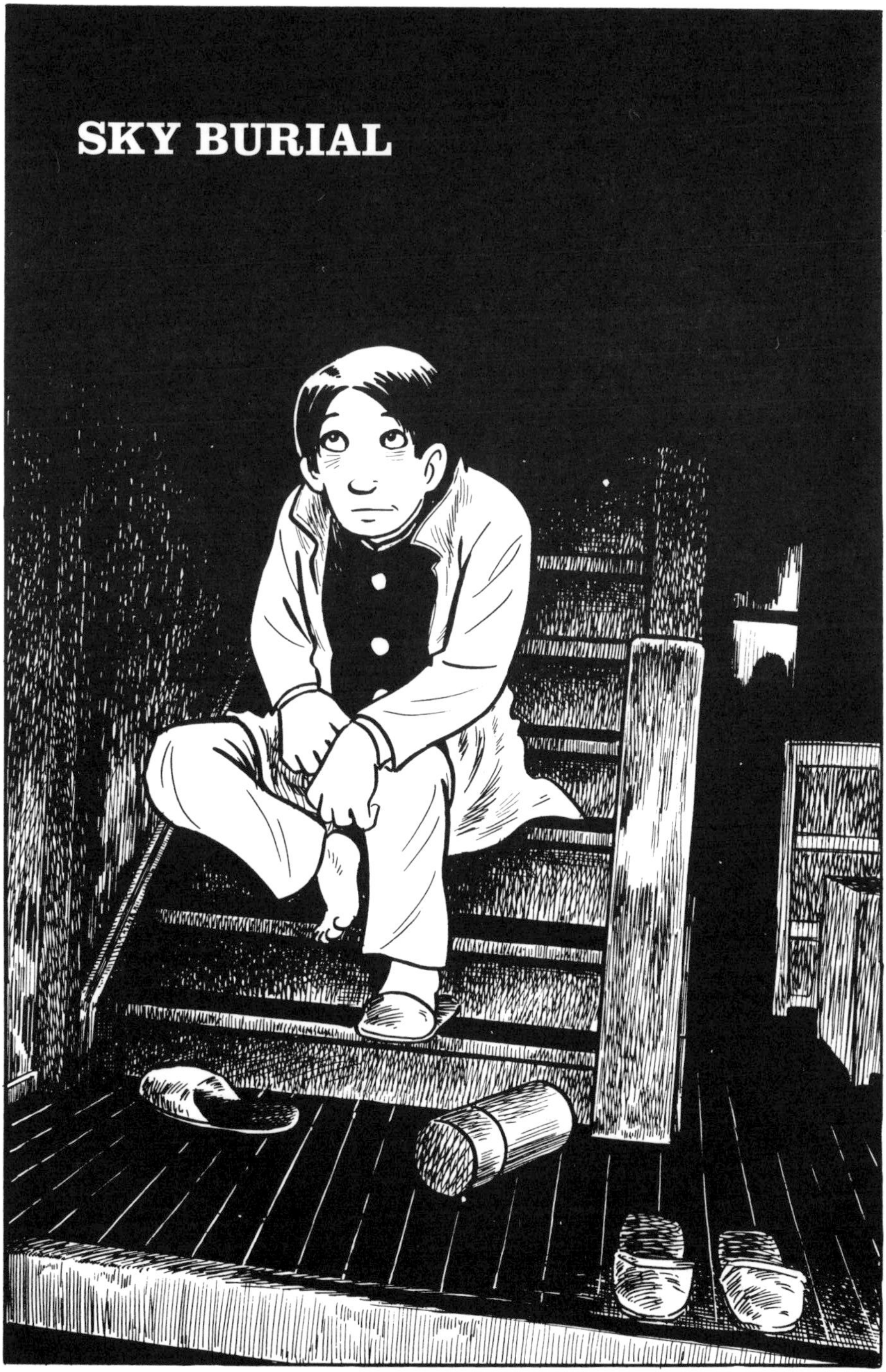
SKY BURIAL

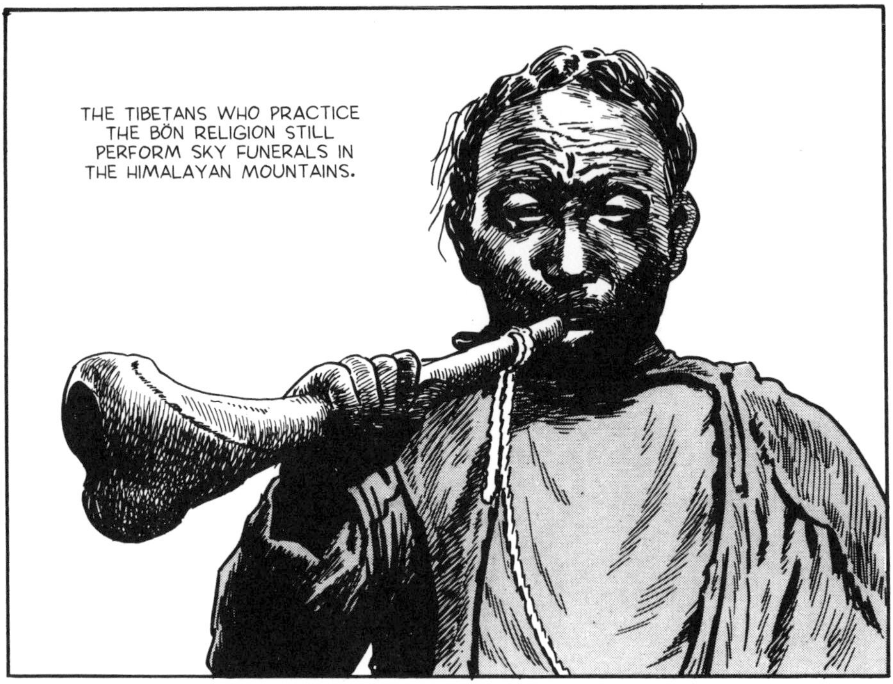
THE TIBETANS WHO PRACTICE THE BÖN RELIGION STILL PERFORM SKY FUNERALS IN THE HIMALAYAN MOUNTAINS.

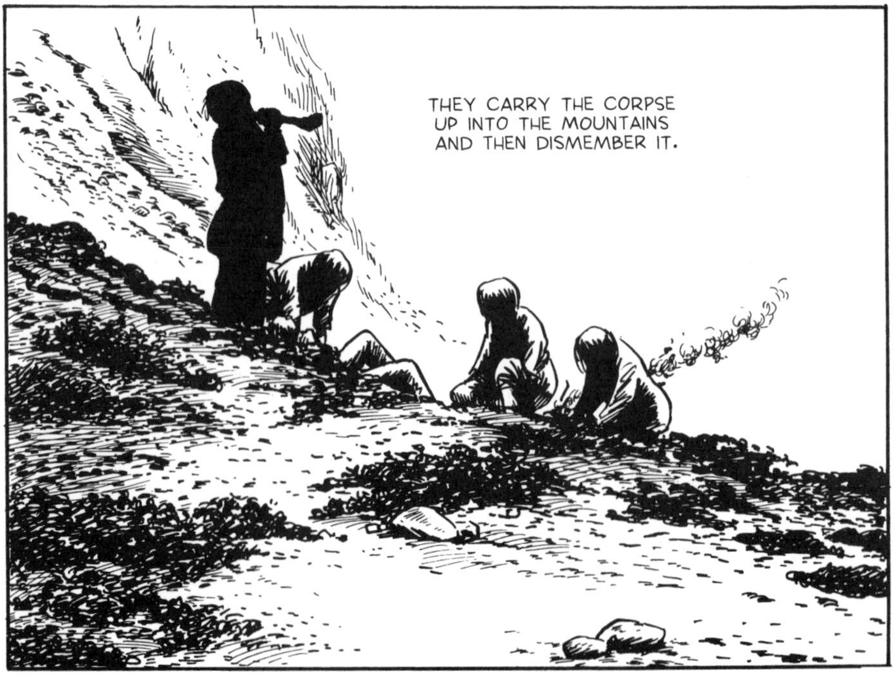
THEY CARRY THE CORPSE UP INTO THE MOUNTAINS AND THEN DISMEMBER IT.

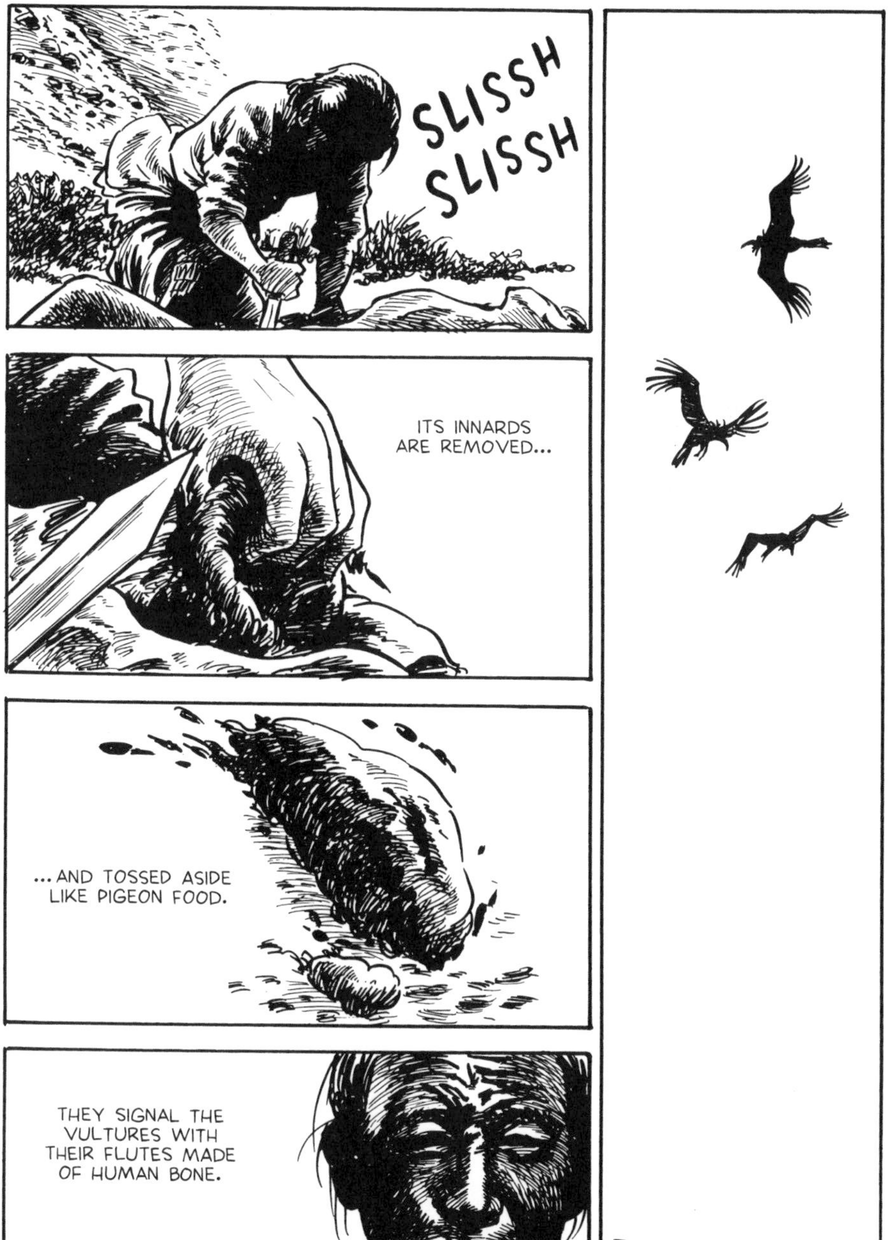
SLISSH SLISSH
ITS INNARDS ARE REMOVED...
...AND TOSSED ASIDE LIKE PIGEON FOOD.
THEY SIGNAL THE VULTURES WITH THEIR FLUTES MADE OF HUMAN BONE.

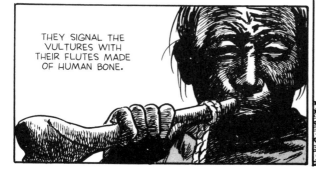

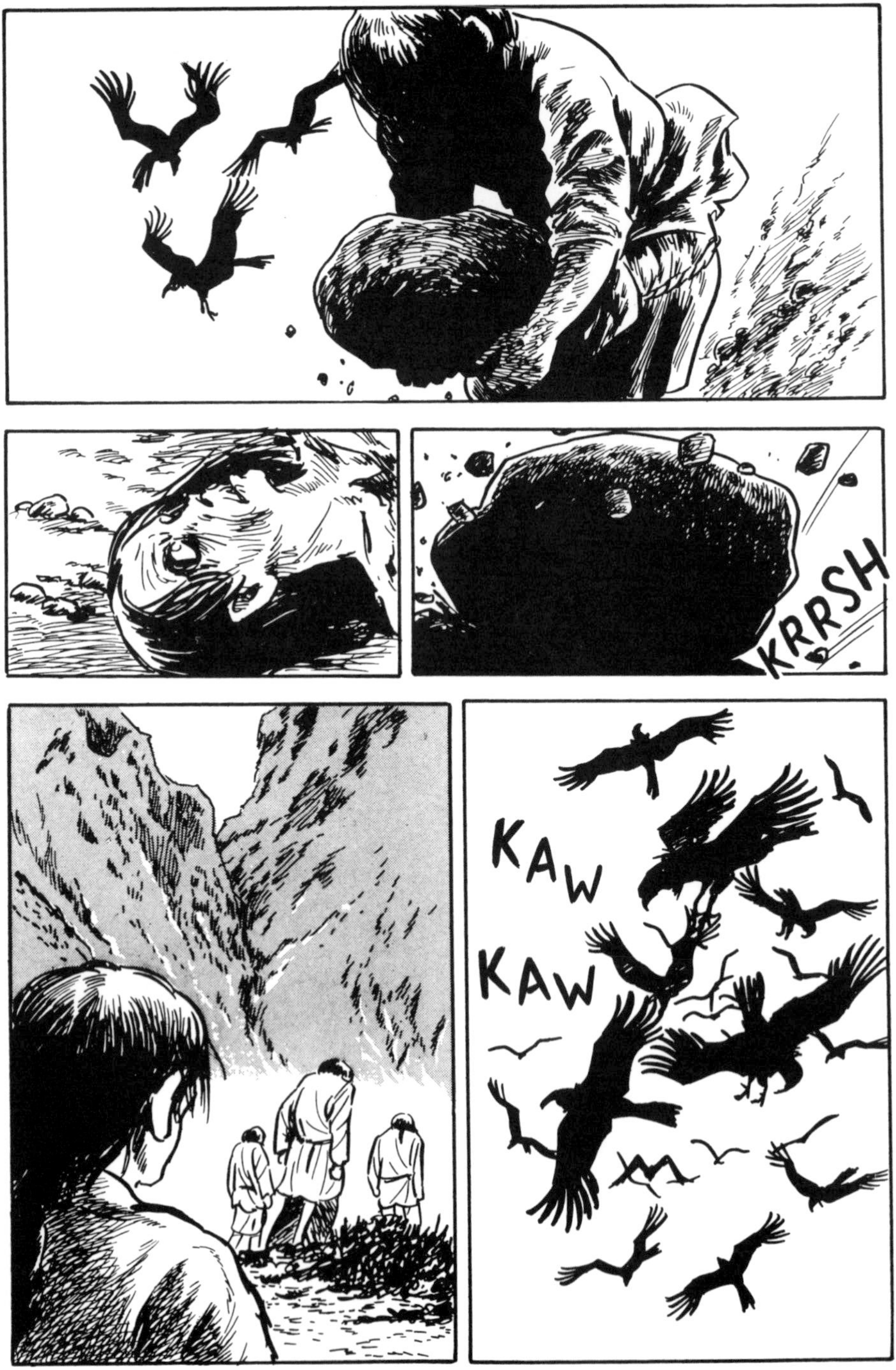
KRRSH
KAW
KAW

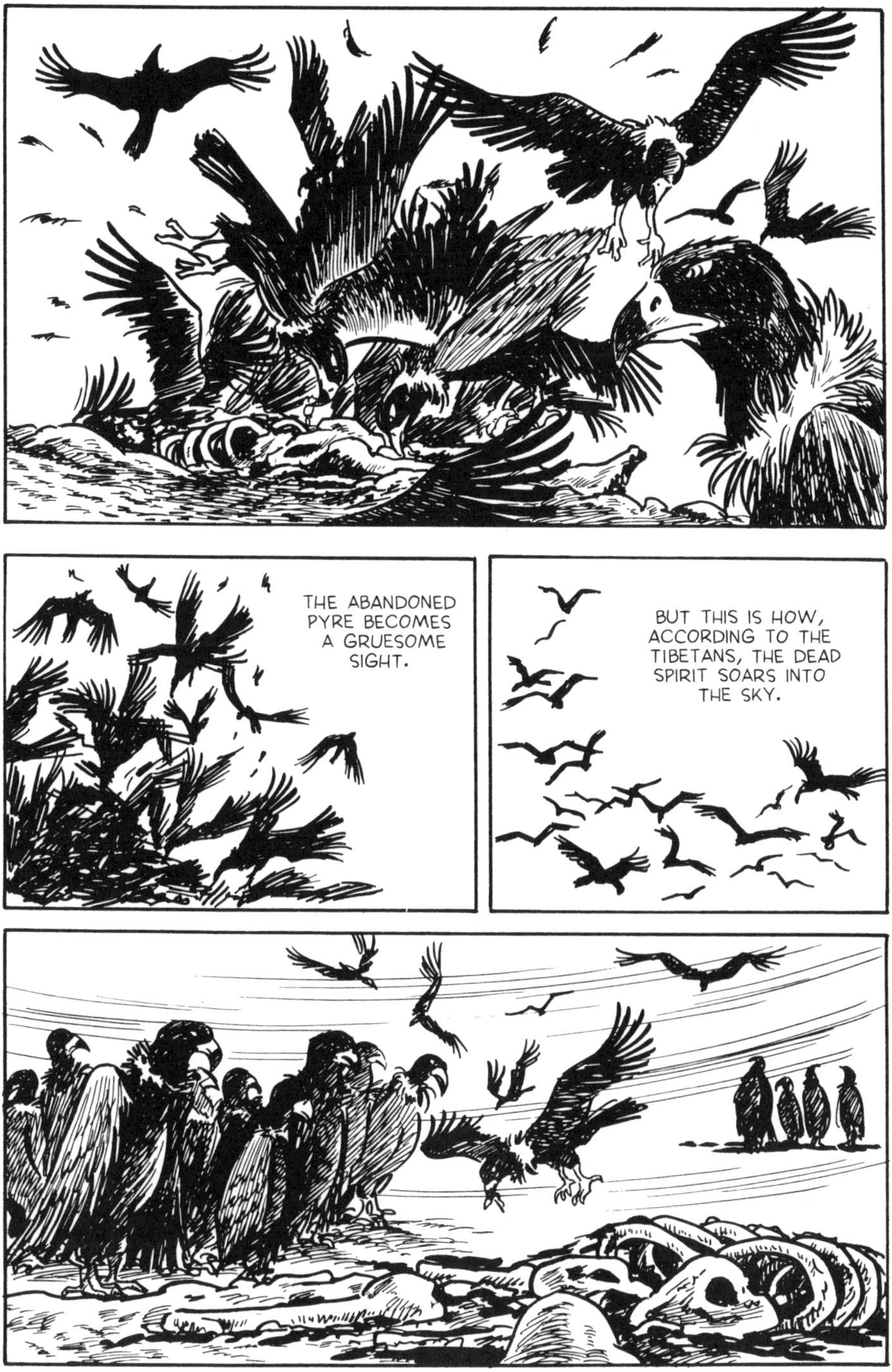
THE ABANDONED PYRE BECOMES A GRUESOME SIGHT.
BUT THIS IS HOW, ACCORDING TO THE TIBETANS, THE DEAD SPIRIT SOARS INTO THE SKY.

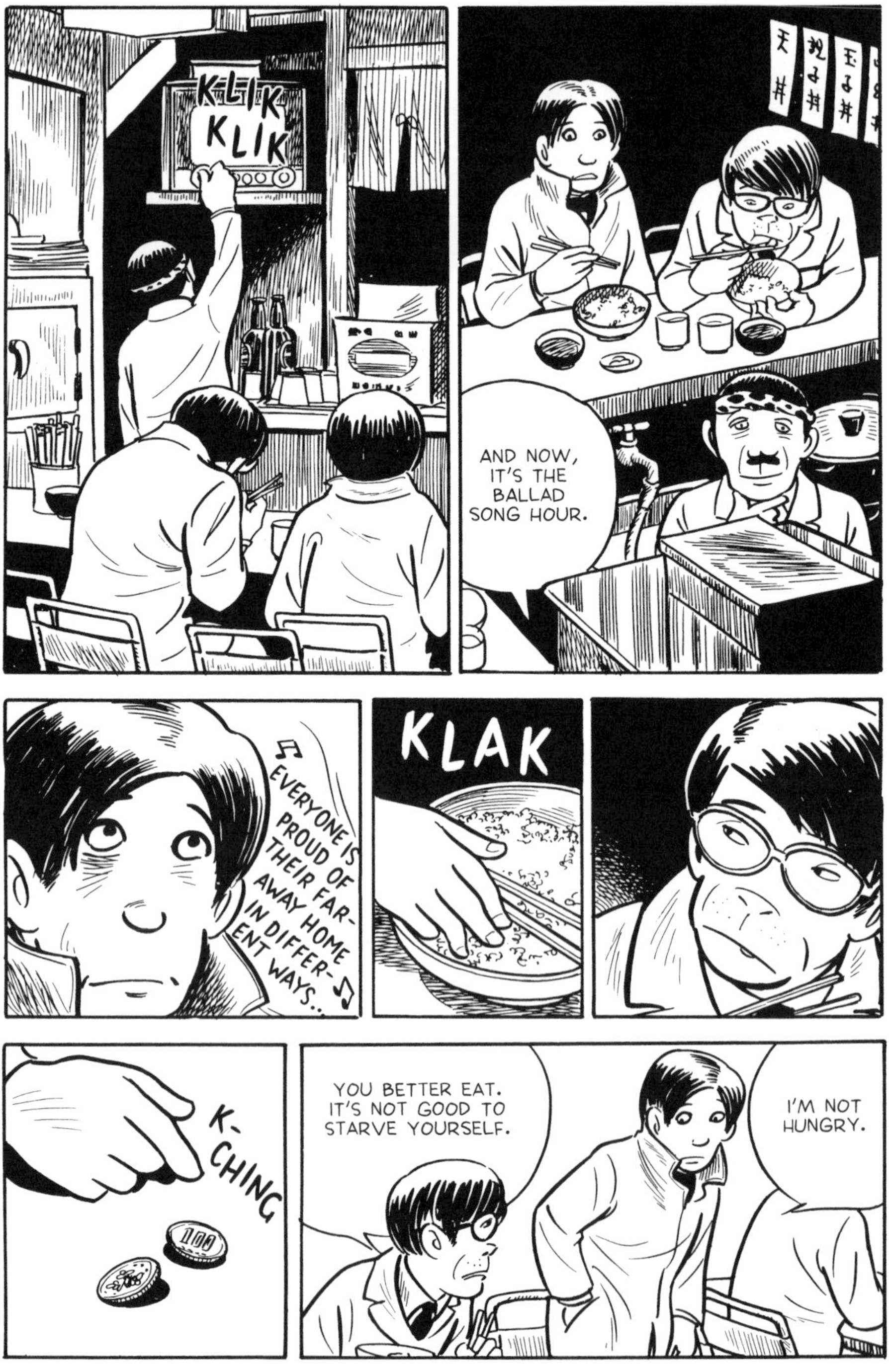
KLIK
KLIK
AND NOW, IT'S THE BALLAD SONG HOUR.
♫ EVERYONE IS PROUD OF THEIR FAR-AWAY HOME IN DIFFER-ENT WAYS... ♪
KLAK
K-CHING
100
YOU BETTER EAT. IT'S NOT GOOD TO STARVE YOURSELF.
I'M NOT HUNGRY.

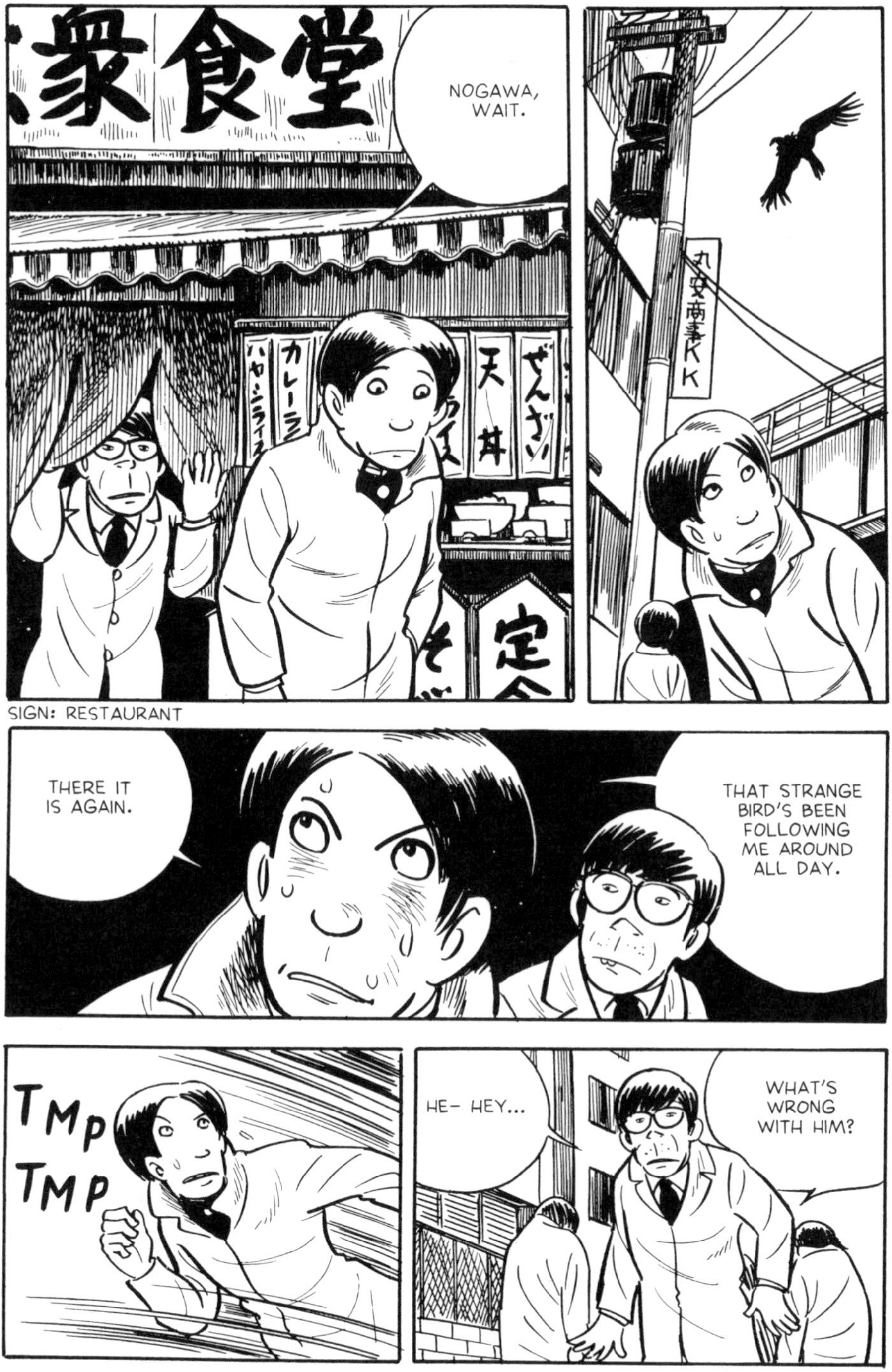
象食堂
NOGAWA, WAIT.
天丼
ぜんざい
丸安商事KK
SIGN: RESTAURANT
THERE IT IS AGAIN.
THAT STRANGE BIRD'S BEEN FOLLOWING ME AROUND ALL DAY.
TMP TMP
HE- HEY...
WHAT'S WRONG WITH HIM?

うなぎ
KLAKETTA
KLAKETTA
KLIK
大人
30
60
80
100
120
SIGN: ADULTS

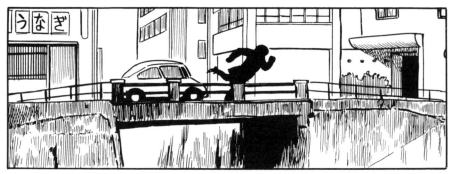

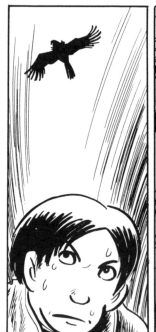

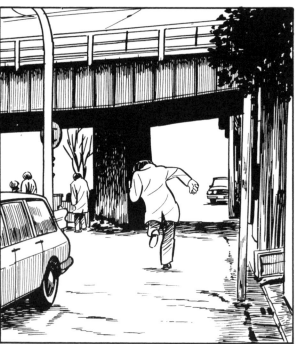

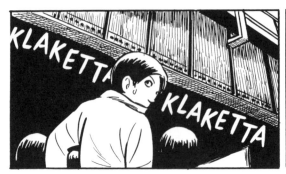

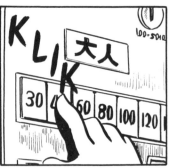

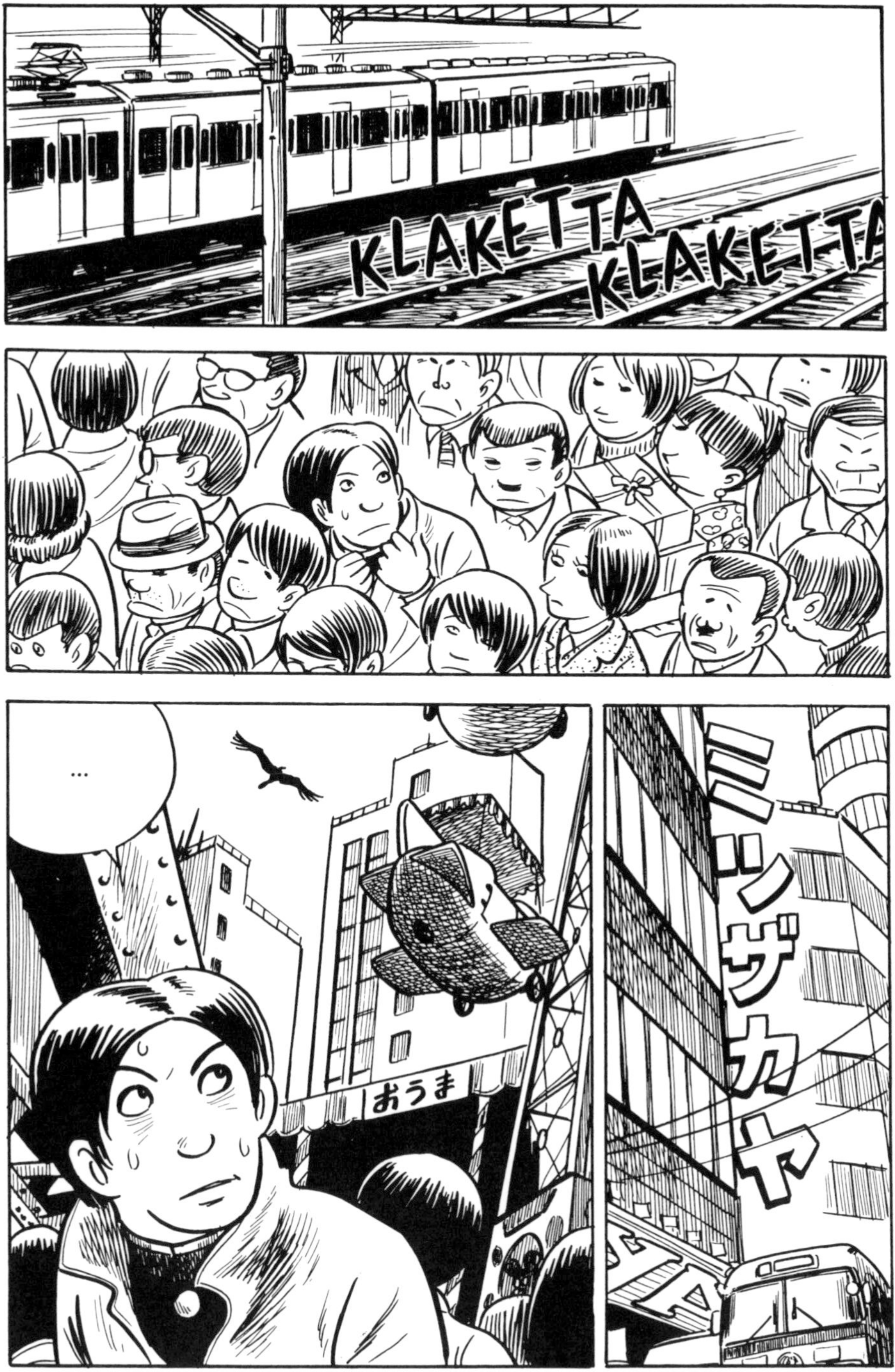
KLAKETTA
KLAKETTA
...
おうま
ミツザカヤ

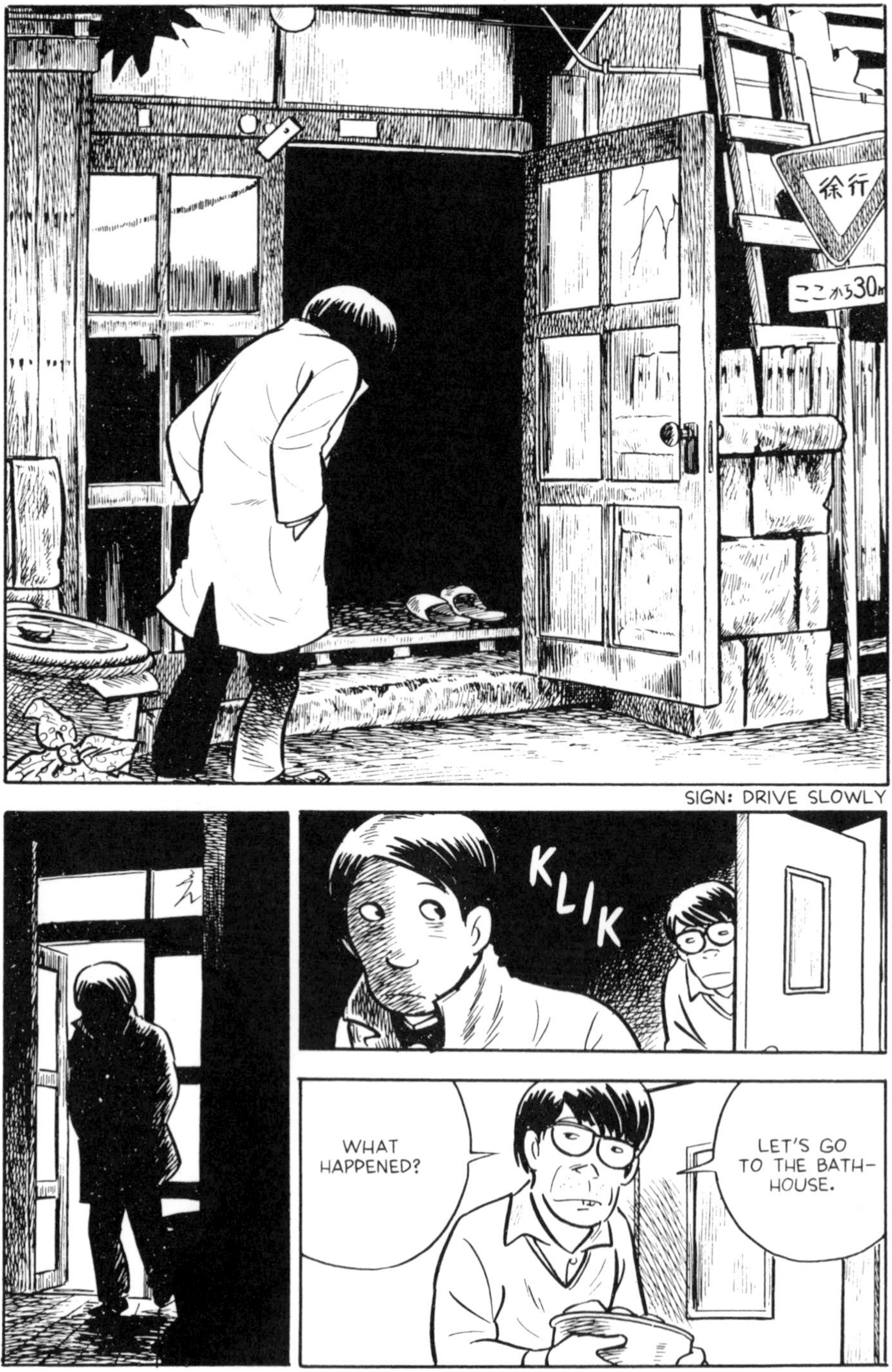
徐行
ここから30
SIGN: DRIVE SLOWLY
KLIK
WHAT HAPPENED?
LET'S GO TO THE BATH-HOUSE.

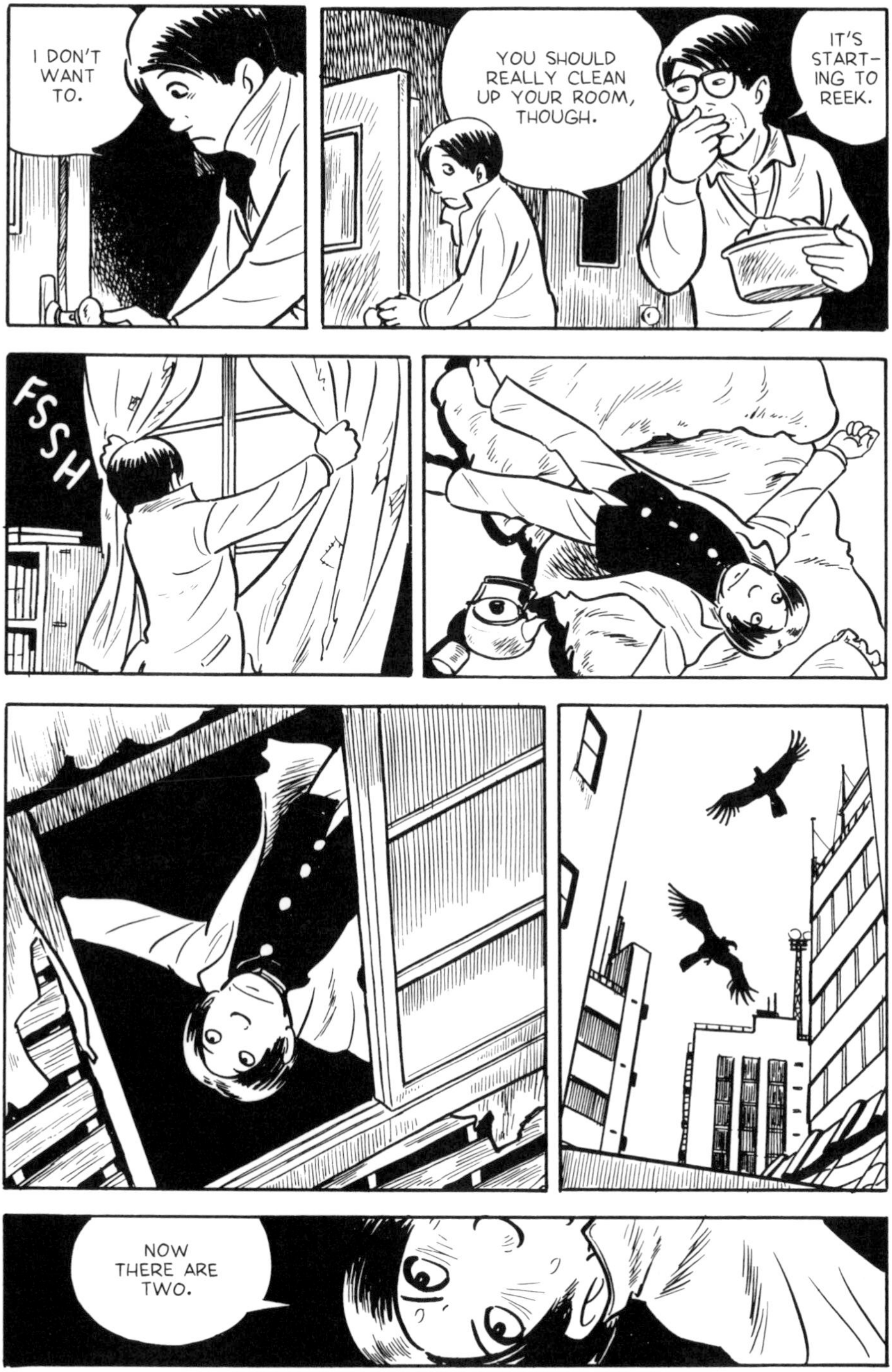
I DON'T WANT TO.
YOU SHOULD REALLY CLEAN UP YOUR ROOM, THOUGH.
IT'S STARTING TO REEK.
FSSH
NOW THERE ARE TWO.

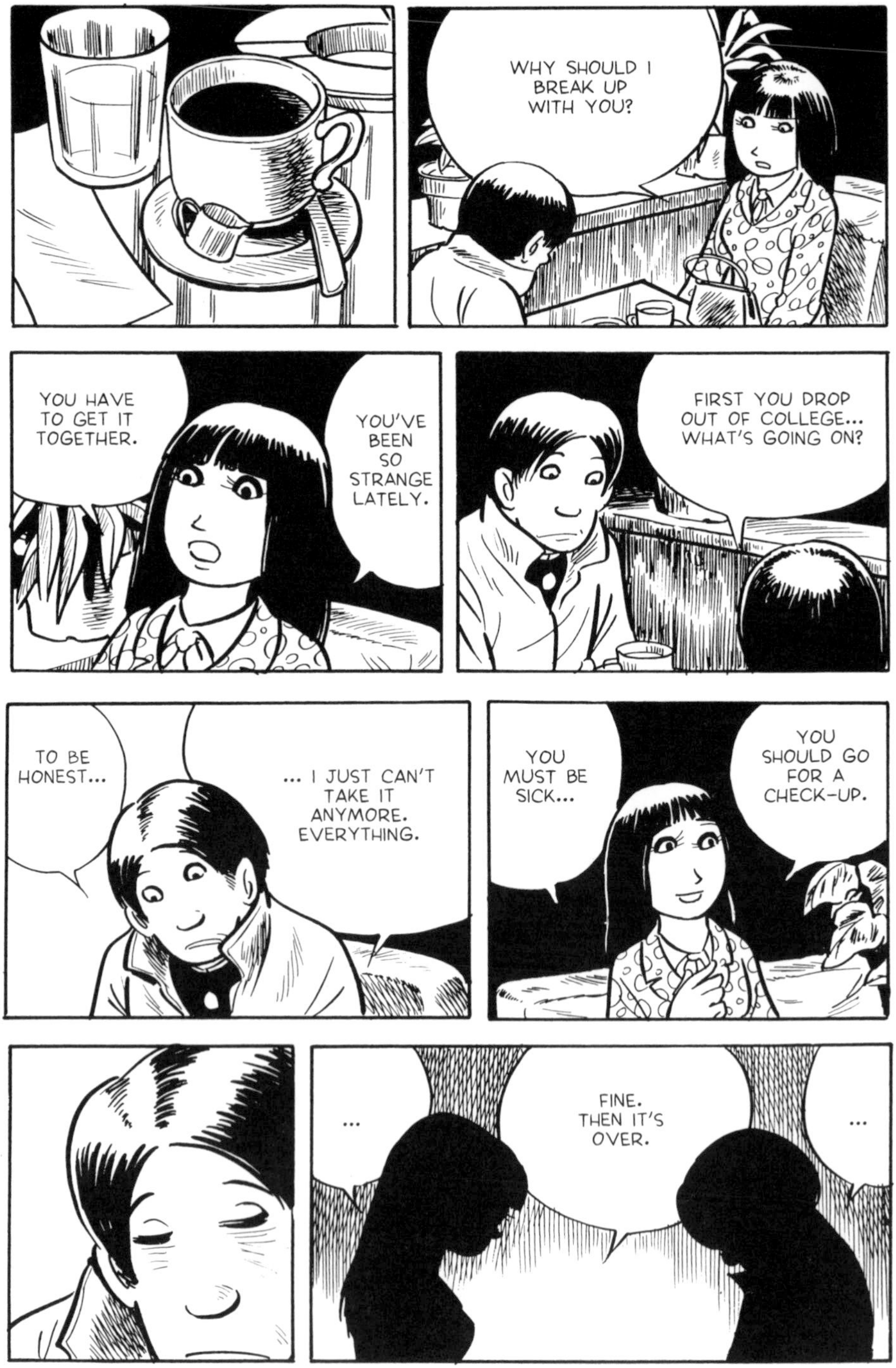
WHY SHOULD I BREAK UP WITH YOU?
YOU HAVE TO GET IT TOGETHER.
YOU'VE BEEN SO STRANGE LATELY.
FIRST YOU DROP OUT OF COLLEGE... WHAT'S GOING ON?
TO BE HONEST...
... I JUST CAN'T TAKE IT ANYMORE. EVERYTHING.
YOU MUST BE SICK...
YOU SHOULD GO FOR A CHECK-UP.
...
FINE. THEN IT'S OVER.
...

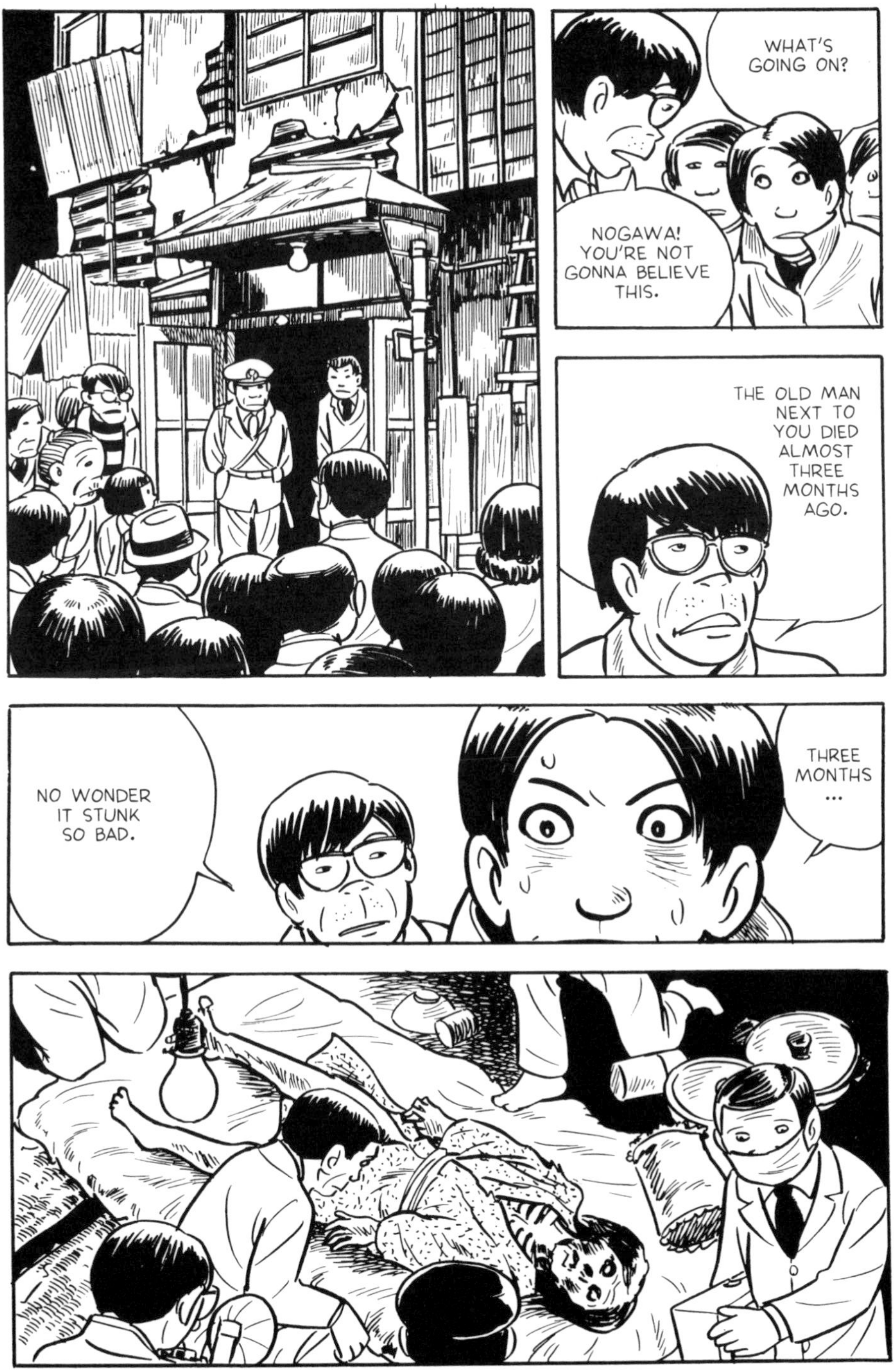
WHAT'S GOING ON?
NOGAWA! YOU'RE NOT GONNA BELIEVE THIS.
THE OLD MAN NEXT TO YOU DIED ALMOST THREE MONTHS AGO.
NO WONDER IT STUNK SO BAD.
THREE MONTHS ...

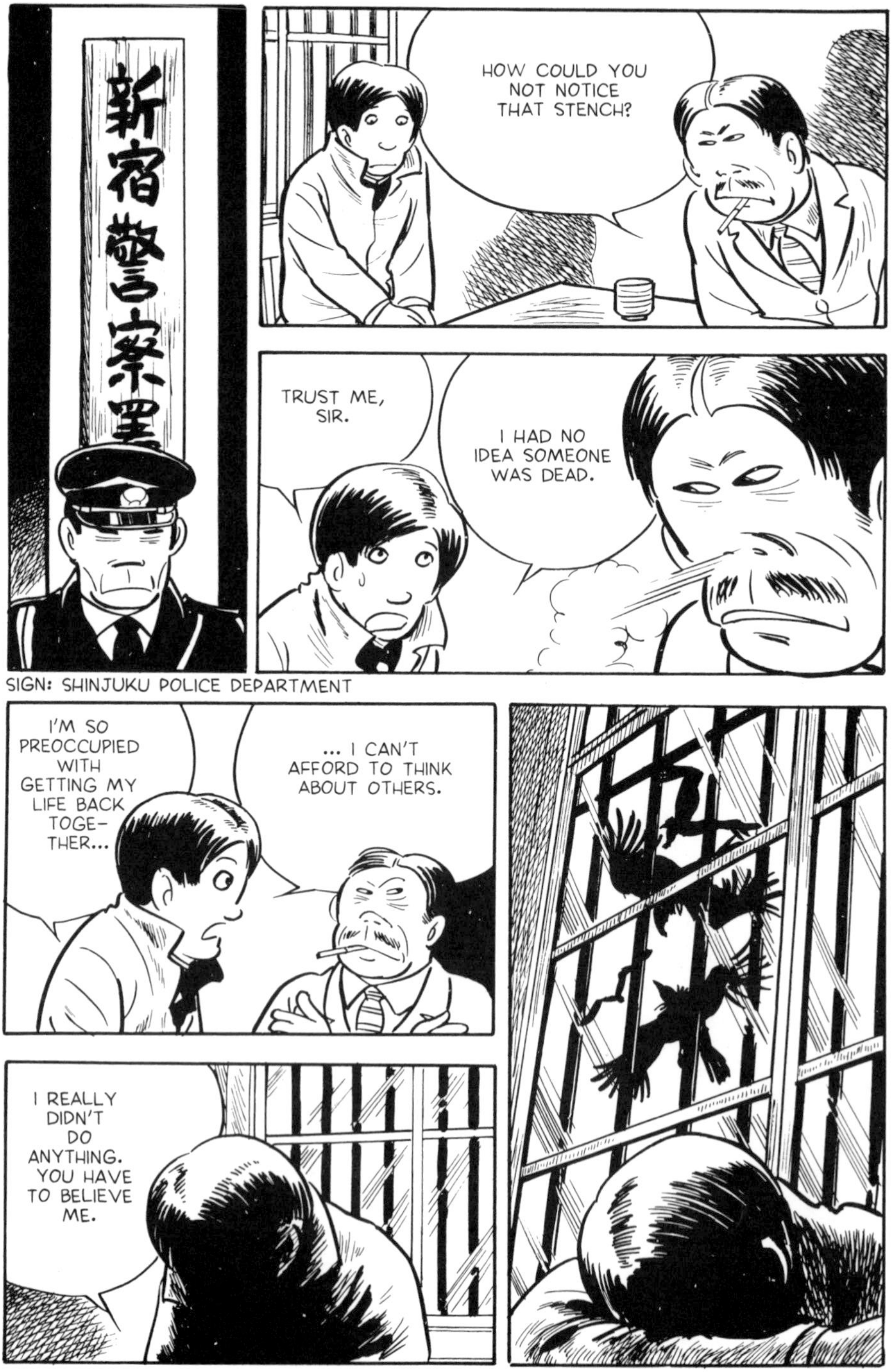
新宿警察署
HOW COULD YOU NOT NOTICE THAT STENCH?
TRUST ME, SIR.
I HAD NO IDEA SOMEONE WAS DEAD.
SIGN: SHINJUKU POLICE DEPARTMENT
I'M SO PREOCCUPIED WITH GETTING MY LIFE BACK TOGE- THER...
... I CAN'T AFFORD TO THINK ABOUT OTHERS.
I REALLY DIDN'T DO ANYTHING. YOU HAVE TO BELIEVE ME.

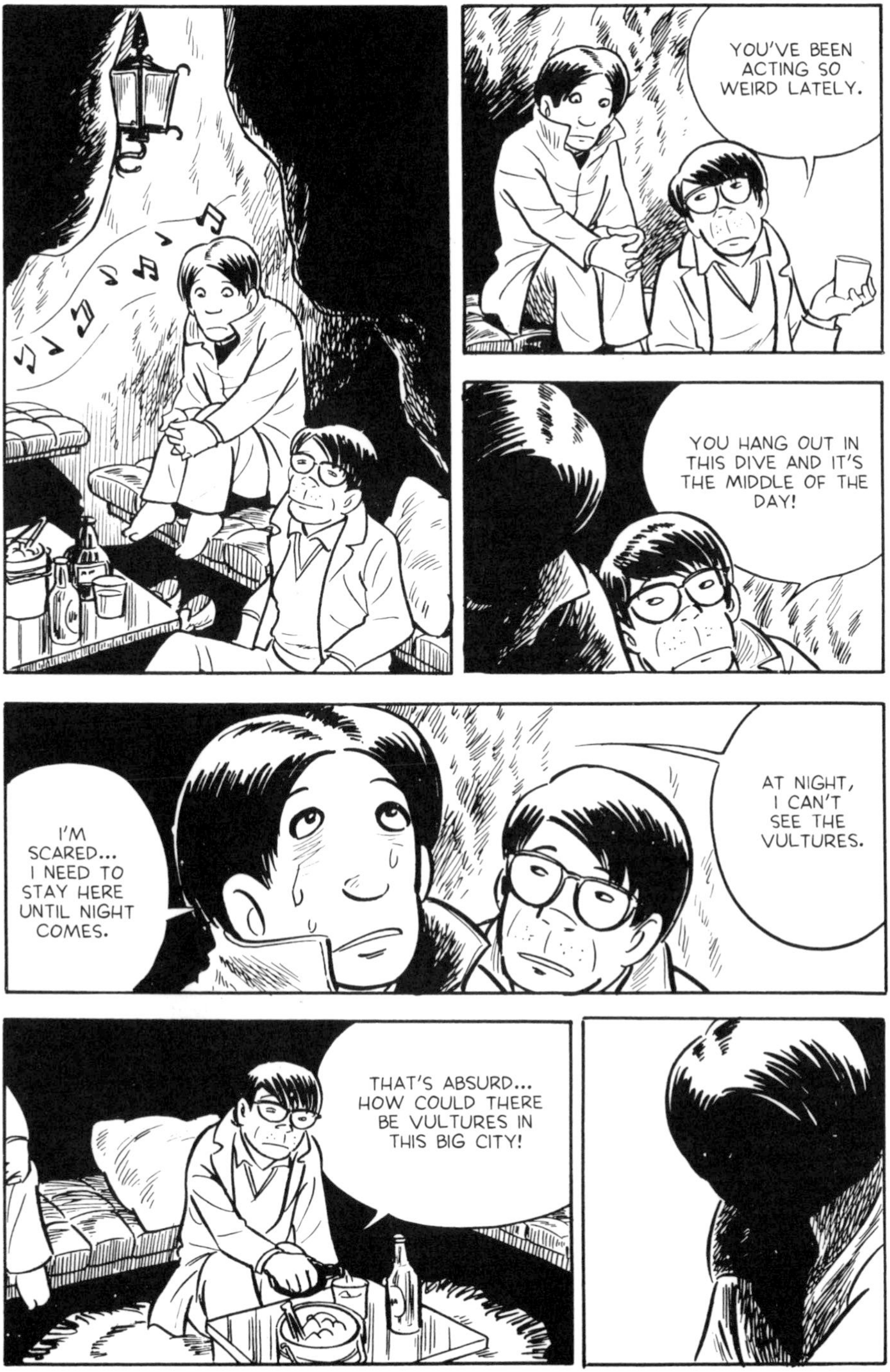
YOU'VE BEEN ACTING SO WEIRD LATELY.
YOU HANG OUT IN THIS DIVE AND IT'S THE MIDDLE OF THE DAY!
I'M SCARED... I NEED TO STAY HERE UNTIL NIGHT COMES.
AT NIGHT, I CAN'T SEE THE VULTURES.
THAT'S ABSURD... HOW COULD THERE BE VULTURES IN THIS BIG CITY!

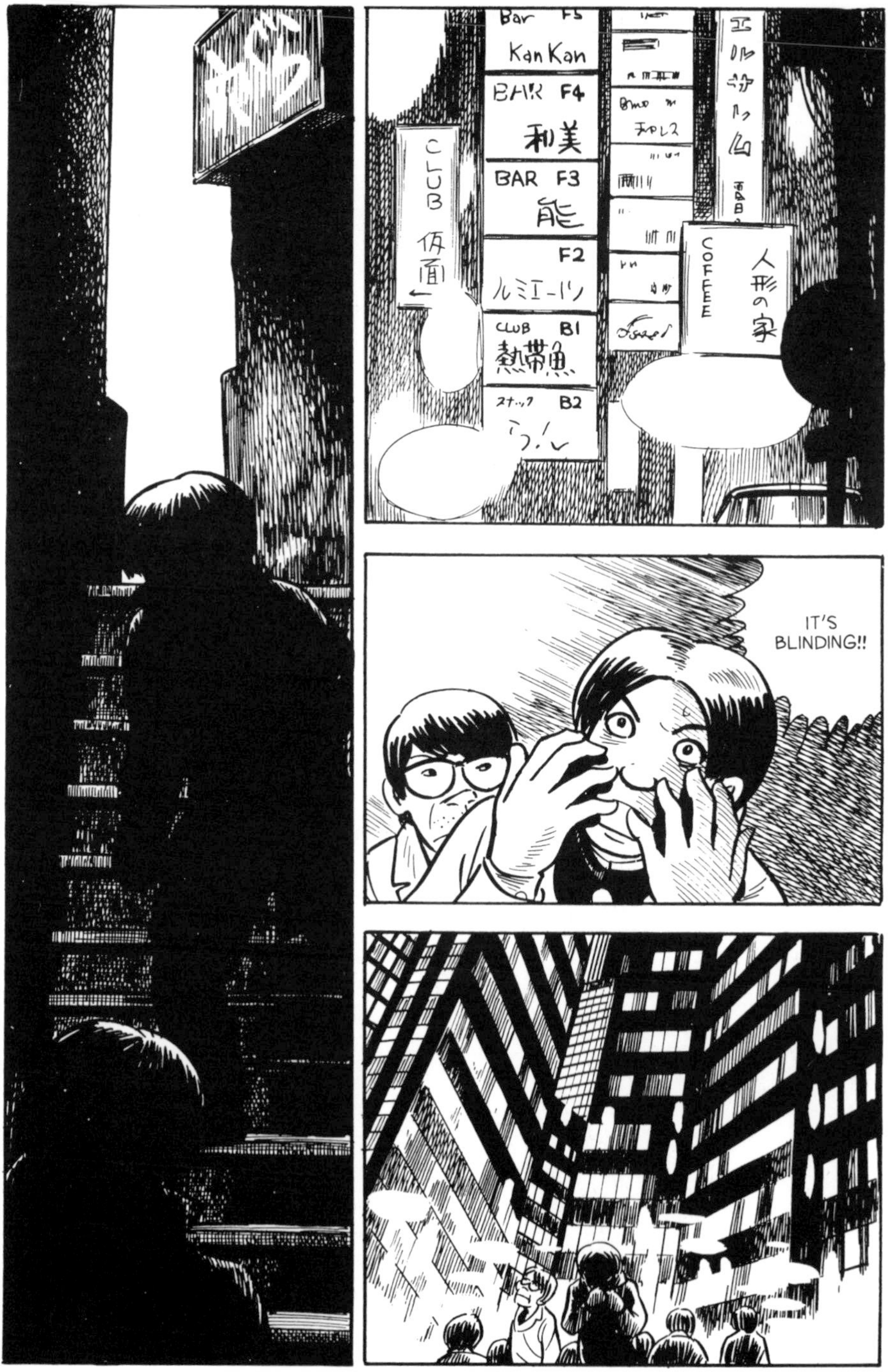
Bar F5
Kan Kan
BAR F4
和美
BAR F3
能
F2
ルミエール
CLUB B1
熱帯魚
B2
CLUB
仮面
COFFEE
人形の家
IT'S BLINDING!!

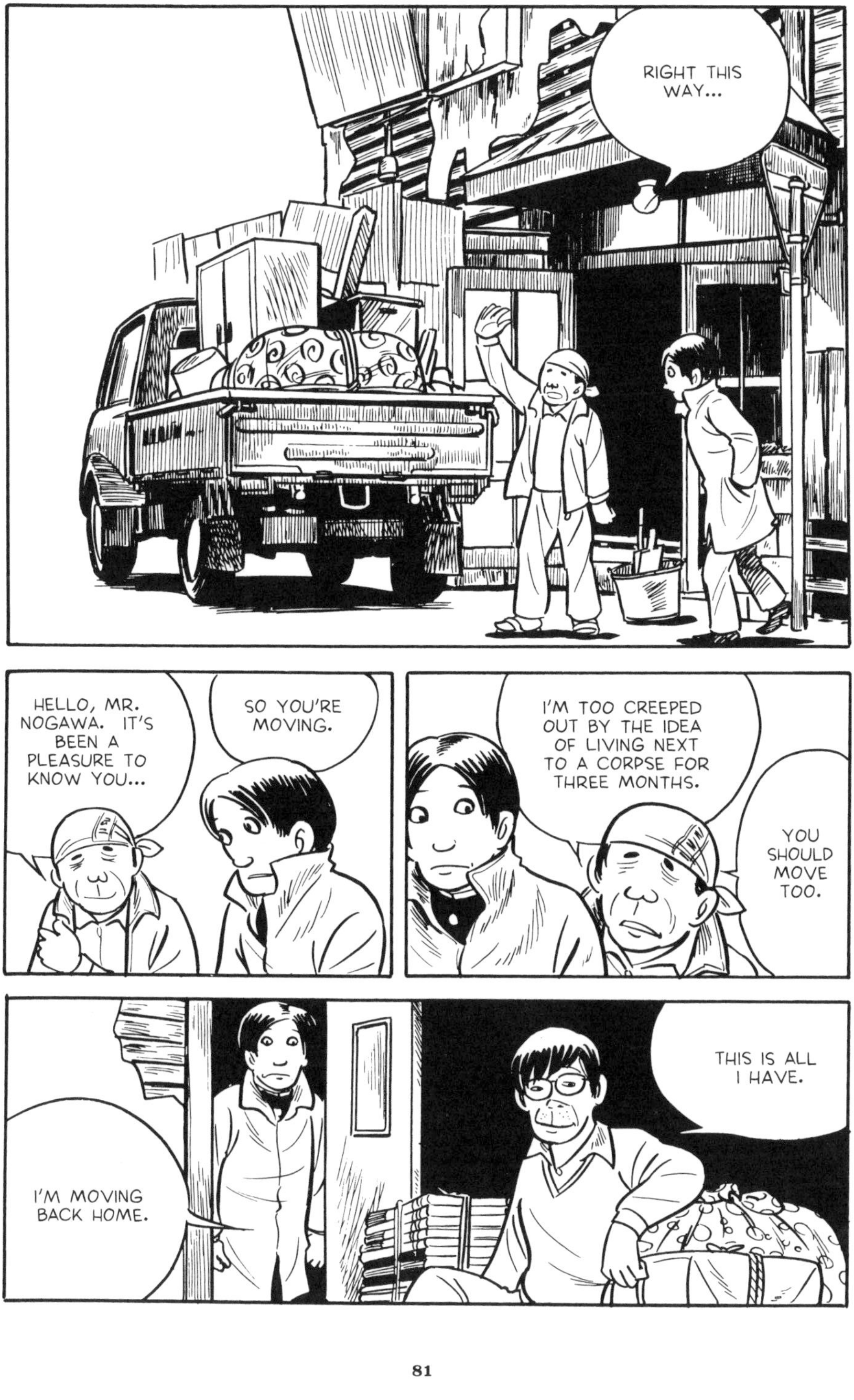
RIGHT THIS WAY...
HELLO, MR. NOGAWA. IT'S BEEN A PLEASURE TO KNOW YOU...
SO YOU'RE MOVING.
I'M TOO CREEPED OUT BY THE IDEA OF LIVING NEXT TO A CORPSE FOR THREE MONTHS.
YOU SHOULD MOVE TOO.
I'M MOVING BACK HOME.
THIS IS ALL I HAVE.

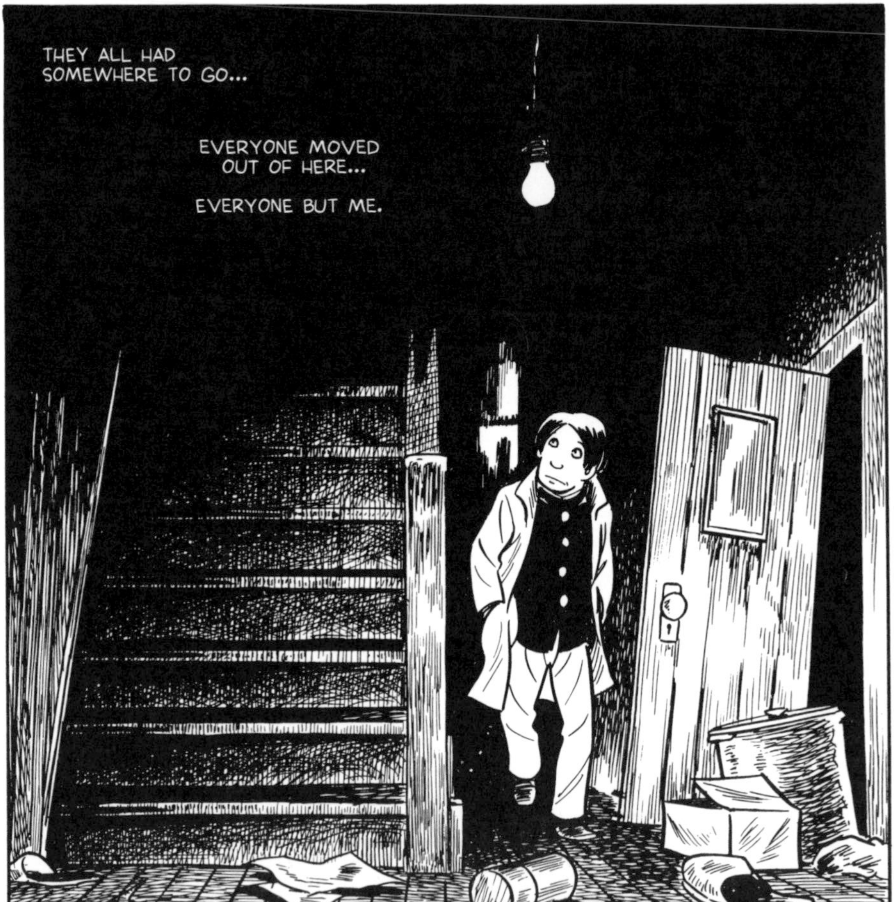
THEY ALL HAD SOMEWHERE TO GO...
EVERYONE MOVED OUT OF HERE...
EVERYONE BUT ME.

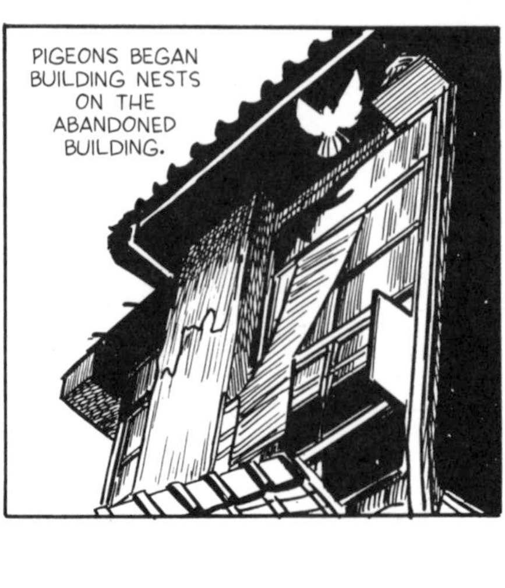
PIGEONS BEGAN BUILDING NESTS ON THE ABANDONED BUILDING.

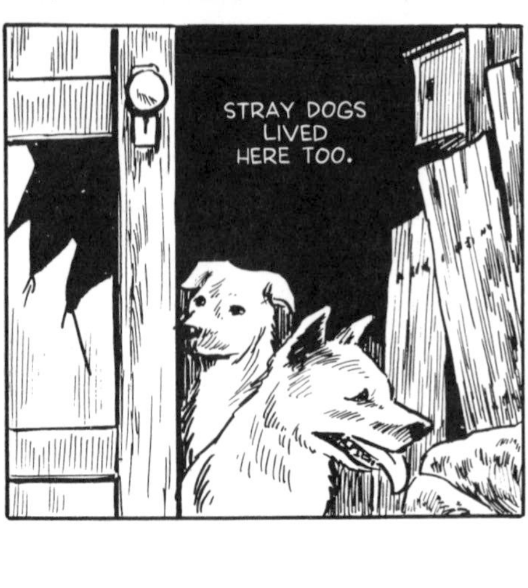
STRAY DOGS LIVED HERE TOO.

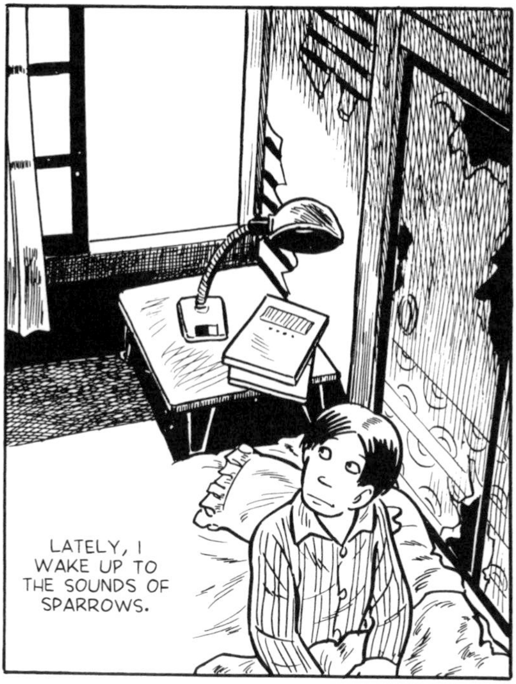
LATELY, I WAKE UP TO THE SOUNDS OF SPARROWS.

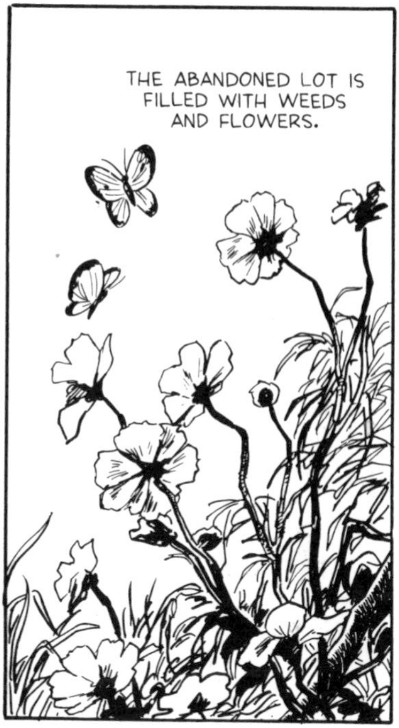
THE ABANDONED LOT IS FILLED WITH WEEDS AND FLOWERS.

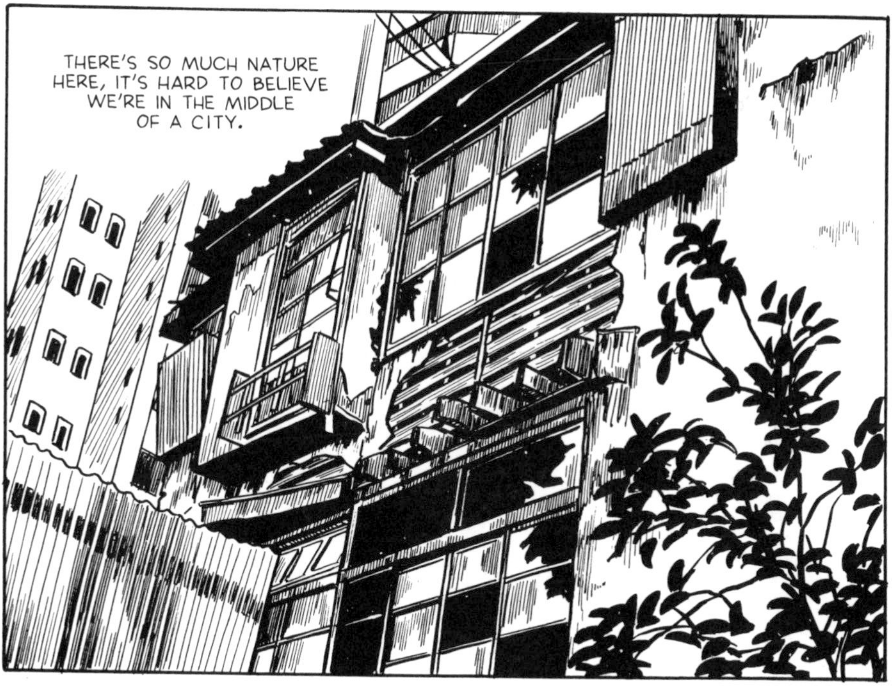
THERE'S SO MUCH NATURE HERE, IT'S HARD TO BELIEVE WE'RE IN THE MIDDLE OF A CITY.

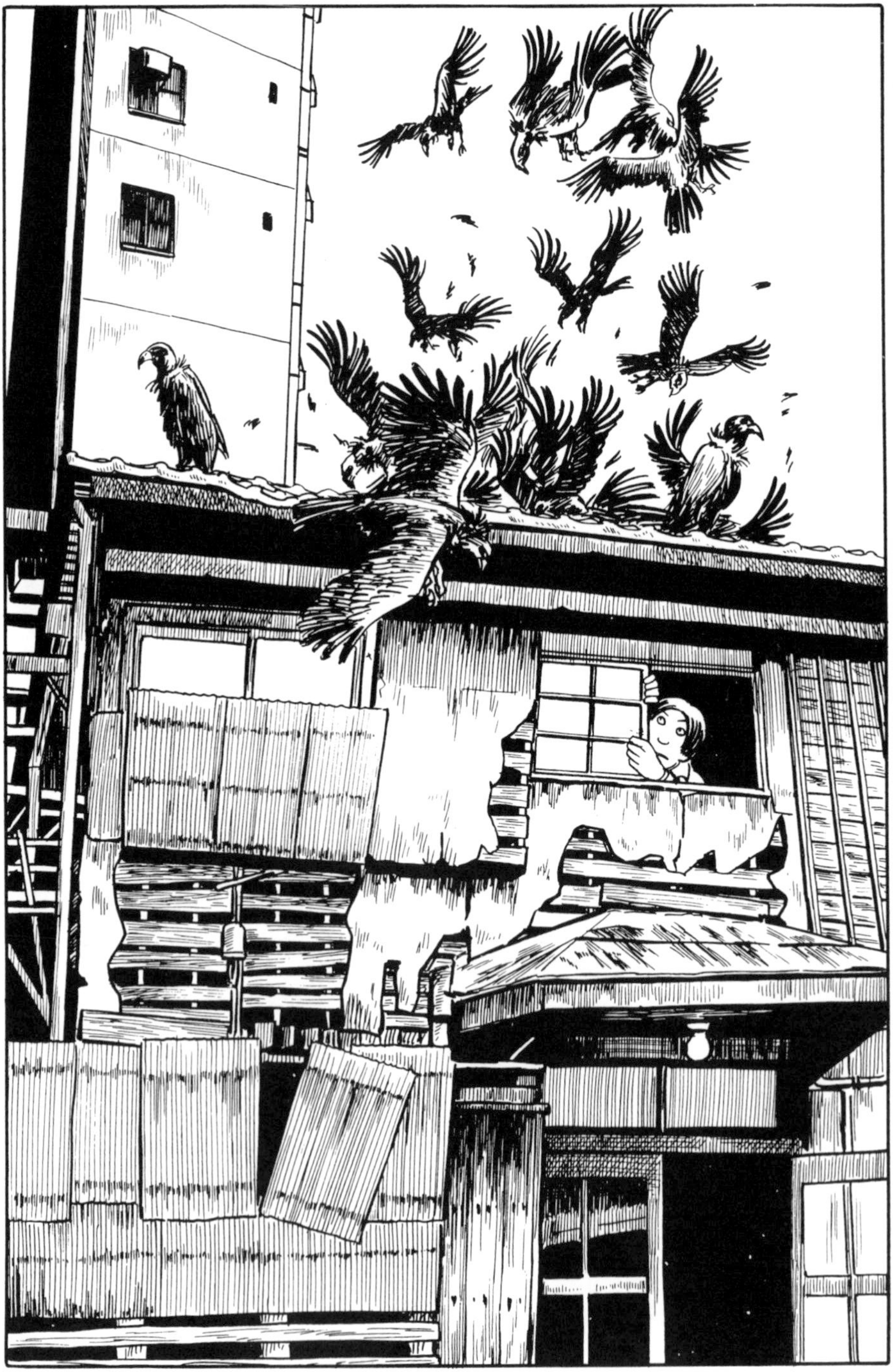

RASH

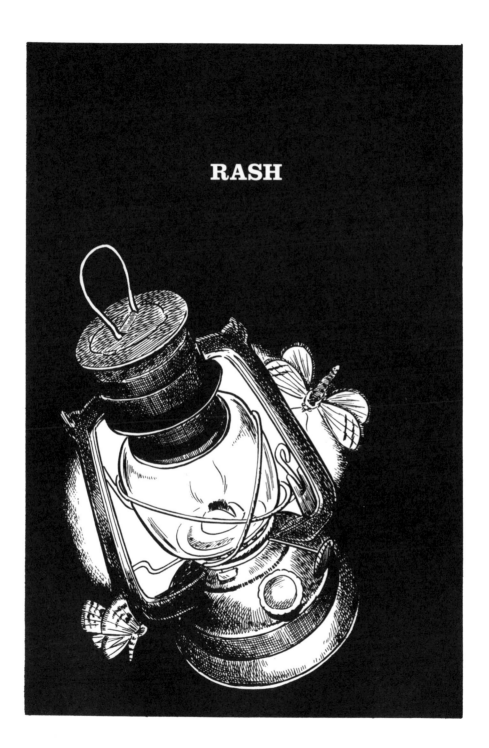

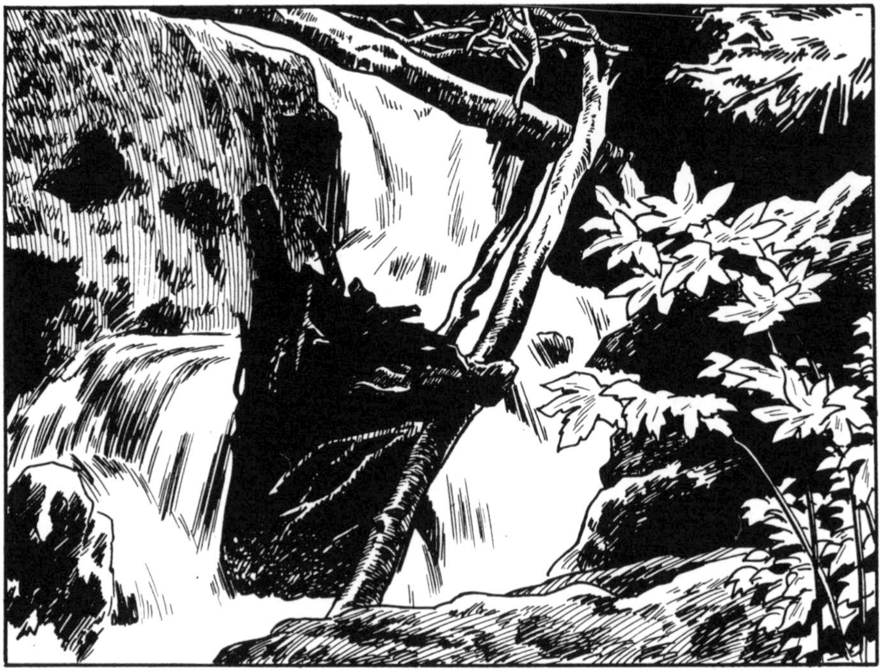

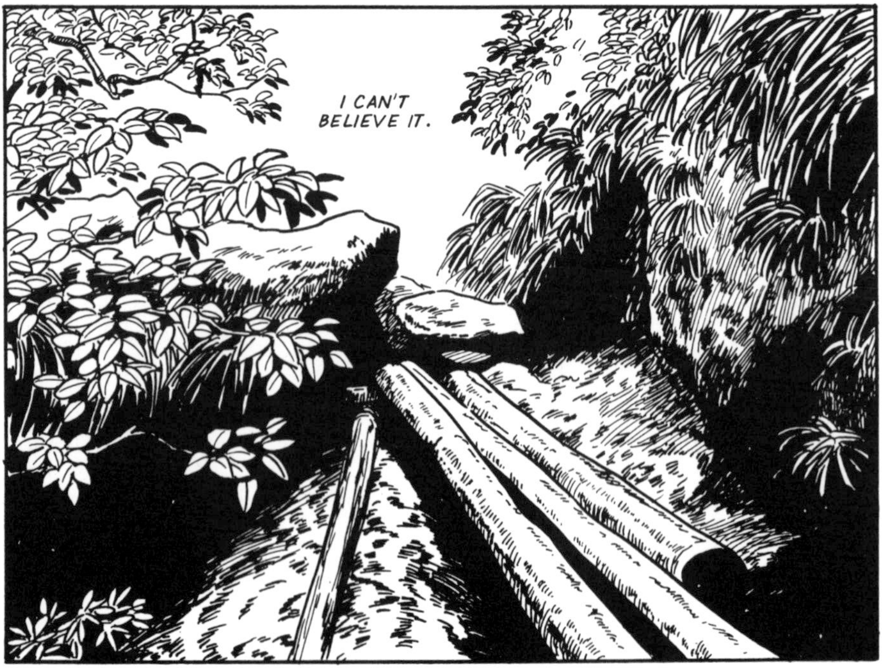
I CAN'T
BELIEVE IT.

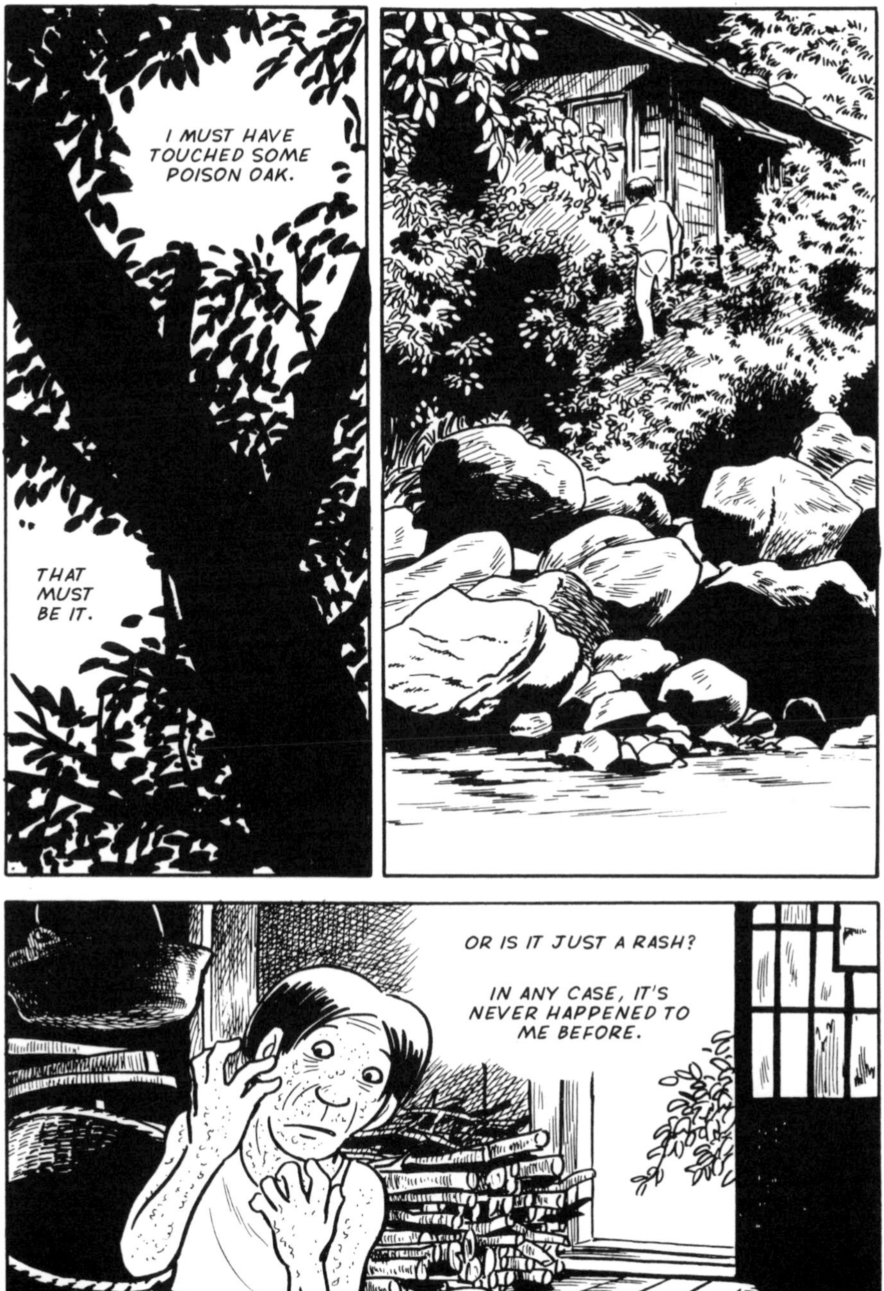
I MUST HAVE TOUCHED SOME POISON OAK.
THAT MUST BE IT.
OR IS IT JUST A RASH?
IN ANY CASE, IT'S NEVER HAPPENED TO ME BEFORE.

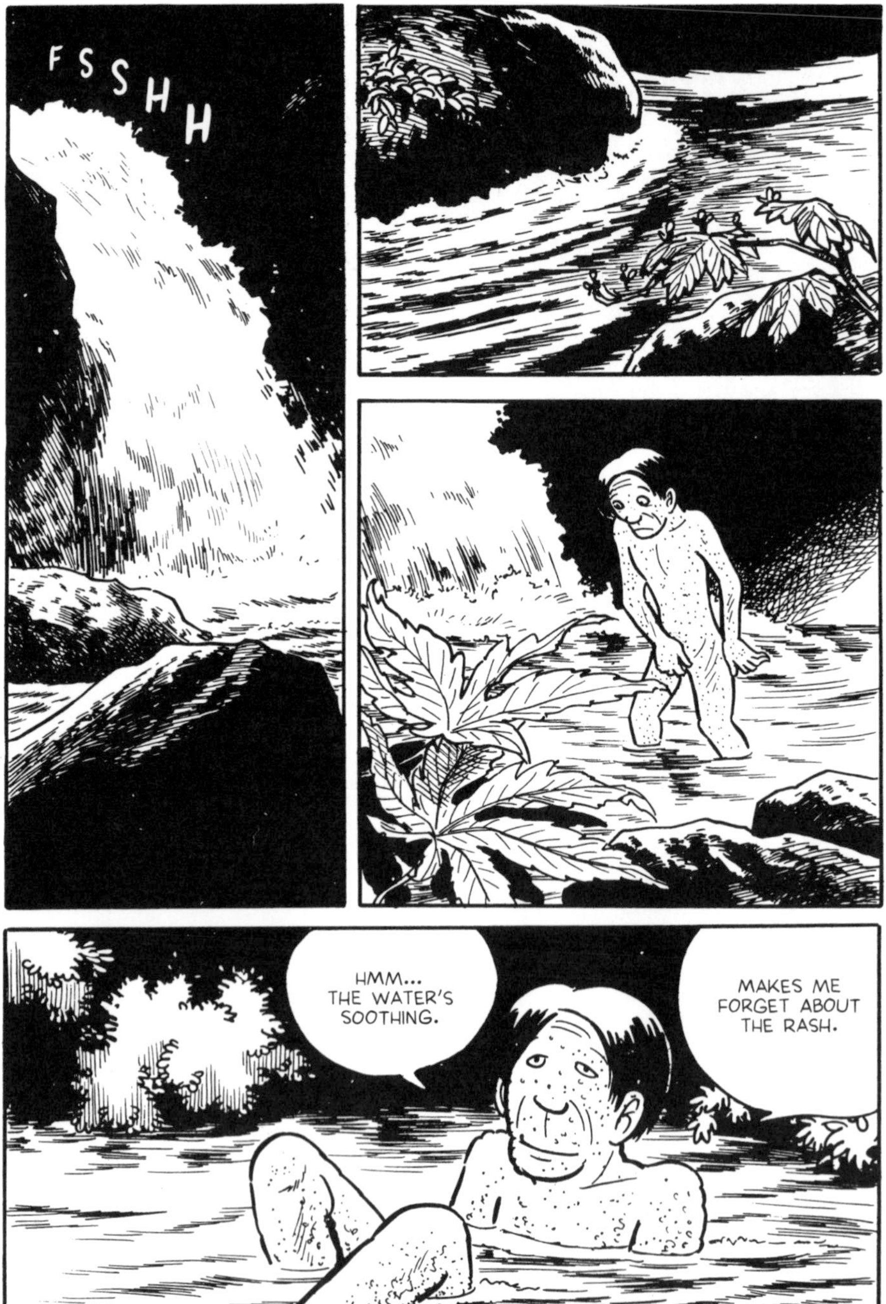
FSSHH
HMM... THE WATER'S SOOTHING.
MAKES ME FORGET ABOUT THE RASH.

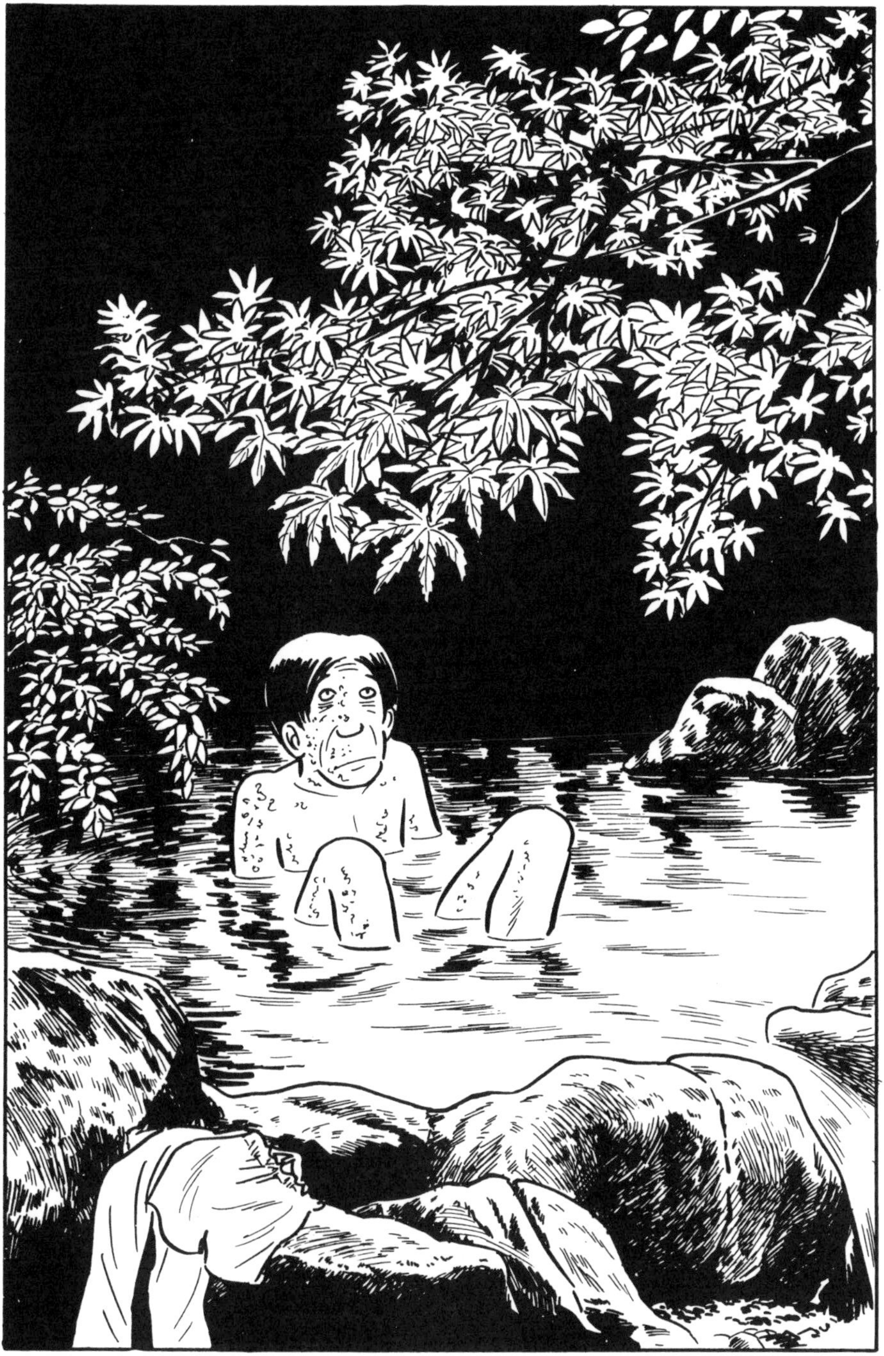

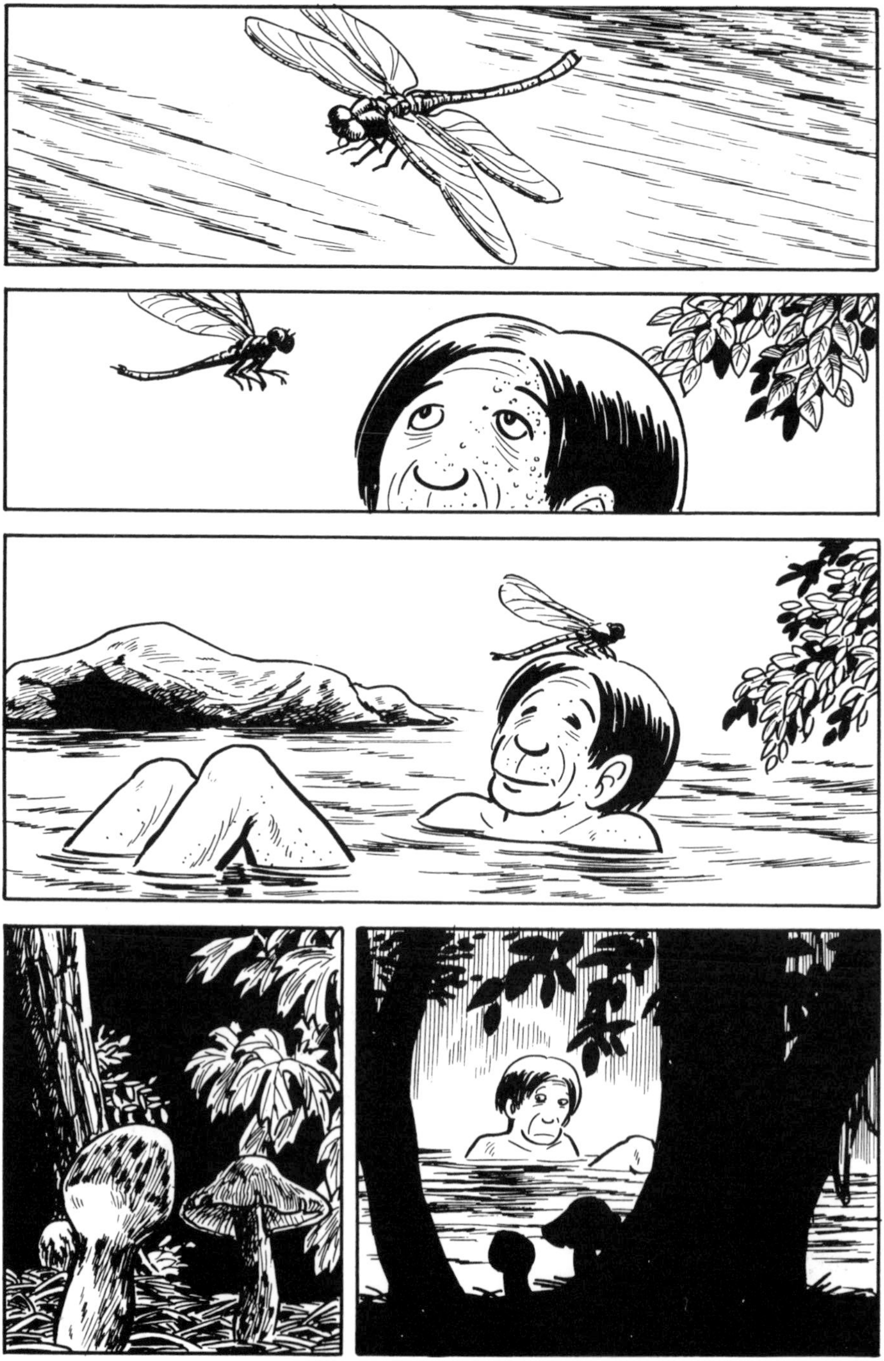

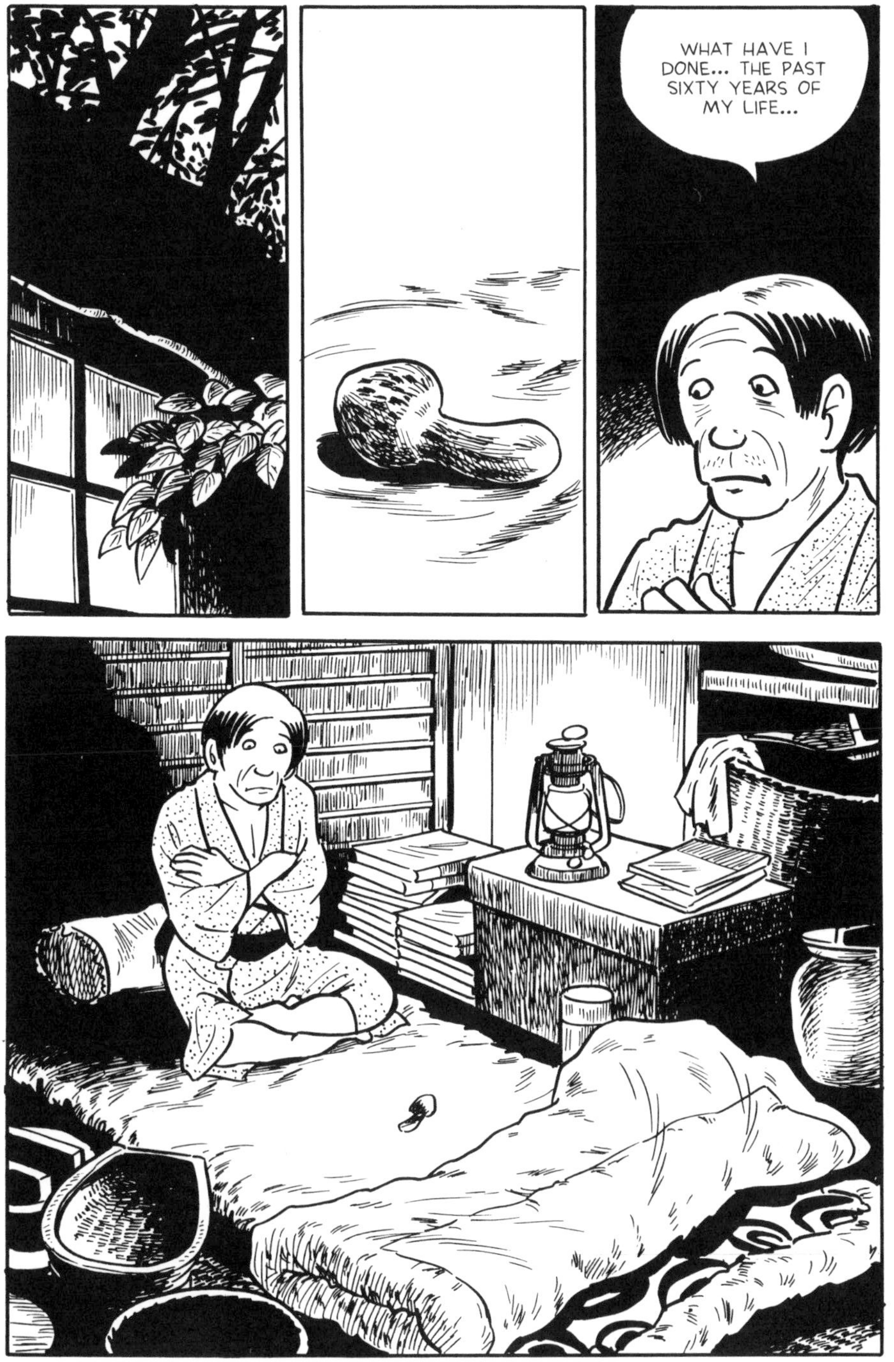
WHAT HAVE I DONE... THE PAST SIXTY YEARS OF MY LIFE...

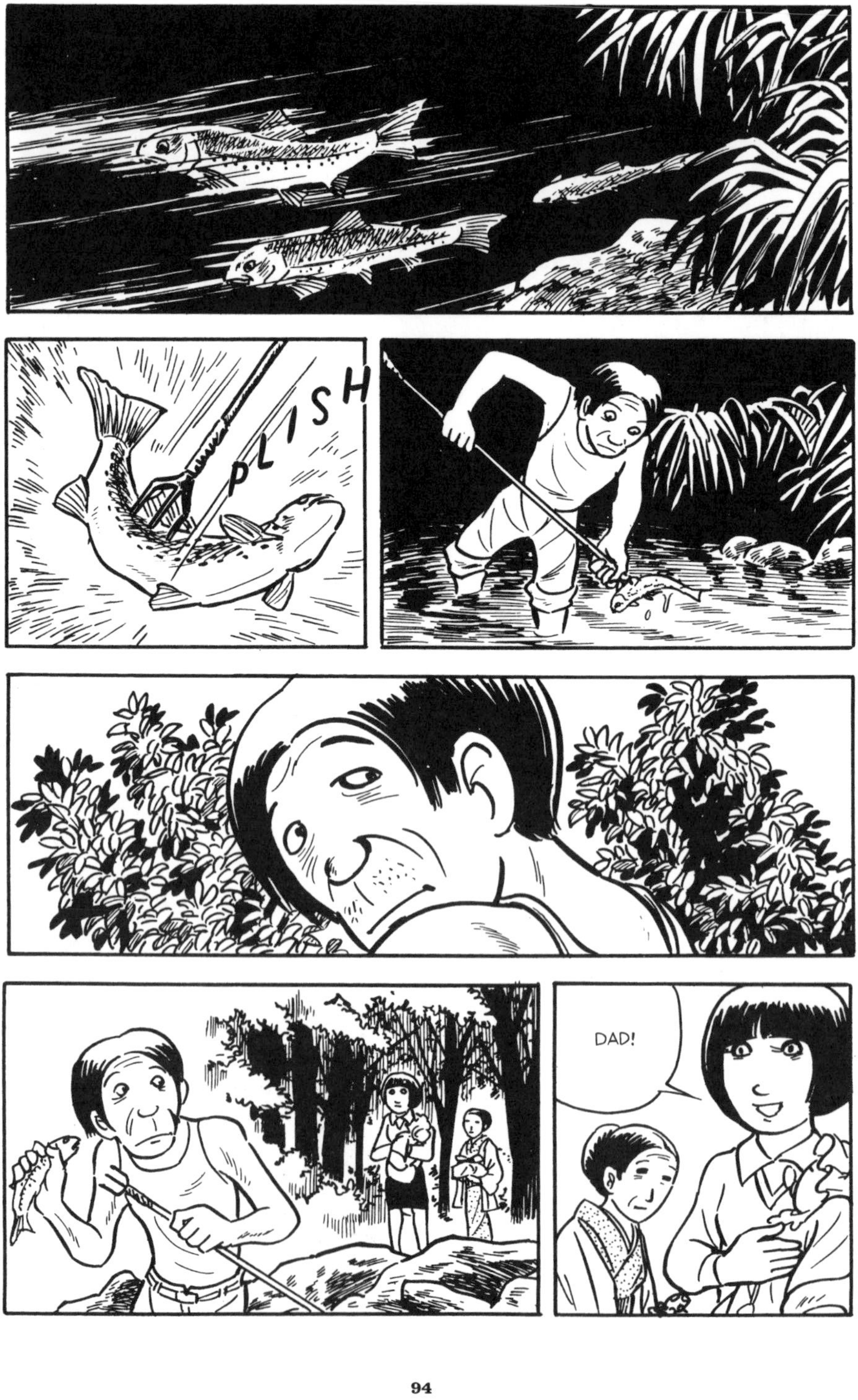
PLISH
DAD!

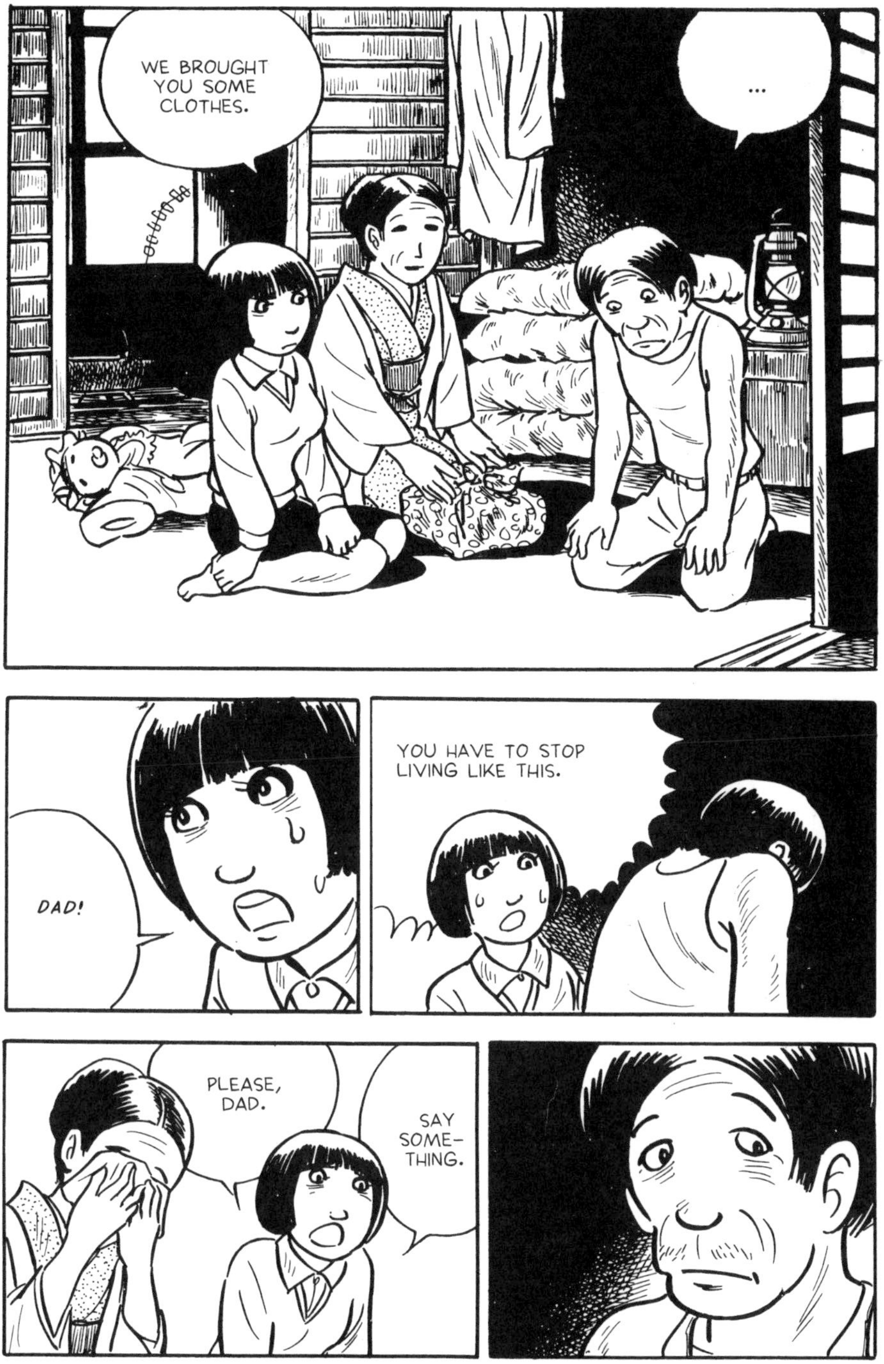
WE BROUGHT YOU SOME CLOTHES.
...
DAD!
YOU HAVE TO STOP LIVING LIKE THIS.
PLEASE, DAD.
SAY SOME-THING.

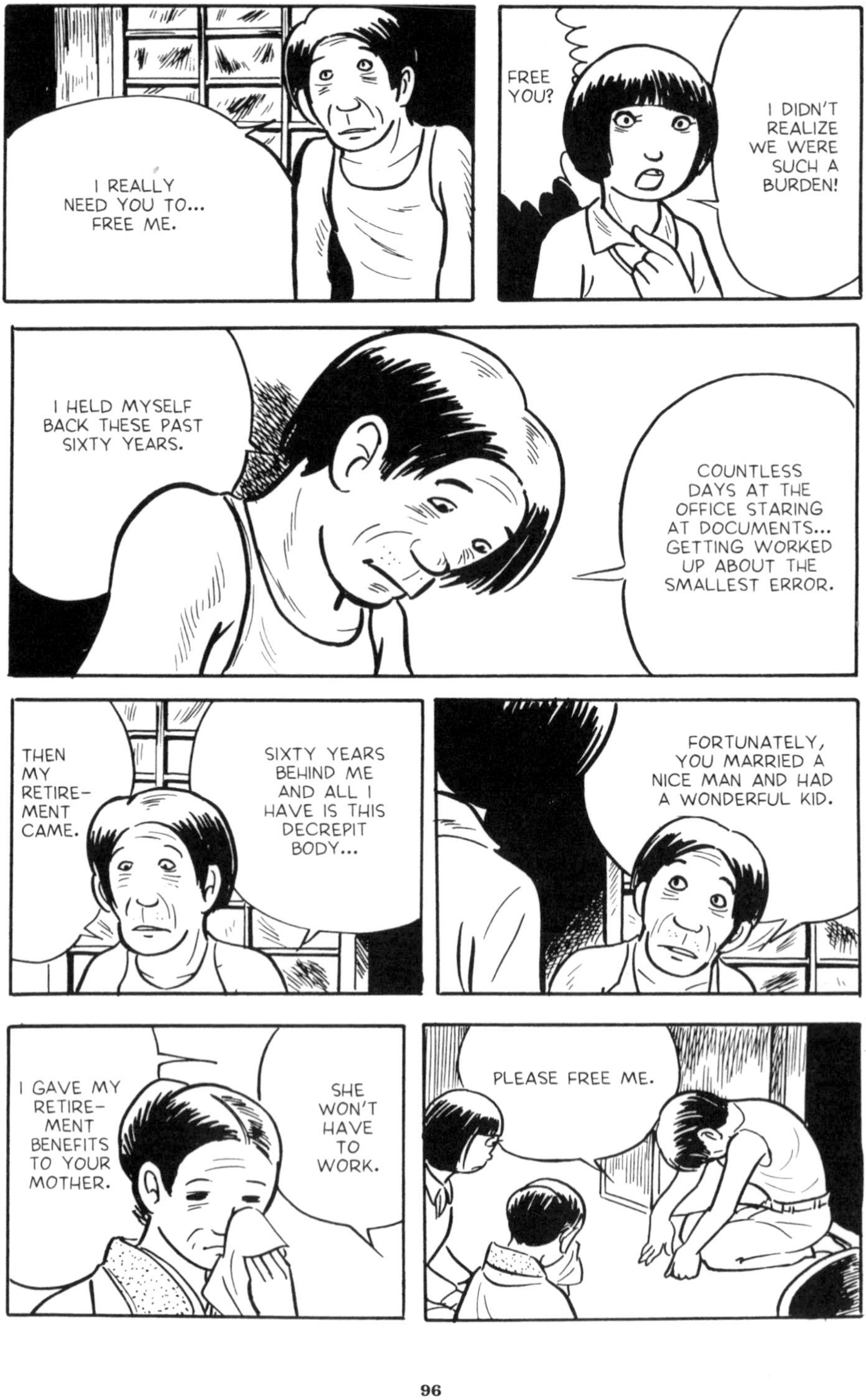
I REALLY NEED YOU TO... FREE ME.
FREE YOU?
I DIDN'T REALIZE WE WERE SUCH A BURDEN!
I HELD MYSELF BACK THESE PAST SIXTY YEARS.
COUNTLESS DAYS AT THE OFFICE STARING AT DOCUMENTS... GETTING WORKED UP ABOUT THE SMALLEST ERROR.
THEN MY RETIRE-MENT CAME.
SIXTY YEARS BEHIND ME AND ALL I HAVE IS THIS DECREPIT BODY...
FORTUNATELY, YOU MARRIED A NICE MAN AND HAD A WONDERFUL KID.
I GAVE MY RETIRE-MENT BENEFITS TO YOUR MOTHER.
SHE WON'T HAVE TO WORK.
PLEASE FREE ME.

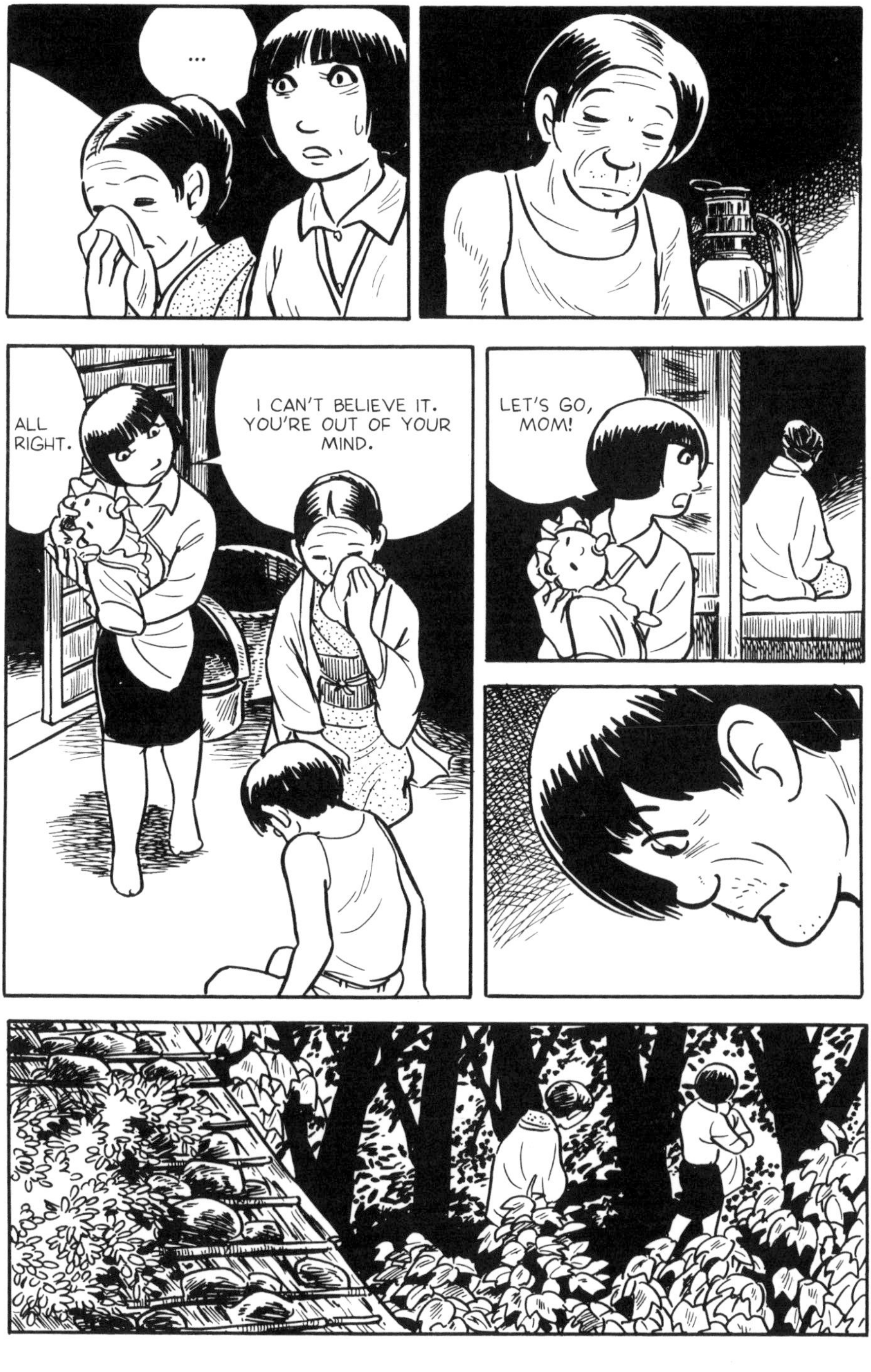
...
ALL RIGHT.
I CAN'T BELIEVE IT. YOU'RE OUT OF YOUR MIND.
LET'S GO, MOM!

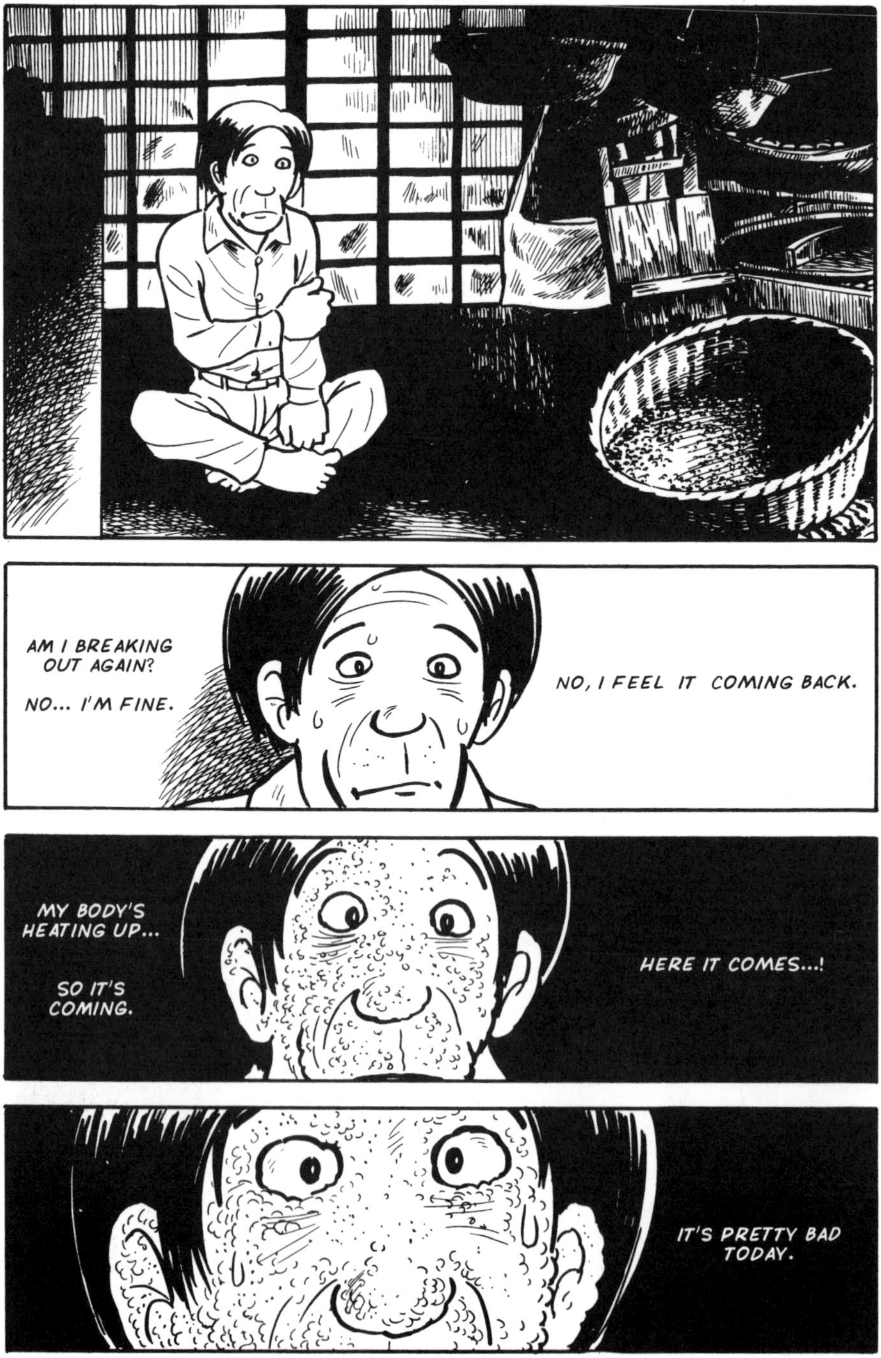
AM I BREAKING OUT AGAIN?
NO... I'M FINE.
NO, I FEEL IT COMING BACK.
MY BODY'S HEATING UP...
SO IT'S COMING.
HERE IT COMES...!
IT'S PRETTY BAD TODAY.

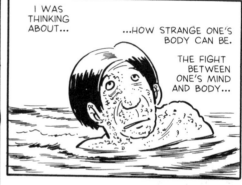

I WAS THINKING ABOUT...

...HOW STRANGE ONE'S BODY CAN BE.

THE FIGHT BETWEEN ONE'S MIND AND BODY...

IF THE RASH COMES WHEN I THINK IT WILL, THEN MAYBE I CAN SUPPRESS IT WITH MY MIND AS WELL.

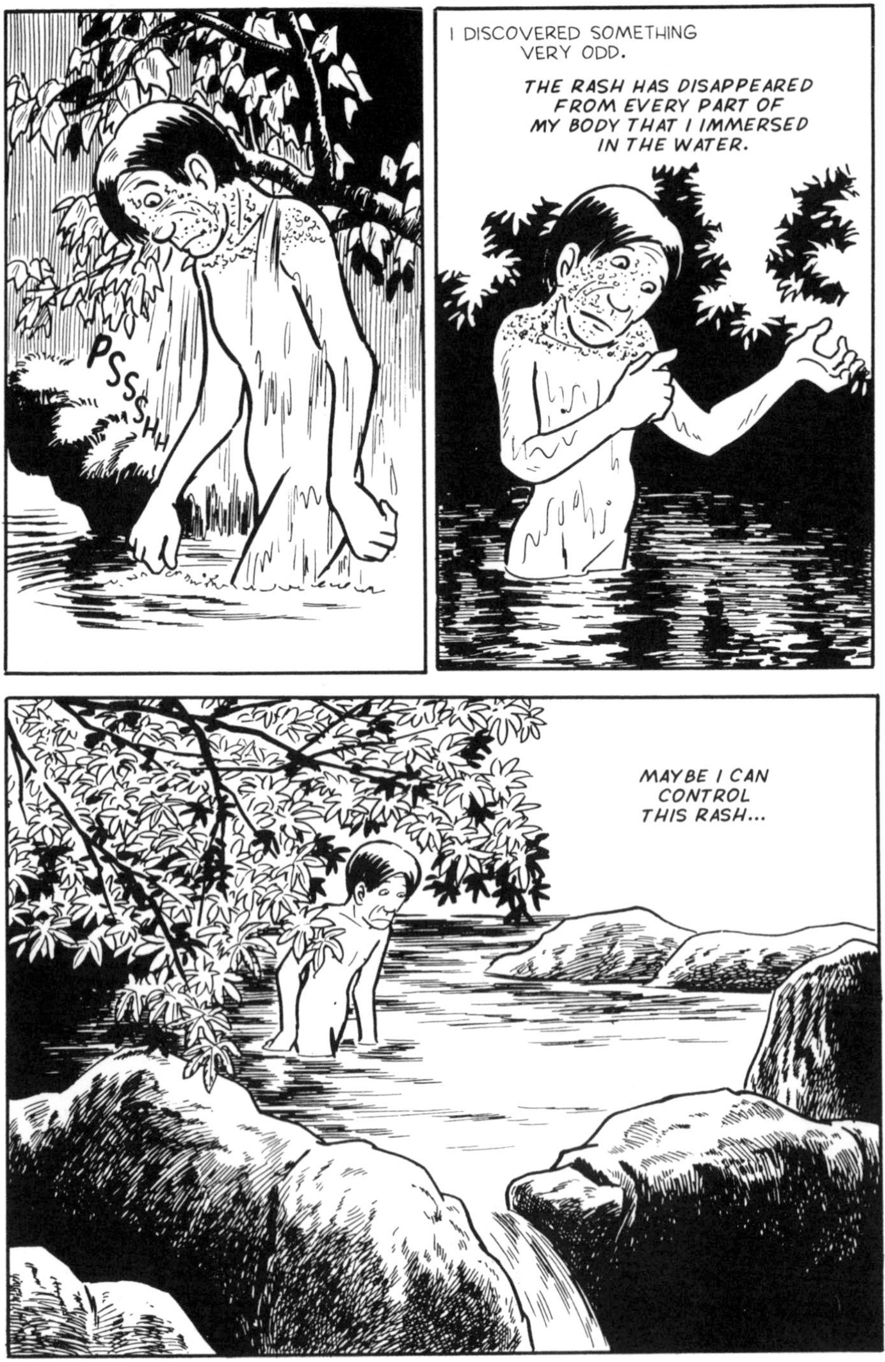
PSSSHH
I DISCOVERED SOMETHING VERY ODD.
THE RASH HAS DISAPPEARED FROM EVERY PART OF MY BODY THAT I IMMERSED IN THE WATER.
MAYBE I CAN CONTROL THIS RASH...

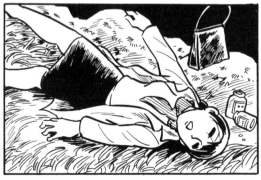

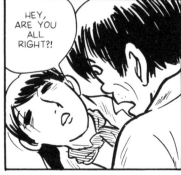

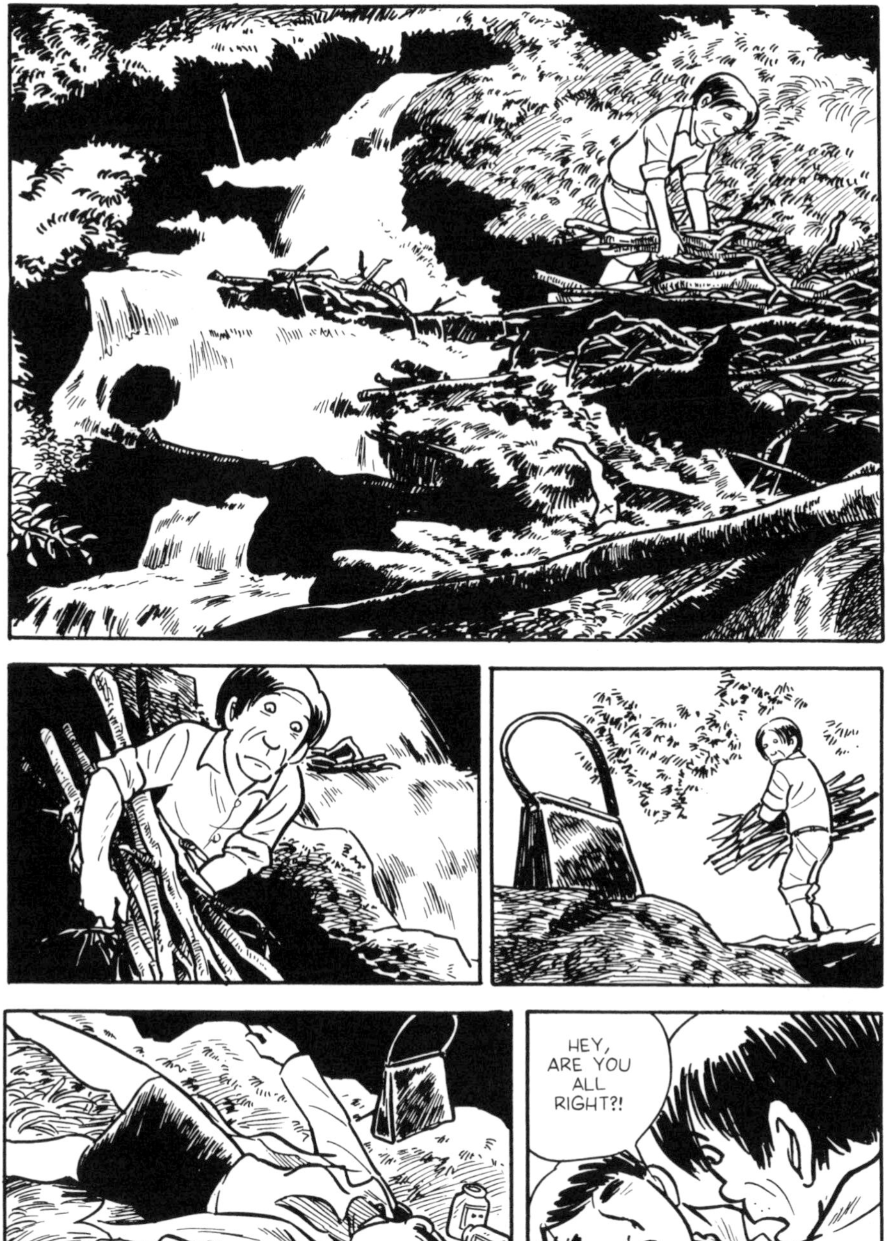
HEY, ARE YOU ALL RIGHT?!

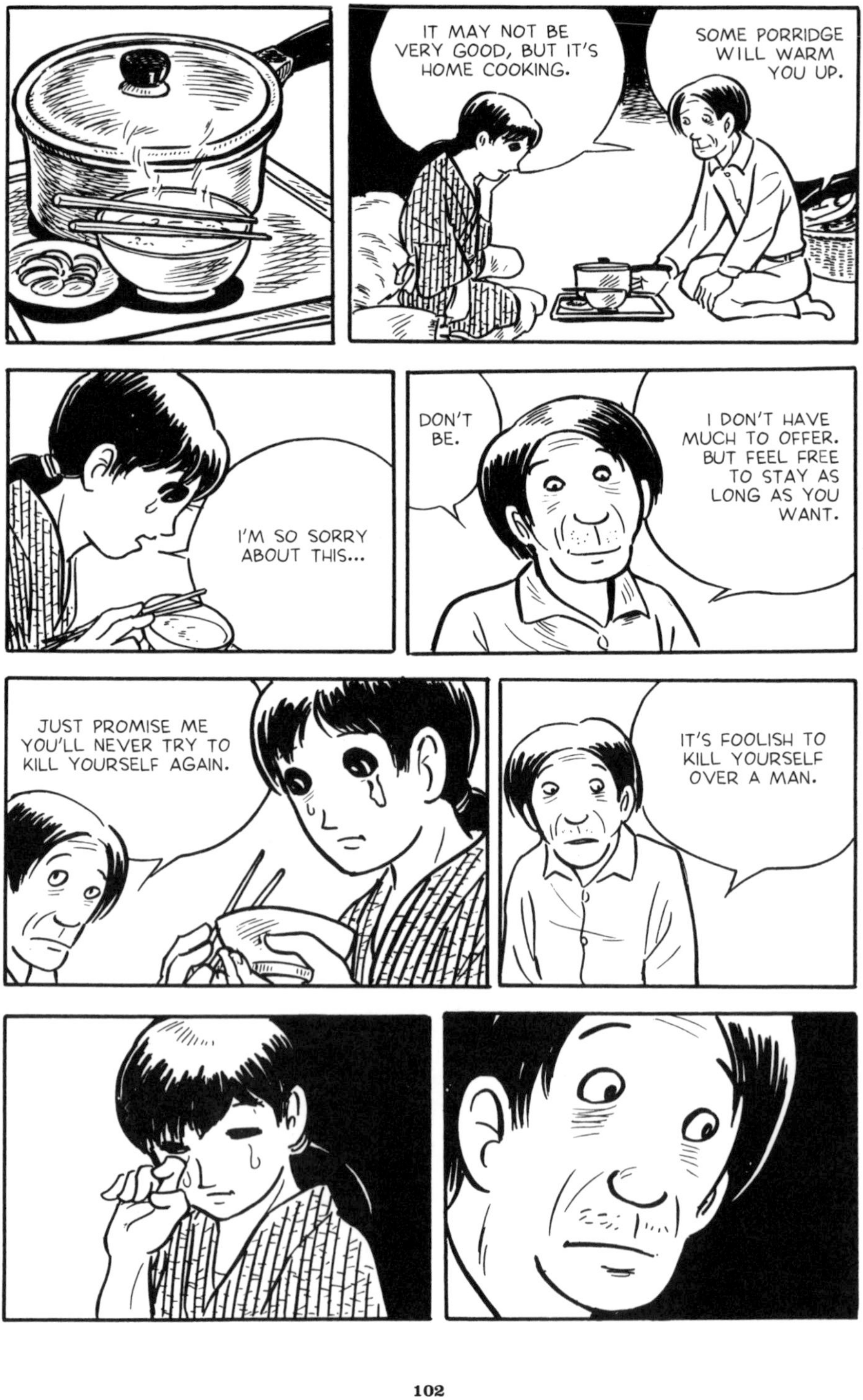
IT MAY NOT BE VERY GOOD, BUT IT'S HOME COOKING.
SOME PORRIDGE WILL WARM YOU UP.
I'M SO SORRY ABOUT THIS...
DON'T BE.
I DON'T HAVE MUCH TO OFFER. BUT FEEL FREE TO STAY AS LONG AS YOU WANT.
JUST PROMISE ME YOU'LL NEVER TRY TO KILL YOURSELF AGAIN.
IT'S FOOLISH TO KILL YOURSELF OVER A MAN.

FSSSHHH

MY FACE AND LEFT LEG AREN'T IMMERSED.

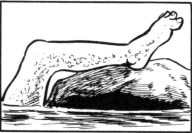

I CONCENTRATED ON RESTRICTING THE RASH ONLY TO MY FACE AND LEFT LEG.

IT TOOK A LOT OF WILL...

IT'S NOT WORKING...

SO I CAN'T CONTROL THE RASH AFTER ALL.

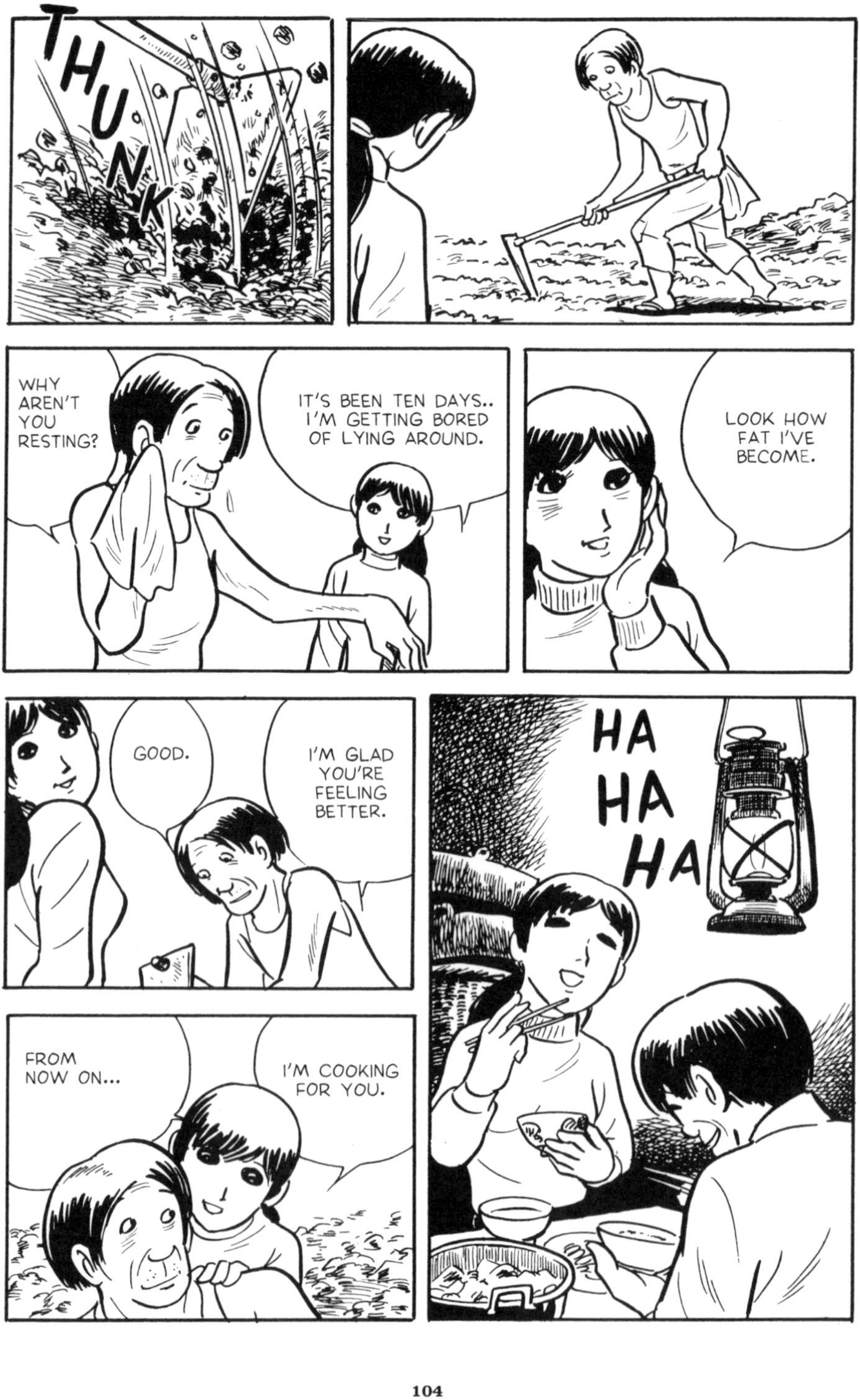
THUNK
WHY AREN'T YOU RESTING?
IT'S BEEN TEN DAYS.. I'M GETTING BORED OF LYING AROUND.
LOOK HOW FAT I'VE BECOME.
GOOD.
I'M GLAD YOU'RE FEELING BETTER.
FROM NOW ON...
I'M COOKING FOR YOU.
HA HA HA

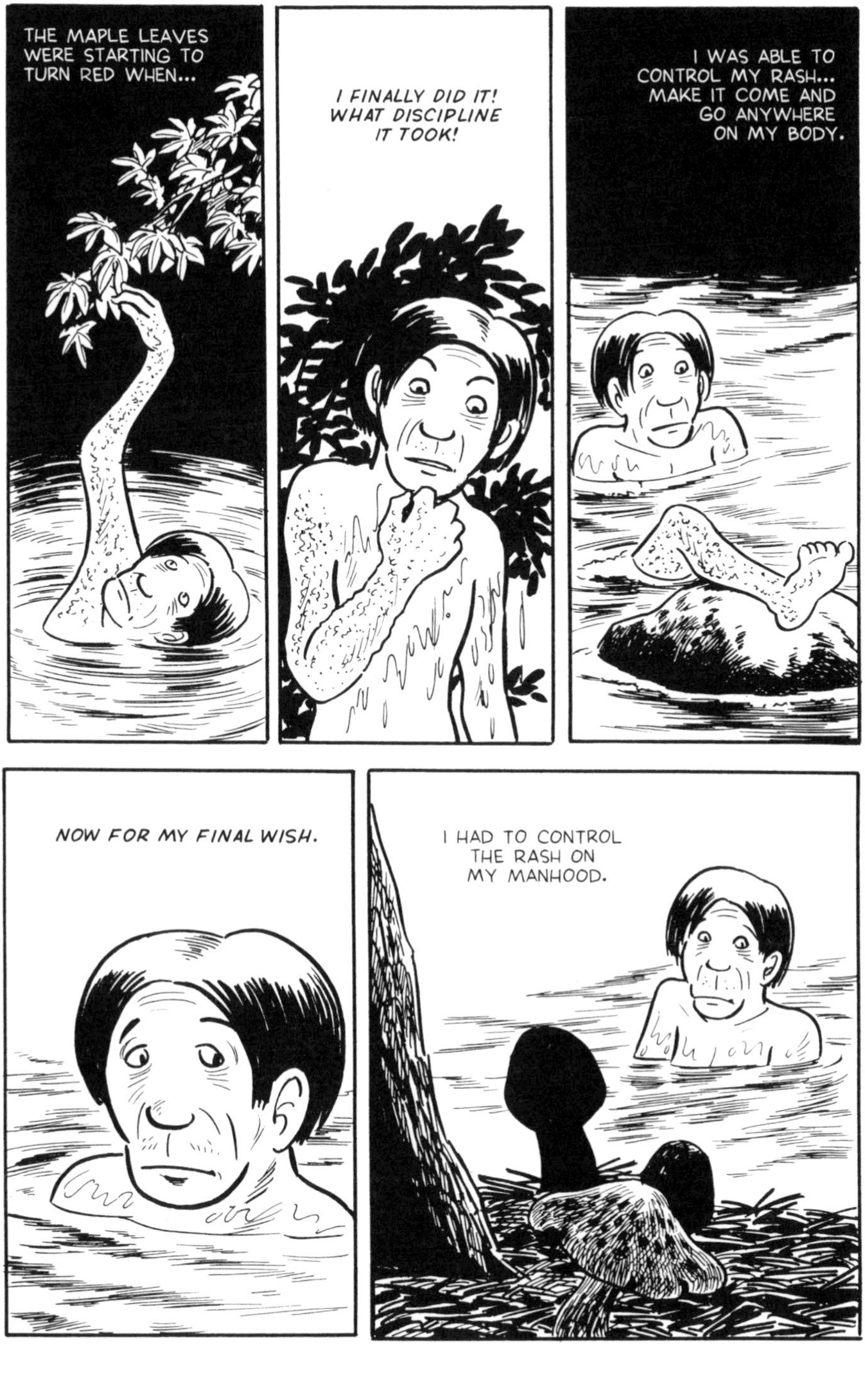
THE MAPLE LEAVES WERE STARTING TO TURN RED WHEN...
I FINALLY DID IT! WHAT DISCIPLINE IT TOOK!
I WAS ABLE TO CONTROL MY RASH... MAKE IT COME AND GO ANYWHERE ON MY BODY.
NOW FOR MY FINAL WISH.
I HAD TO CONTROL THE RASH ON MY MANHOOD.

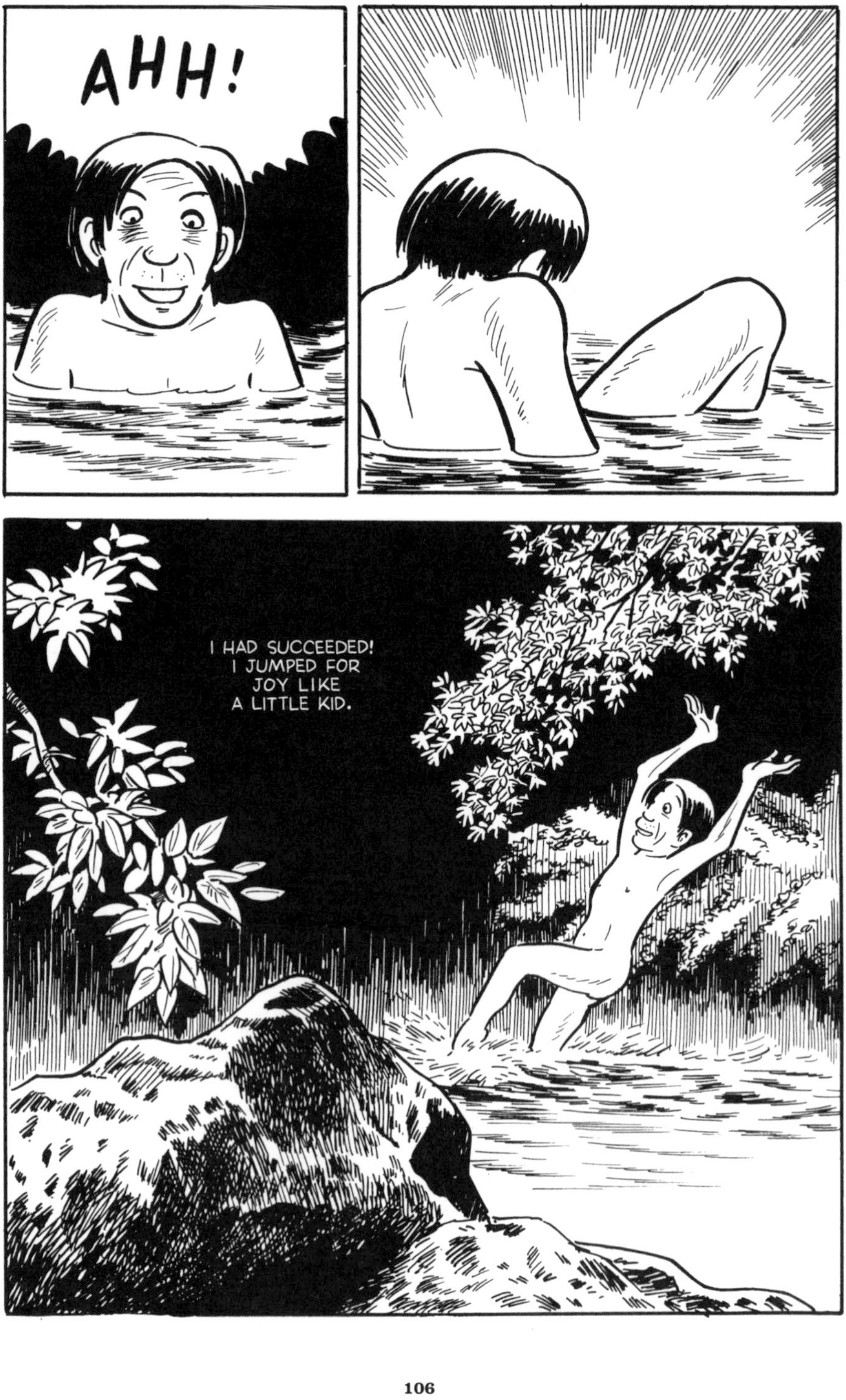
AHH!
I HAD SUCCEEDED! I JUMPED FOR JOY LIKE A LITTLE KID.

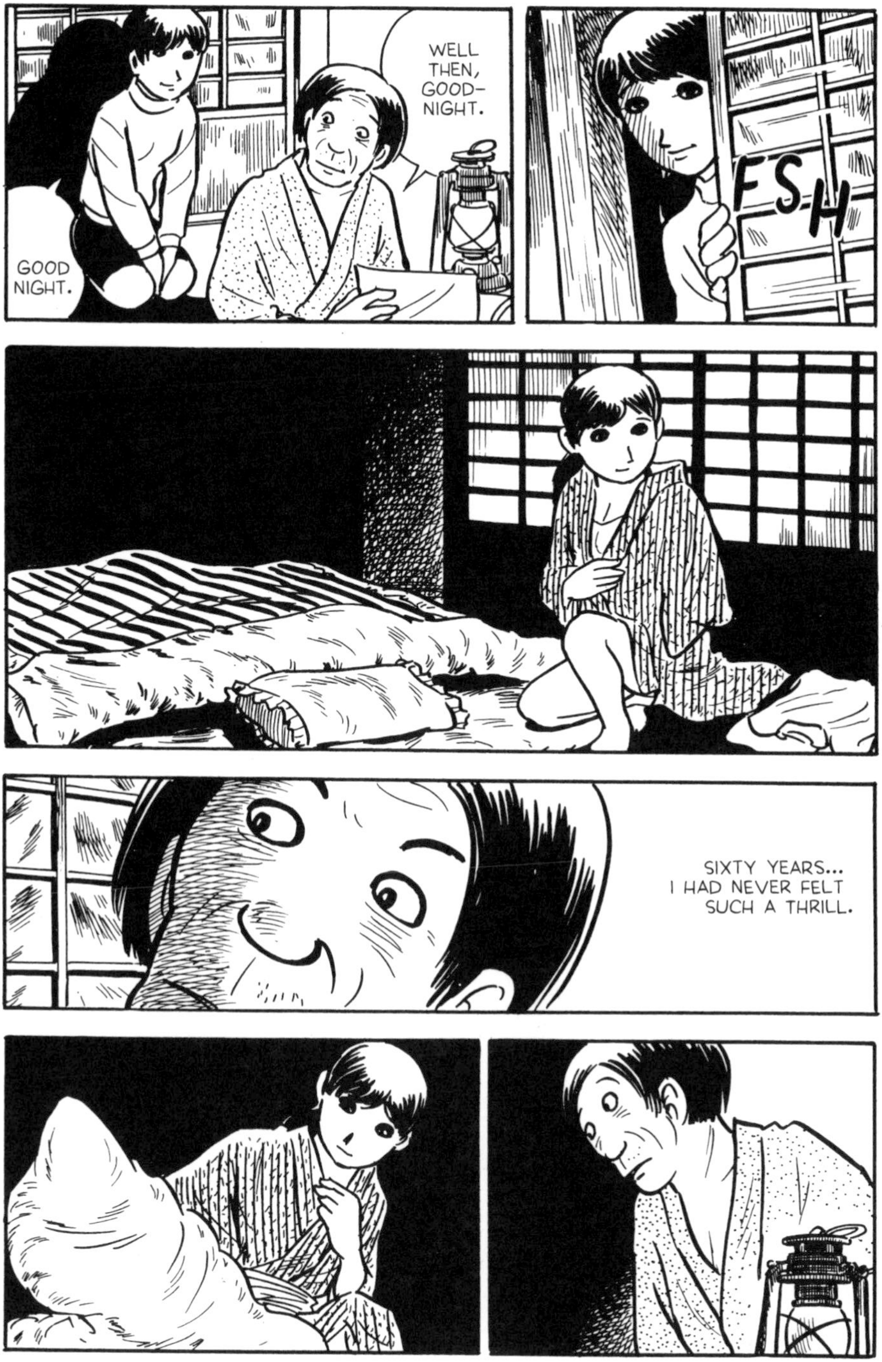

WELL THEN, GOOD-NIGHT.
GOOD NIGHT.
FSH
SIXTY YEARS... I HAD NEVER FELT SUCH A THRILL.

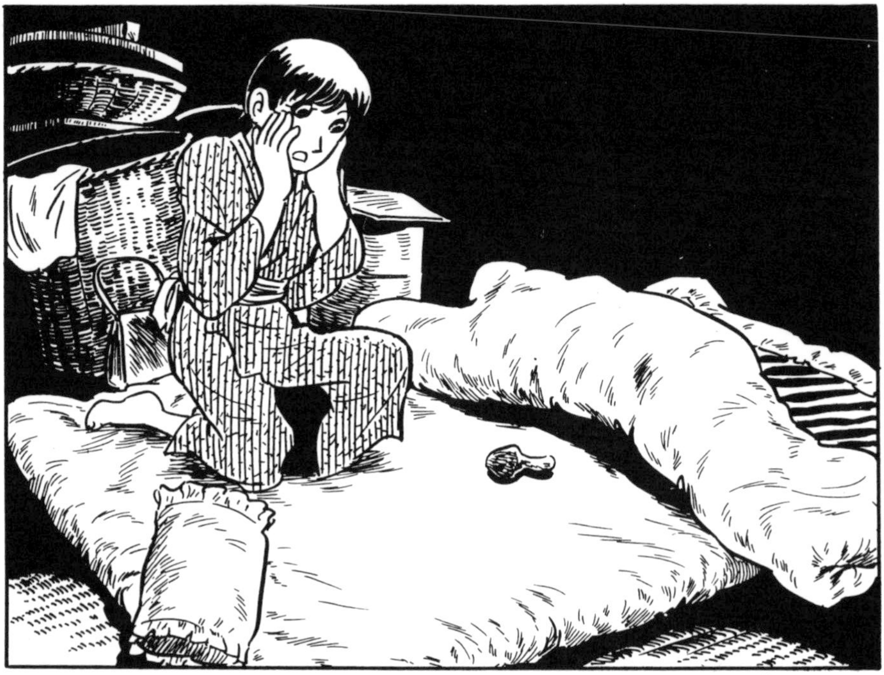

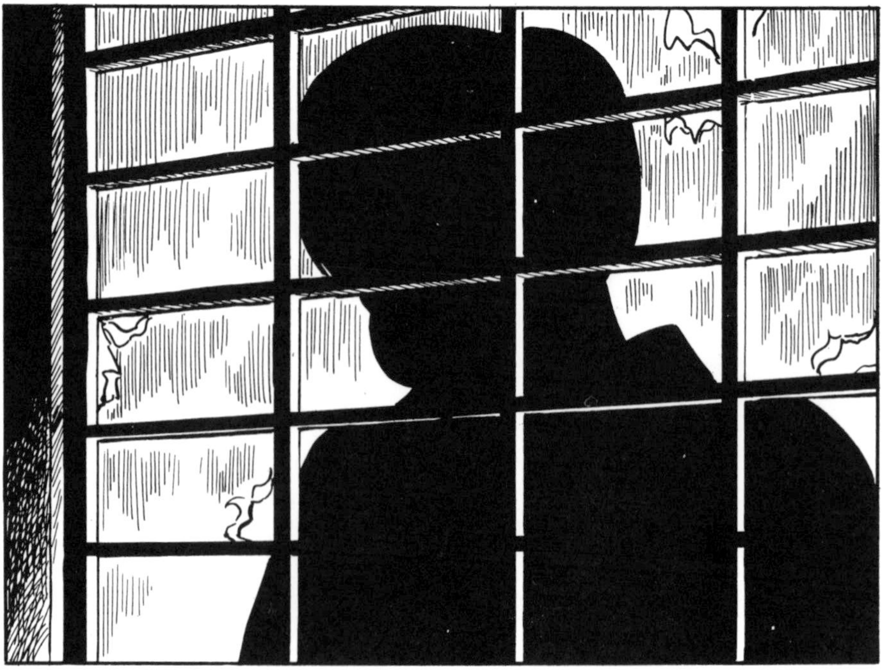

WOMAN IN THE MIRROR

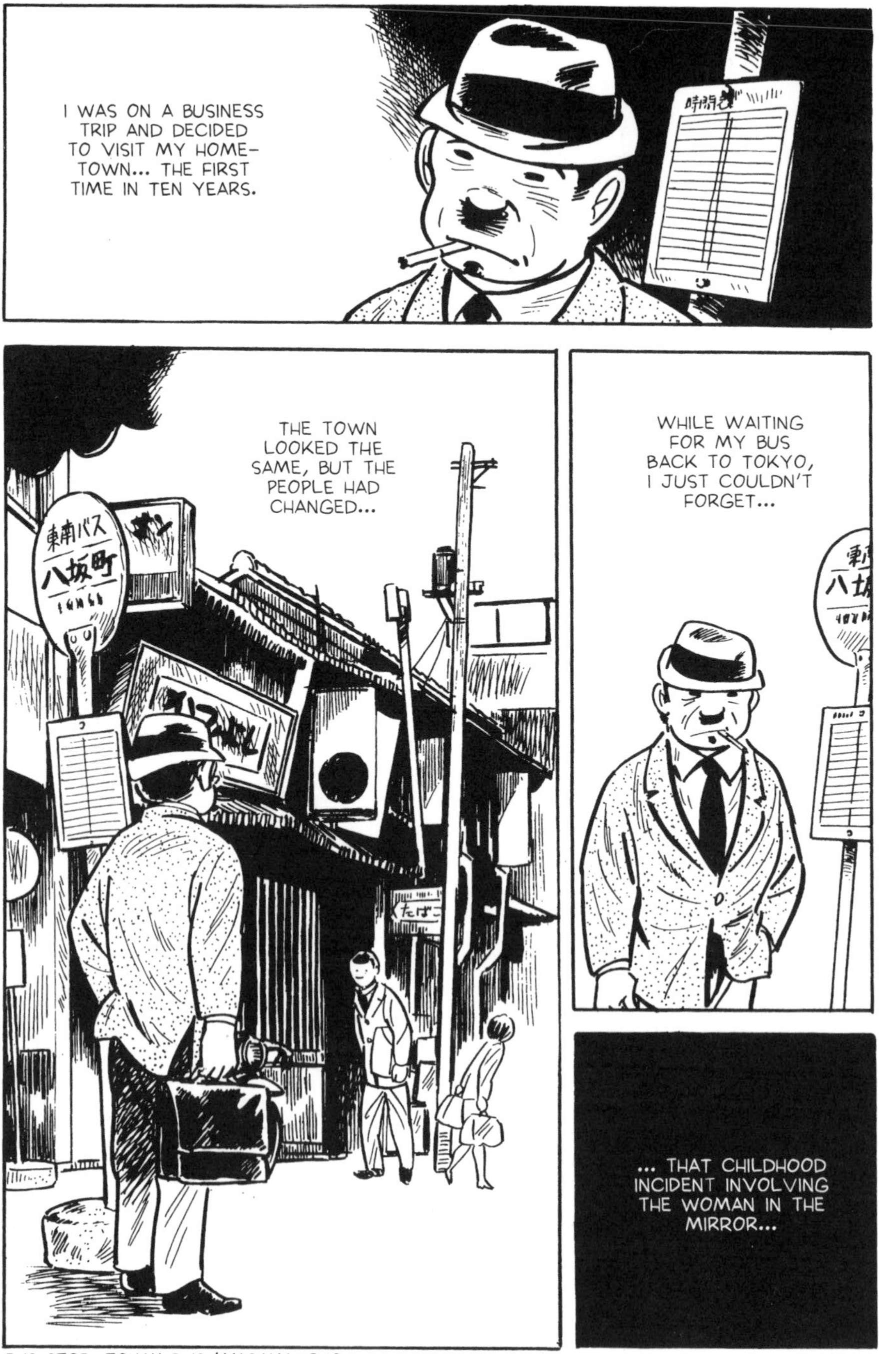
I WAS ON A BUSINESS TRIP AND DECIDED TO VISIT MY HOME-TOWN... THE FIRST TIME IN TEN YEARS.
東南バス
八坂町
たばこ
THE TOWN LOOKED THE SAME, BUT THE PEOPLE HAD CHANGED...
WHILE WAITING FOR MY BUS BACK TO TOKYO, I JUST COULDN'T FORGET...
... THAT CHILDHOOD INCIDENT INVOLVING THE WOMAN IN THE MIRROR...

BUS STOP: TONAN BUS / YASAKA-CHO

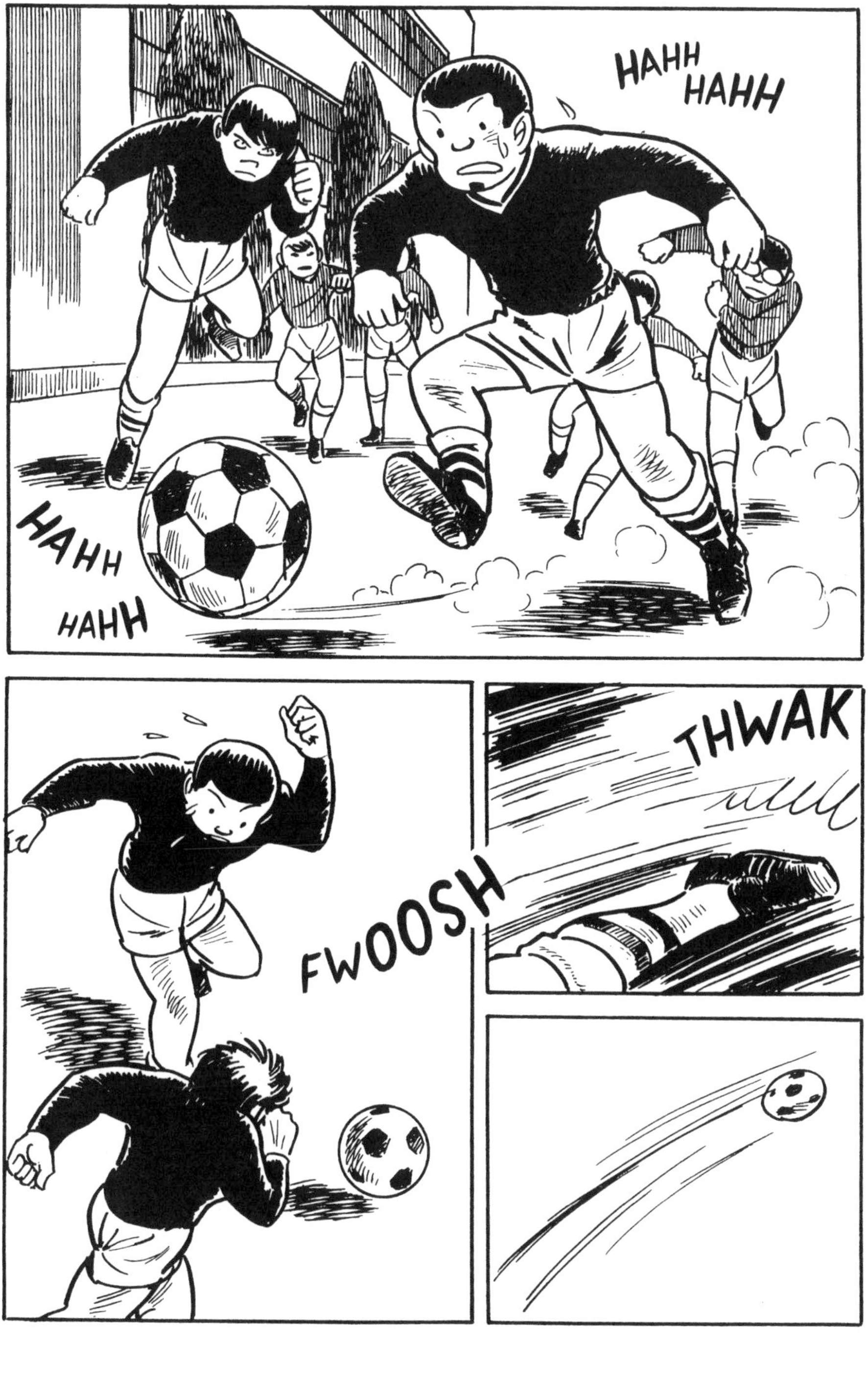
HAHH HAHH
HAHH HAHH
THWAK
FWOOSH

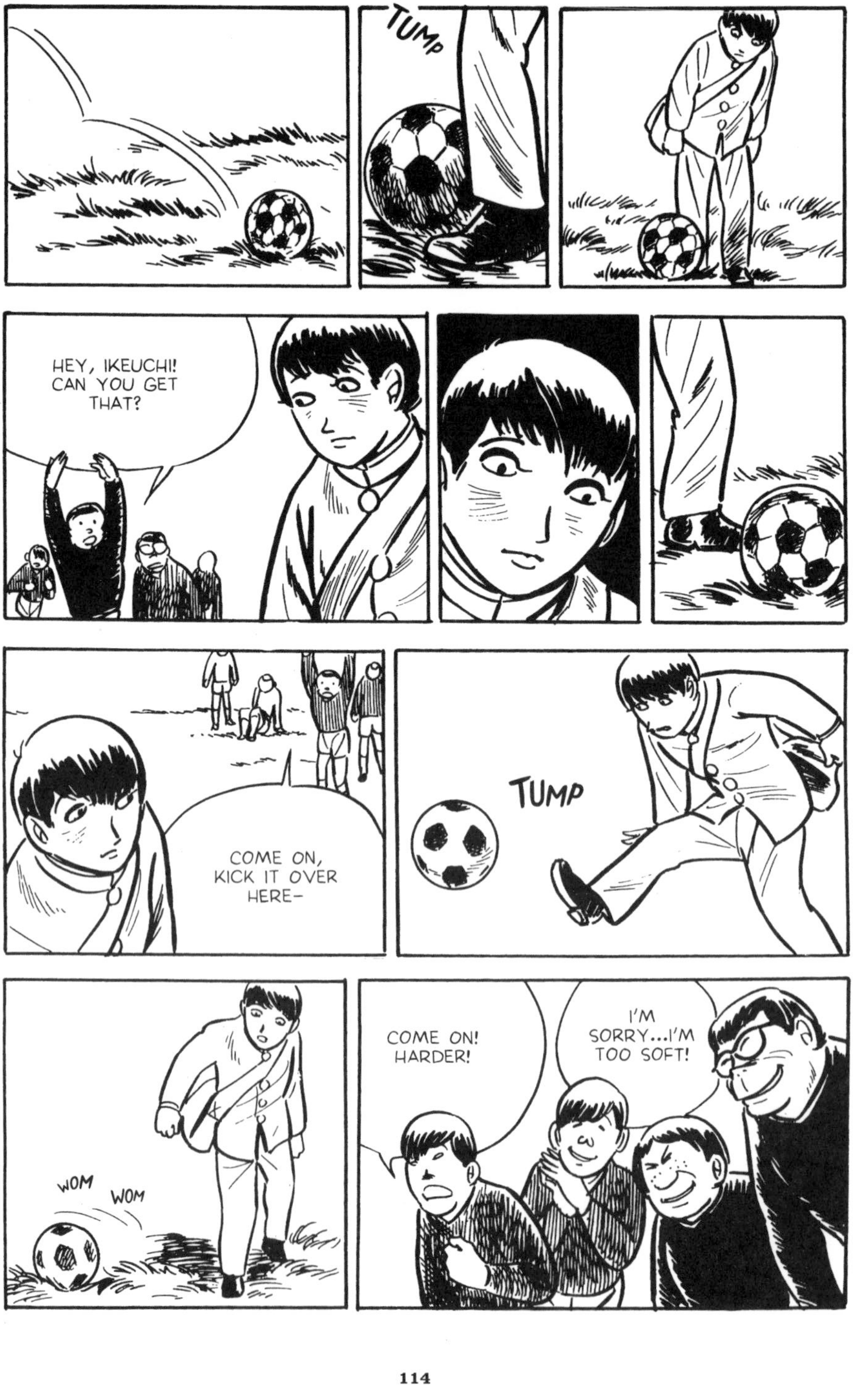
TUMP
HEY, IKEUCHI! CAN YOU GET THAT?
COME ON, KICK IT OVER HERE–
TUMP
WOM
WOM
COME ON! HARDER!
I'M SORRY...I'M TOO SOFT!

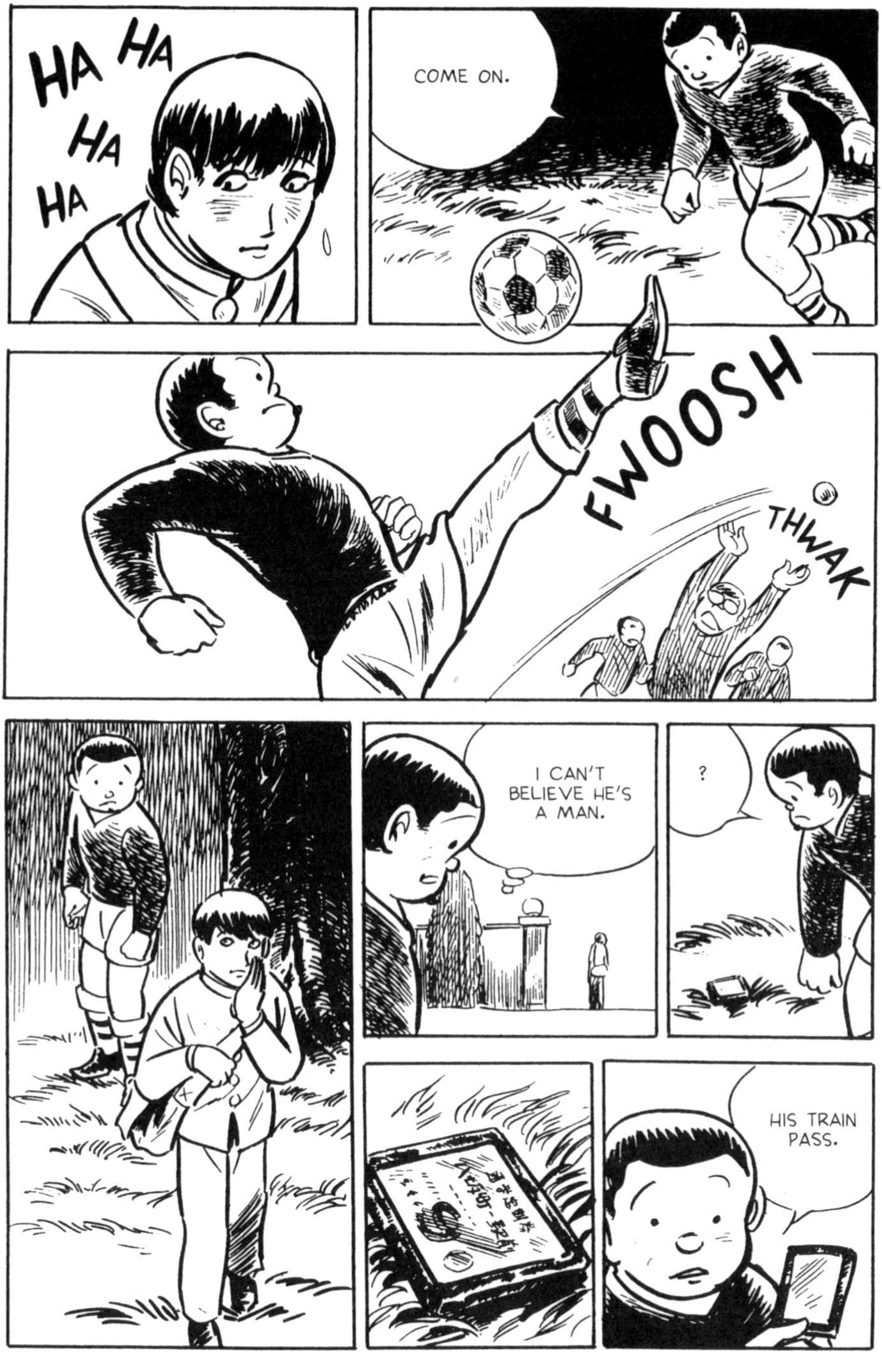
HA HA
HA
HA
COME ON.
FWOOSH
THWAK
I CAN'T BELIEVE HE'S A MAN.
?
HIS TRAIN PASS.

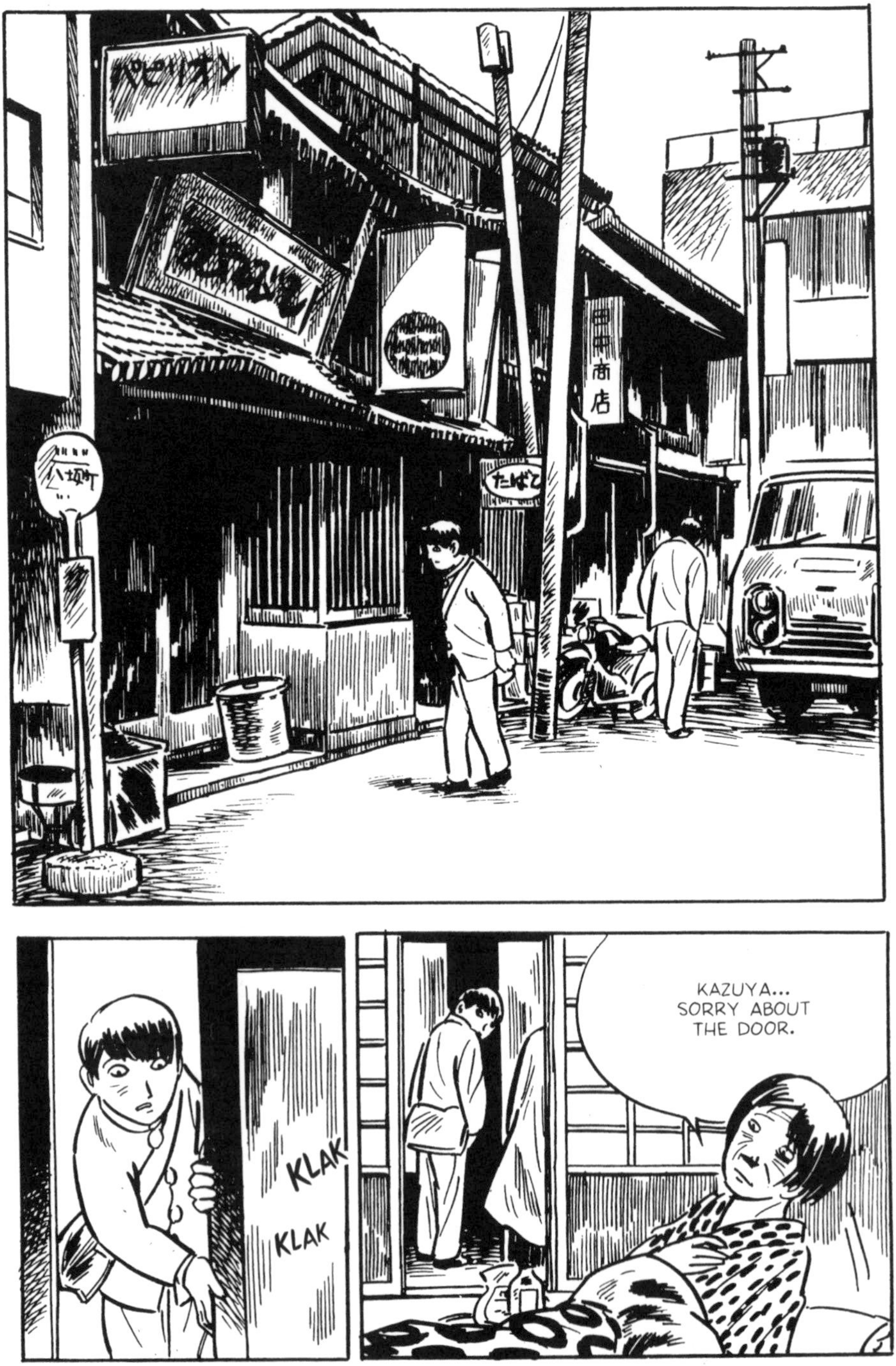
田中商店
たばこ
KLAK
KLAK
KAZUYA... SORRY ABOUT THE DOOR.

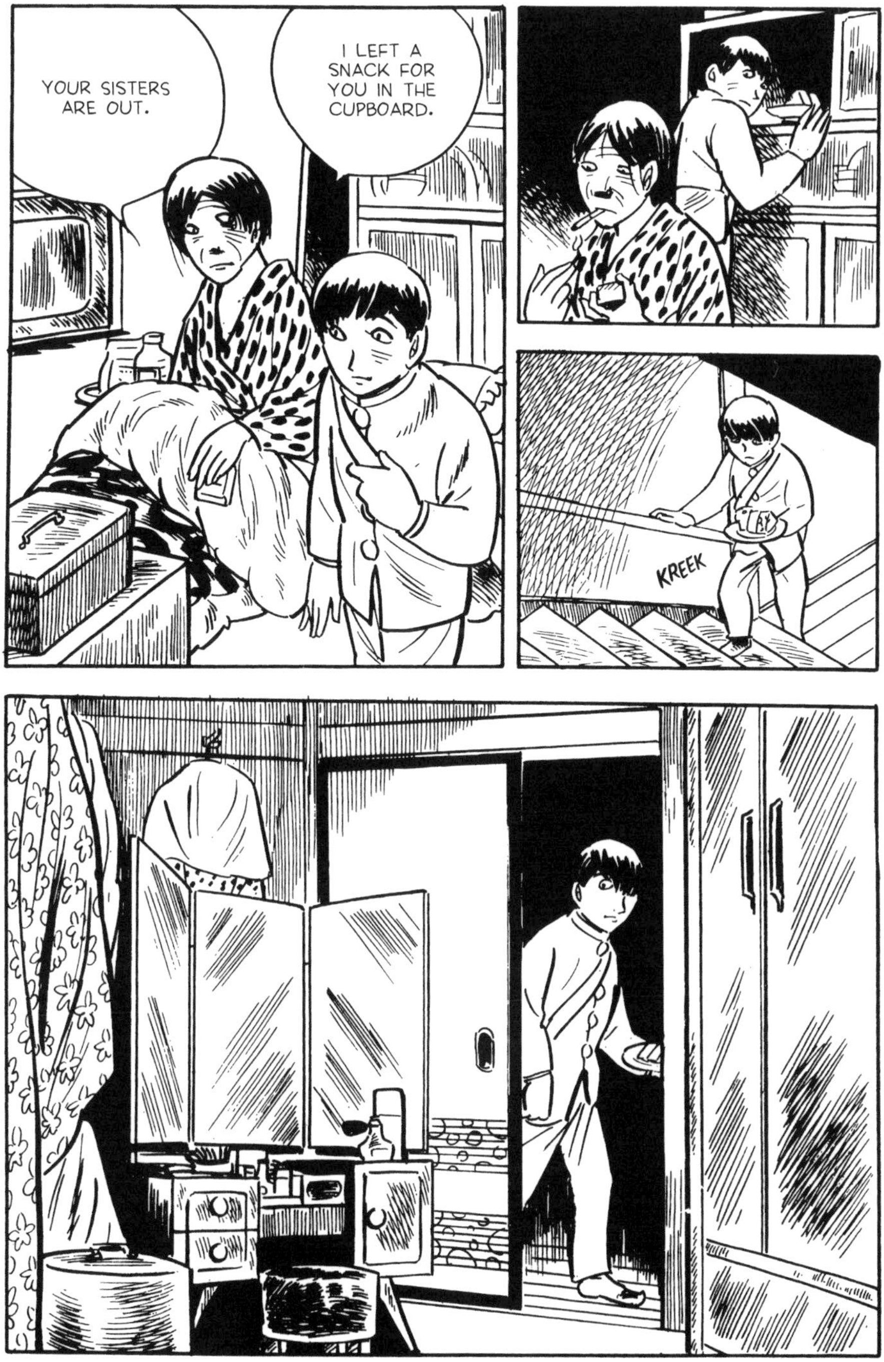
YOUR SISTERS ARE OUT.
I LEFT A SNACK FOR YOU IN THE CUPBOARD.
KREEK

THUMP

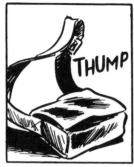

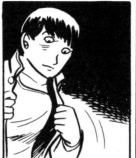

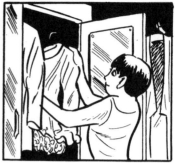

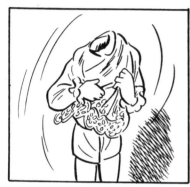

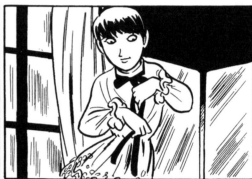

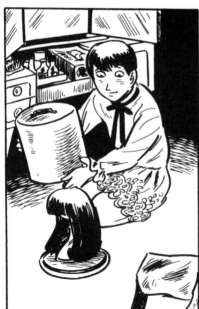

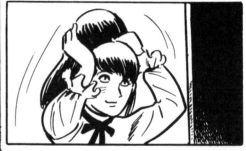

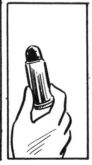

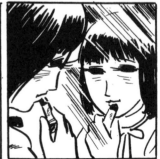

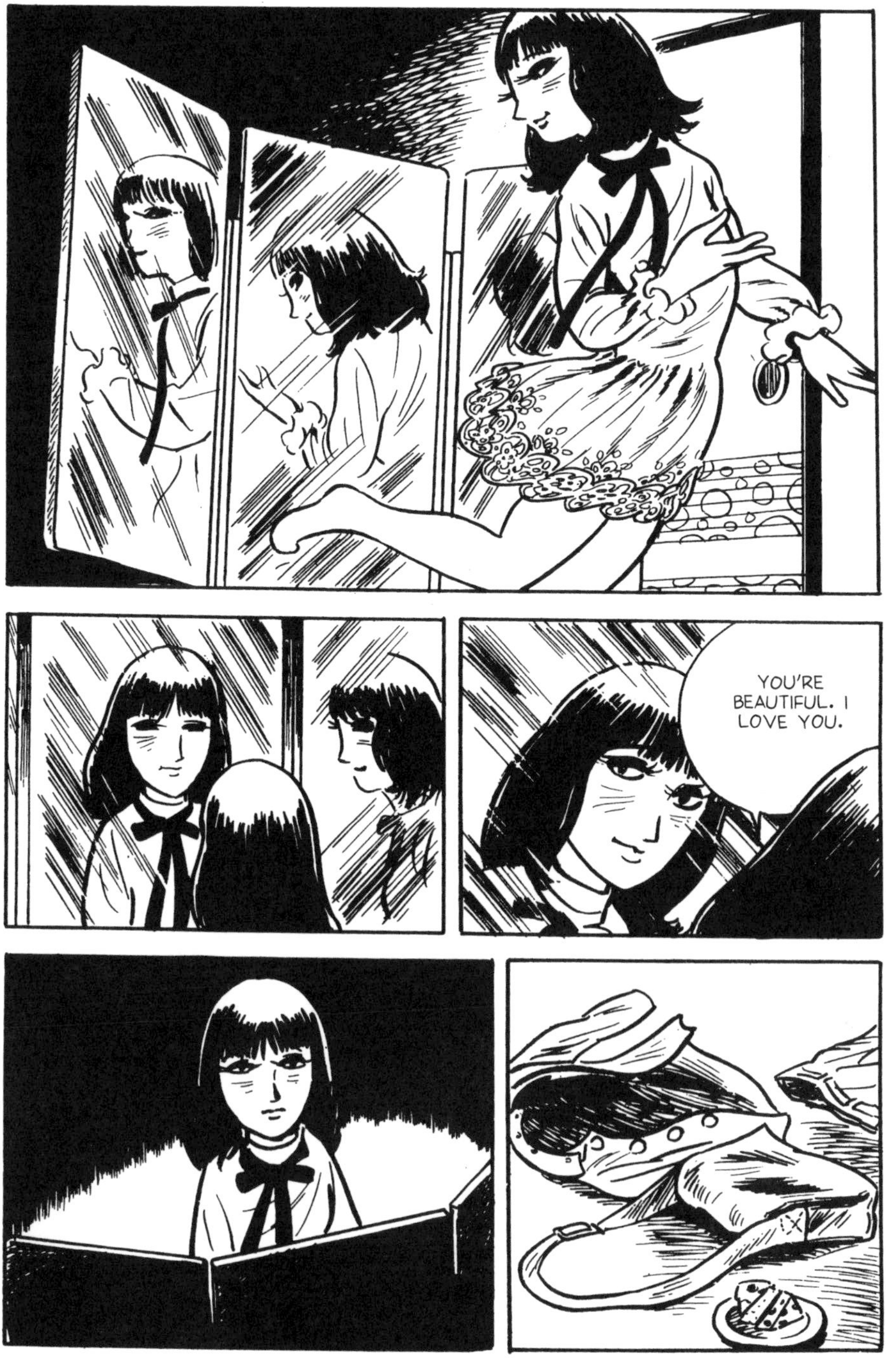
YOU'RE BEAUTIFUL. I LOVE YOU.

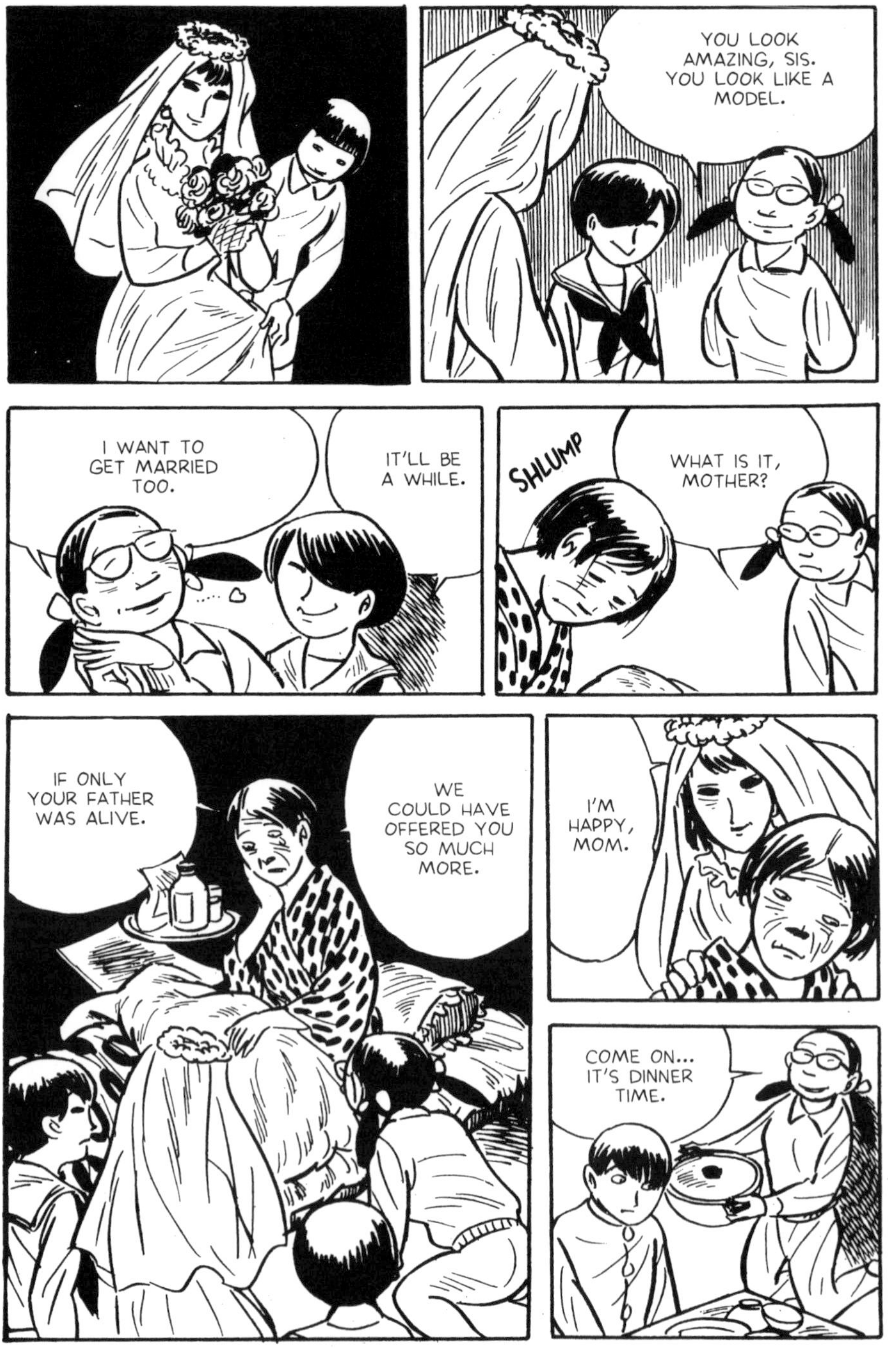
YOU LOOK AMAZING, SIS. YOU LOOK LIKE A MODEL.
I WANT TO GET MARRIED TOO.
IT'LL BE A WHILE.
SHLUMP
WHAT IS IT, MOTHER?
IF ONLY YOUR FATHER WAS ALIVE.
WE COULD HAVE OFFERED YOU SO MUCH MORE.
I'M HAPPY, MOM.
COME ON... IT'S DINNER TIME.

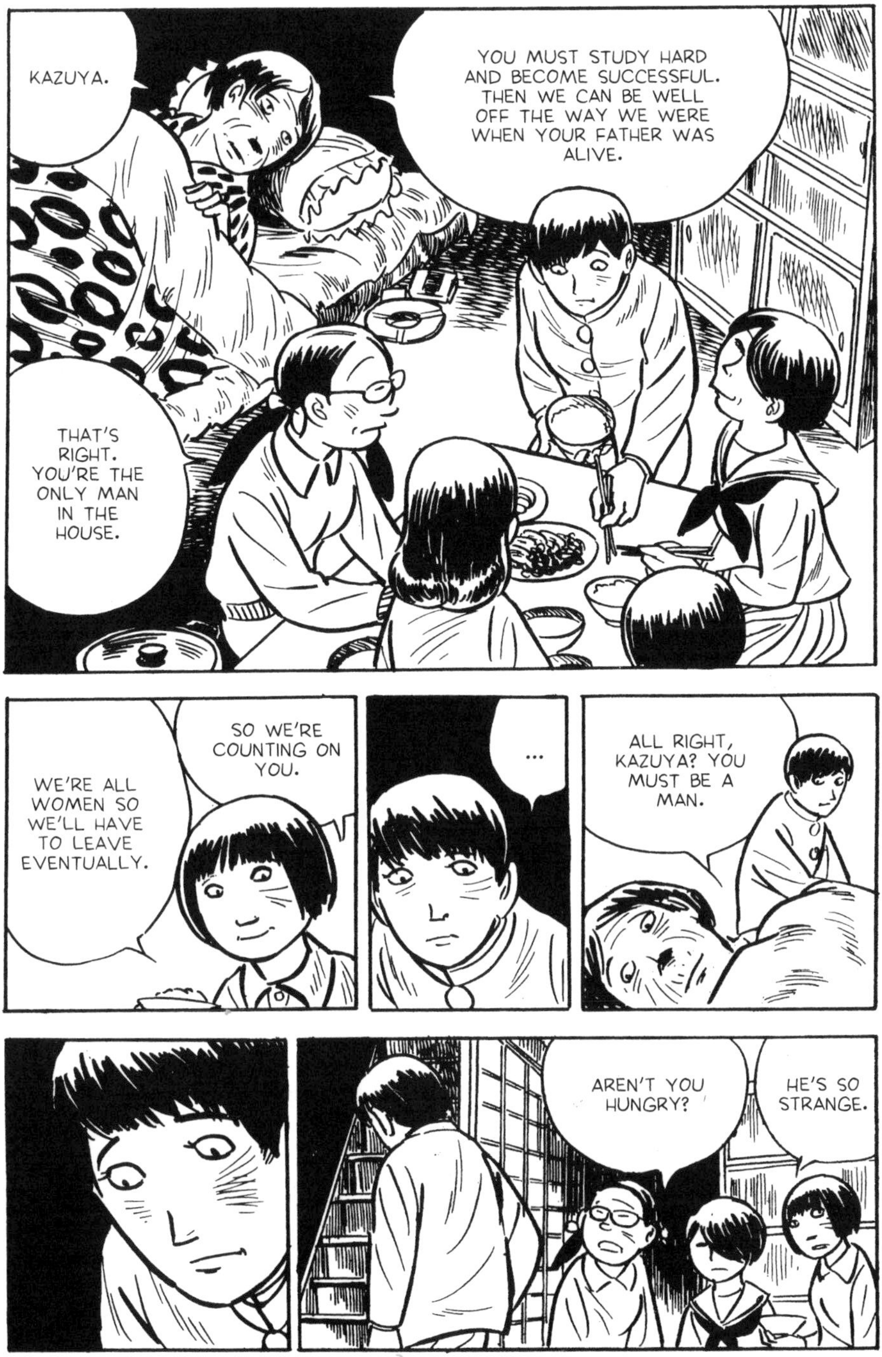
KAZUYA.
YOU MUST STUDY HARD AND BECOME SUCCESSFUL. THEN WE CAN BE WELL OFF THE WAY WE WERE WHEN YOUR FATHER WAS ALIVE.
THAT'S RIGHT. YOU'RE THE ONLY MAN IN THE HOUSE.
WE'RE ALL WOMEN SO WE'LL HAVE TO LEAVE EVENTUALLY.
SO WE'RE COUNTING ON YOU.
...
ALL RIGHT, KAZUYA? YOU MUST BE A MAN.
AREN'T YOU HUNGRY?
HE'S SO STRANGE.

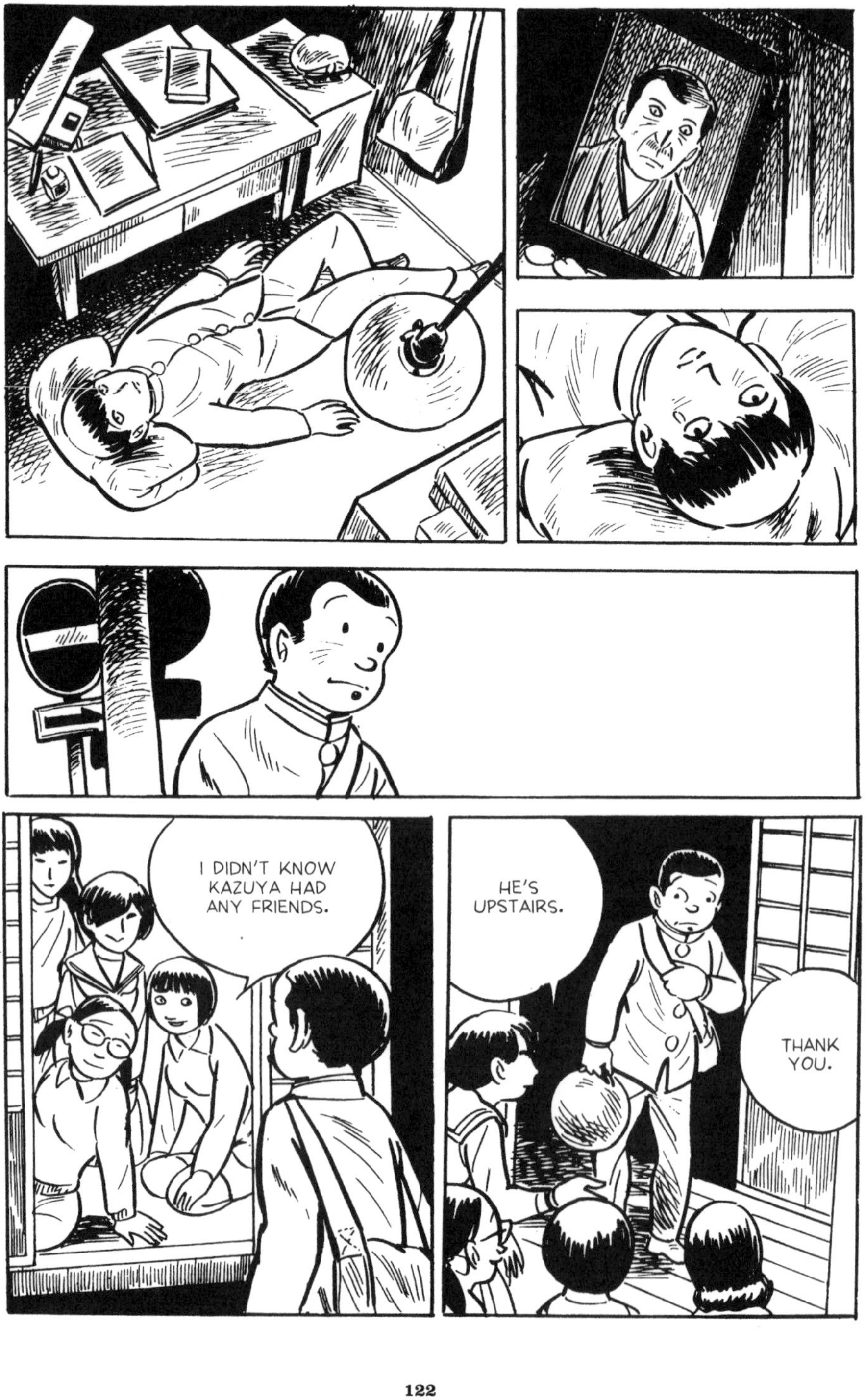
I DIDN'T KNOW KAZUYA HAD ANY FRIENDS.
HE'S UPSTAIRS.
THANK YOU.

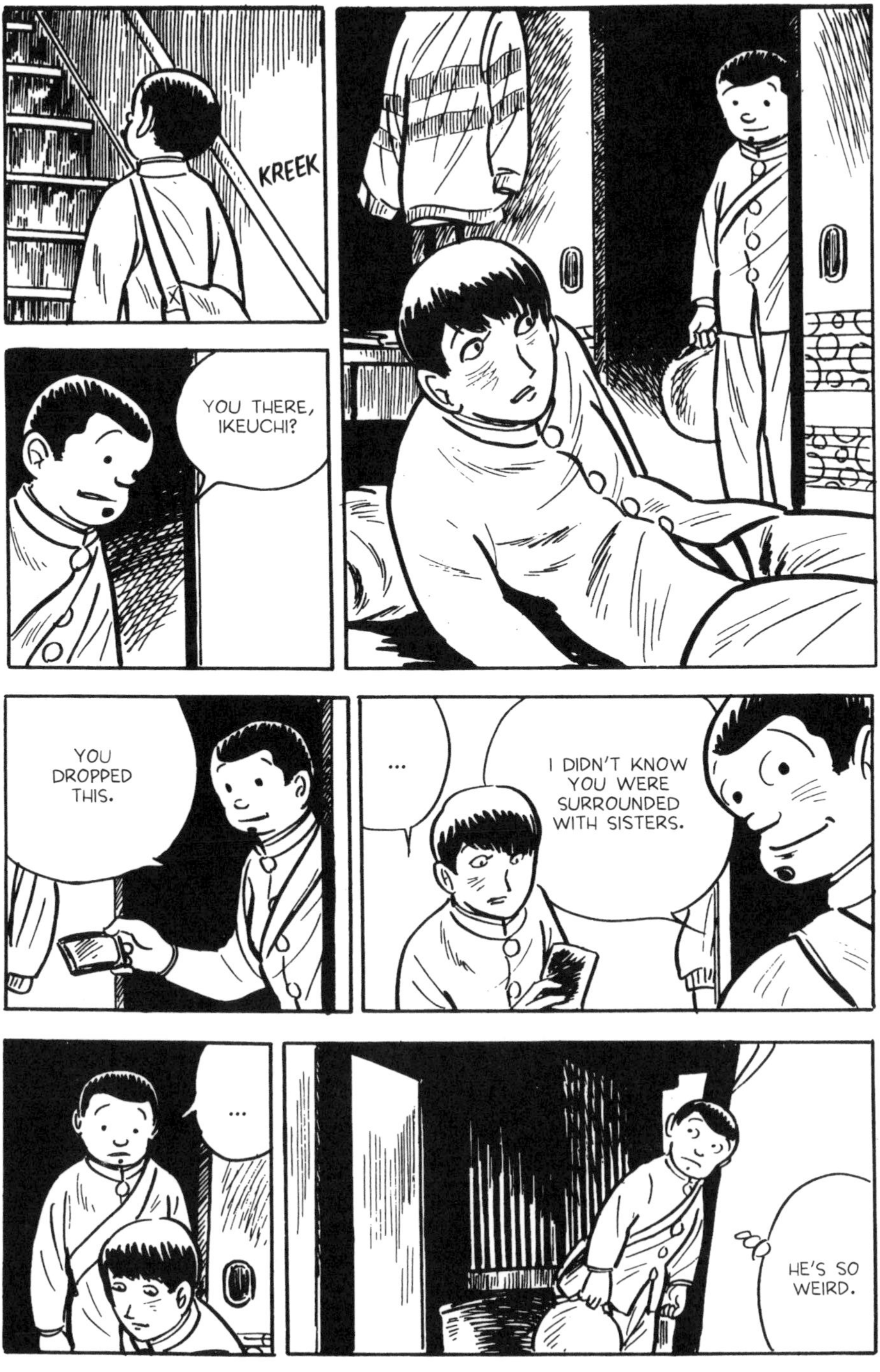
KREEK
YOU THERE, IKEUCHI?
YOU DROPPED THIS.
...
I DIDN'T KNOW YOU WERE SURROUNDED WITH SISTERS.
...
HE'S SO WEIRD.

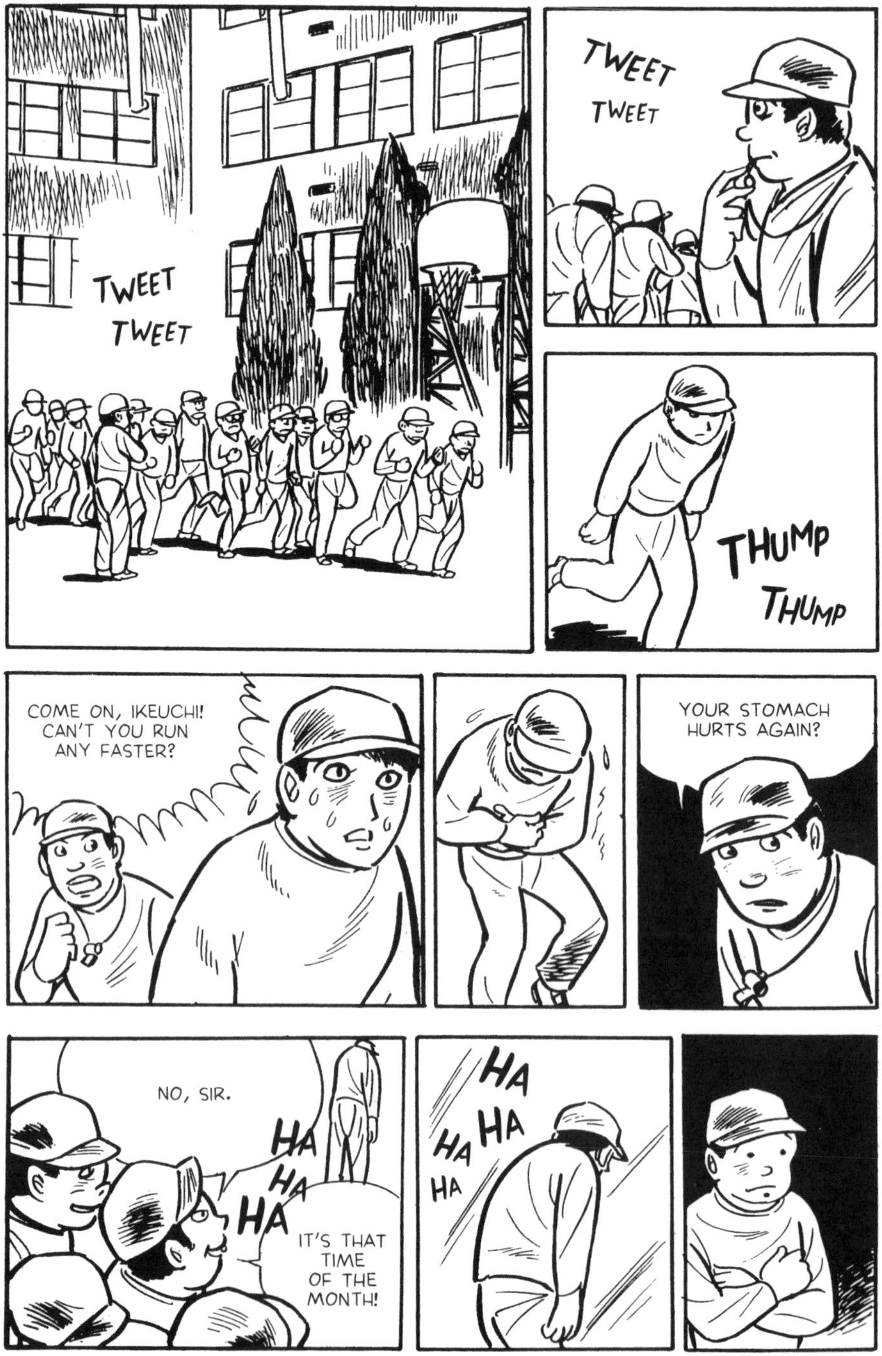
TWEET
TWEET
TWEET
TWEET
THUMP
THUMP
COME ON, IKEUCHI! CAN'T YOU RUN ANY FASTER?
YOUR STOMACH HURTS AGAIN?
NO, SIR.
HA
HA
HA
IT'S THAT TIME OF THE MONTH!
HA
HA
HA
HA

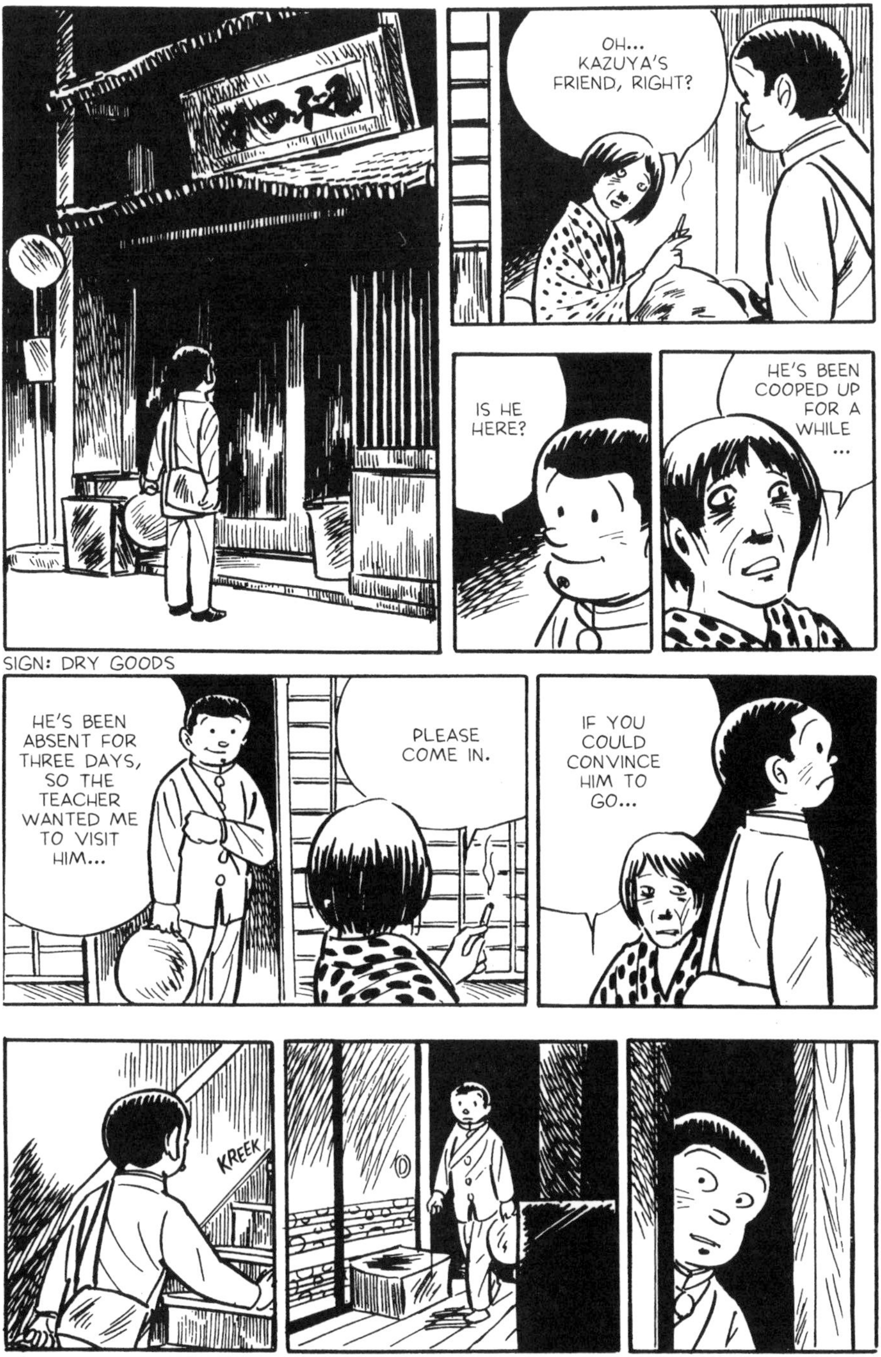
SIGN: DRY GOODS
OH... KAZUYA'S FRIEND, RIGHT?
IS HE HERE?
HE'S BEEN COOPED UP FOR A WHILE ...
HE'S BEEN ABSENT FOR THREE DAYS, SO THE TEACHER WANTED ME TO VISIT HIM...
PLEASE COME IN.
IF YOU COULD CONVINCE HIM TO GO...
KREEK

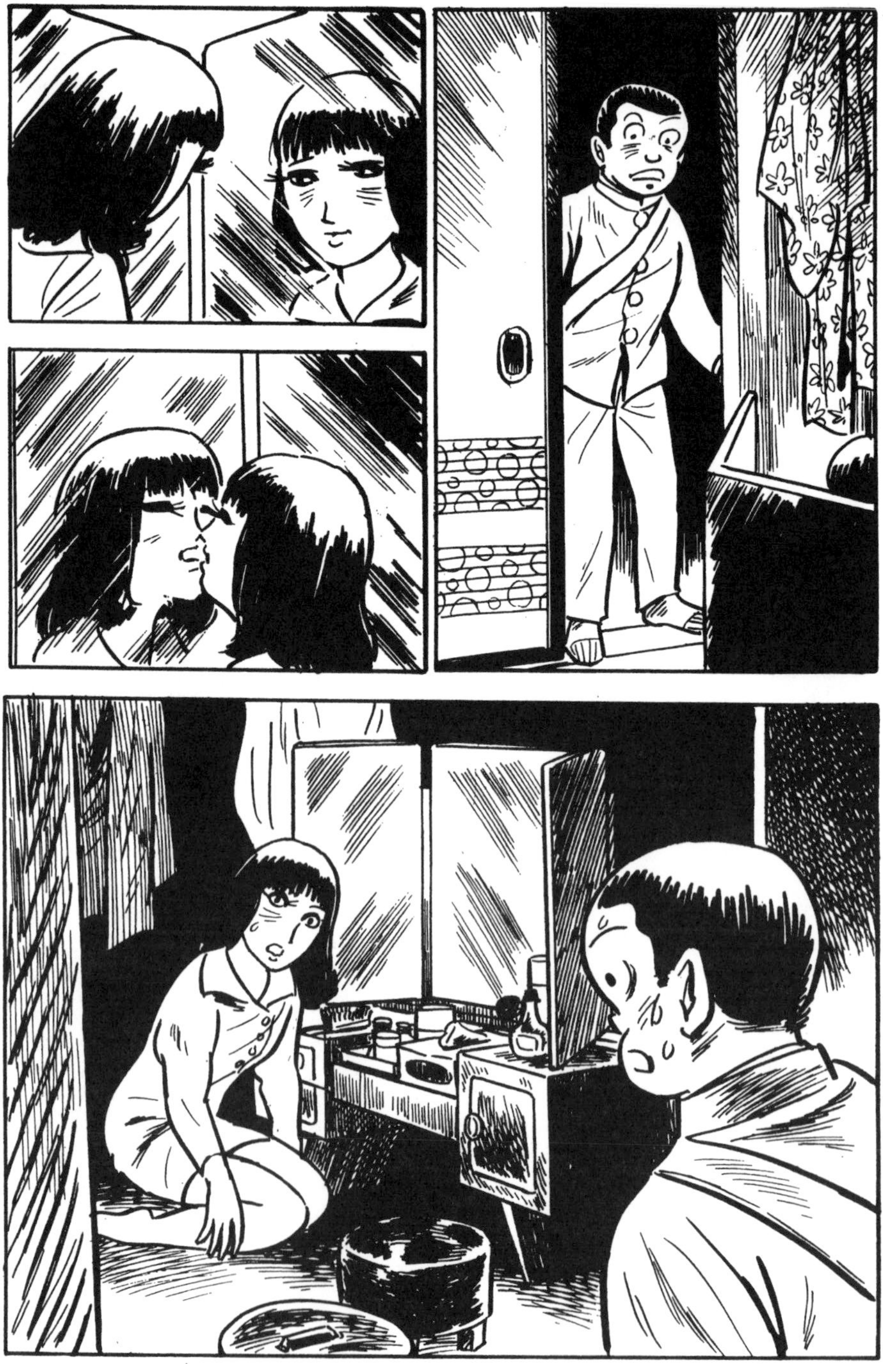

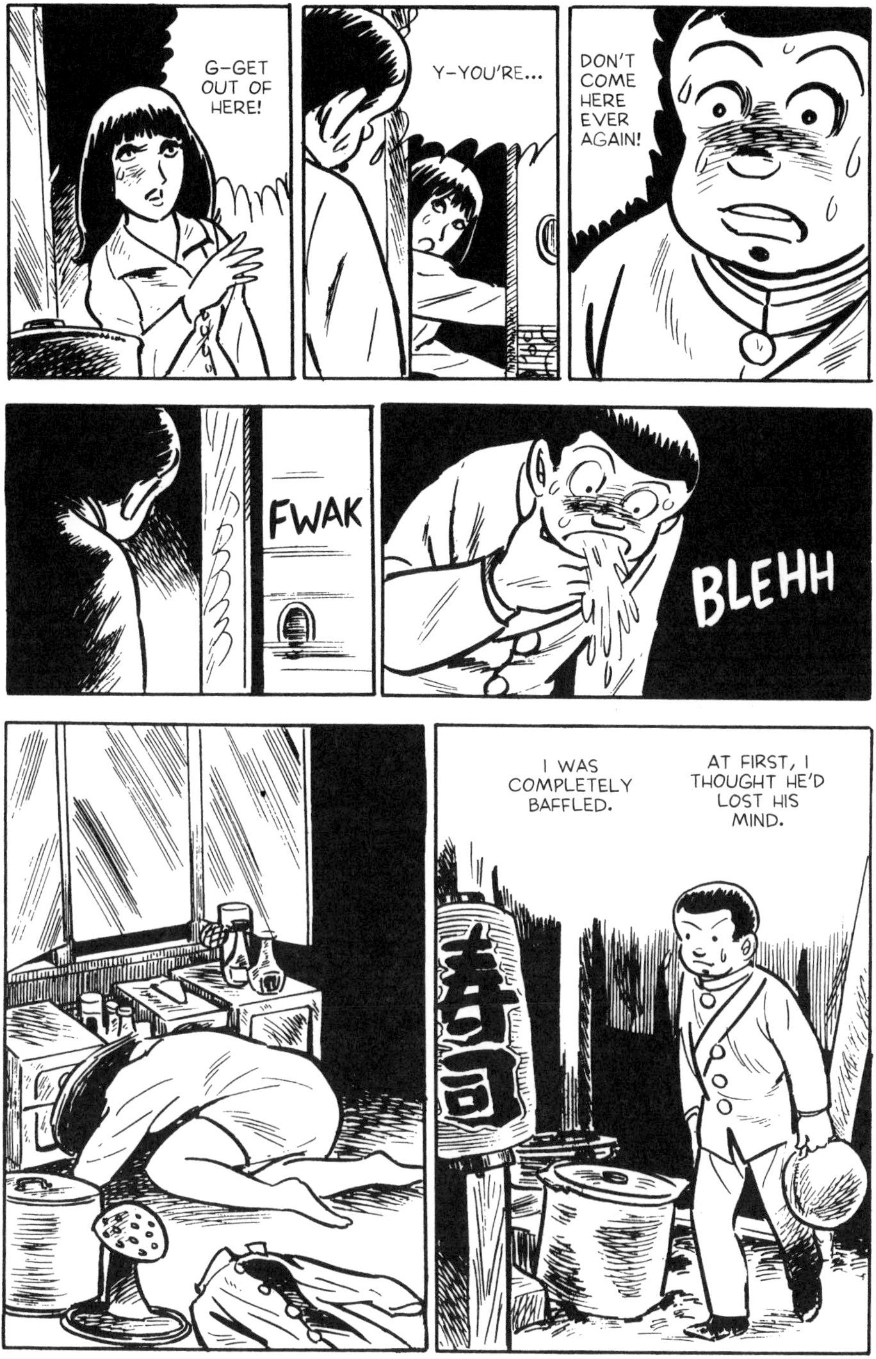
G-GET OUT OF HERE!
Y-YOU'RE...
DON'T COME HERE EVER AGAIN!
FWAK
BLEHH
I WAS COMPLETELY BAFFLED.
AT FIRST, I THOUGHT HE'D LOST HIS MIND.
寿司

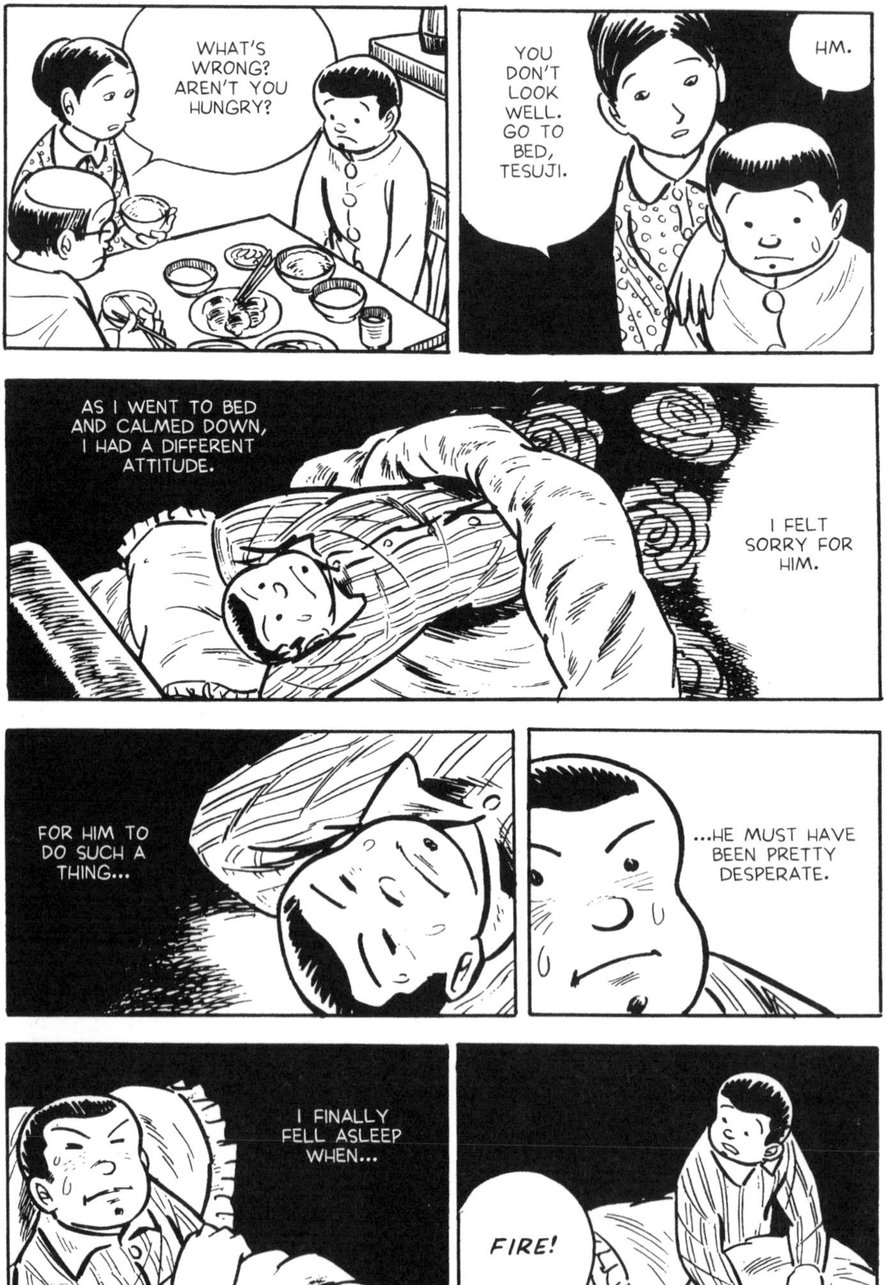
WHAT'S WRONG? AREN'T YOU HUNGRY?
YOU DON'T LOOK WELL. GO TO BED, TESUJI.
HM.
AS I WENT TO BED AND CALMED DOWN, I HAD A DIFFERENT ATTITUDE.
I FELT SORRY FOR HIM.
FOR HIM TO DO SUCH A THING...
...HE MUST HAVE BEEN PRETTY DESPERATE.
I FINALLY FELL ASLEEP WHEN...
FIRE!

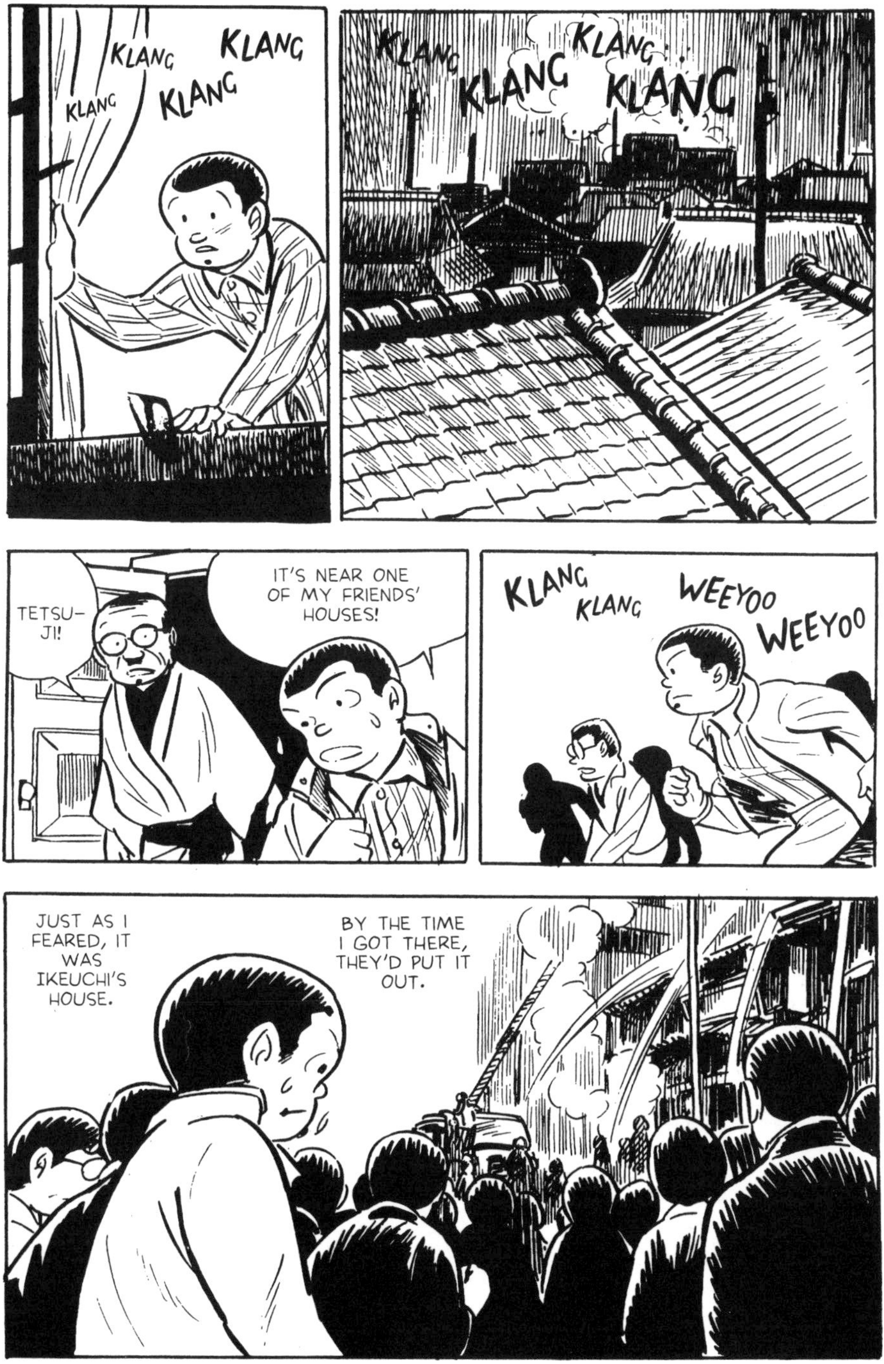
KLANG
KLANG
KLANG
KLANG
KLANG
KLANG
KLANG
KLANG
TETSU-JI!
IT'S NEAR ONE OF MY FRIENDS' HOUSES!
KLANG
KLANG
WEEYOO
WEEYOO
JUST AS I FEARED, IT WAS IKEUCHI'S HOUSE.
BY THE TIME I GOT THERE, THEY'D PUT IT OUT.

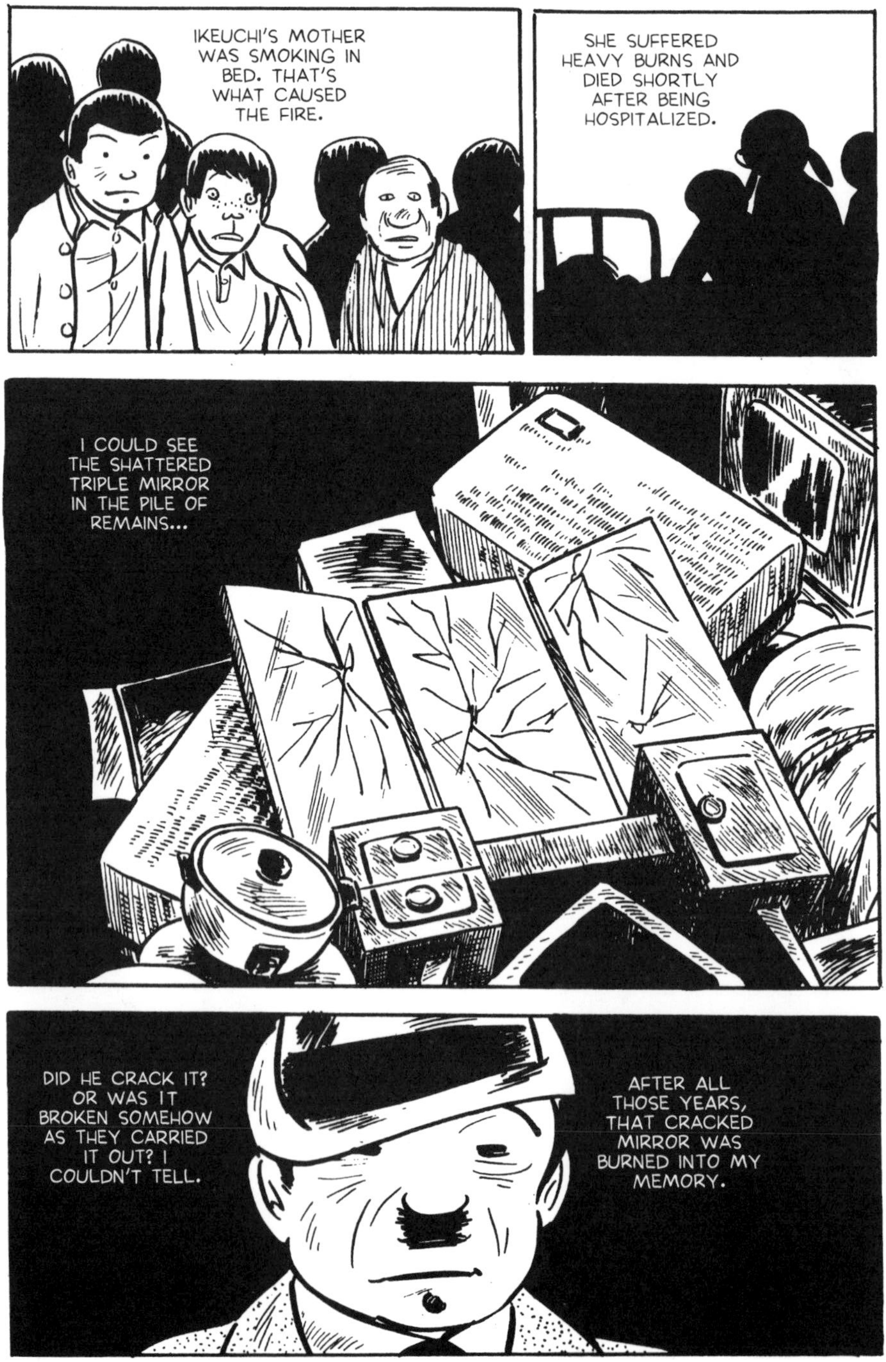
IKEUCHI'S MOTHER WAS SMOKING IN BED. THAT'S WHAT CAUSED THE FIRE.
SHE SUFFERED HEAVY BURNS AND DIED SHORTLY AFTER BEING HOSPITALIZED.
I COULD SEE THE SHATTERED TRIPLE MIRROR IN THE PILE OF REMAINS...
DID HE CRACK IT? OR WAS IT BROKEN SOMEHOW AS THEY CARRIED IT OUT? I COULDN'T TELL.
AFTER ALL THOSE YEARS, THAT CRACKED MIRROR WAS BURNED INTO MY MEMORY.

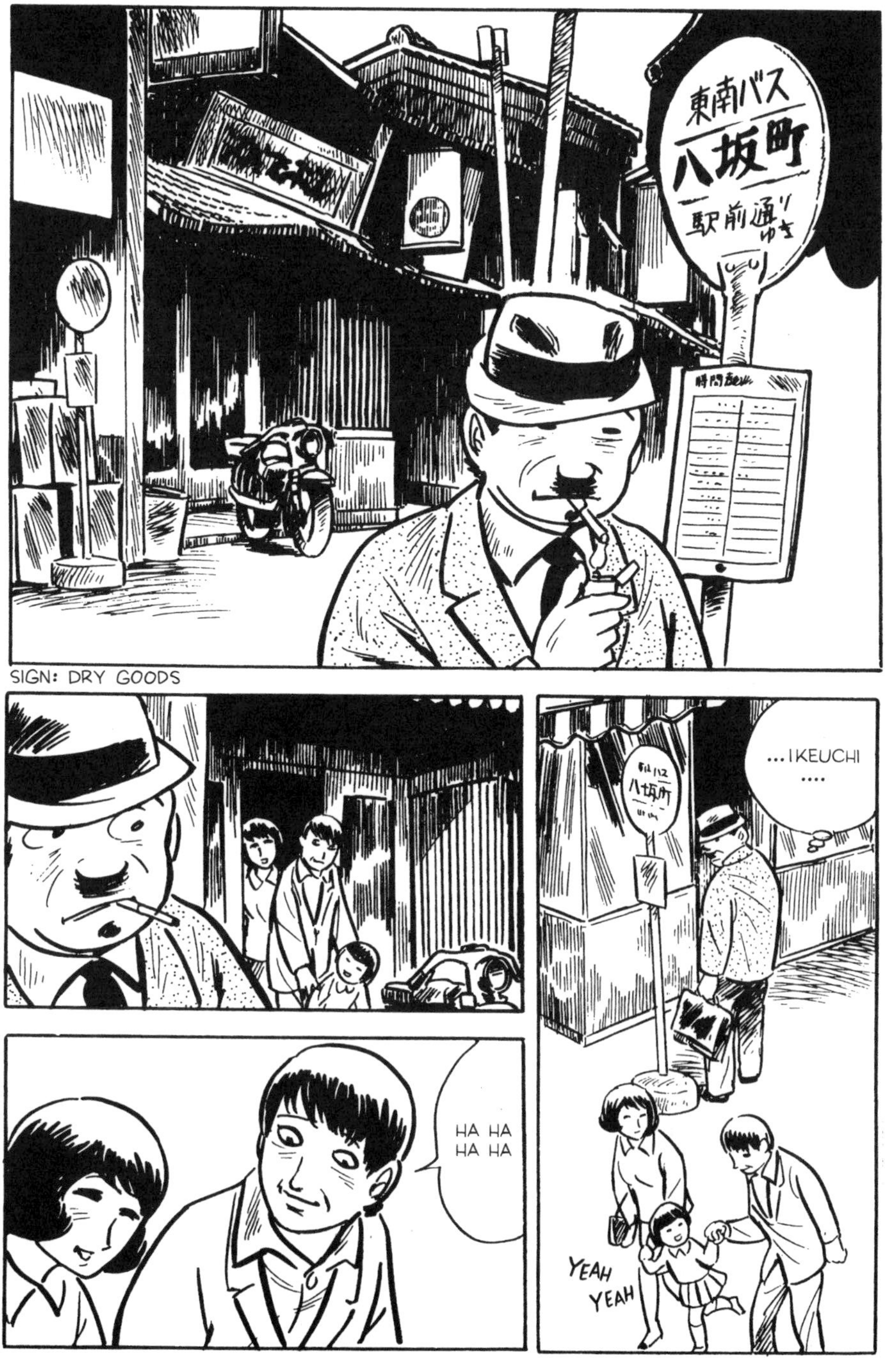
東南バス
八坂町
駅前通りゆき
SIGN: DRY GOODS
HA HA HA HA
...IKEUCHI ....
YEAH YEAH

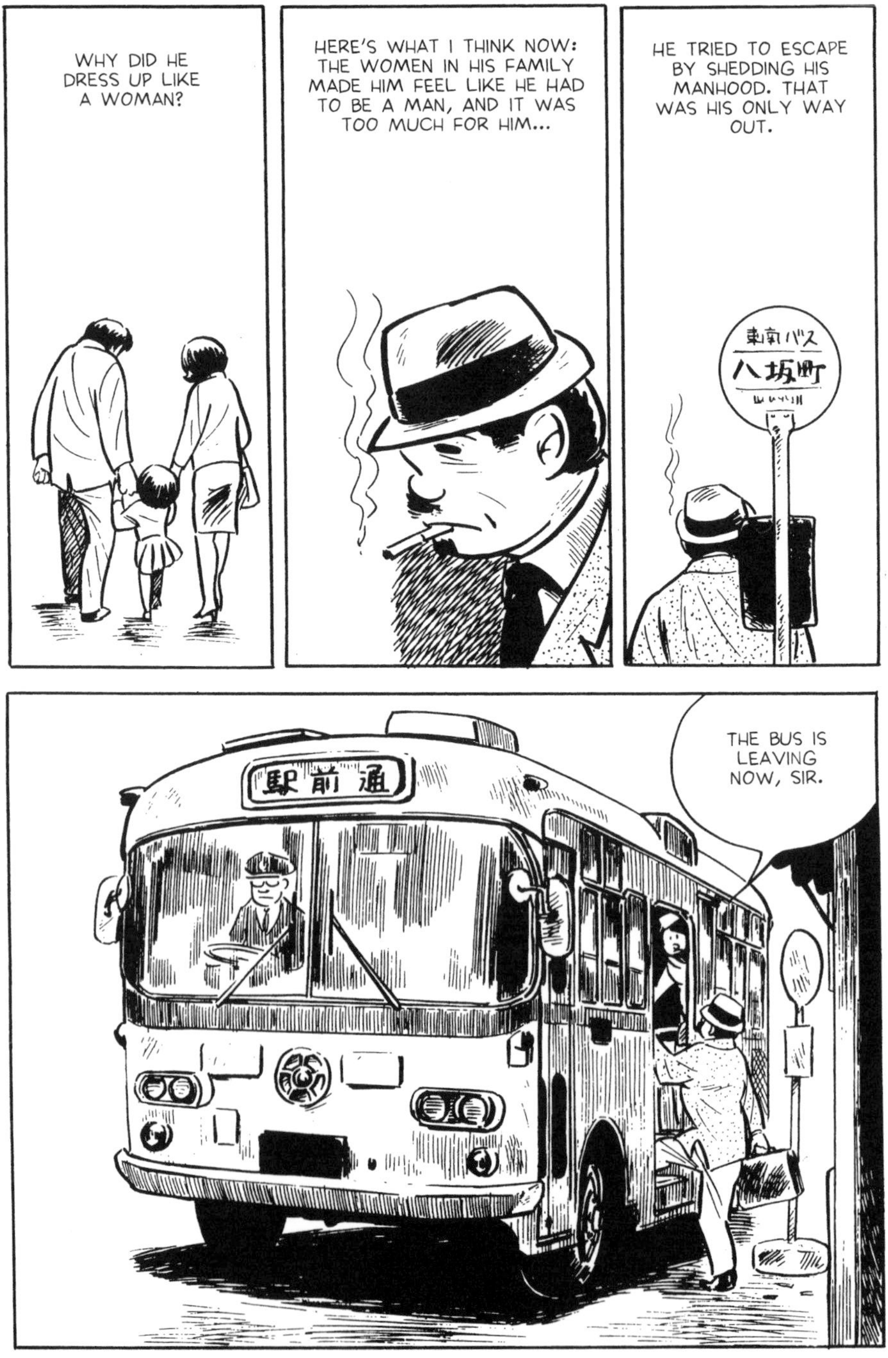
WHY DID HE DRESS UP LIKE A WOMAN?
HERE'S WHAT I THINK NOW: THE WOMEN IN HIS FAMILY MADE HIM FEEL LIKE HE HAD TO BE A MAN, AND IT WAS TOO MUCH FOR HIM...
HE TRIED TO ESCAPE BY SHEDDING HIS MANHOOD. THAT WAS HIS ONLY WAY OUT.
東南バス
八坂町
駅前通
THE BUS IS LEAVING NOW, SIR.

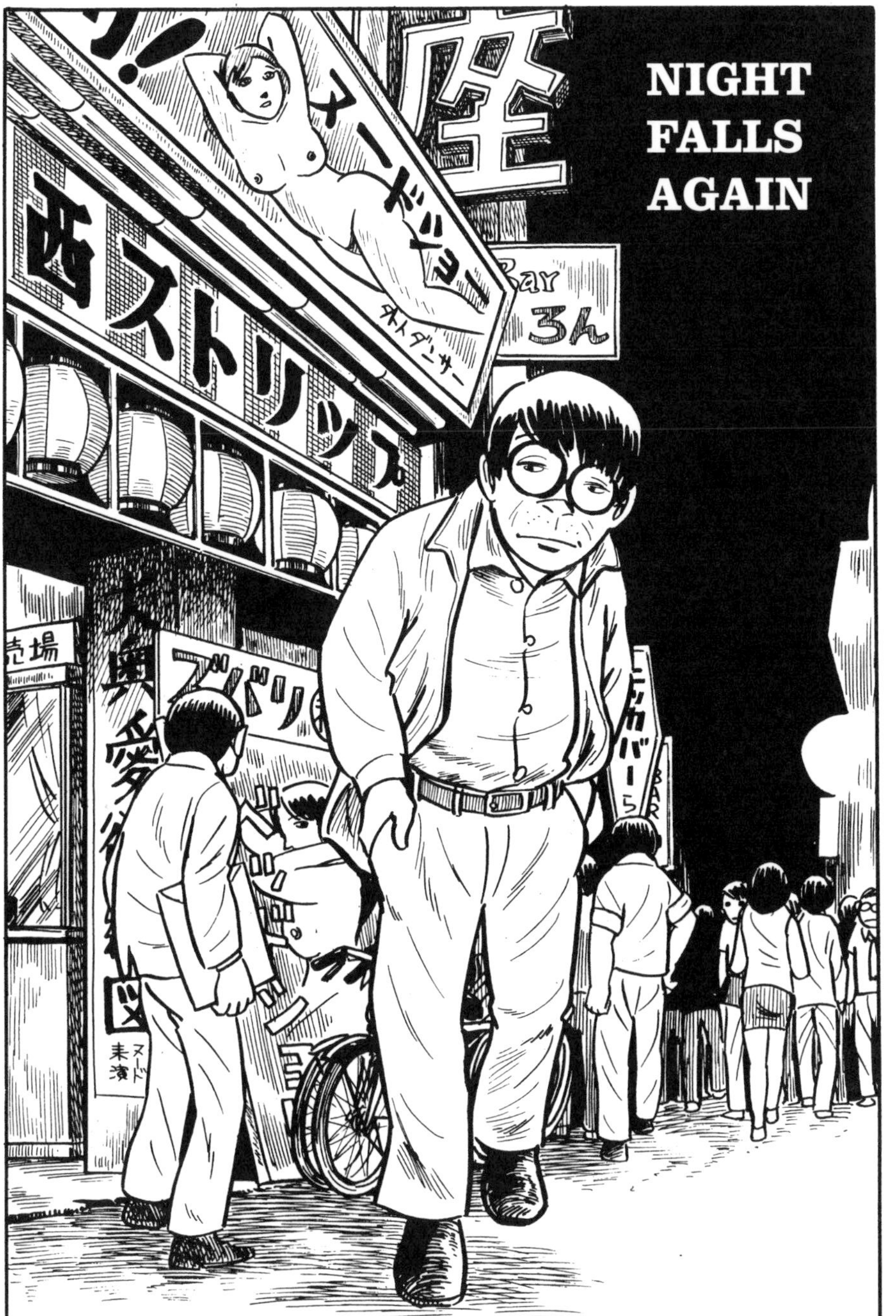
NIGHT
FALLS
AGAIN
座
ヌードショー
外人ダンサー
西ストリップ
Bar
ろん
売場
ニッカバー
BAR
ヌード
来演

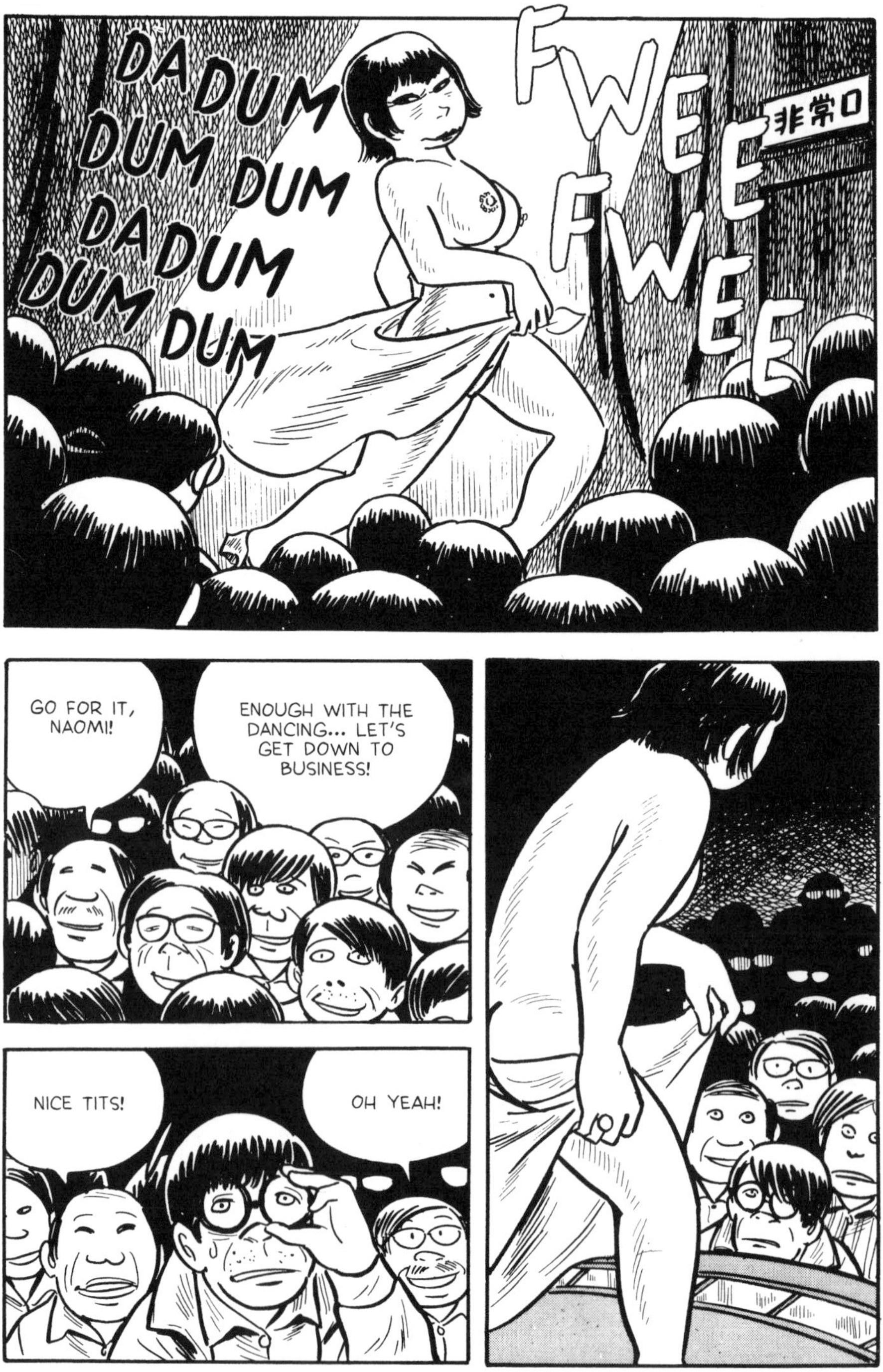
DADUM DUM
DUM DUM
DADUM
DUM DUM
FWEE
FWEE
非常口
GO FOR IT, NAOMI!
ENOUGH WITH THE DANCING... LET'S GET DOWN TO BUSINESS!
NICE TITS!
OH YEAH!

BADOOM

TUGG

THIS FOUR-EYED FREAK SURE HAS A THING FOR ME.

PER-VERT.

HEE HEE HA HA HA HA HA HA

DADUM DADUM DADUM

通天閣
たばこ
洋食
めし
スマートボー

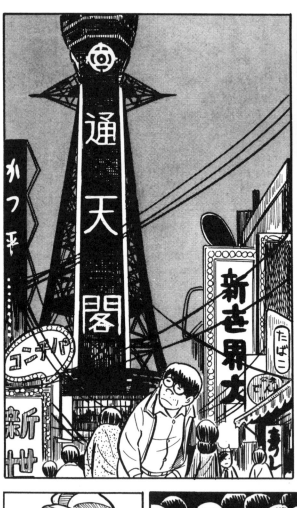

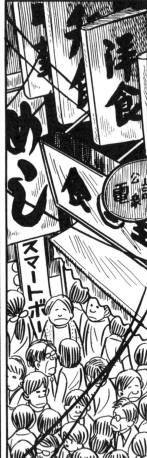

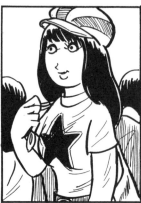

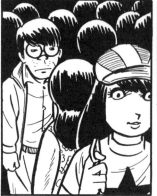

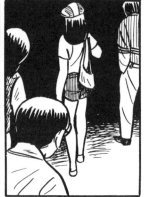

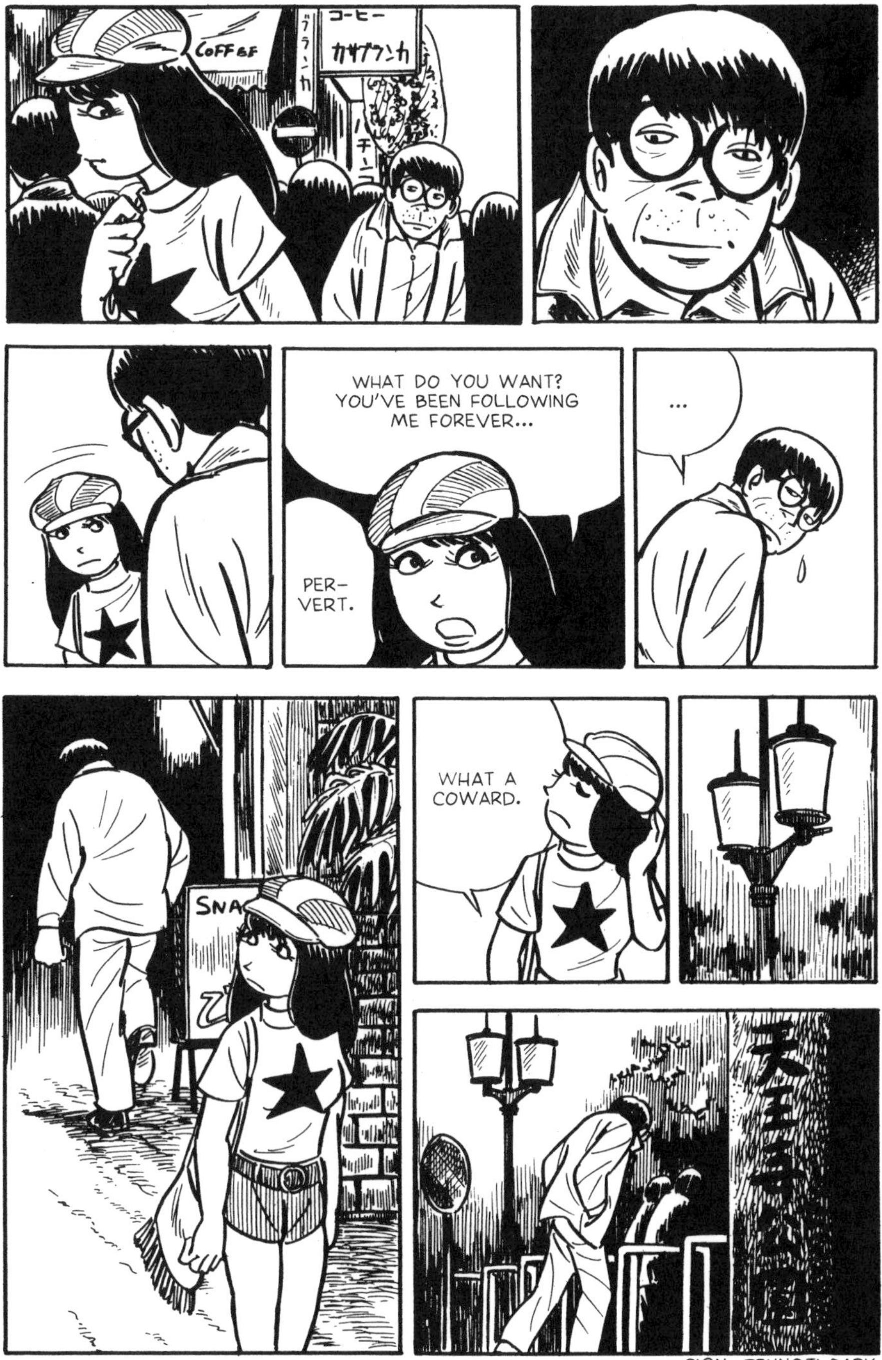
コーヒー
カサブランカ
WHAT DO YOU WANT? YOU'VE BEEN FOLLOWING ME FOREVER...
PER- VERT.
...
WHAT A COWARD.
SIGN: TENNOJI PARK

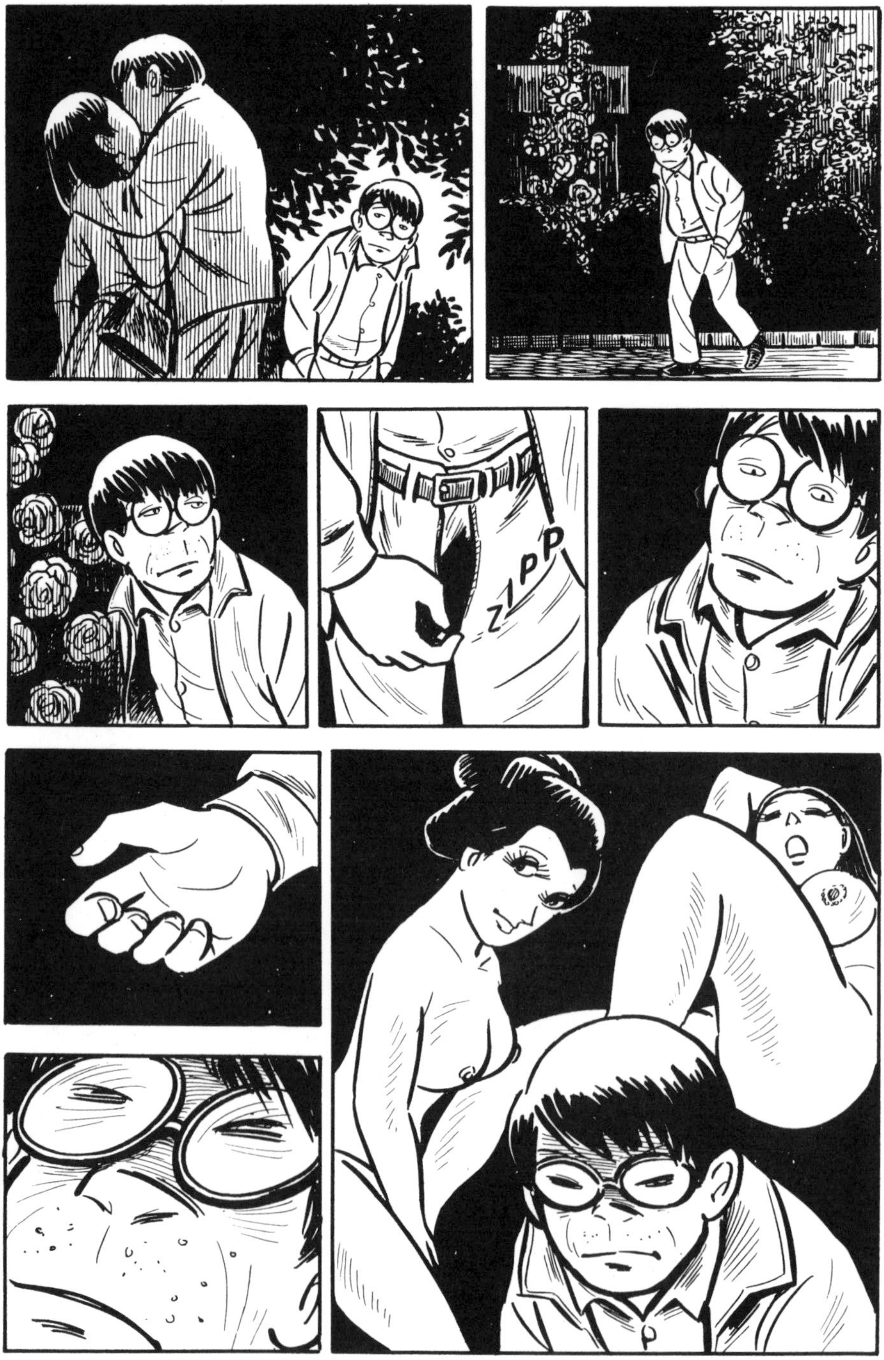
ZIPP

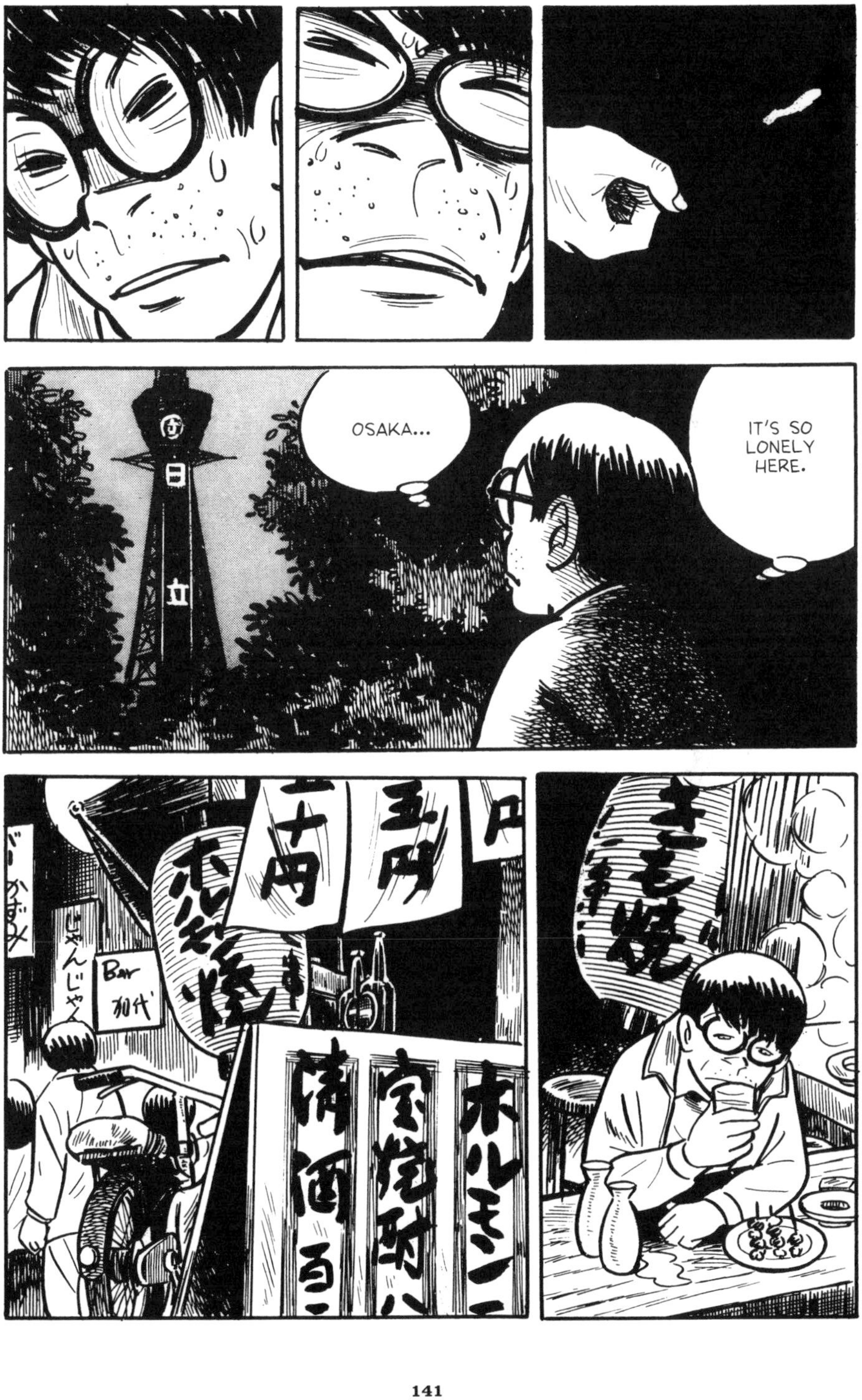
OSAKA...
IT'S SO LONELY HERE.
Bar
加代

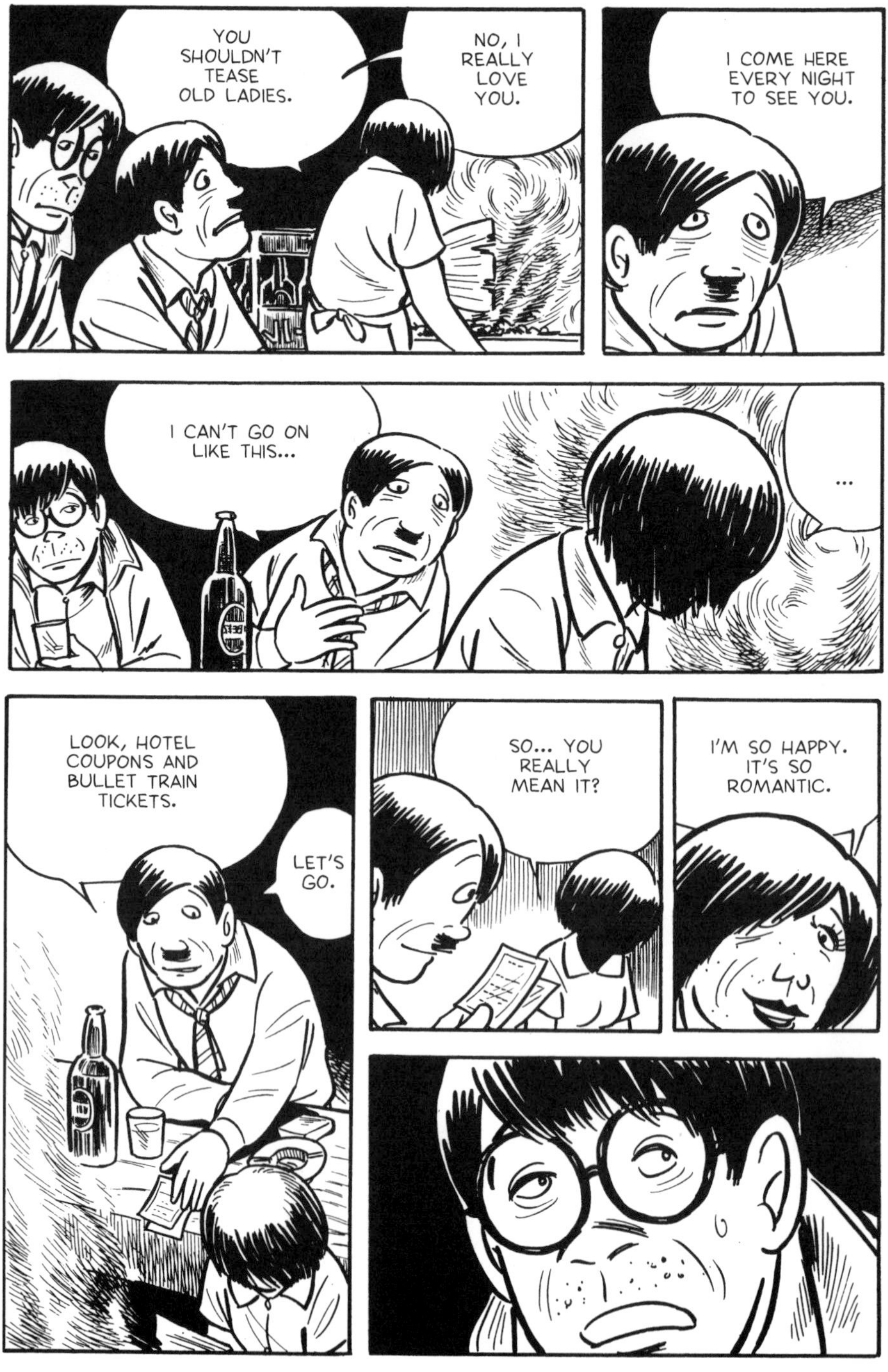
YOU SHOULDN'T TEASE OLD LADIES.
NO, I REALLY LOVE YOU.
I COME HERE EVERY NIGHT TO SEE YOU.
I CAN'T GO ON LIKE THIS...
...
LOOK, HOTEL COUPONS AND BULLET TRAIN TICKETS.
LET'S GO.
SO... YOU REALLY MEAN IT?
I'M SO HAPPY. IT'S SO ROMANTIC.

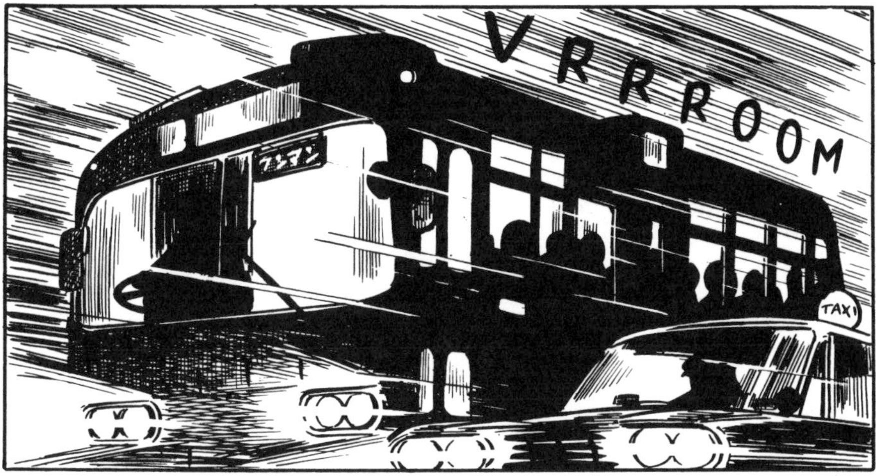
VRRROOM
ワンマン
TAXI

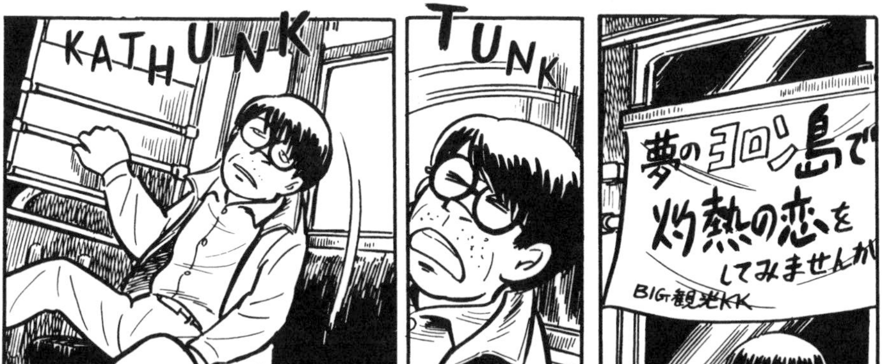
KATHUNK
TUNK
夢のヨロン島で
灼熱の恋を
してみませんか
BIG観光KK

BANNER: HOW ABOUT SOME HOT LOVE ON THE YORON ISLANDS?! BIG TRAVEL AGENCY

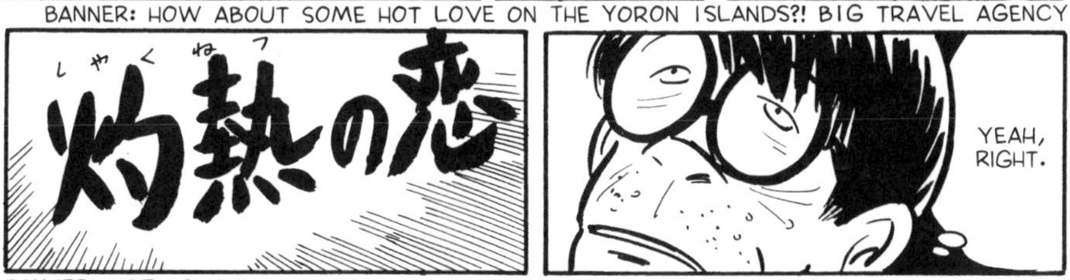
しゃくねつ
灼熱の恋
YEAH, RIGHT.

BANNER: HOT LOVE

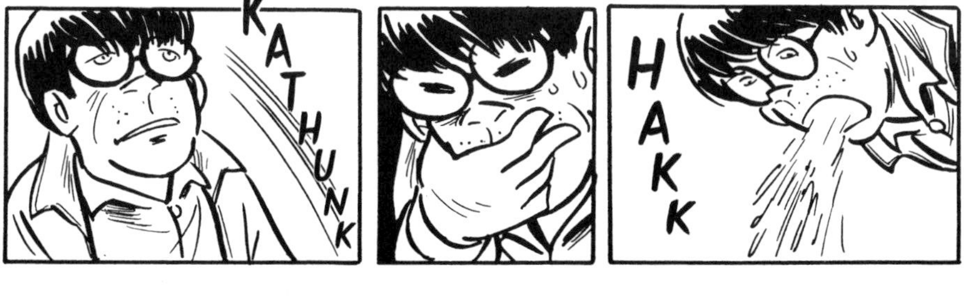
KATHUNK
HAKK

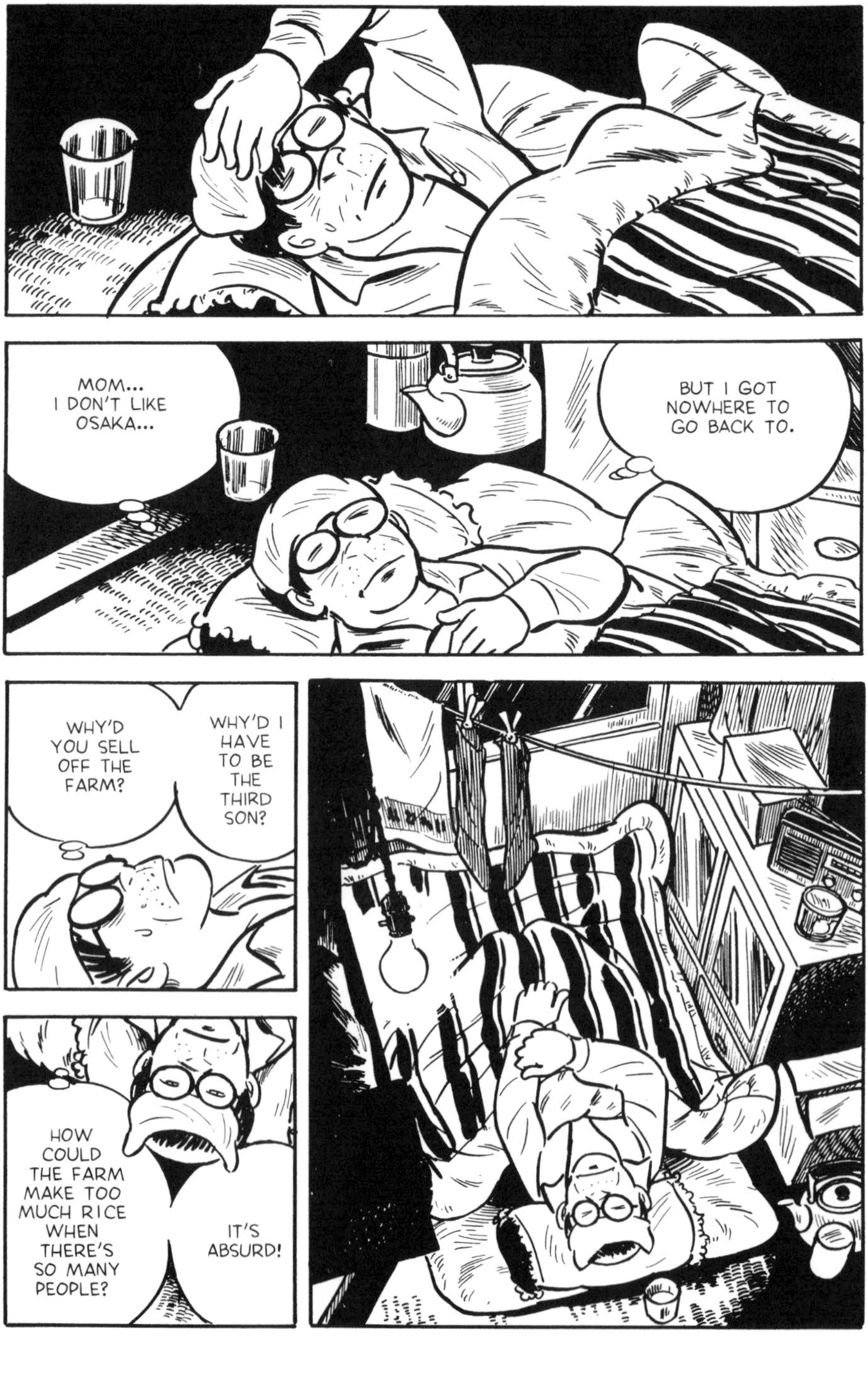
MOM... I DON'T LIKE OSAKA...
BUT I GOT NOWHERE TO GO BACK TO.
WHY'D YOU SELL OFF THE FARM?
WHY'D I HAVE TO BE THE THIRD SON?
HOW COULD THE FARM MAKE TOO MUCH RICE WHEN THERE'S SO MANY PEOPLE?
IT'S ABSURD!

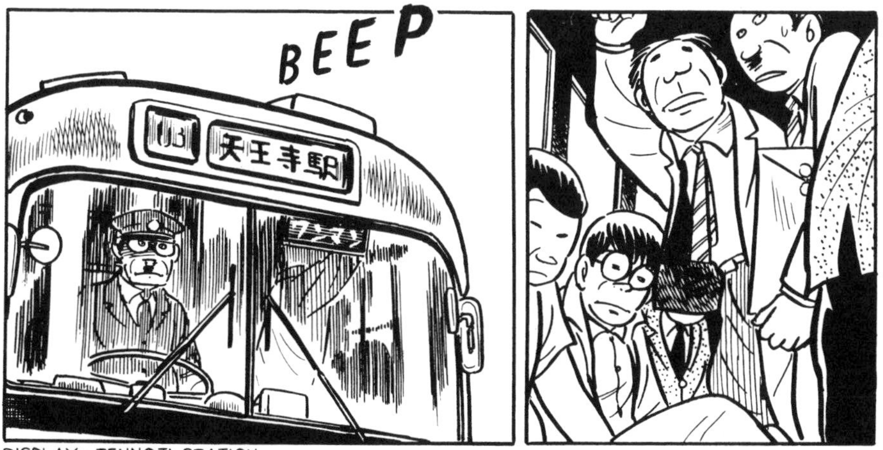
BEEP
天王寺駅

DISPLAY: TENNOJI STATION

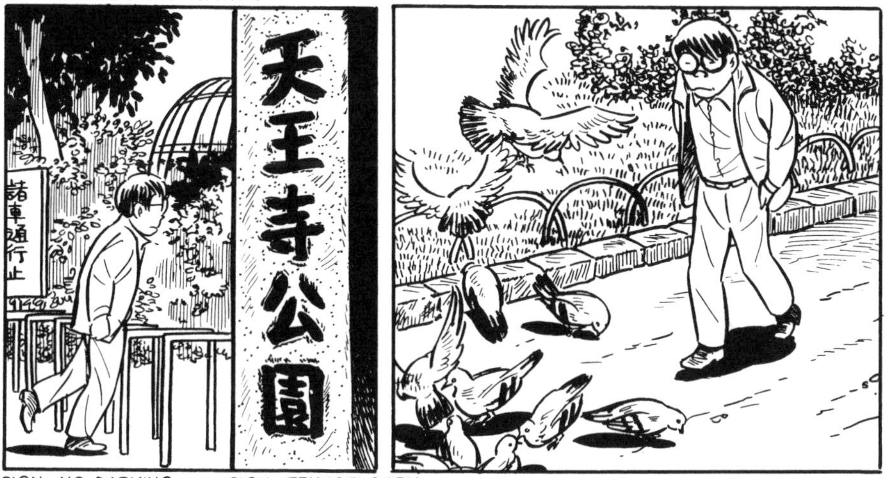
諸車通行止
天王寺公園

SIGN: NO PARKING SIGN: TENNOJI PARK

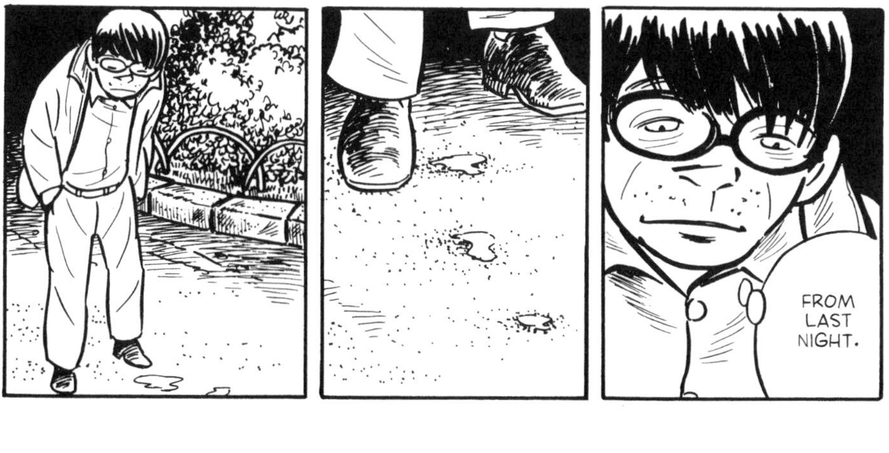
FROM LAST NIGHT.

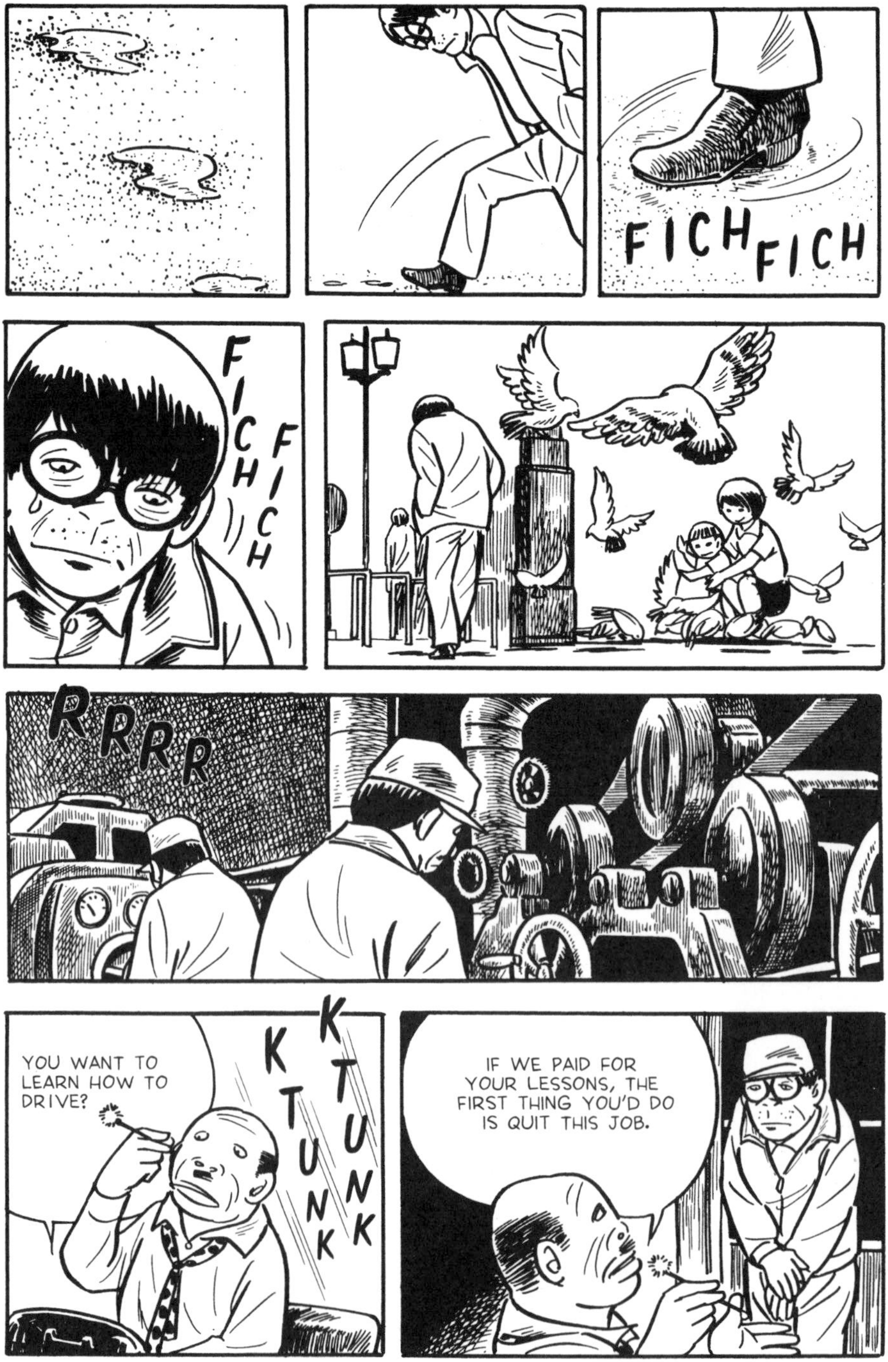
FICH FICH
FICH FICH
RRRRR
YOU WANT TO LEARN HOW TO DRIVE?
KTUNK KTUNK
IF WE PAID FOR YOUR LESSONS, THE FIRST THING YOU'D DO IS QUIT THIS JOB.

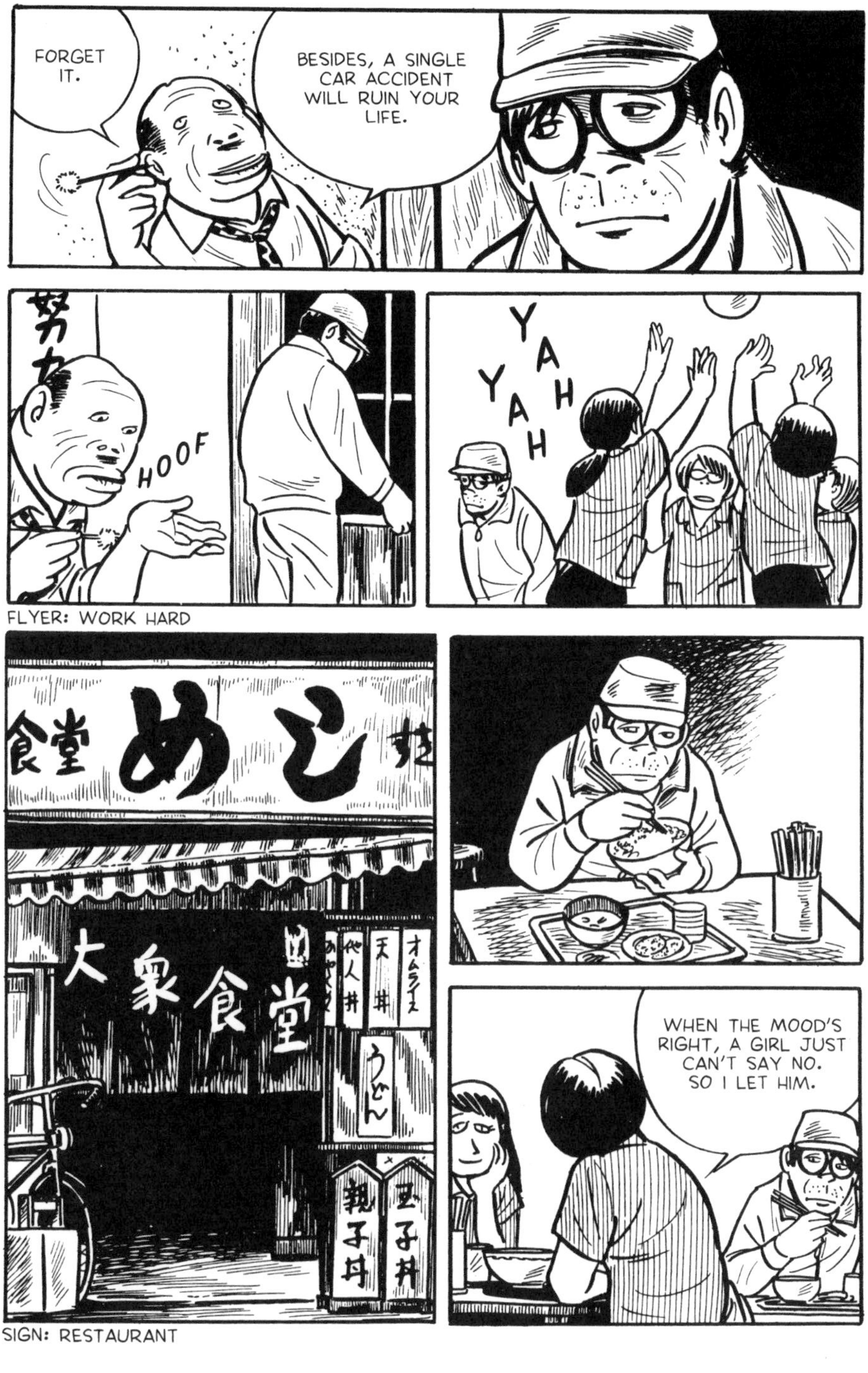
FORGET IT.
BESIDES, A SINGLE CAR ACCIDENT WILL RUIN YOUR LIFE.
HOOF
YAH YAH
食堂 めし
大衆食堂
他人丼
天丼
オムライス
うどん
親子丼
玉子丼
WHEN THE MOOD'S RIGHT, A GIRL JUST CAN'T SAY NO. SO I LET HIM.
FLYER: WORK HARD
SIGN: RESTAURANT

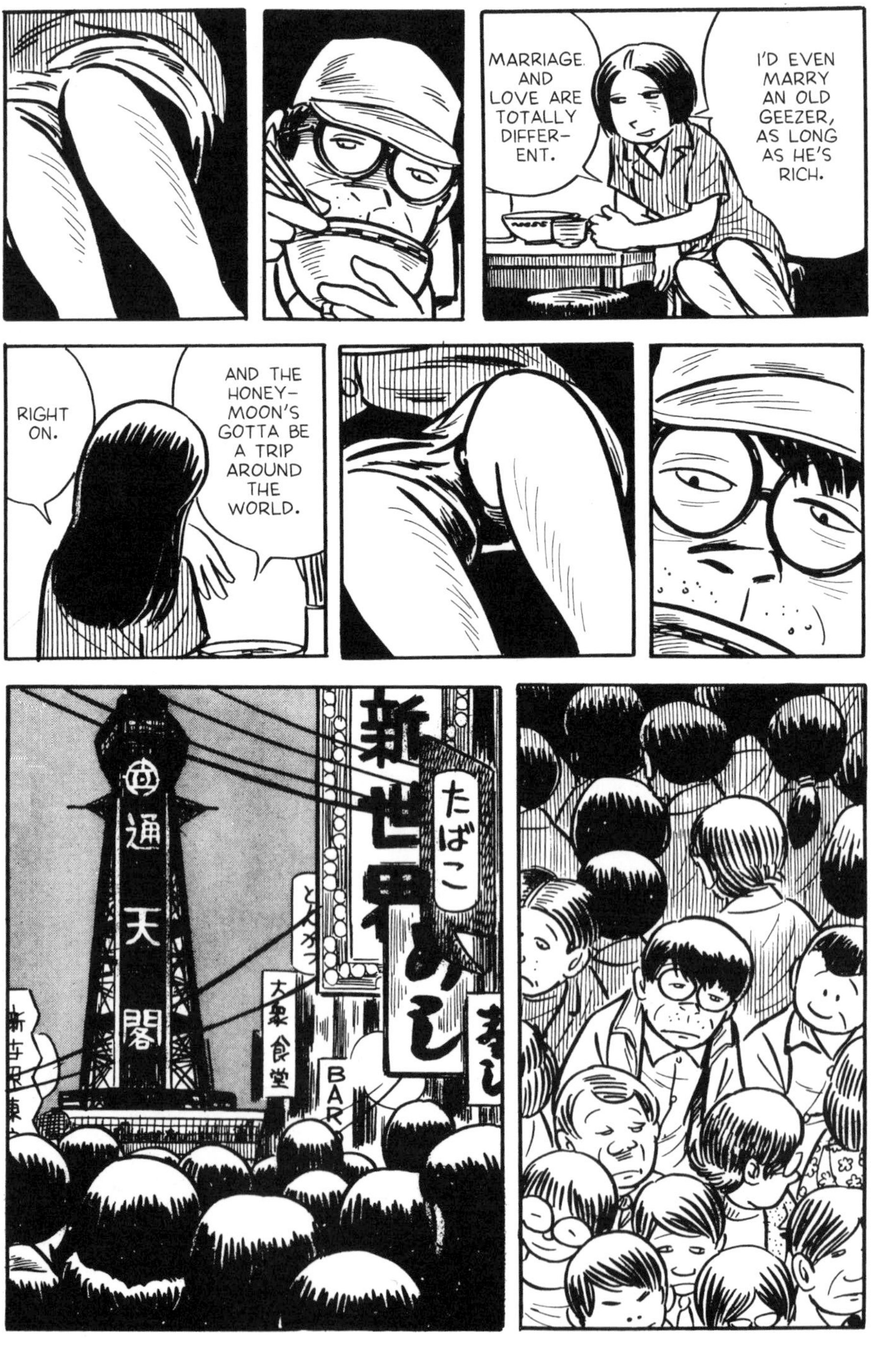
MARRIAGE AND LOVE ARE TOTALLY DIFFER-ENT.
I'D EVEN MARRY AN OLD GEEZER, AS LONG AS HE'S RICH.
RIGHT ON.
AND THE HONEY-MOON'S GOTTA BE A TRIP AROUND THE WORLD.
通天閣
新世界
たばこ
めし
大衆食堂
BAR

とろんと
レストラン
女湯のぞき
すごい!
ベッドショー
濡れて泣いた女

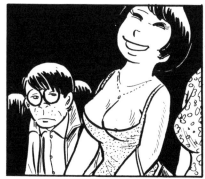

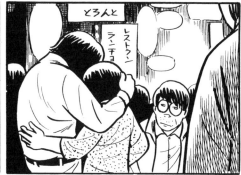

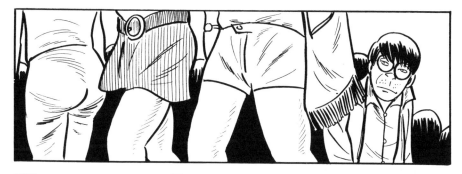

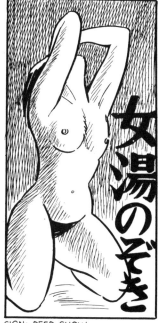

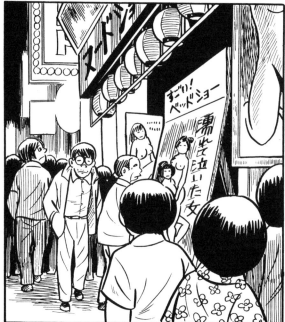

SIGN: PEEP SHOW

SIGNS: WOW! / BED SHOW / WET WOMEN IN TEARS

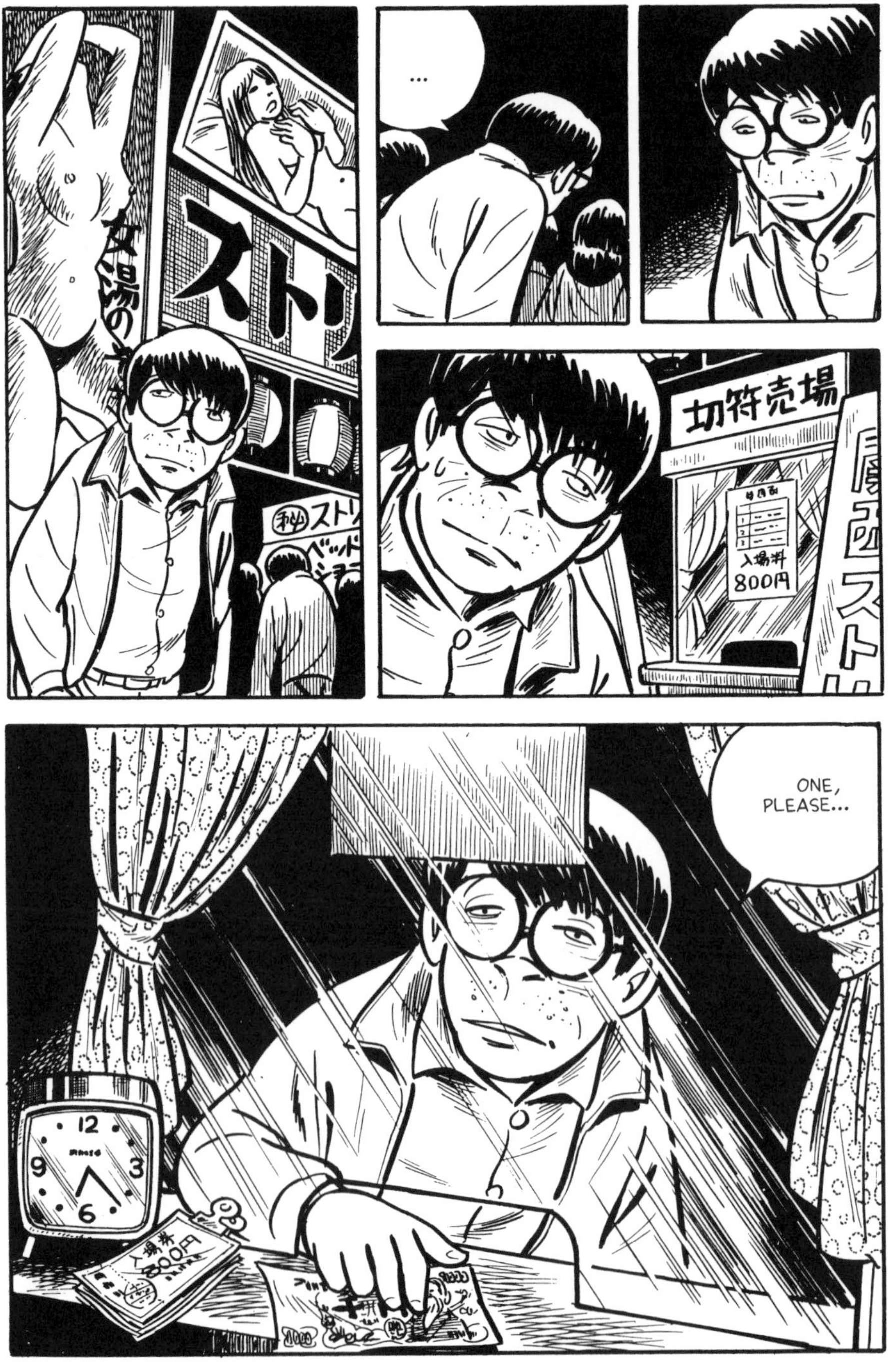
女湯の
ストリ
...
切符売場
入場料
800円
ONE, PLEASE...

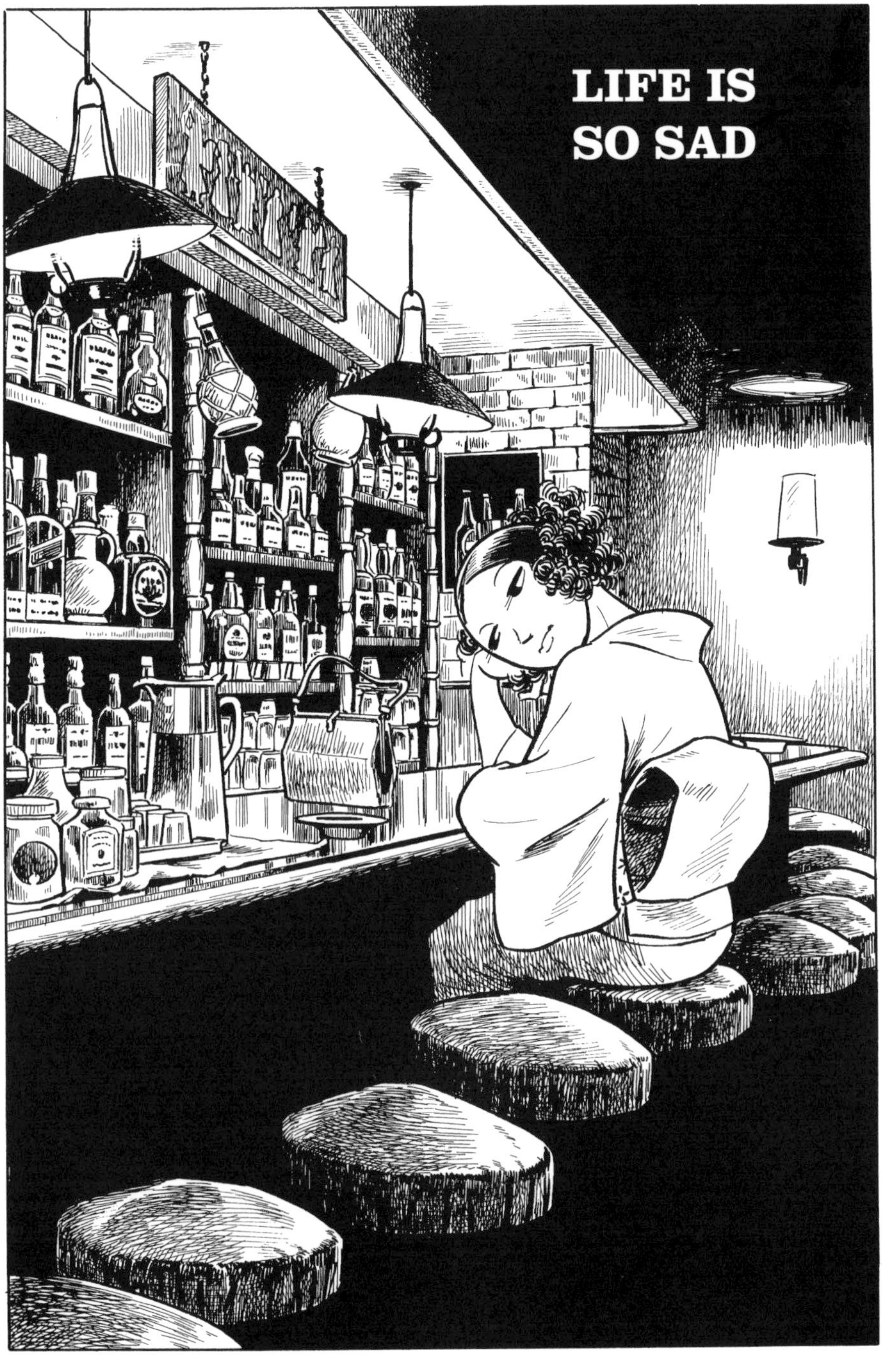
LIFE IS
SO SAD

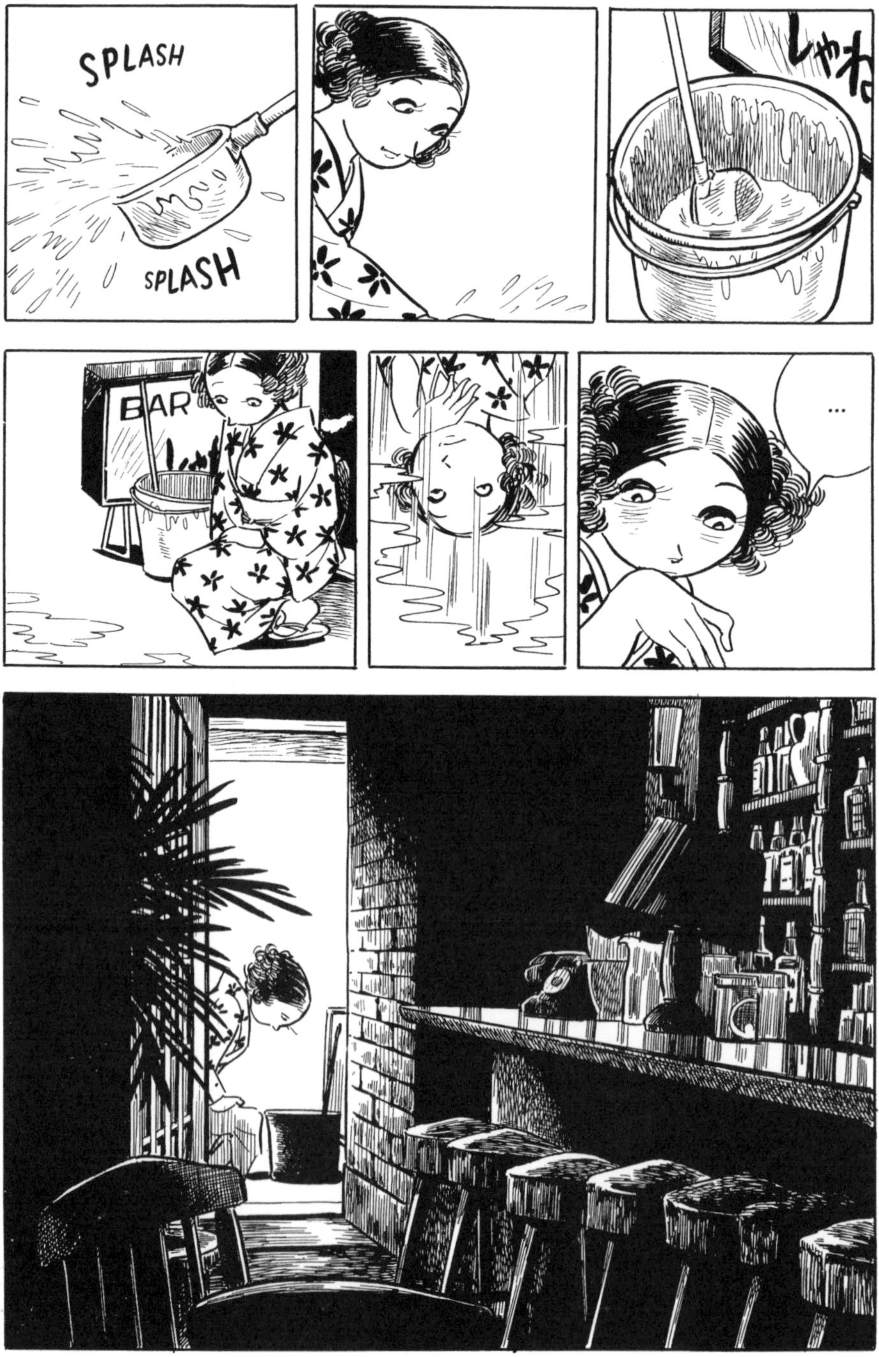
SPLASH
SPLASH
BAR
...

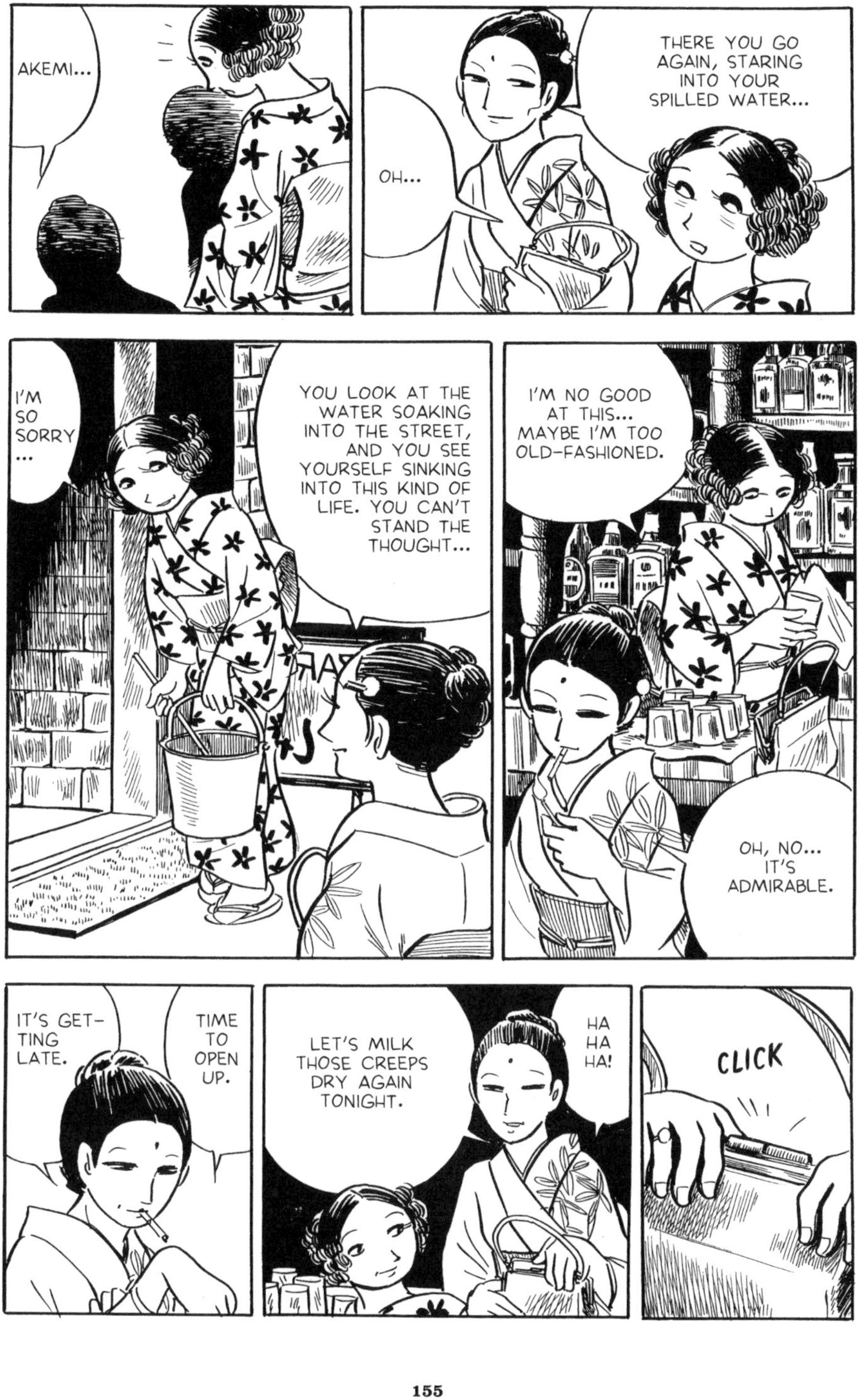
AKEMI...
THERE YOU GO AGAIN, STARING INTO YOUR SPILLED WATER...
OH...
I'M SO SORRY ...
YOU LOOK AT THE WATER SOAKING INTO THE STREET, AND YOU SEE YOURSELF SINKING INTO THIS KIND OF LIFE. YOU CAN'T STAND THE THOUGHT...
I'M NO GOOD AT THIS... MAYBE I'M TOO OLD-FASHIONED.
OH, NO... IT'S ADMIRABLE.
IT'S GET-TING LATE.
TIME TO OPEN UP.
LET'S MILK THOSE CREEPS DRY AGAIN TONIGHT.
HA HA HA!
CLICK

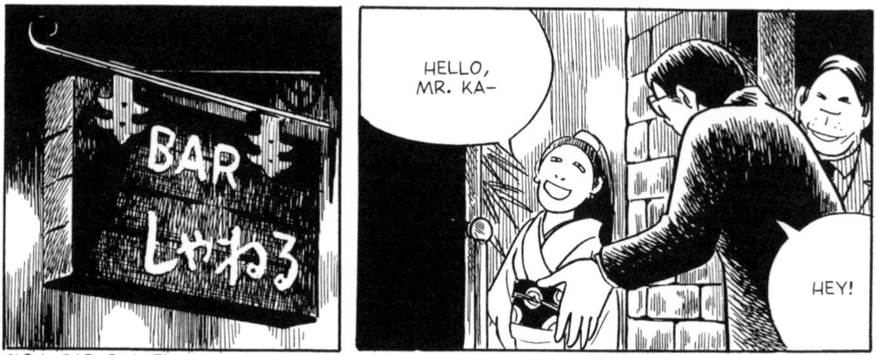
BAR
しゃねる
HELLO, MR. KA-
HEY!
SIGN: BAR CHANEL

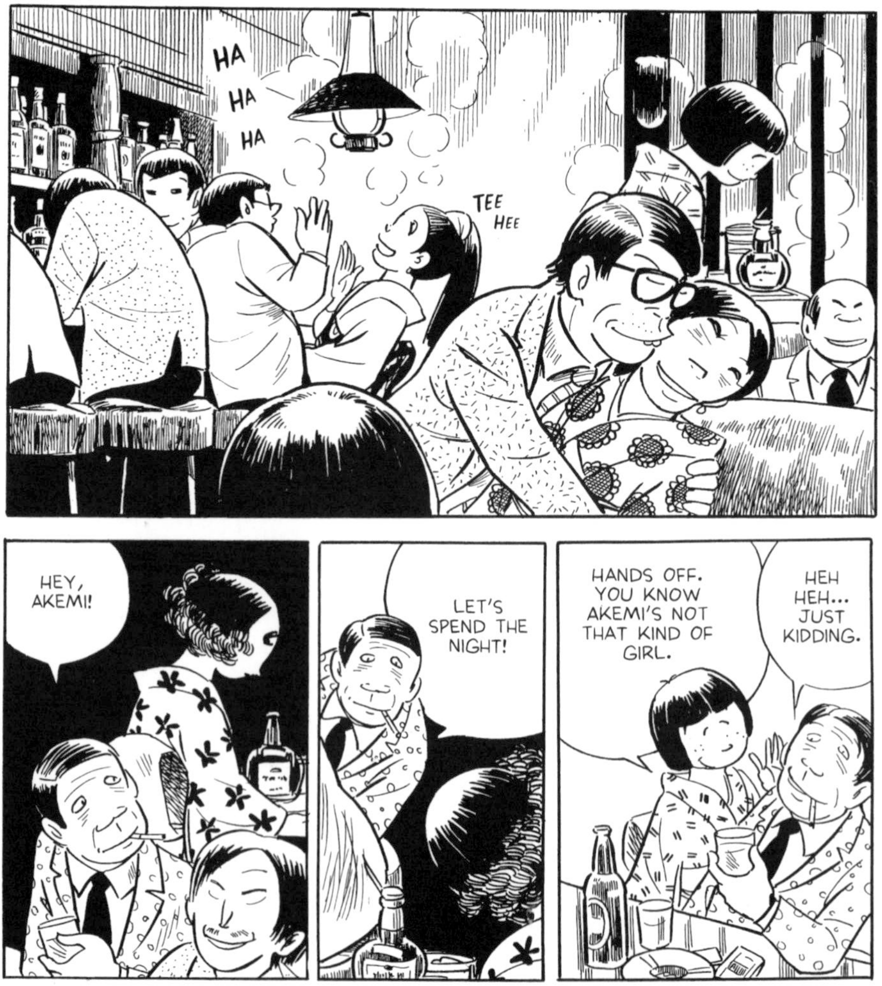
HA
HA
HA
TEE HEE
HEY, AKEMI!
LET'S SPEND THE NIGHT!
HANDS OFF. YOU KNOW AKEMI'S NOT THAT KIND OF GIRL.
HEH HEH... JUST KIDDING.

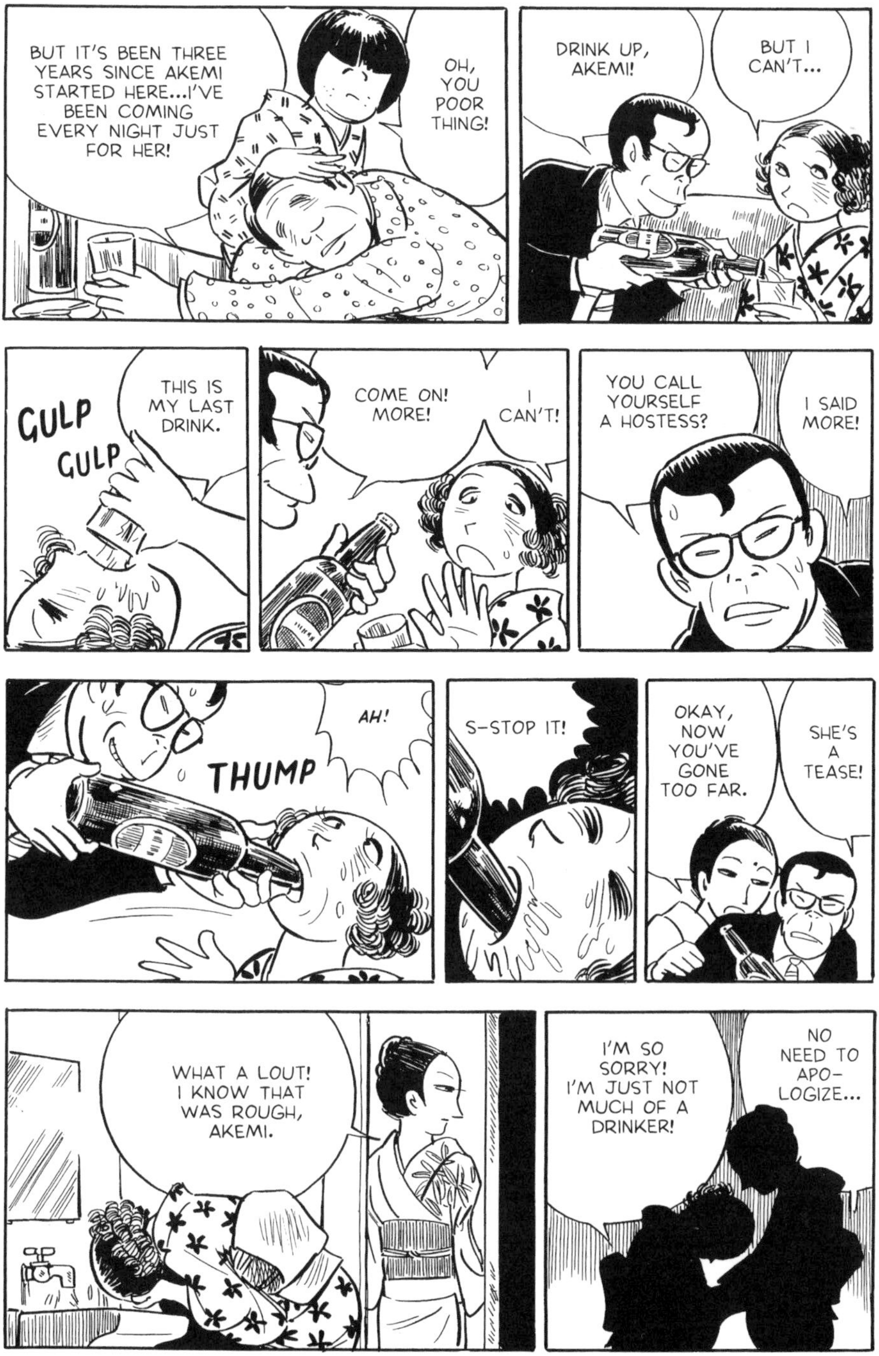
BUT IT'S BEEN THREE YEARS SINCE AKEMI STARTED HERE...I'VE BEEN COMING EVERY NIGHT JUST FOR HER!
OH, YOU POOR THING!
DRINK UP, AKEMI!
BUT I CAN'T...
GULP
GULP
THIS IS MY LAST DRINK.
COME ON! MORE!
I CAN'T!
YOU CALL YOURSELF A HOSTESS?
I SAID MORE!
AH!
THUMP
S-STOP IT!
OKAY, NOW YOU'VE GONE TOO FAR.
SHE'S A TEASE!
WHAT A LOUT! I KNOW THAT WAS ROUGH, AKEMI.
I'M SO SORRY! I'M JUST NOT MUCH OF A DRINKER!
NO NEED TO APO-LOGIZE...

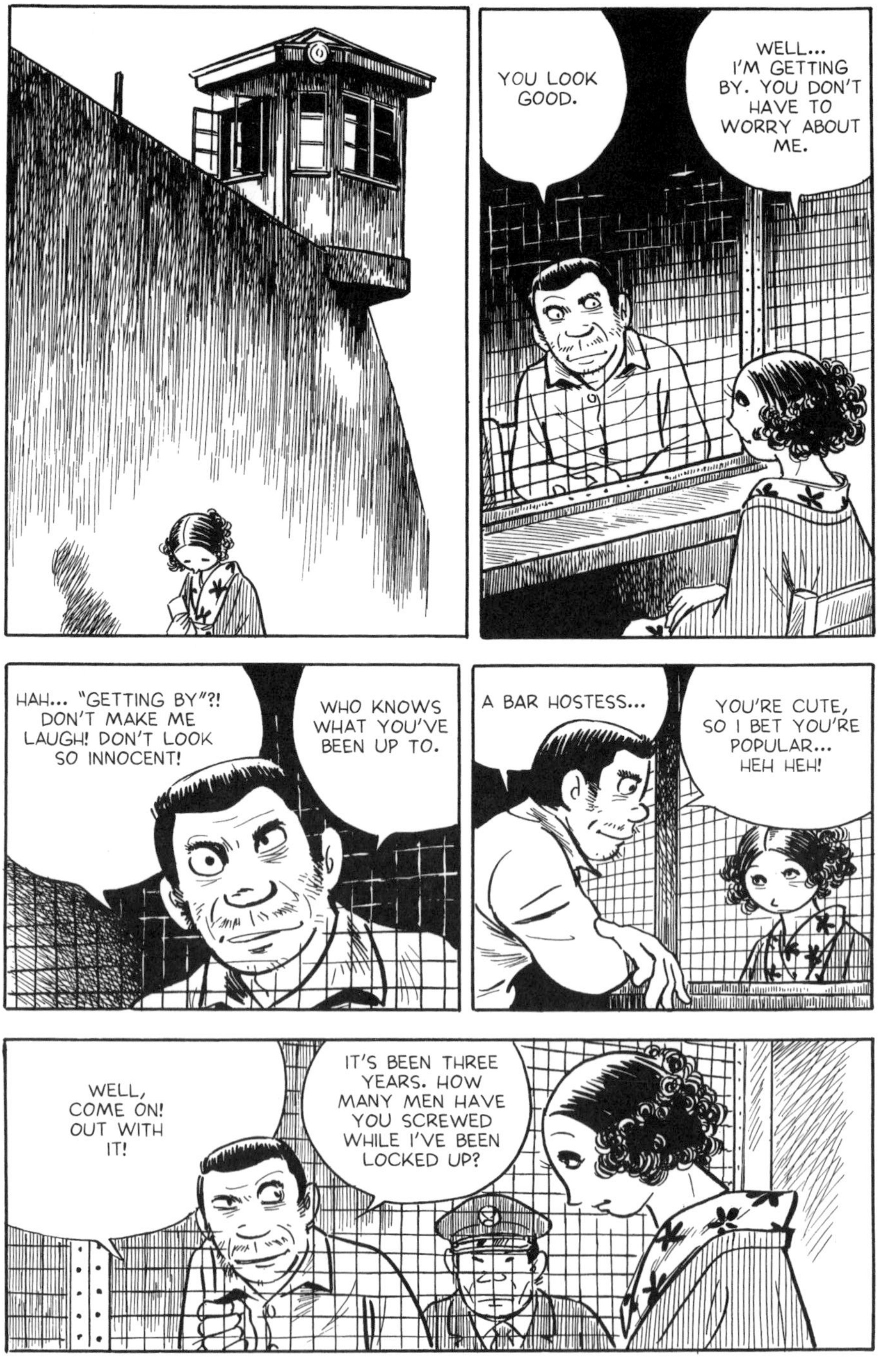
YOU LOOK GOOD.
WELL... I'M GETTING BY. YOU DON'T HAVE TO WORRY ABOUT ME.
HAH... "GETTING BY"?! DON'T MAKE ME LAUGH! DON'T LOOK SO INNOCENT!
WHO KNOWS WHAT YOU'VE BEEN UP TO.
A BAR HOSTESS...
YOU'RE CUTE, SO I BET YOU'RE POPULAR... HEH HEH!
WELL, COME ON! OUT WITH IT!
IT'S BEEN THREE YEARS. HOW MANY MEN HAVE YOU SCREWED WHILE I'VE BEEN LOCKED UP?

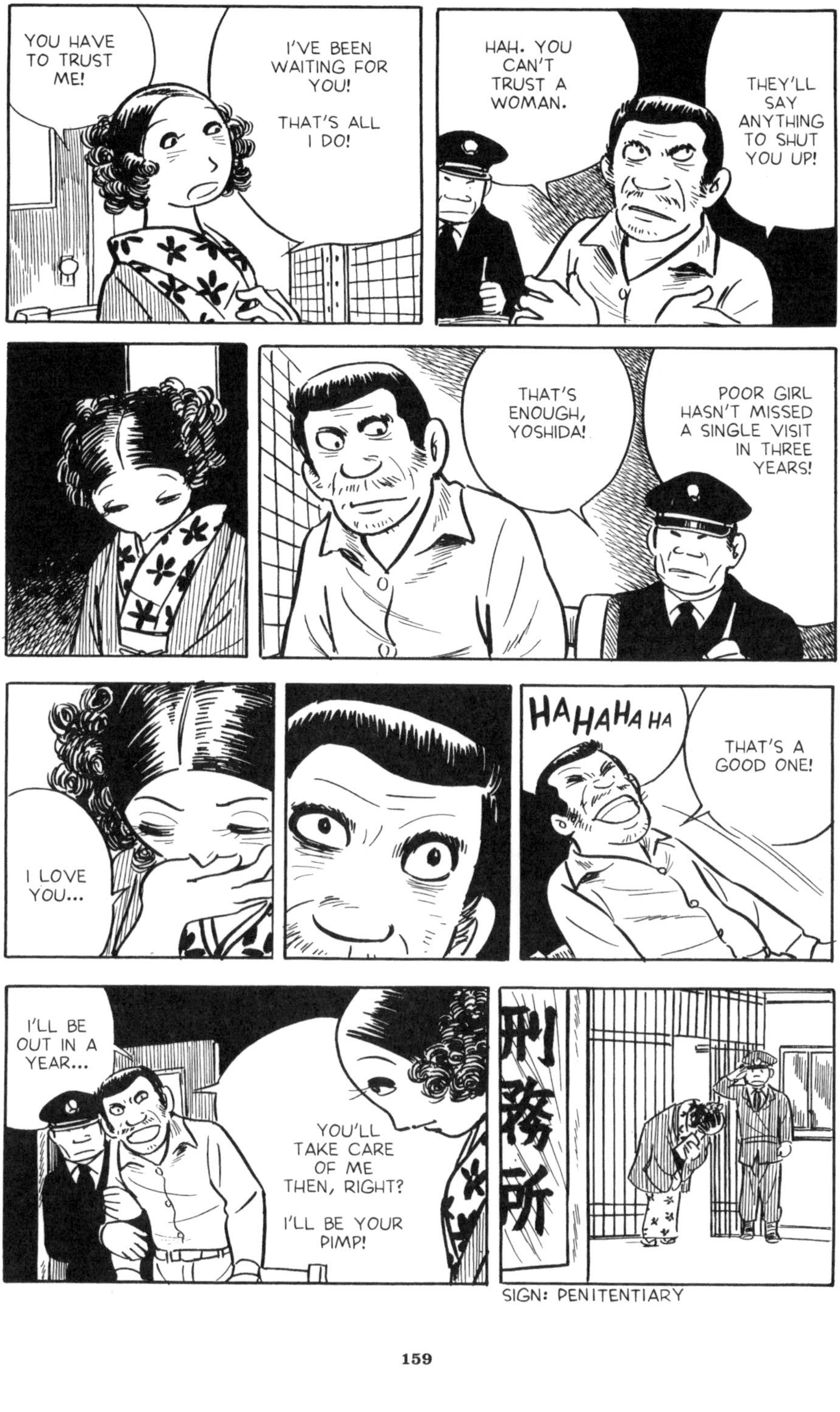
YOU HAVE TO TRUST ME!
I'VE BEEN WAITING FOR YOU!
THAT'S ALL I DO!
HAH. YOU CAN'T TRUST A WOMAN.
THEY'LL SAY ANYTHING TO SHUT YOU UP!
THAT'S ENOUGH, YOSHIDA!
POOR GIRL HASN'T MISSED A SINGLE VISIT IN THREE YEARS!
I LOVE YOU...
HAHAHAHA
THAT'S A GOOD ONE!
I'LL BE OUT IN A YEAR...
YOU'LL TAKE CARE OF ME THEN, RIGHT?
I'LL BE YOUR PIMP!
刑務所
SIGN: PENITENTIARY

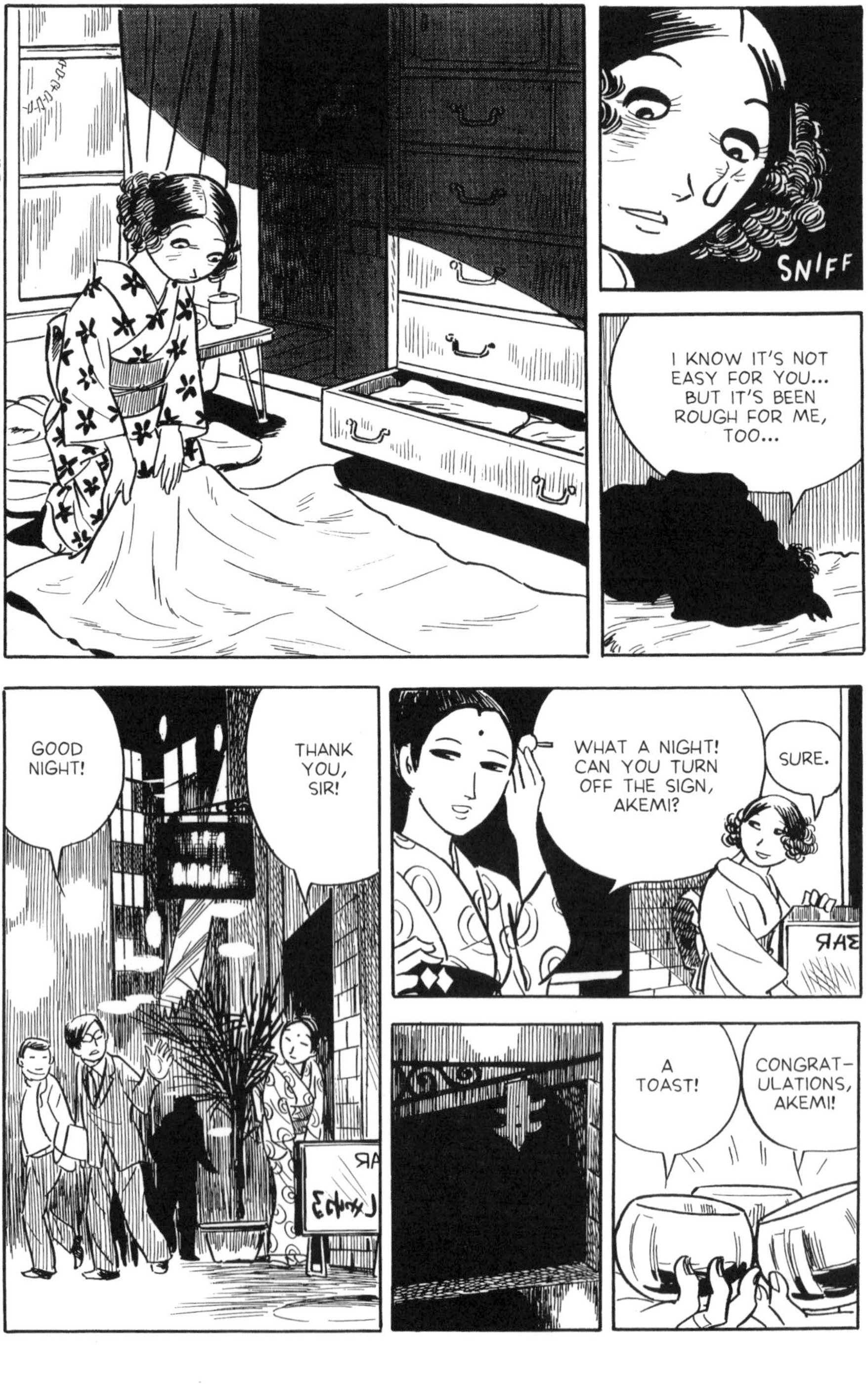
SNIFF
I KNOW IT'S NOT EASY FOR YOU... BUT IT'S BEEN ROUGH FOR ME, TOO...
GOOD NIGHT!
THANK YOU, SIR!
WHAT A NIGHT! CAN YOU TURN OFF THE SIGN, AKEMI?
SURE.
A TOAST!
CONGRAT-ULATIONS, AKEMI!

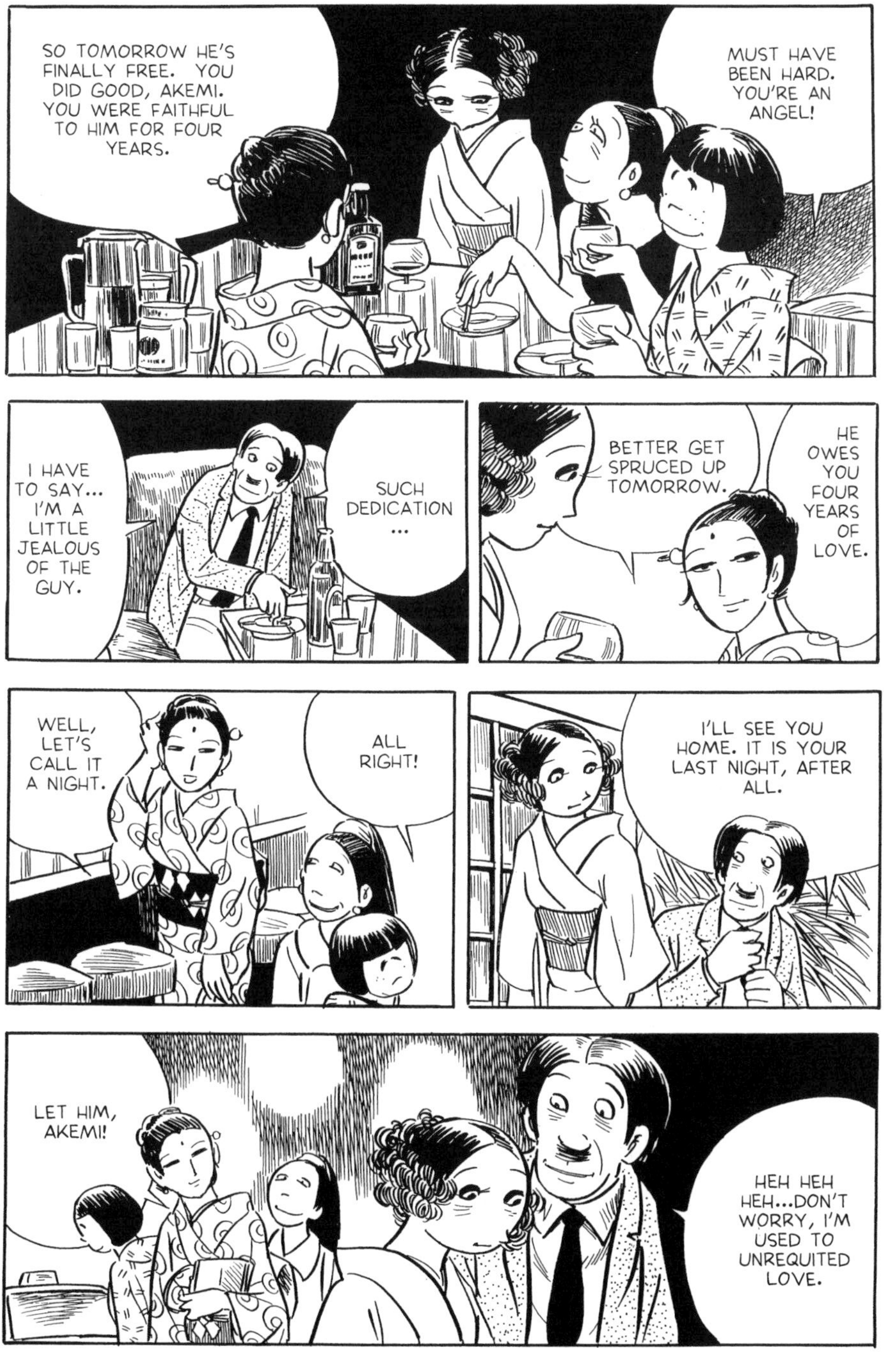

SO TOMORROW HE'S FINALLY FREE. YOU DID GOOD, AKEMI. YOU WERE FAITHFUL TO HIM FOR FOUR YEARS.
MUST HAVE BEEN HARD. YOU'RE AN ANGEL!
I HAVE TO SAY... I'M A LITTLE JEALOUS OF THE GUY.
SUCH DEDICATION ...
BETTER GET SPRUCED UP TOMORROW.
HE OWES YOU FOUR YEARS OF LOVE.
WELL, LET'S CALL IT A NIGHT.
ALL RIGHT!
I'LL SEE YOU HOME. IT IS YOUR LAST NIGHT, AFTER ALL.
LET HIM, AKEMI!
HEH HEH HEH...DON'T WORRY, I'M USED TO UNREQUITED LOVE.

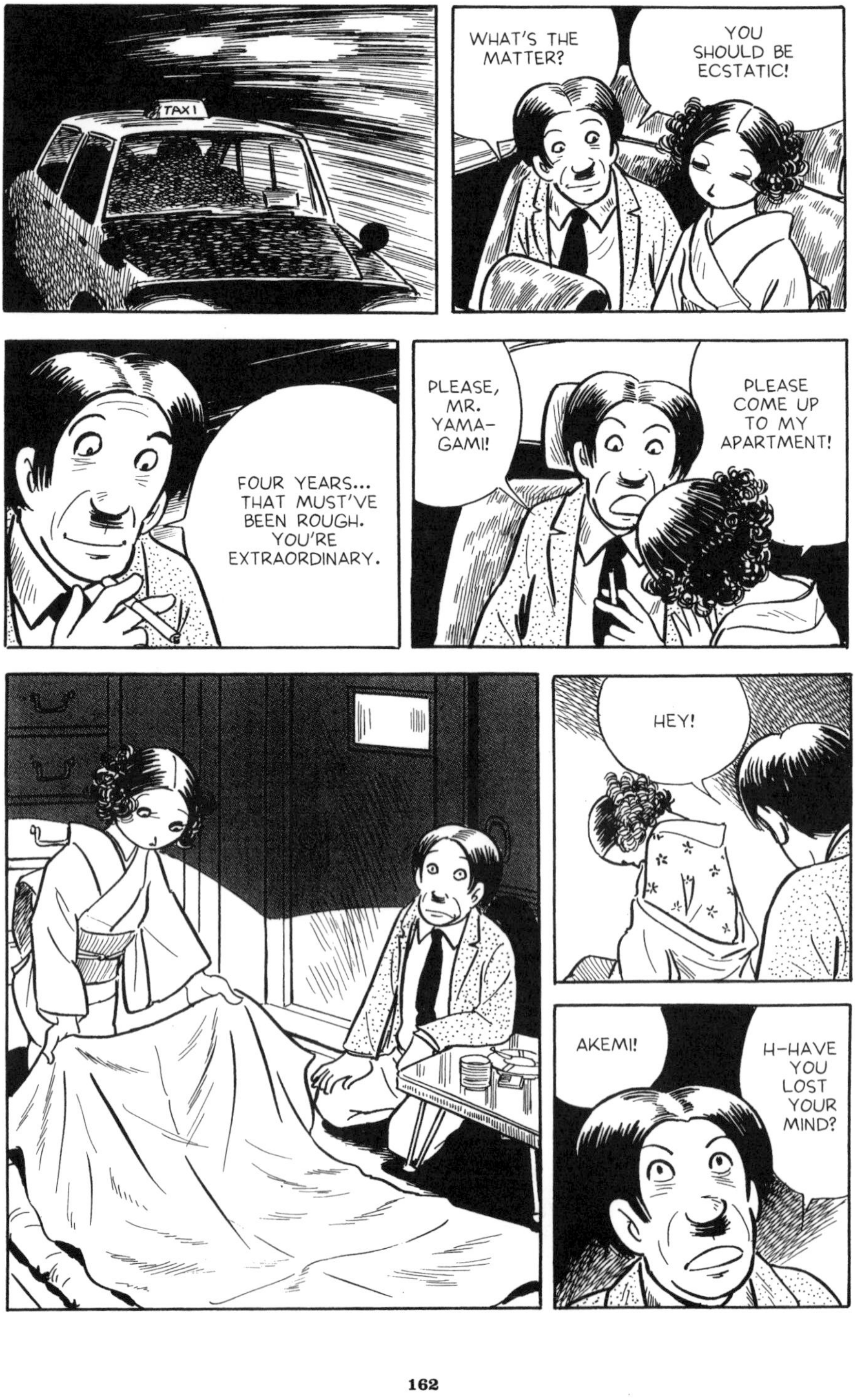
WHAT'S THE MATTER?
YOU SHOULD BE ECSTATIC!
FOUR YEARS... THAT MUST'VE BEEN ROUGH. YOU'RE EXTRAORDINARY.
PLEASE, MR. YAMA-GAMI!
PLEASE COME UP TO MY APARTMENT!
HEY!
AKEMI!
H-HAVE YOU LOST YOUR MIND?

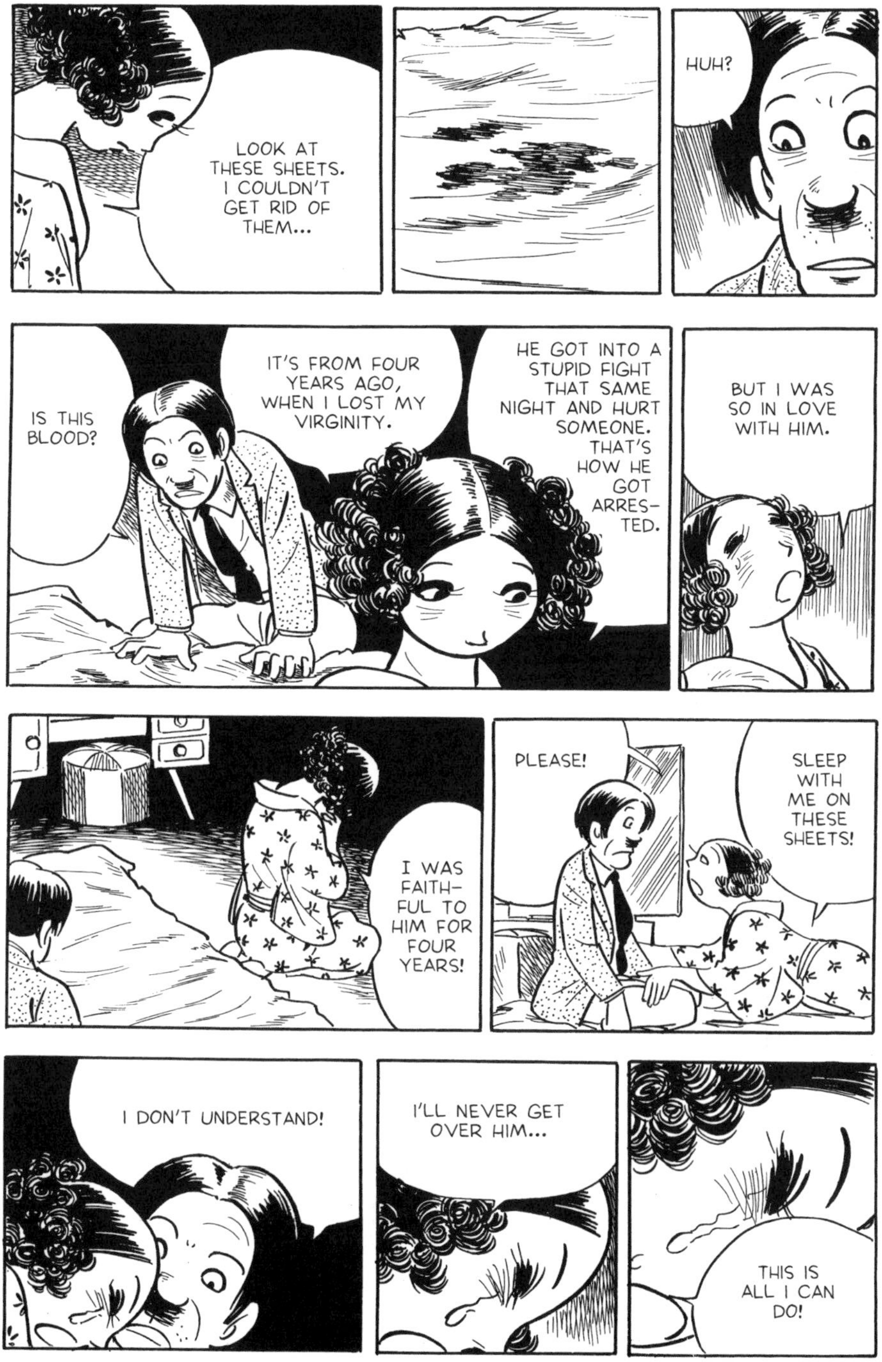
LOOK AT THESE SHEETS. I COULDN'T GET RID OF THEM...
HUH?
IS THIS BLOOD?
IT'S FROM FOUR YEARS AGO, WHEN I LOST MY VIRGINITY.
HE GOT INTO A STUPID FIGHT THAT SAME NIGHT AND HURT SOMEONE. THAT'S HOW HE GOT ARRES-TED.
BUT I WAS SO IN LOVE WITH HIM.
I WAS FAITH-FUL TO HIM FOR FOUR YEARS!
PLEASE!
SLEEP WITH ME ON THESE SHEETS!
I DON'T UNDERSTAND!
I'LL NEVER GET OVER HIM...
THIS IS ALL I CAN DO!

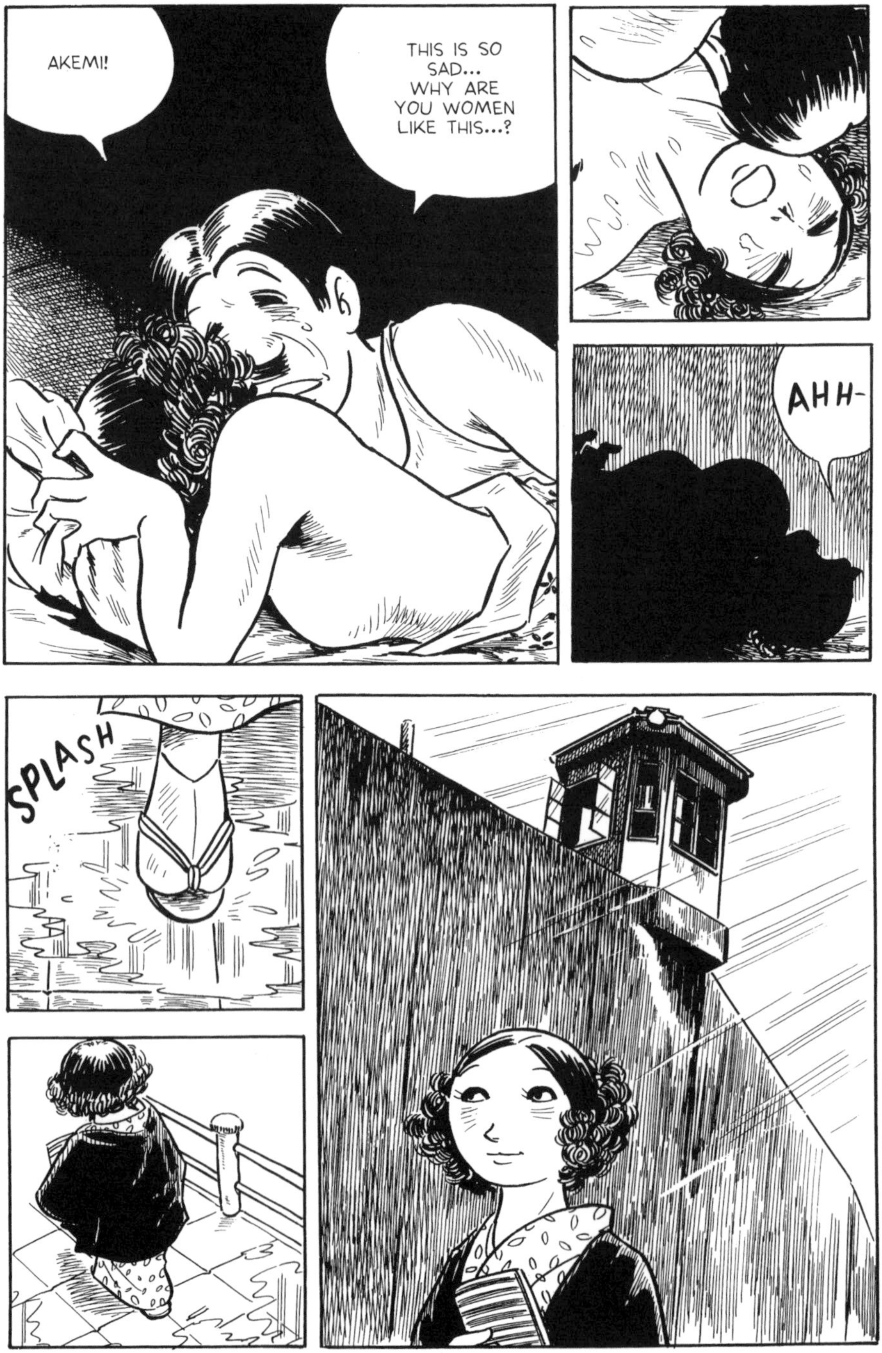
AKEMI!
THIS IS SO SAD... WHY ARE YOU WOMEN LIKE THIS...?
AHH-
SPLASH

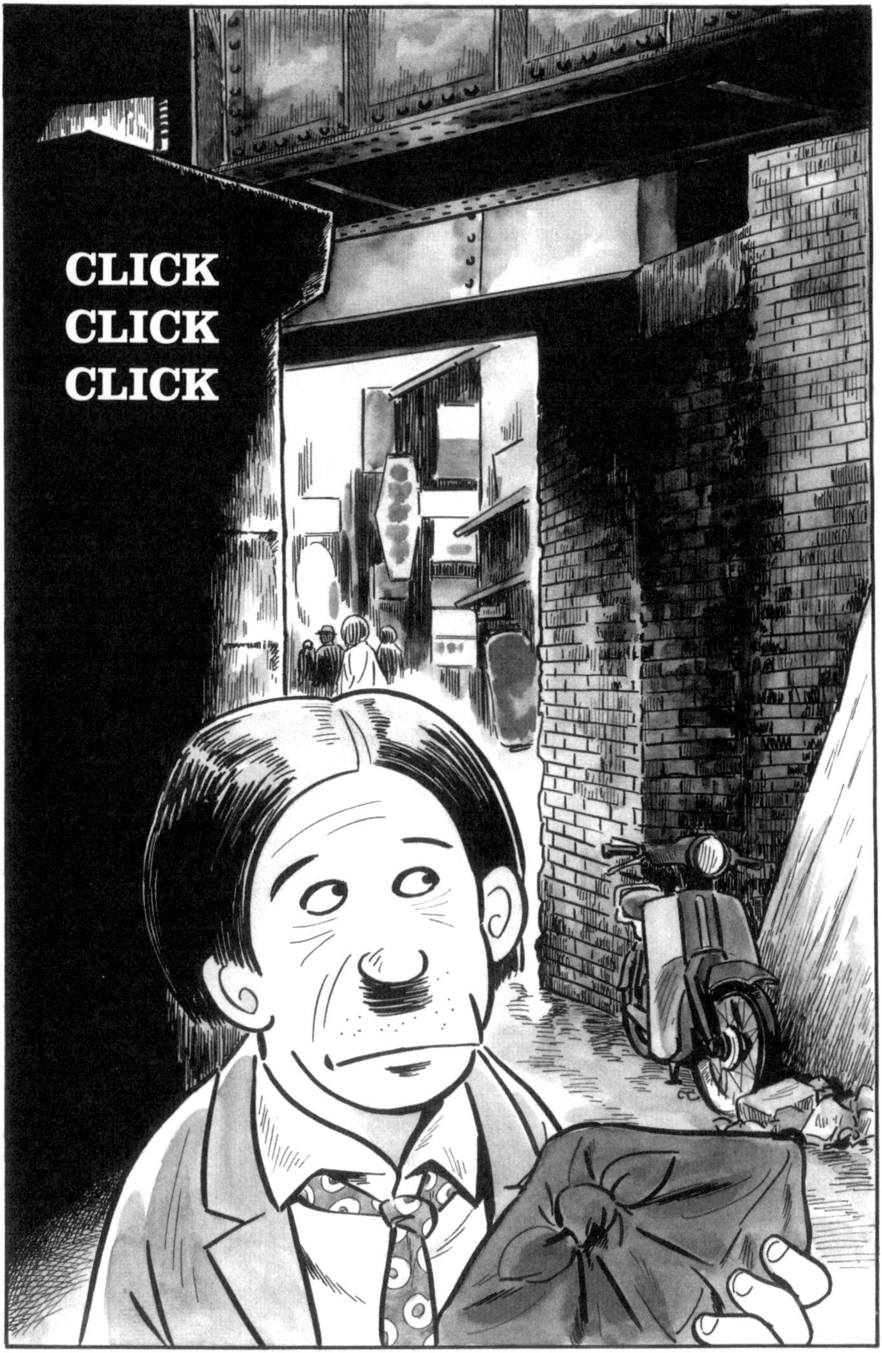
CLICK
CLICK
CLICK

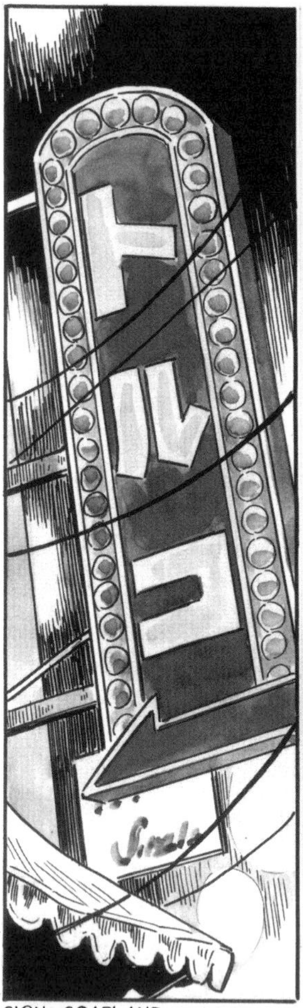
トルコ

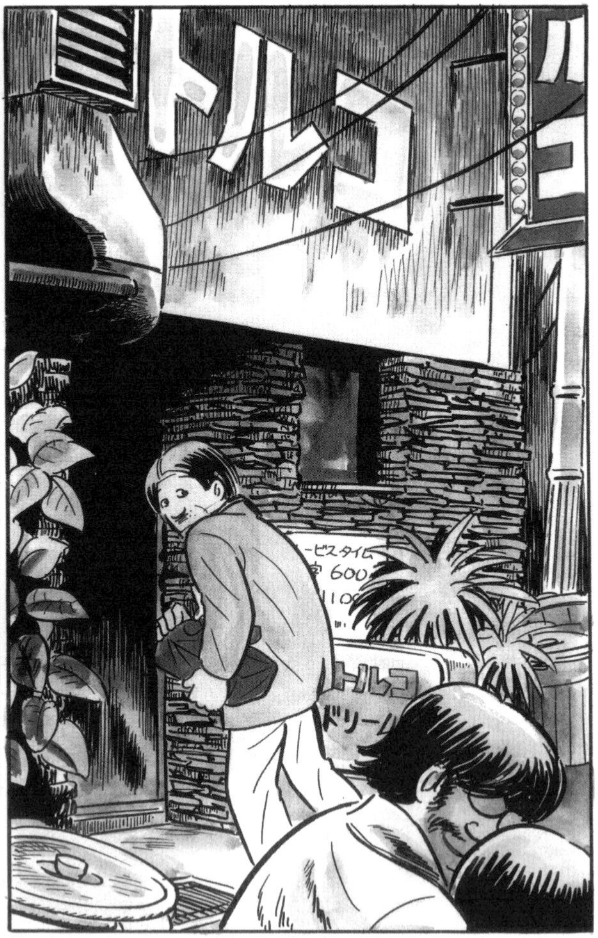
トルコ
トルコ

SIGN: SOAPLAND

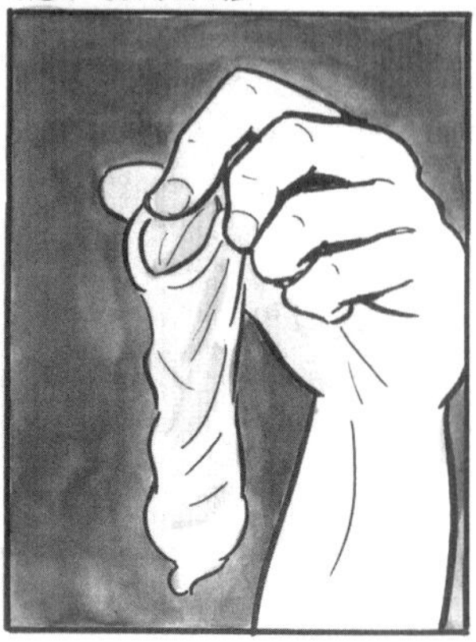

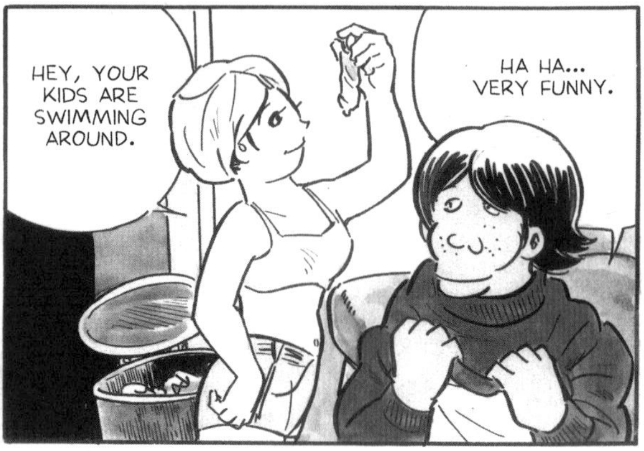
HEY, YOUR KIDS ARE SWIMMING AROUND.
HA HA... VERY FUNNY.

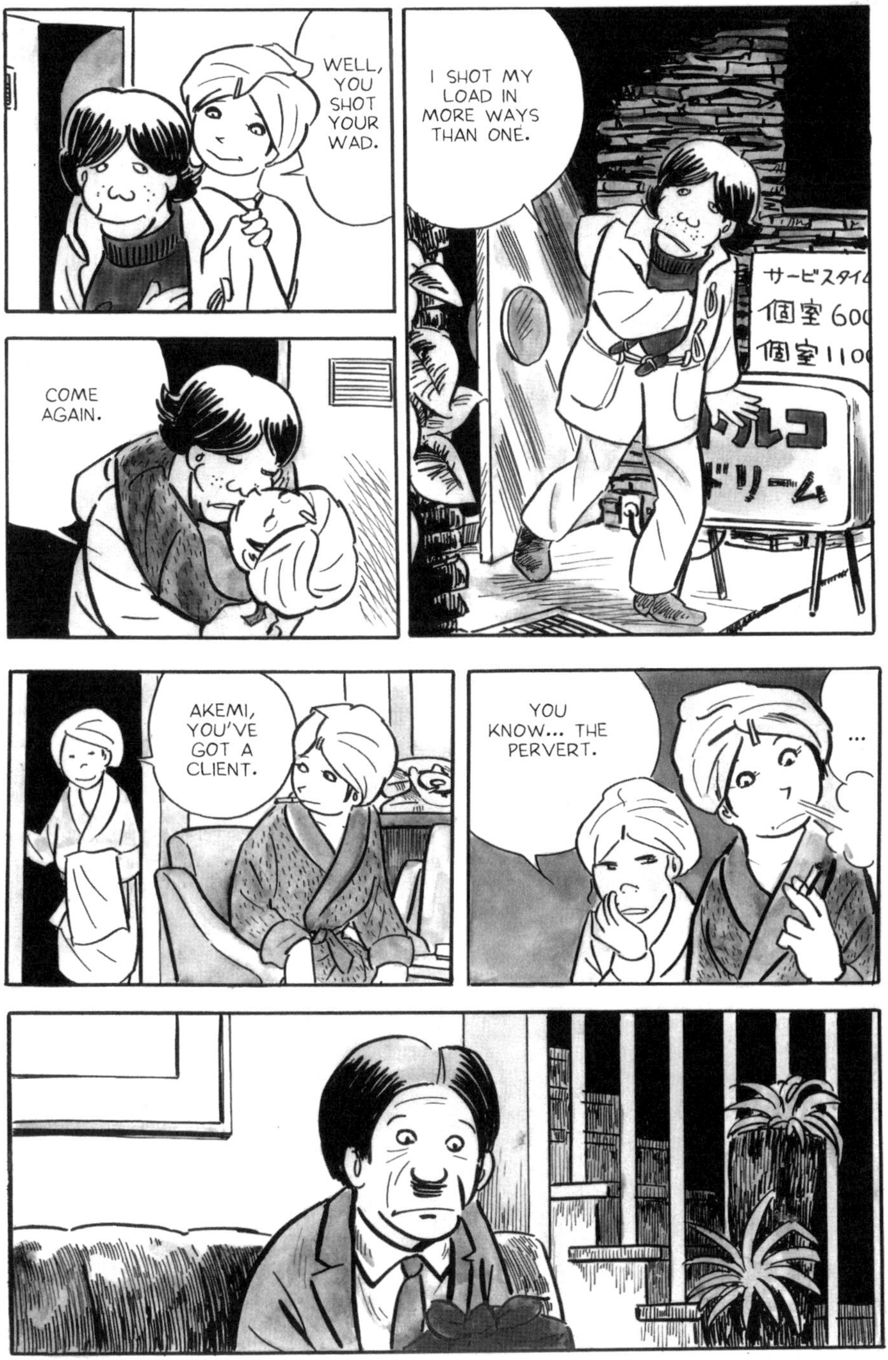
WELL, YOU SHOT YOUR WAD.
COME AGAIN.
I SHOT MY LOAD IN MORE WAYS THAN ONE.
AKEMI, YOU'VE GOT A CLIENT.
YOU KNOW... THE PERVERT.
...

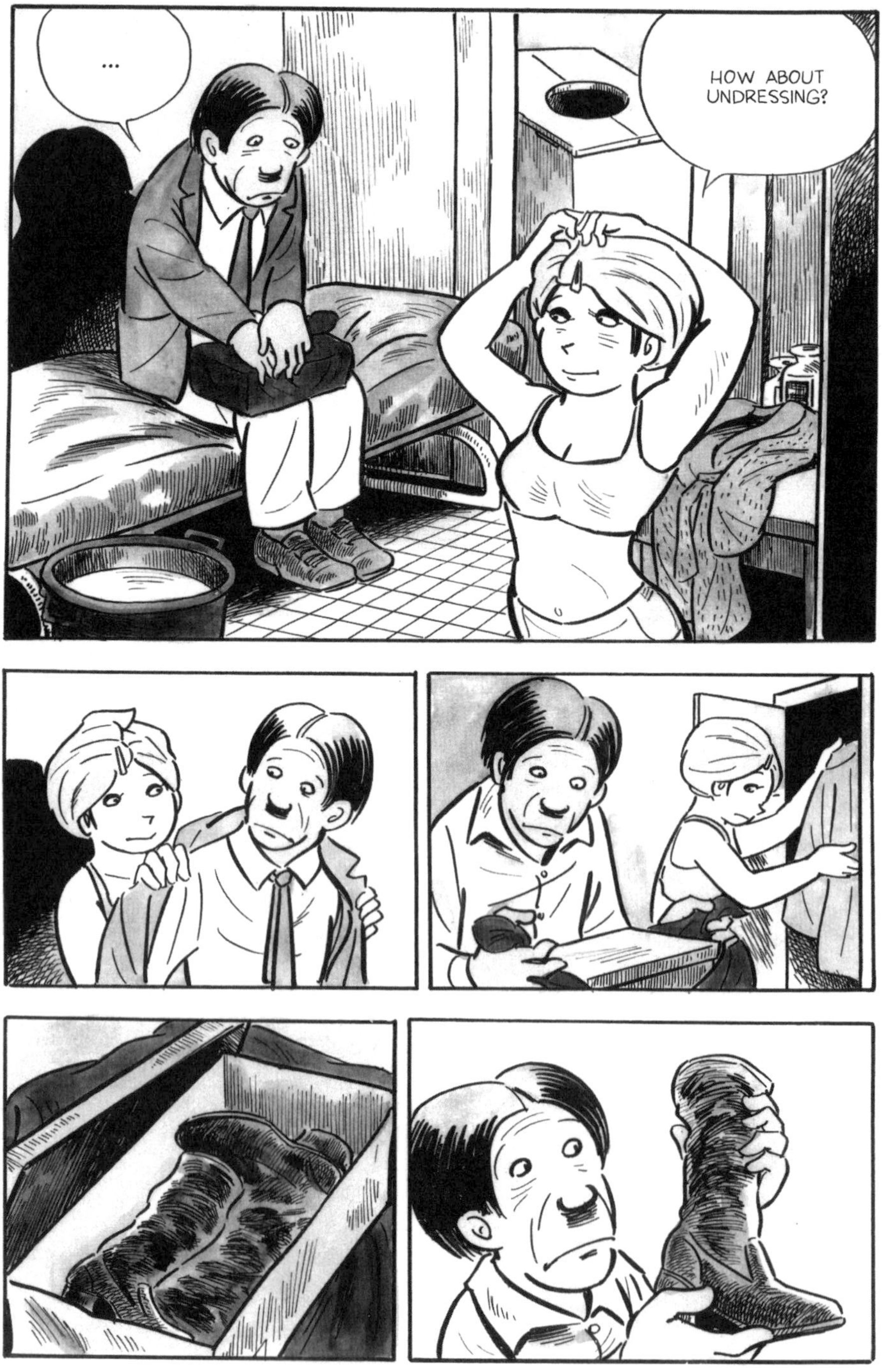
...
HOW ABOUT UNDRESSING?

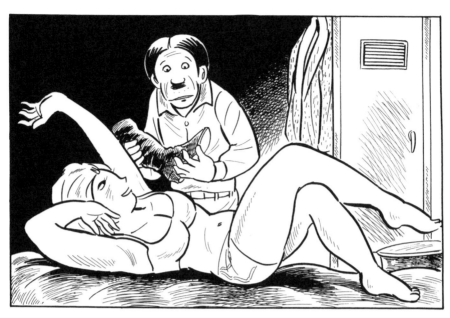

...

MAGNI-
FICENT.

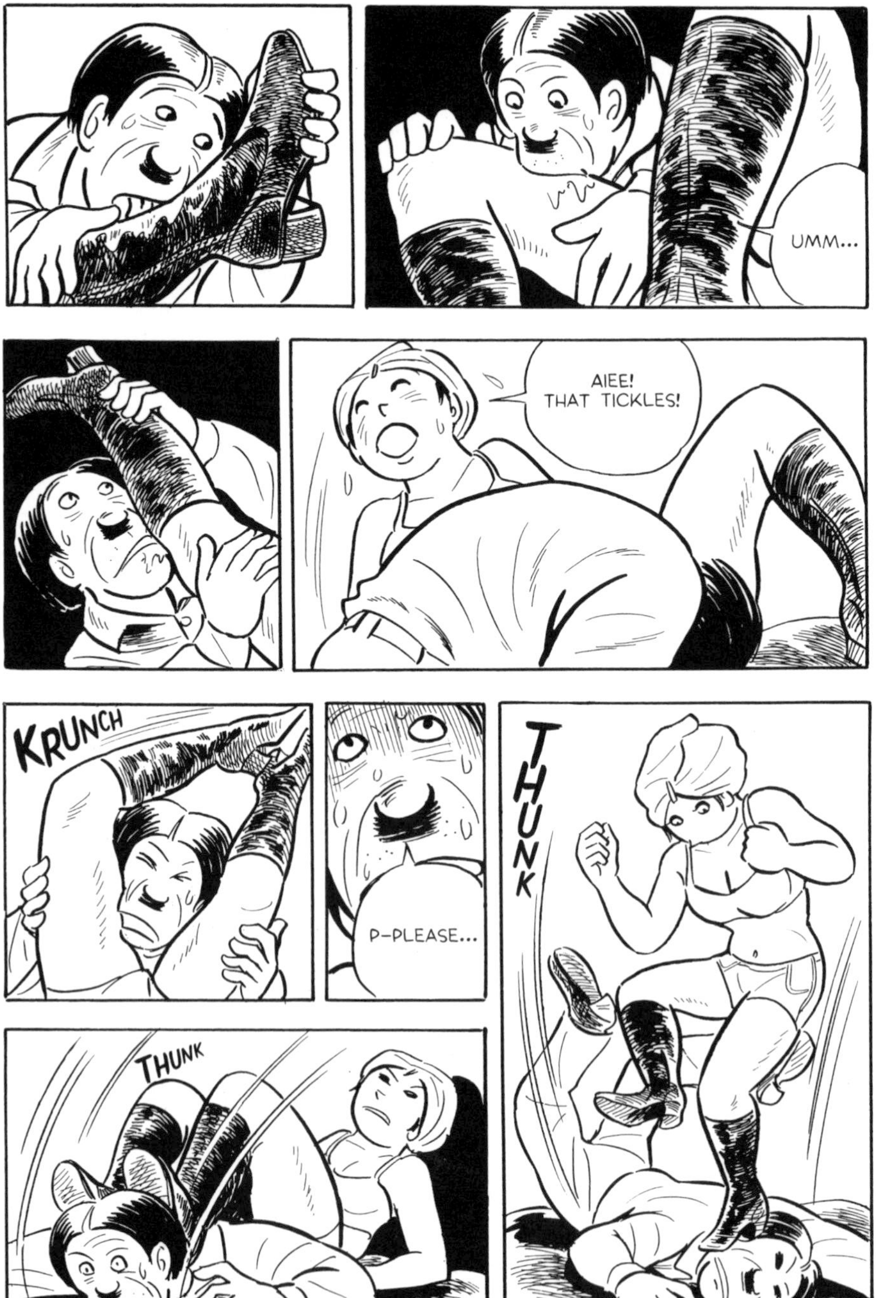
UMM...
AIEE! THAT TICKLES!
KRUNCH
P-PLEASE...
THUNK
THUNK

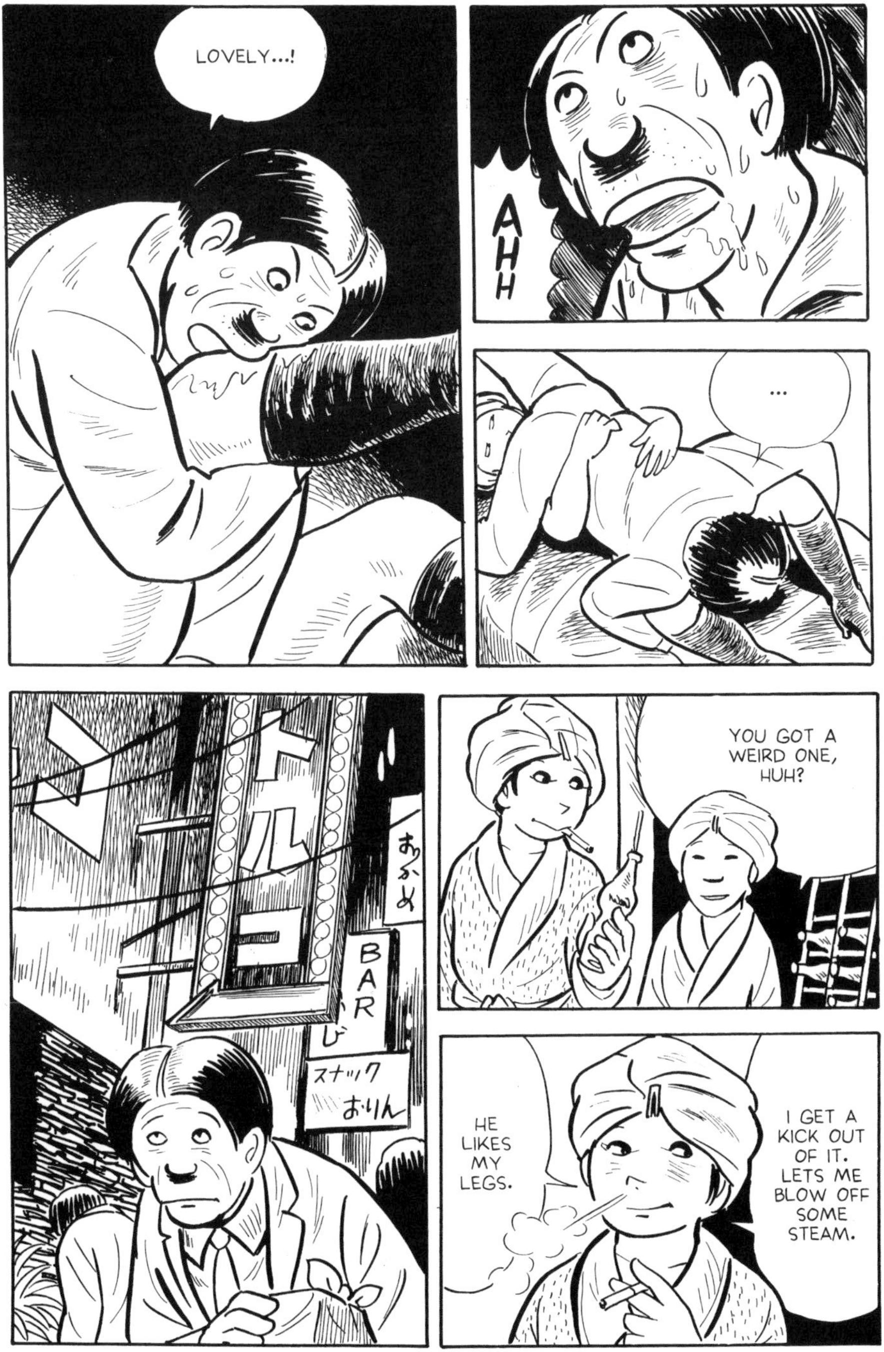
LOVELY...!
AHH
...
トルコ
BAR
スナック
おりん
YOU GOT A WEIRD ONE, HUH?
HE LIKES MY LEGS.
I GET A KICK OUT OF IT. LETS ME BLOW OFF SOME STEAM.

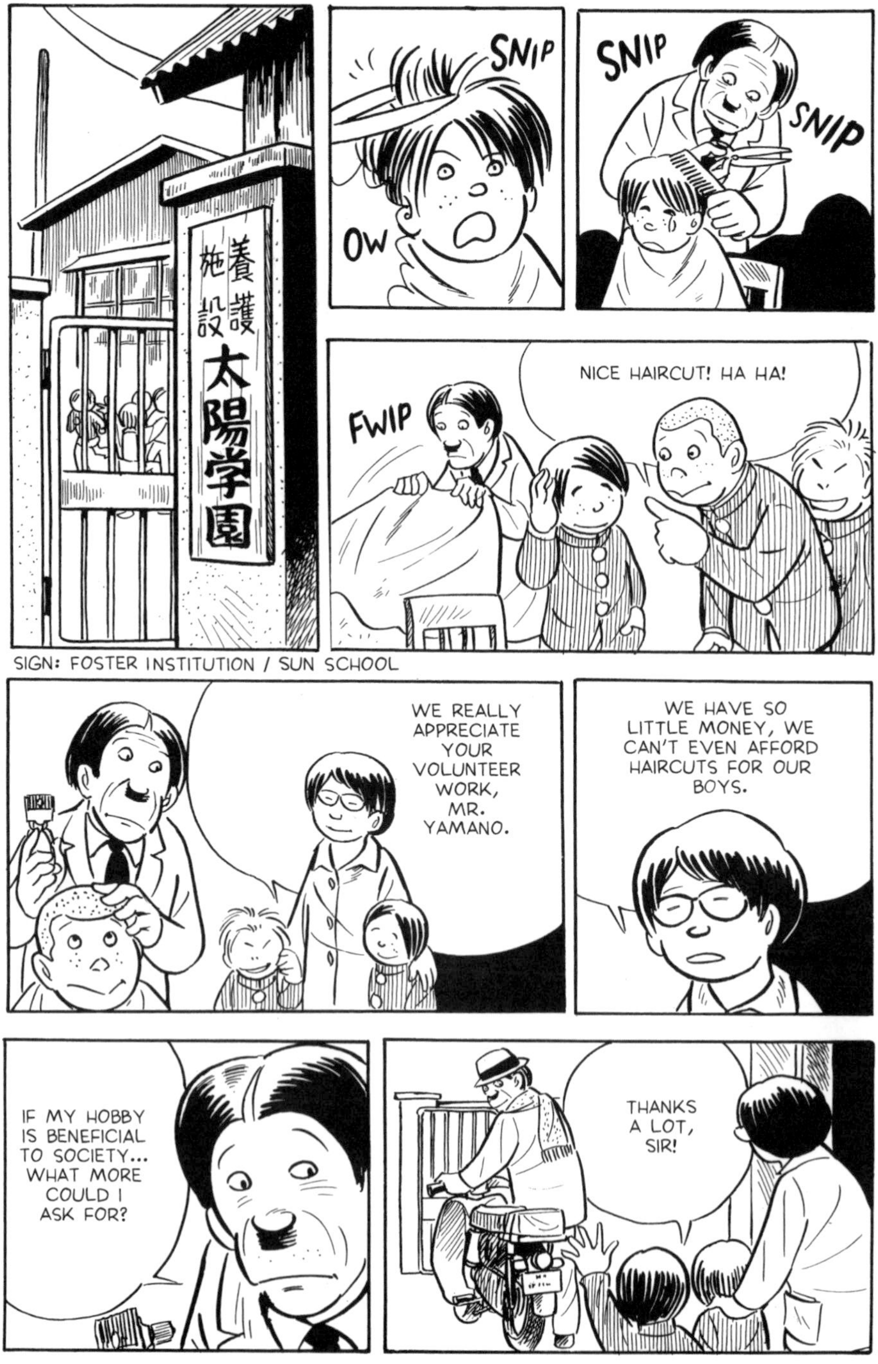
養護施設
太陽学園
SNIP
OW
SNIP
SNIP
FWIP
NICE HAIRCUT! HA HA!
SIGN: FOSTER INSTITUTION / SUN SCHOOL
WE REALLY APPRECIATE YOUR VOLUNTEER WORK, MR. YAMANO.
WE HAVE SO LITTLE MONEY, WE CAN'T EVEN AFFORD HAIRCUTS FOR OUR BOYS.
IF MY HOBBY IS BENEFICIAL TO SOCIETY... WHAT MORE COULD I ASK FOR?
THANKS A LOT, SIR!

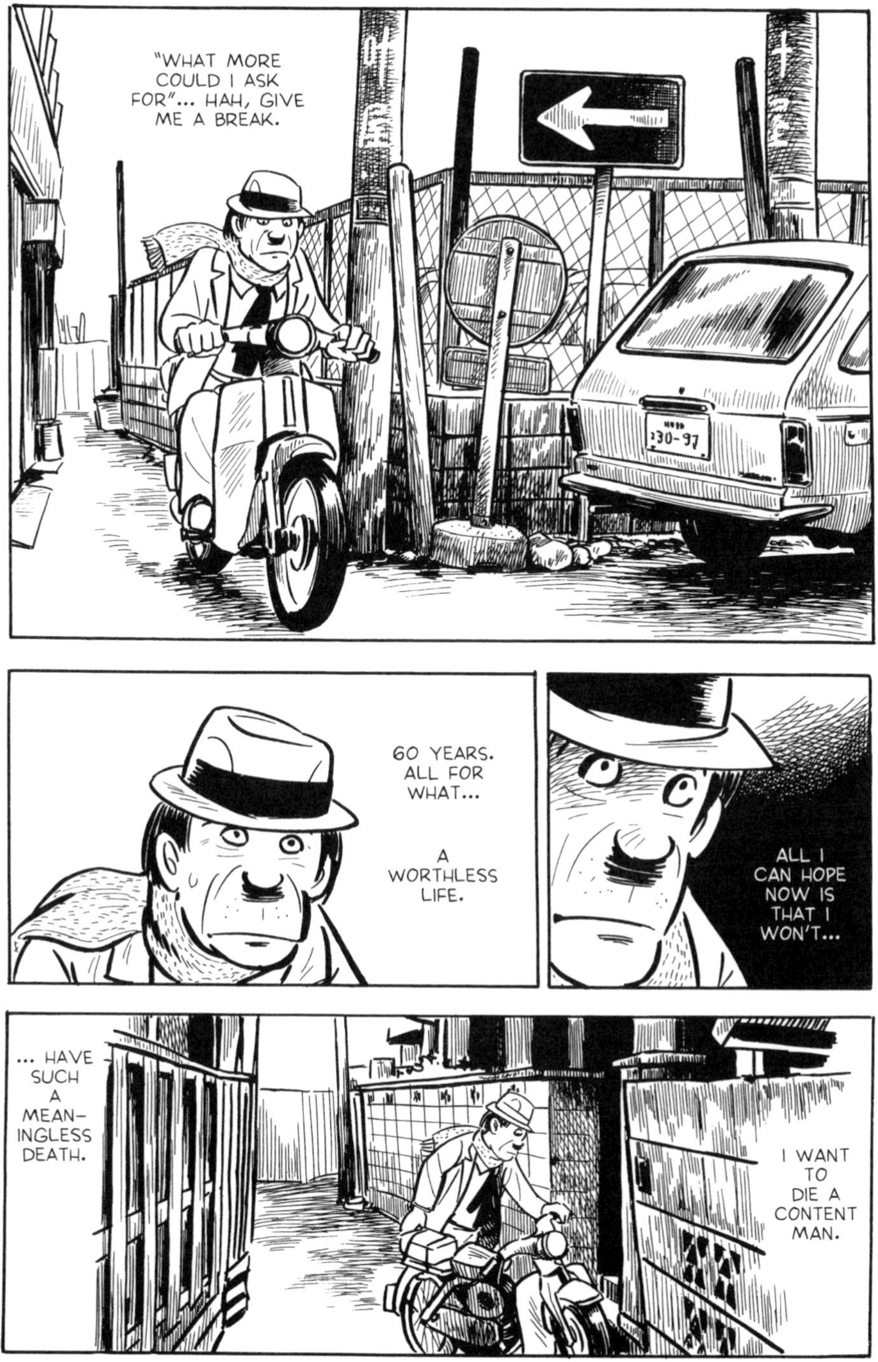
"WHAT MORE COULD I ASK FOR"... HAH, GIVE ME A BREAK.
60 YEARS. ALL FOR WHAT...
A WORTHLESS LIFE.
ALL I CAN HOPE NOW IS THAT I WON'T...
... HAVE SUCH A MEAN-INGLESS DEATH.
I WANT TO DIE A CONTENT MAN.

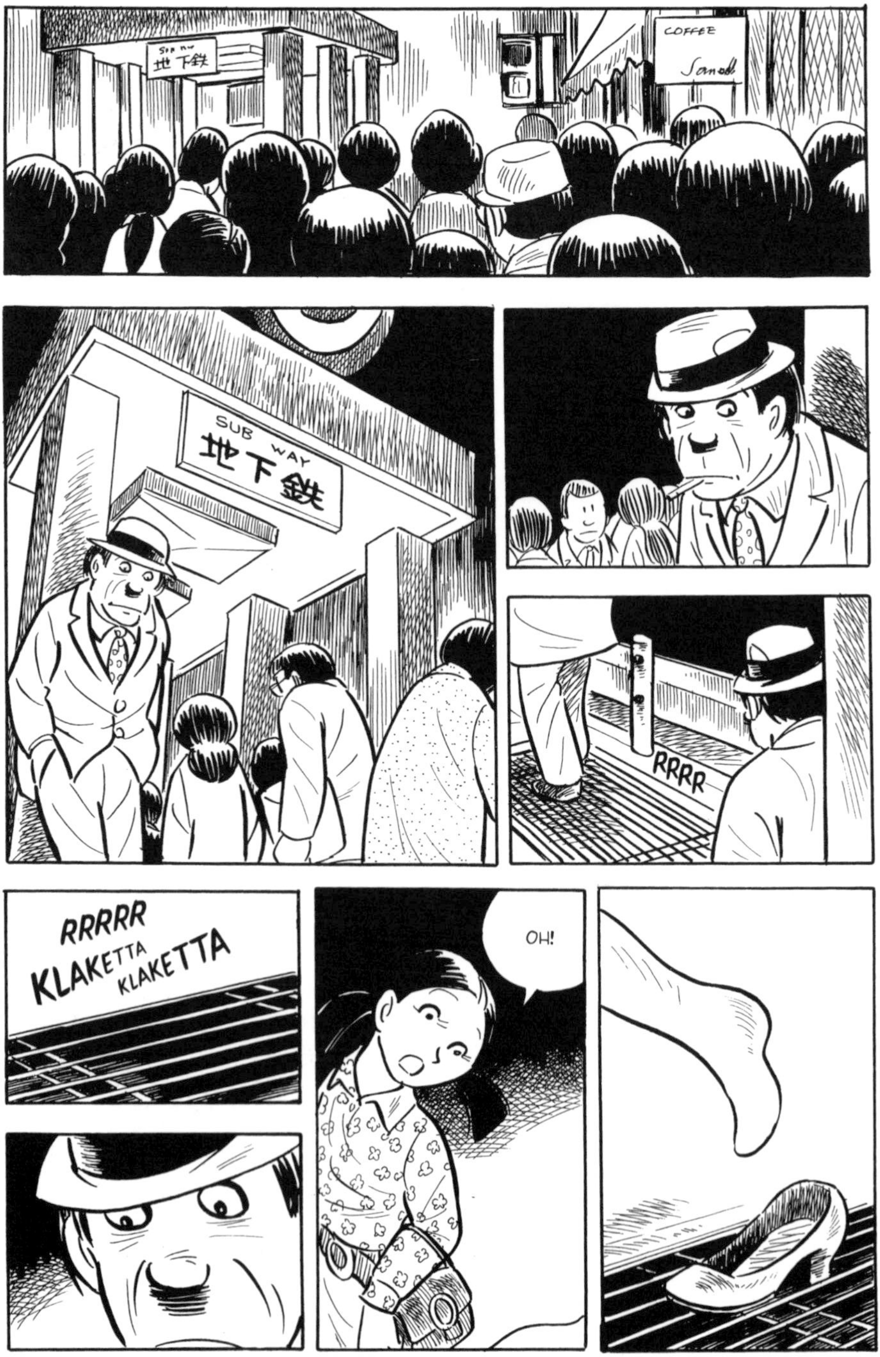

COFFEE
SUB WAY
地下鉄
RRRR
RRRRR
KLAKETTA KLAKETTA
OH!

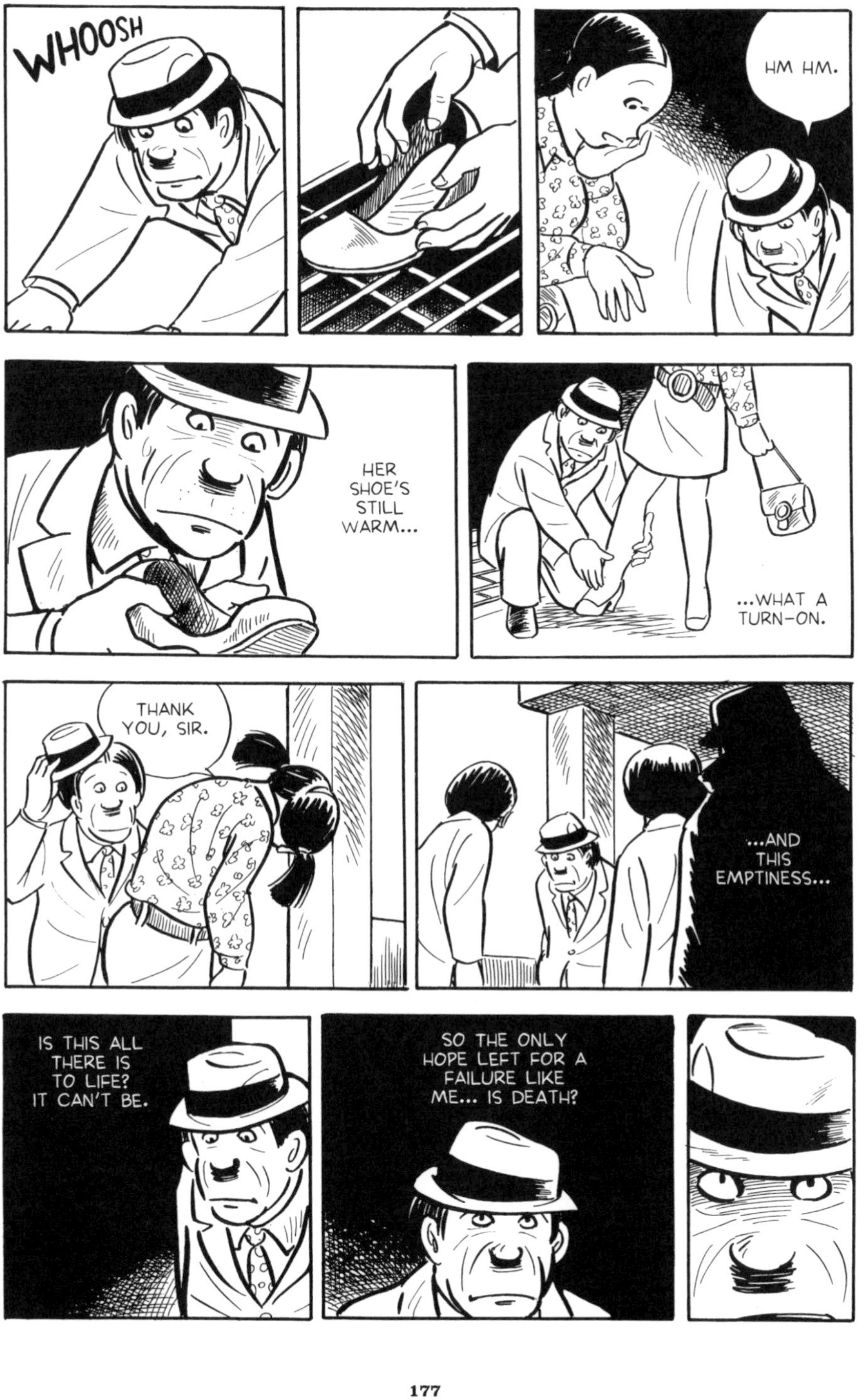
WHOOSH
HM HM.
HER SHOE'S STILL WARM...
...WHAT A TURN-ON.
THANK YOU, SIR.
...AND THIS EMPTINESS...
IS THIS ALL THERE IS TO LIFE? IT CAN'T BE.
SO THE ONLY HOPE LEFT FOR A FAILURE LIKE ME... IS DEATH?

SIGN: CERTIFICATE OF HONOR

WE PRESENT YOU, YASUKE YAMANO, WITH THIS CERTIFICATE FOR YOUR VOLUNTEER WORK.

CLAP CLAP

WE HOPE YOU CONTINUE WORKING WITH US.

YOU'RE A WONDERFUL MAN.

SIGN: TOKYO SOCIAL WELFARE BUREAU

I'M NOT WONDERFUL. JUST LUCKY. I HAVEN'T HAD TO WORK SINCE I STRUCK IT BIG ON THE STOCK MARKET.

MY VOLUNTEER WORK IS JUST AN ACT.

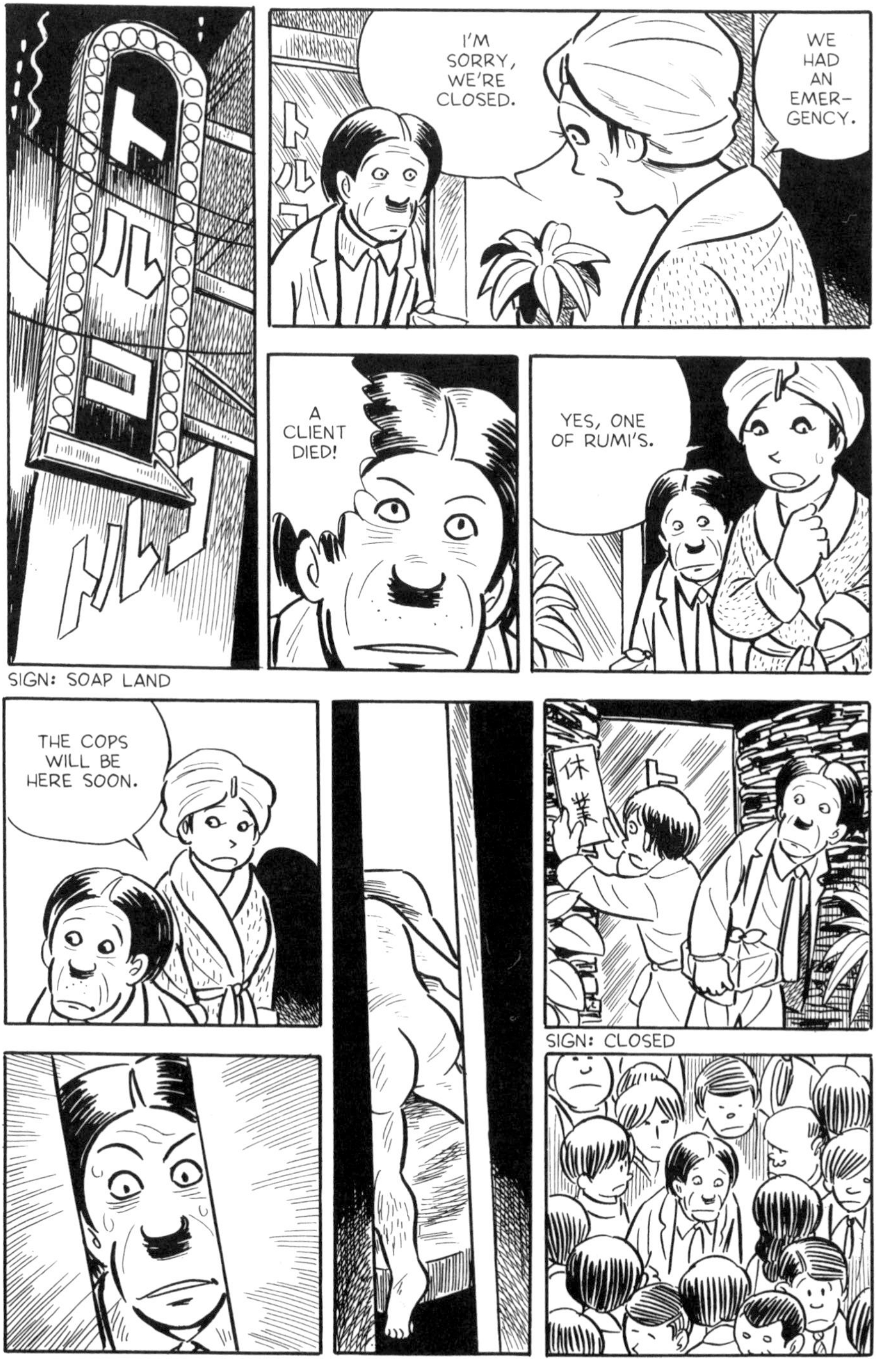
トルコ
SIGN: SOAP LAND
I'M SORRY, WE'RE CLOSED.
WE HAD AN EMERGENCY.
A CLIENT DIED!
YES, ONE OF RUMI'S.
THE COPS WILL BE HERE SOON.
休業
SIGN: CLOSED

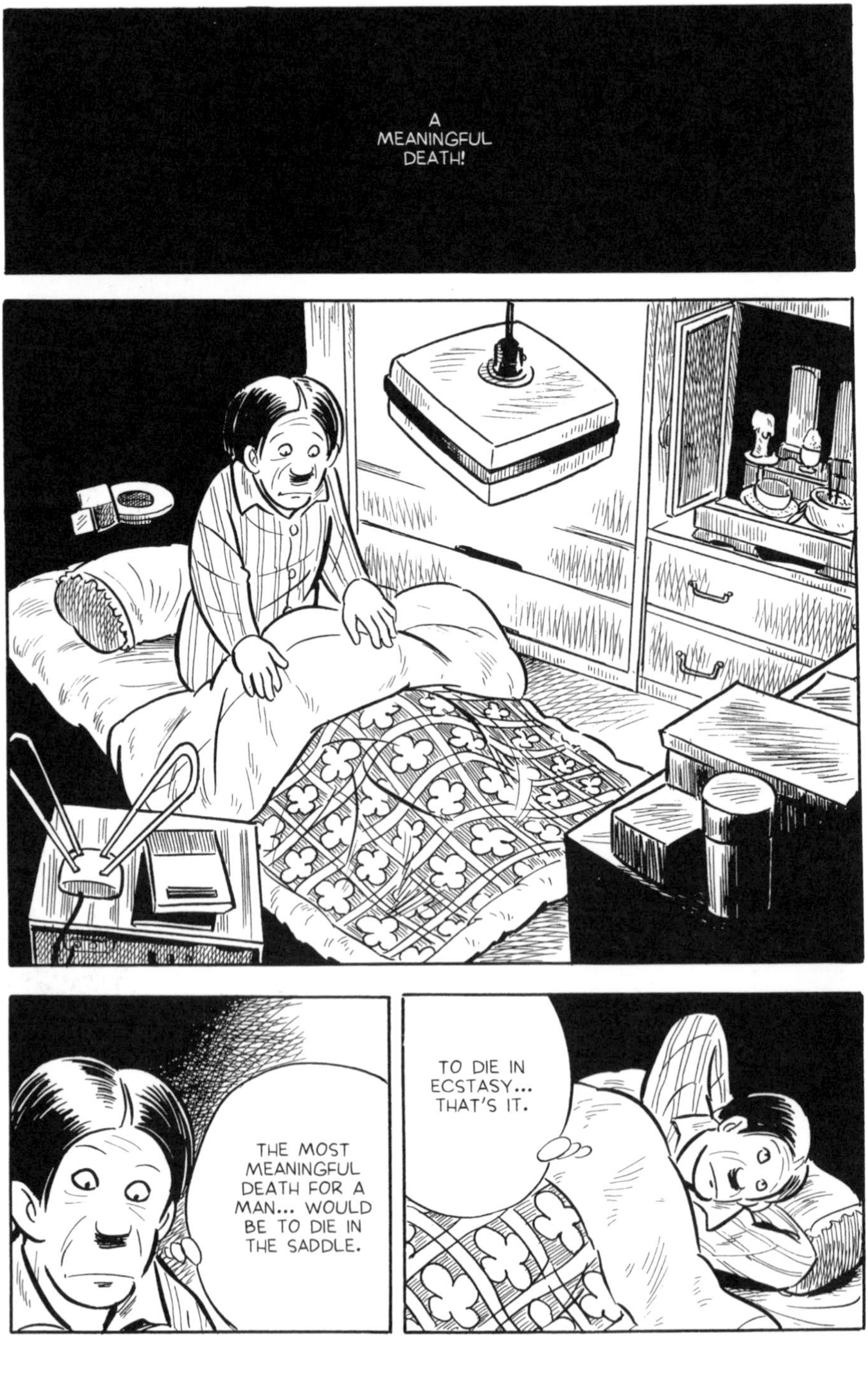
A MEANINGFUL DEATH!
THE MOST MEANINGFUL DEATH FOR A MAN... WOULD BE TO DIE IN THE SADDLE.
TO DIE IN ECSTASY... THAT'S IT.

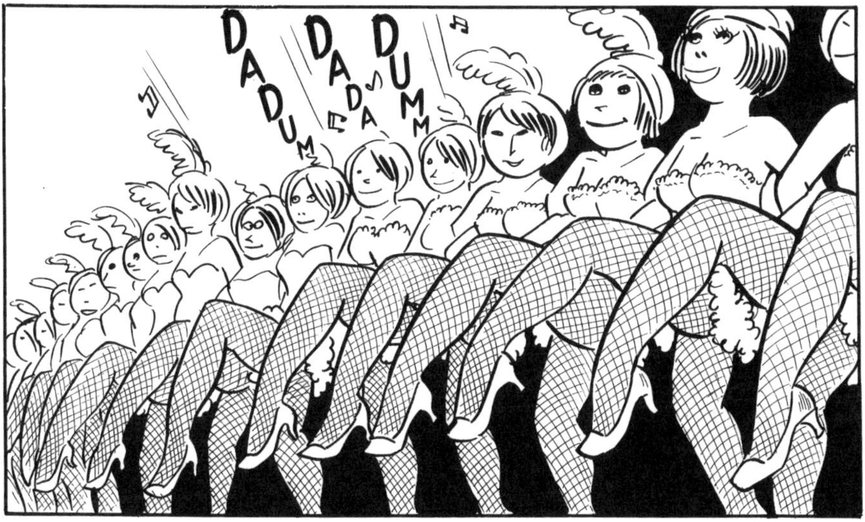
DADUM
DADA
DUMM

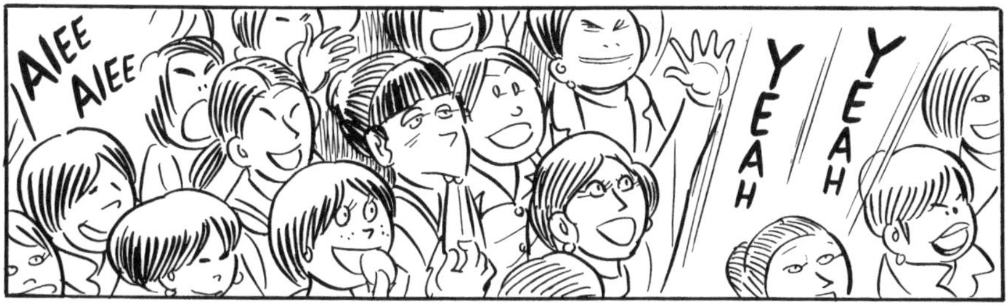
AIEE
AIEE
YEAH
YEAH

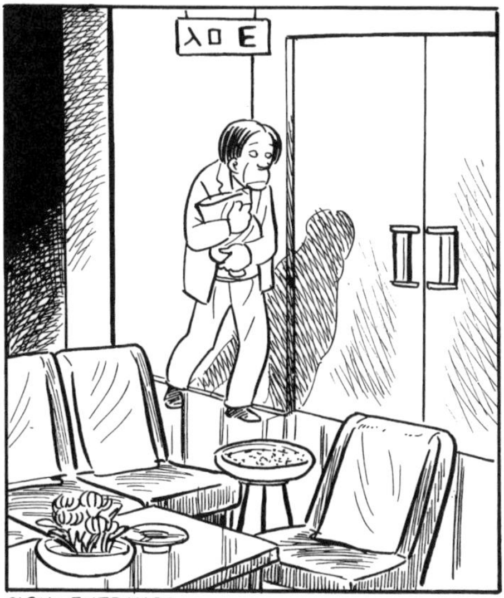
入口 E

SIGN: ENTRANCE

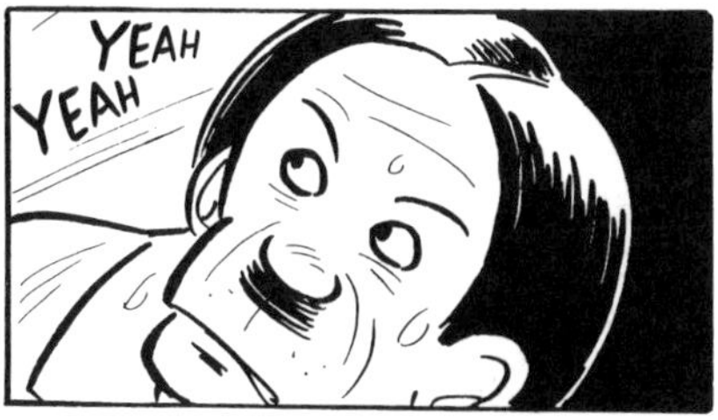
YEAH
YEAH

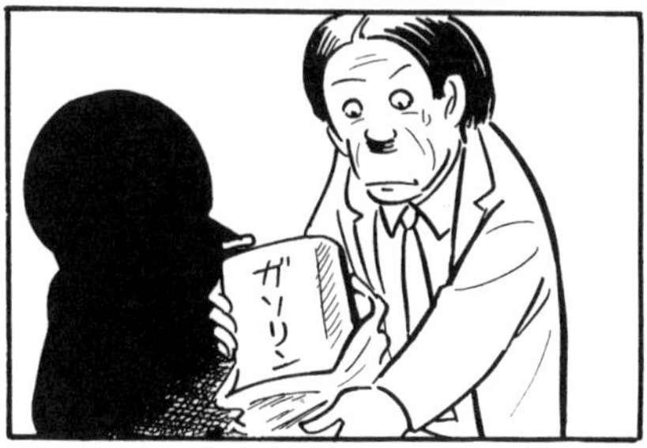
ガソリン

CONTAINER: GASOLINE

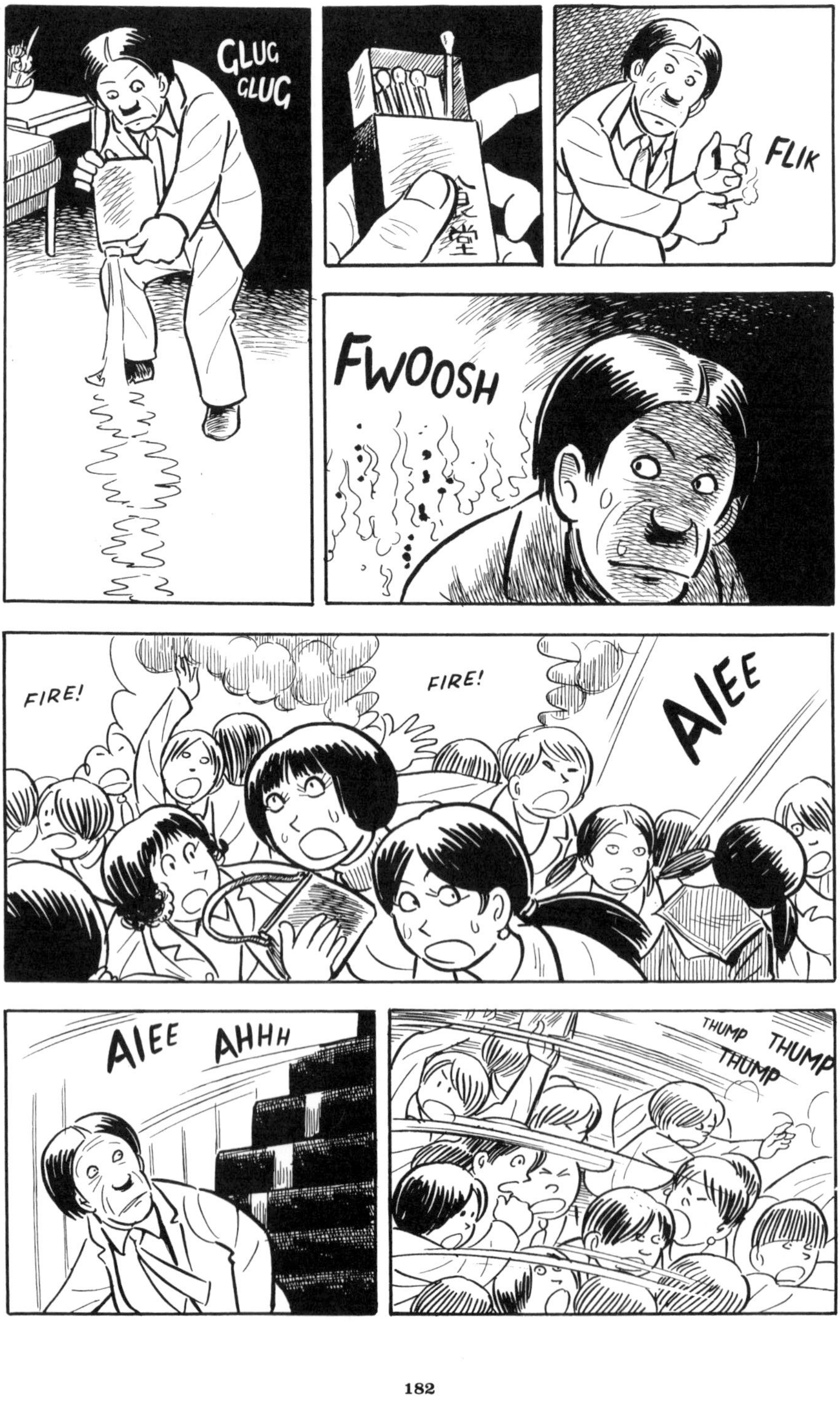
GLUG GLUG
FLIK
FWOOSH
FIRE!
FIRE!
AIEE
AIEE AHHH
THUMP THUMP
THUMP

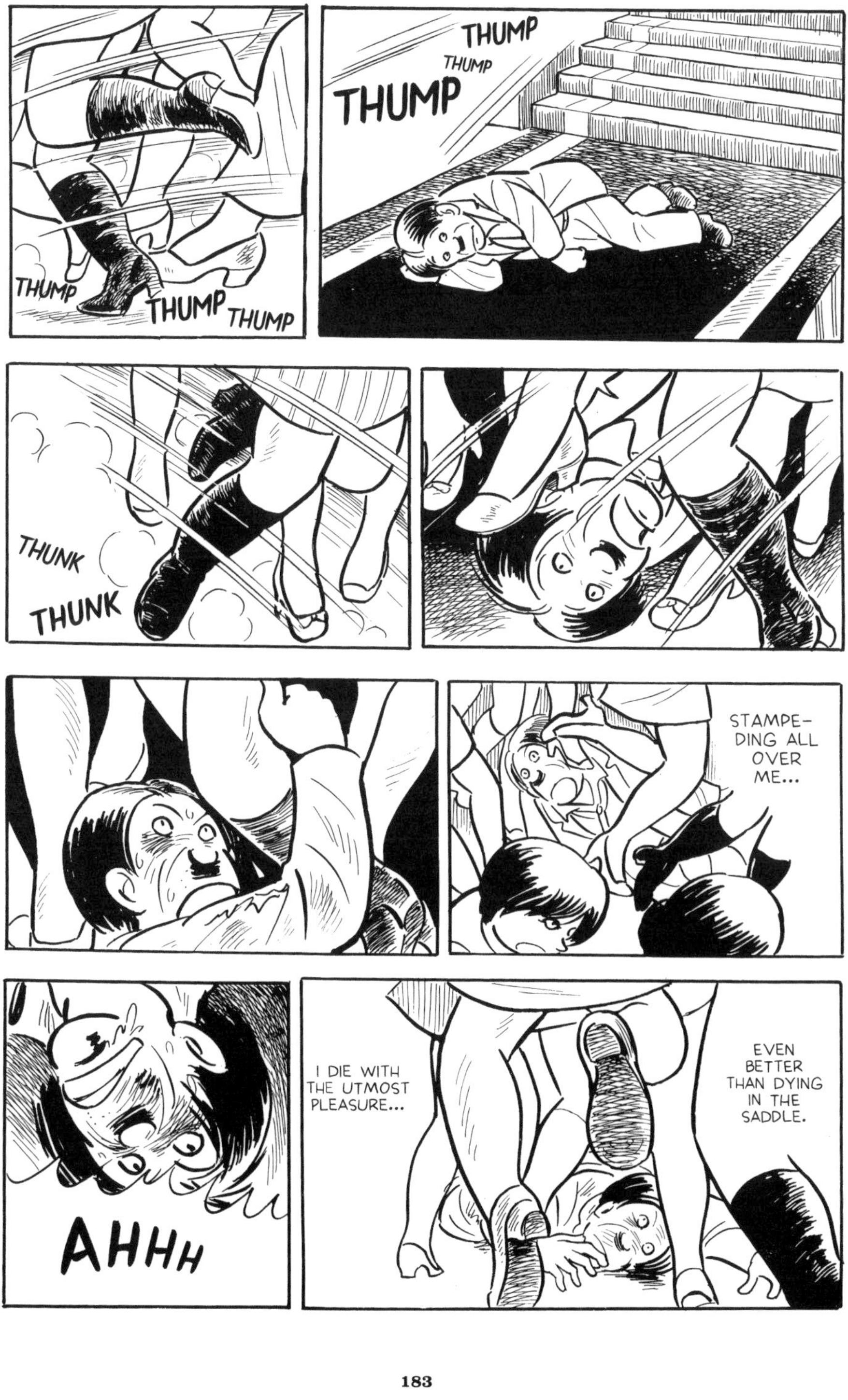
THUMP
THUMP
THUMP
THUMP
THUMP
THUMP
THUNK
THUNK
STAMPE-
DING ALL
OVER
ME...
AHHH
I DIE WITH
THE UTMOST
PLEASURE...
EVEN
BETTER
THAN DYING
IN THE
SADDLE.

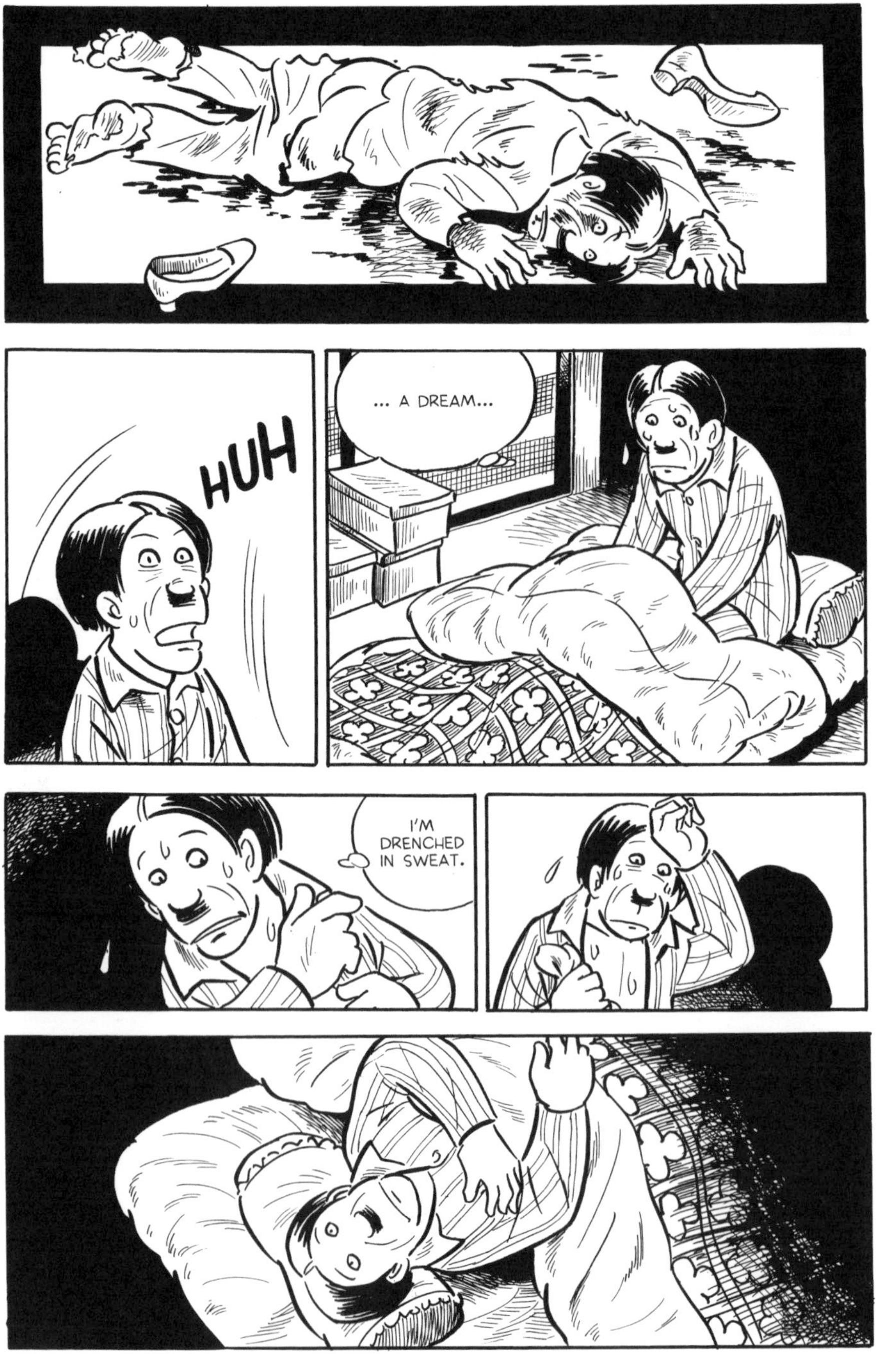
HUH
... A DREAM...
I'M DRENCHED IN SWEAT.

CLICK
CLICK

CLICK
CLICK
CLICK
CLICK

CLICK
CLICK
CLICK
CLICK

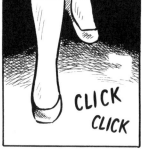

CLICK
CLICK

CLICK CLICK
CLICK

THUD

CLICK

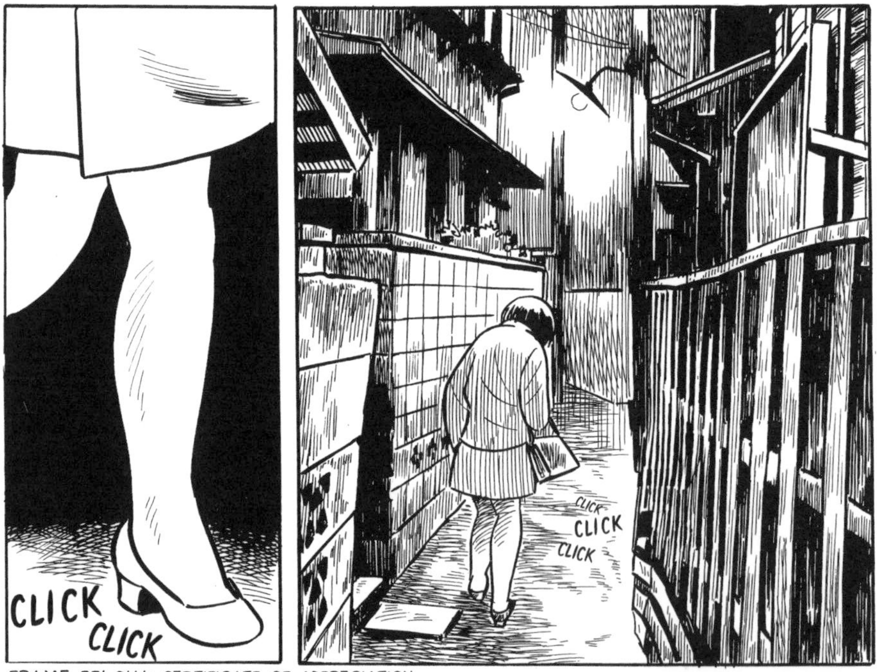
CLICK
CLICK
CLICK
CLICK
CLICK

FRAME BELOW: CERTIFICATE OF APPRECIATION

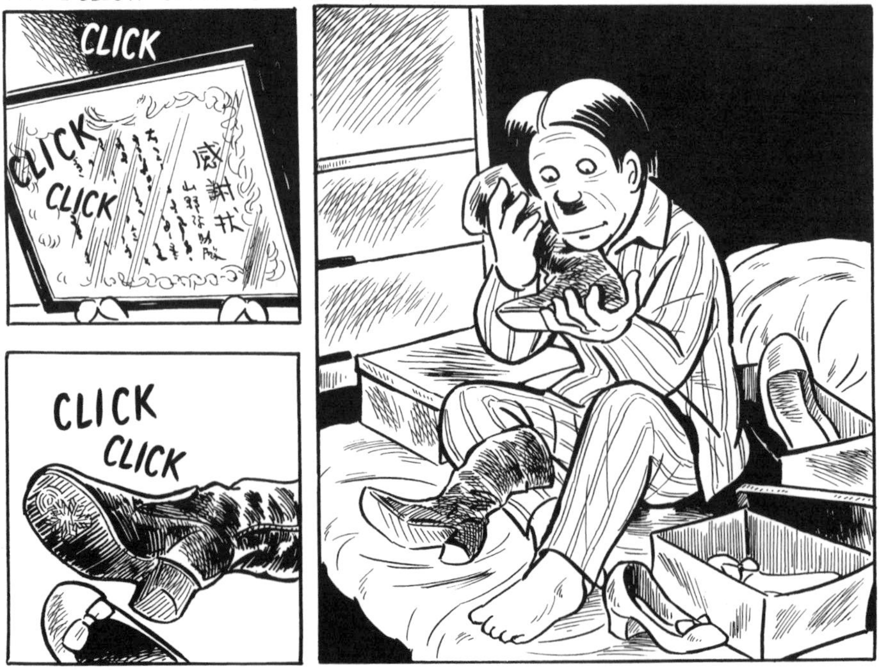
CLICK
CLICK
CLICK
感謝状
CLICK
CLICK

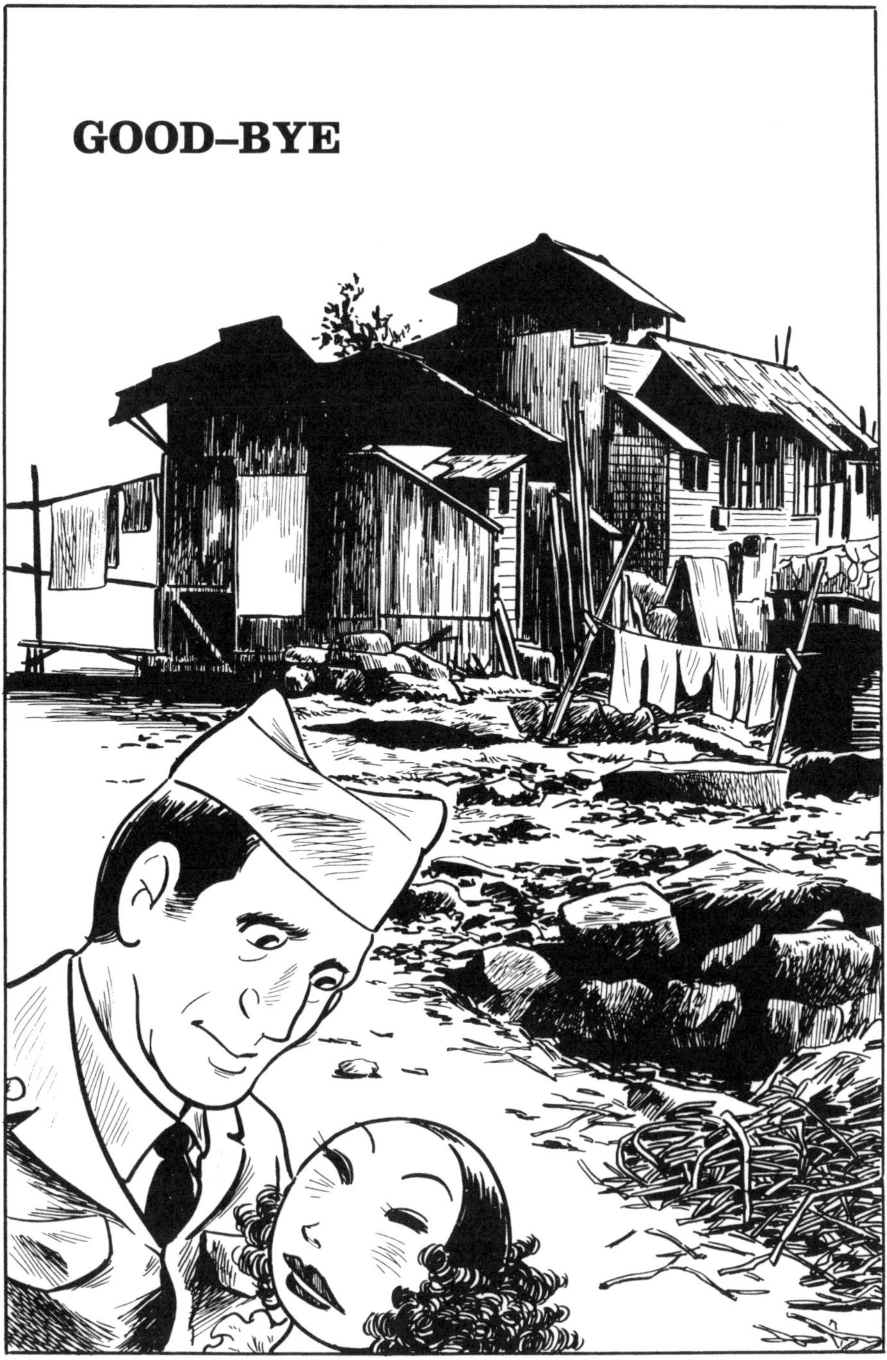
GOOD–BYE

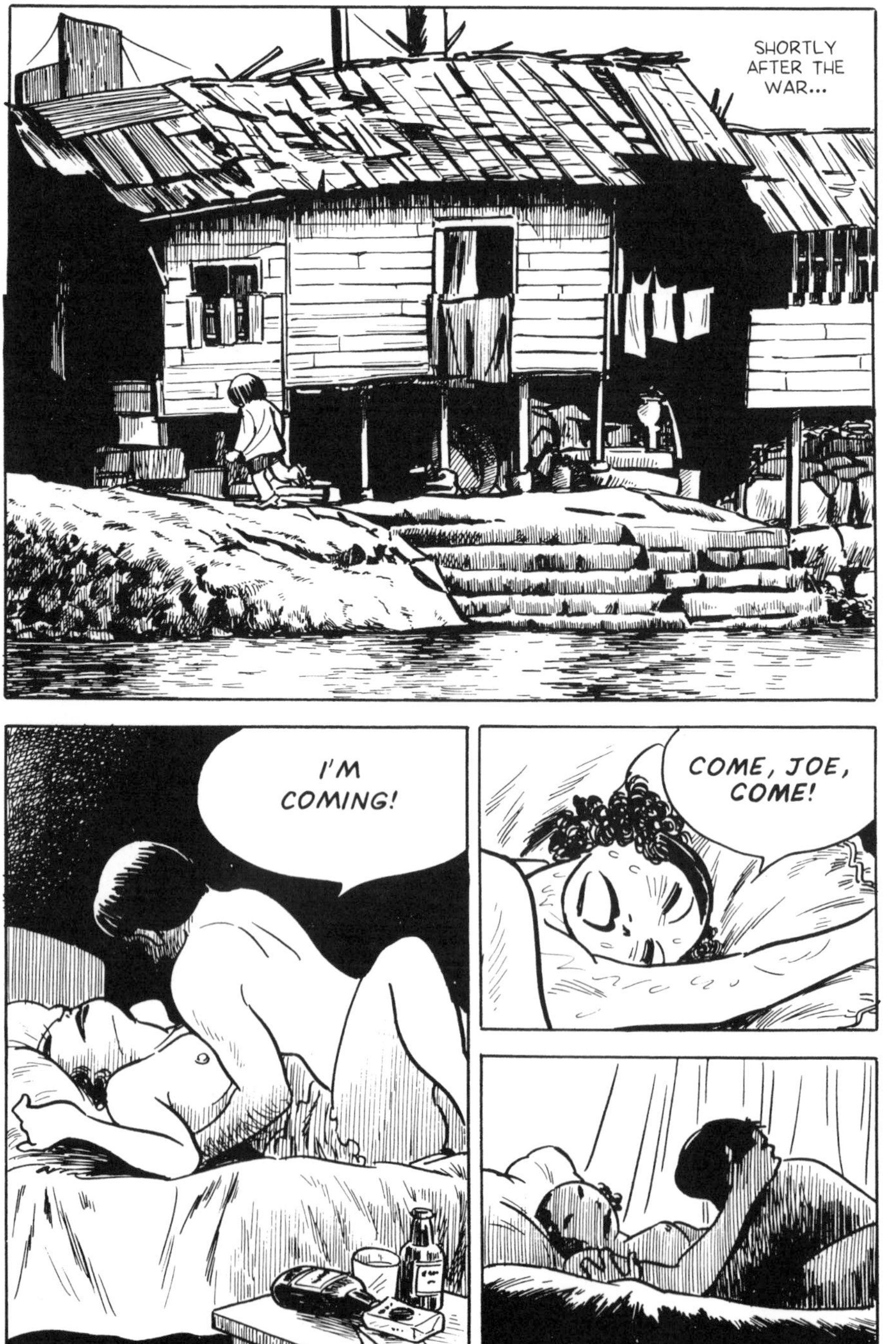
SHORTLY AFTER THE WAR...
I'M COMING!
COME, JOE, COME!

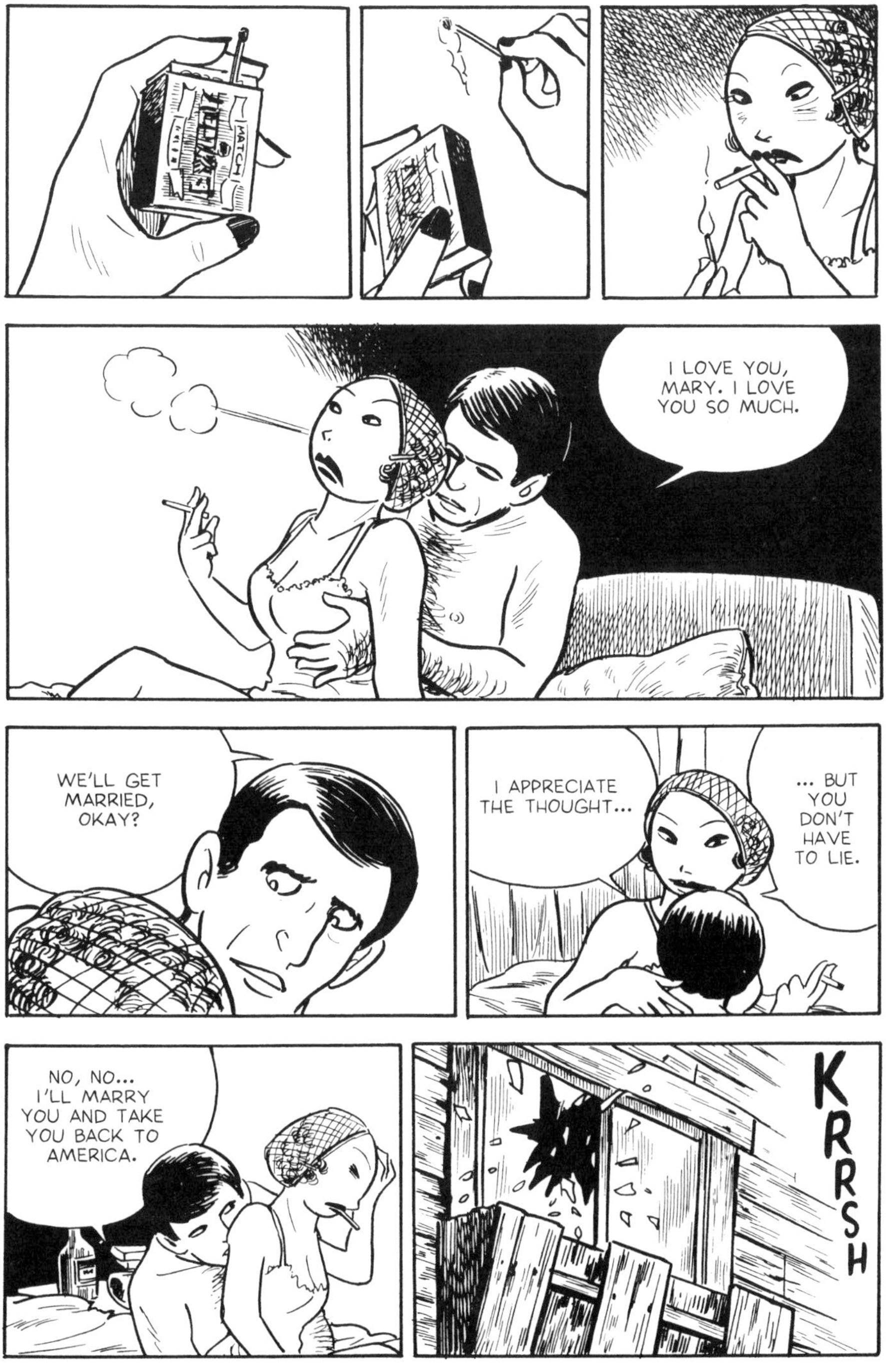
MATCH
I LOVE YOU, MARY. I LOVE YOU SO MUCH.
WE'LL GET MARRIED, OKAY?
I APPRECIATE THE THOUGHT...
... BUT YOU DON'T HAVE TO LIE.
NO, NO... I'LL MARRY YOU AND TAKE YOU BACK TO AMERICA.
KRRSH

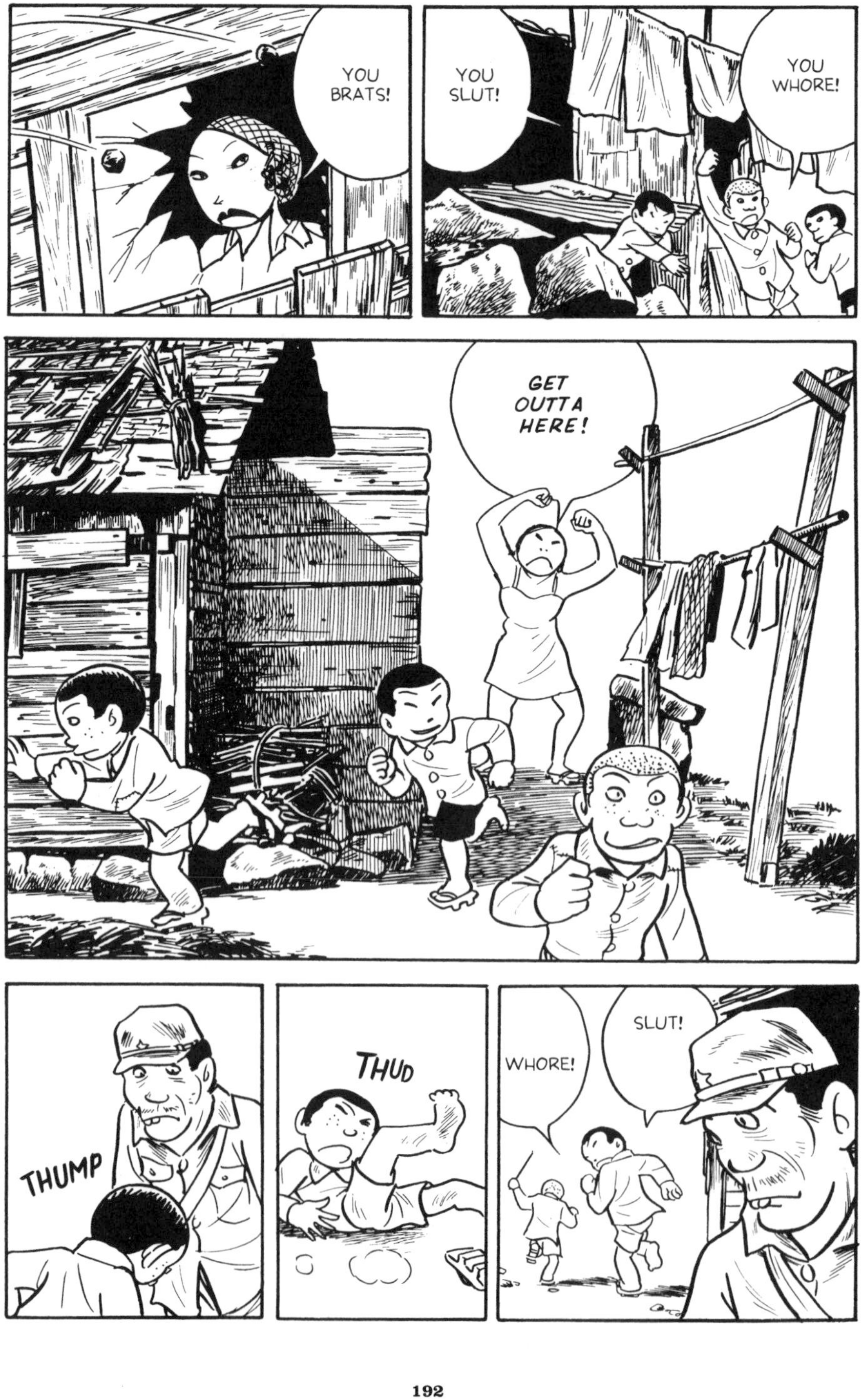
YOU BRATS!
YOU SLUT!
YOU WHORE!
GET OUTTA HERE!
THUMP
THUD
WHORE!
SLUT!

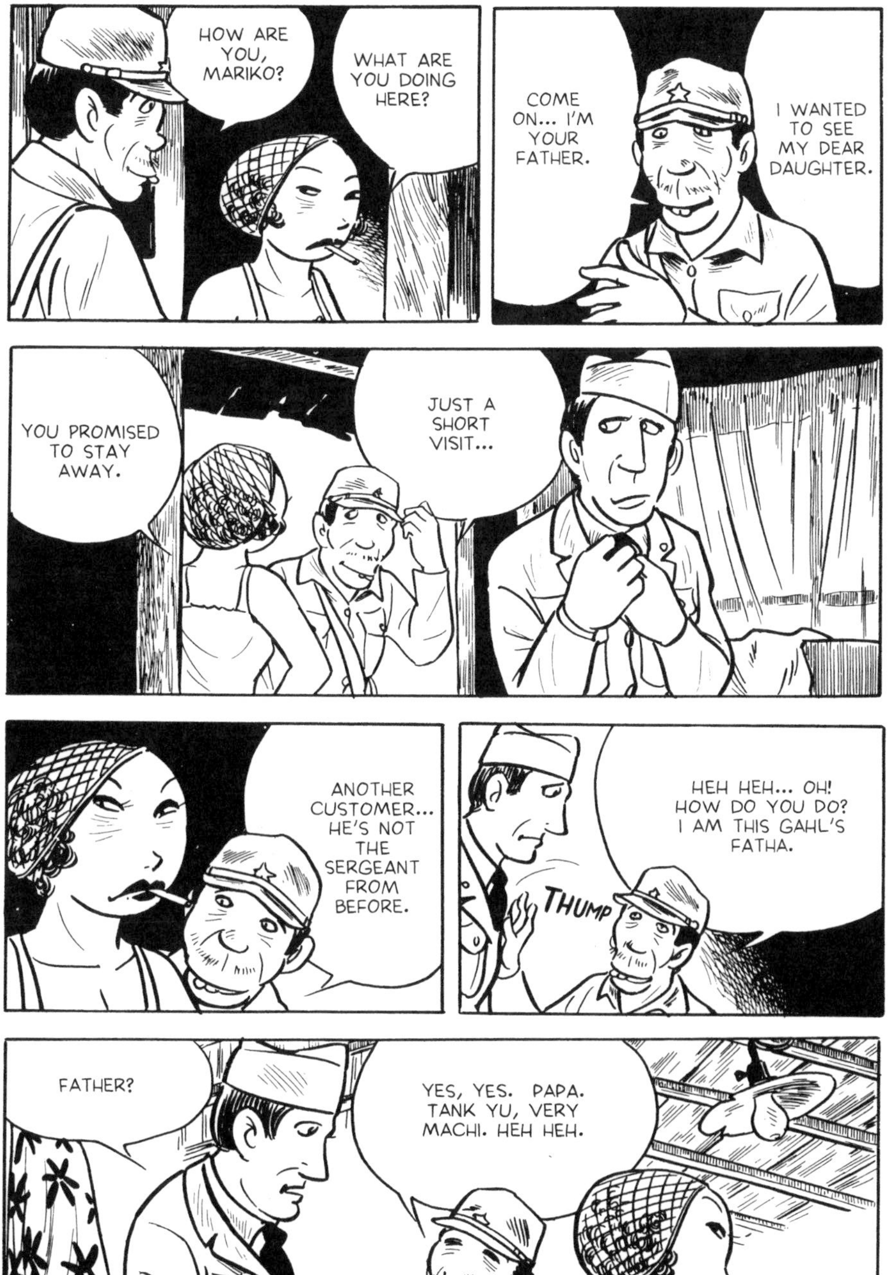
HOW ARE YOU, MARIKO?
WHAT ARE YOU DOING HERE?
COME ON... I'M YOUR FATHER.
I WANTED TO SEE MY DEAR DAUGHTER.
YOU PROMISED TO STAY AWAY.
JUST A SHORT VISIT...
ANOTHER CUSTOMER... HE'S NOT THE SERGEANT FROM BEFORE.
THUMP
HEH HEH... OH! HOW DO YOU DO? I AM THIS GAHL'S FATHA.
FATHER?
YES, YES. PAPA. TANK YU, VERY MACHI. HEH HEH.

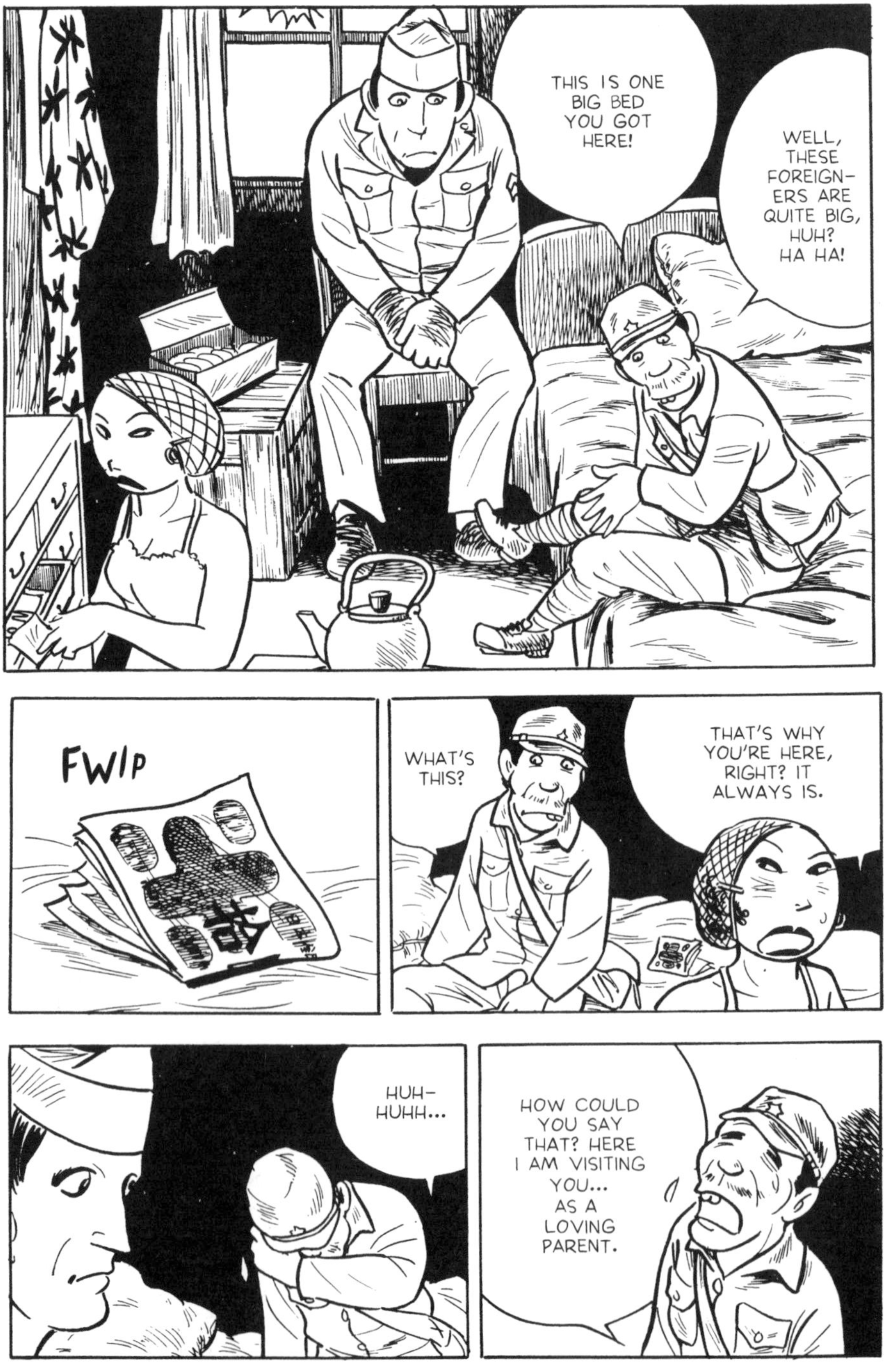
THIS IS ONE BIG BED YOU GOT HERE!
WELL, THESE FOREIGN-ERS ARE QUITE BIG, HUH? HA HA!
FWIP
WHAT'S THIS?
THAT'S WHY YOU'RE HERE, RIGHT? IT ALWAYS IS.
HUH-HUHH...
HOW COULD YOU SAY THAT? HERE I AM VISITING YOU... AS A LOVING PARENT.

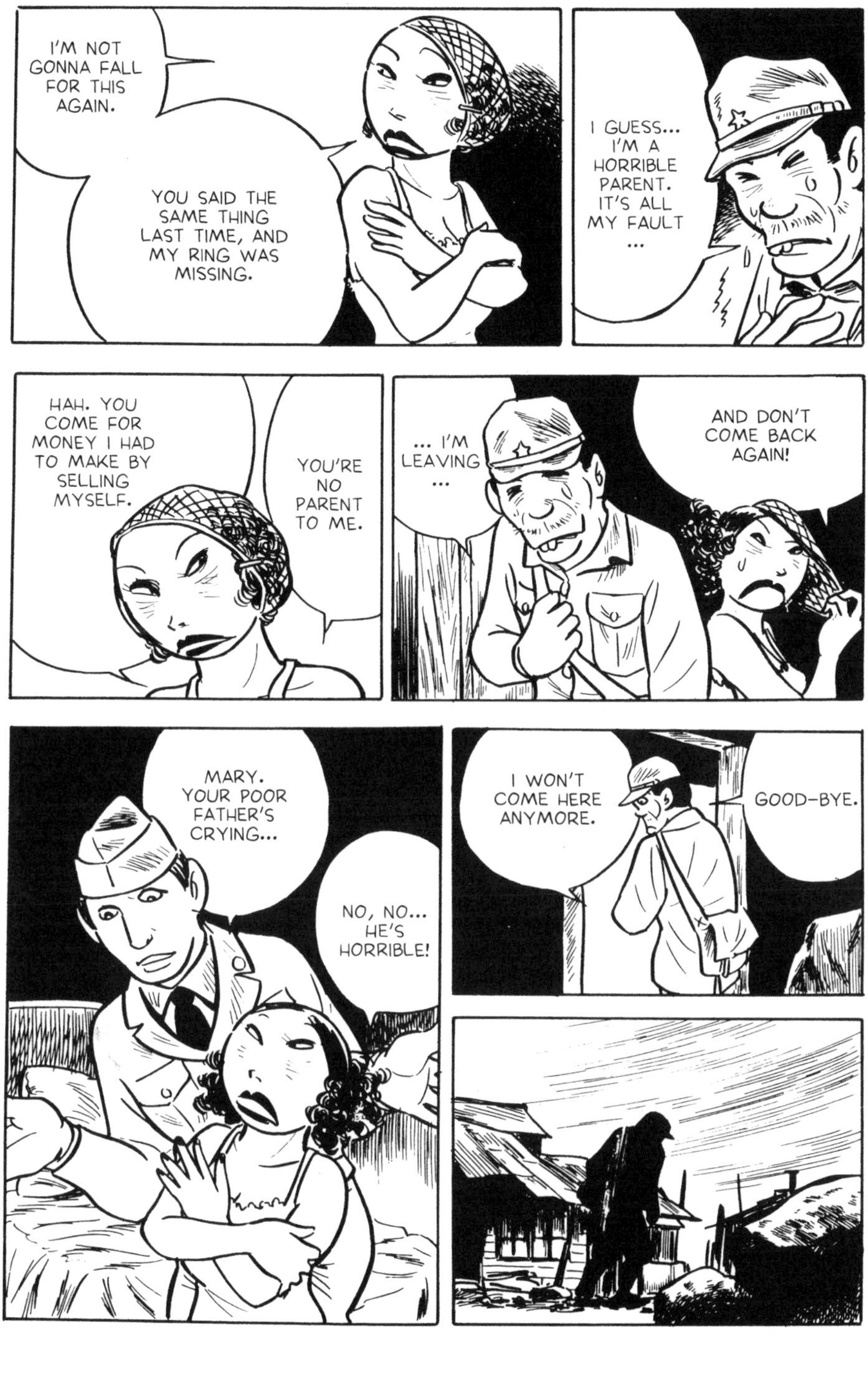
I'M NOT GONNA FALL FOR THIS AGAIN.
YOU SAID THE SAME THING LAST TIME, AND MY RING WAS MISSING.
I GUESS... I'M A HORRIBLE PARENT. IT'S ALL MY FAULT ...
HAH. YOU COME FOR MONEY I HAD TO MAKE BY SELLING MYSELF.
YOU'RE NO PARENT TO ME.
... I'M LEAVING ...
AND DON'T COME BACK AGAIN!
MARY. YOUR POOR FATHER'S CRYING...
NO, NO... HE'S HORRIBLE!
I WON'T COME HERE ANYMORE.
GOOD-BYE.

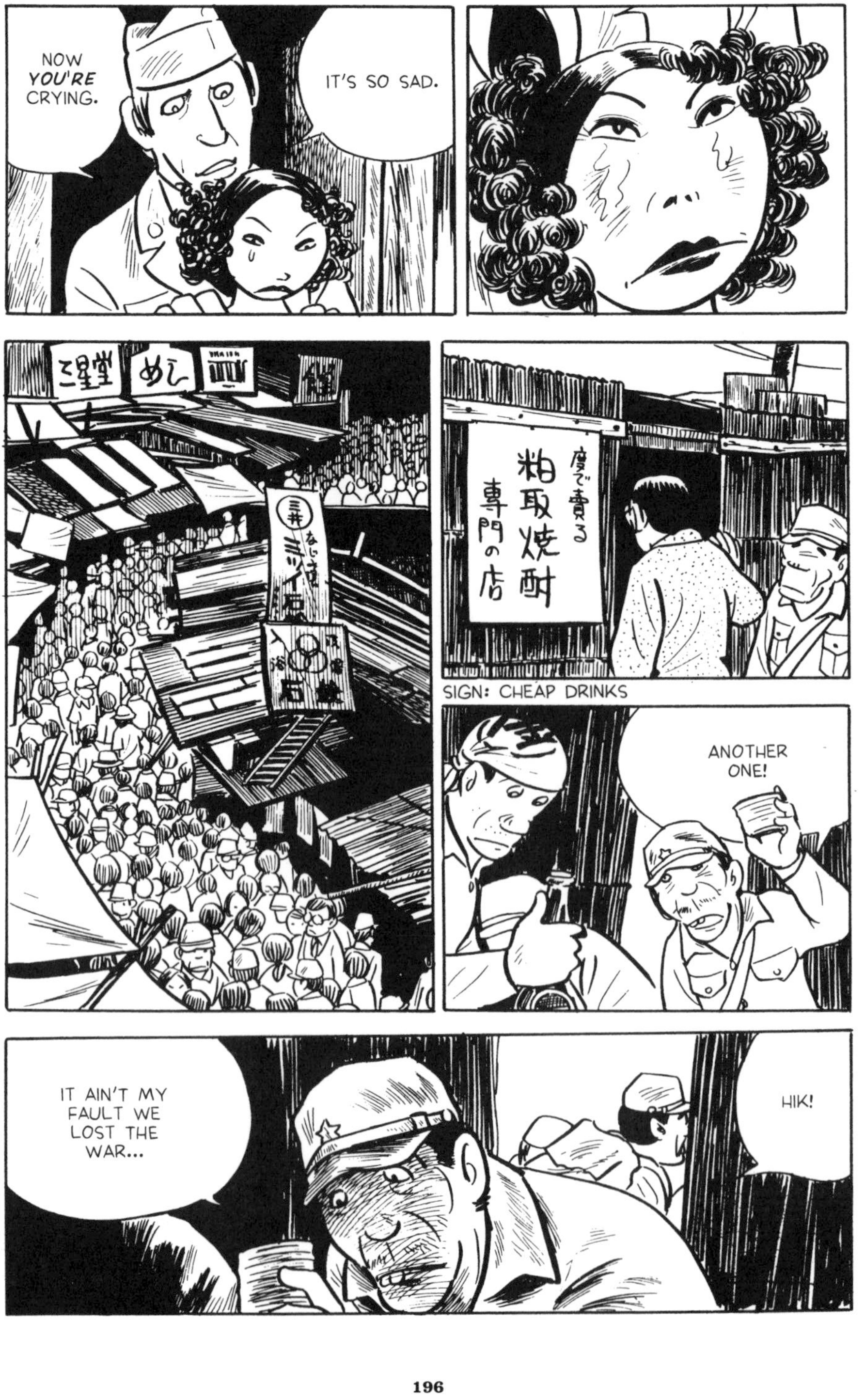
NOW *YOU'RE* CRYING.
IT'S SO SAD.
めし
粕取焼酎
専門の店
SIGN: CHEAP DRINKS
ANOTHER ONE!
IT AIN'T MY FAULT WE LOST THE WAR...
HIK!

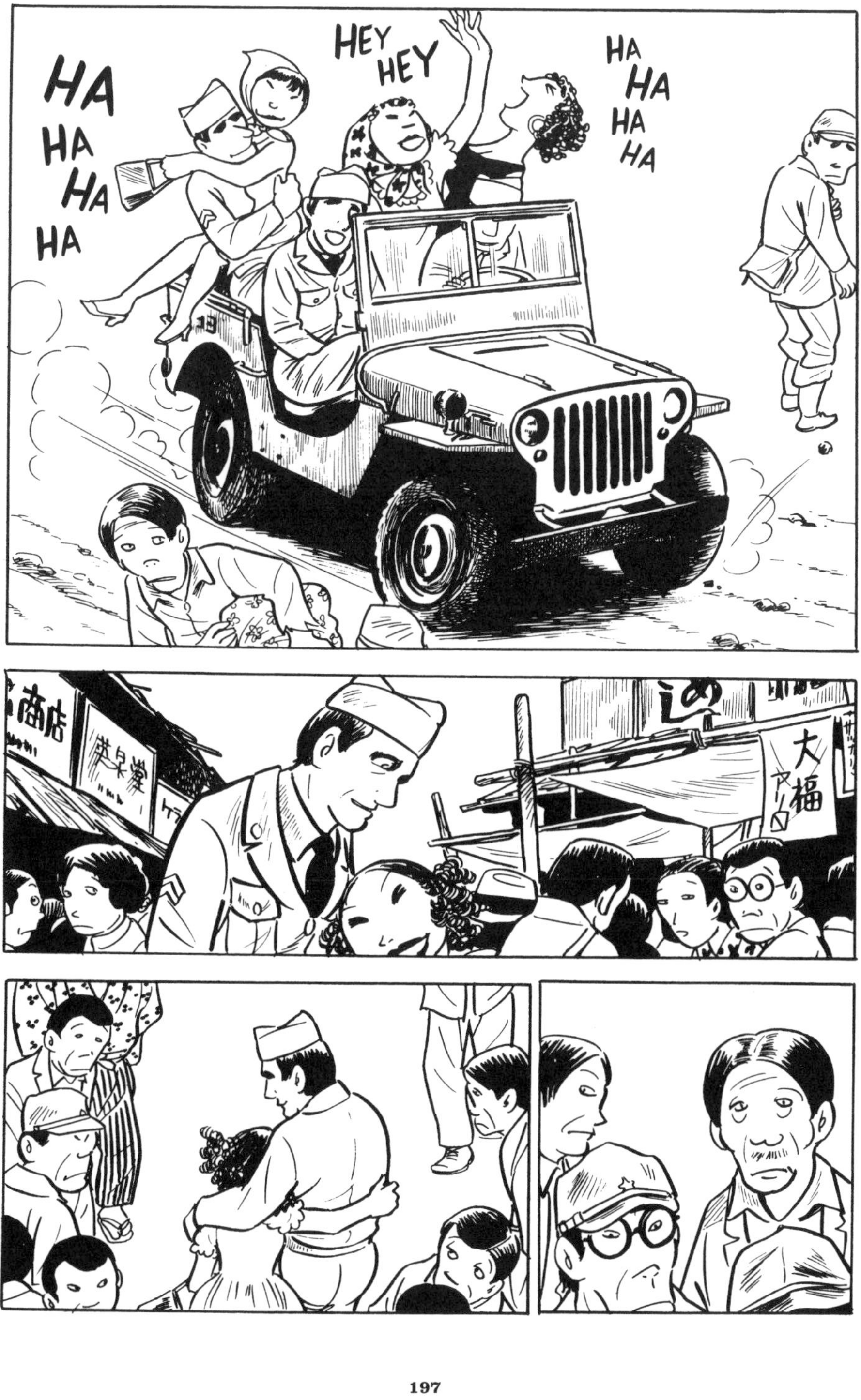
HA HA HA HA
HEY HEY
HA HA HA HA
商店
大福

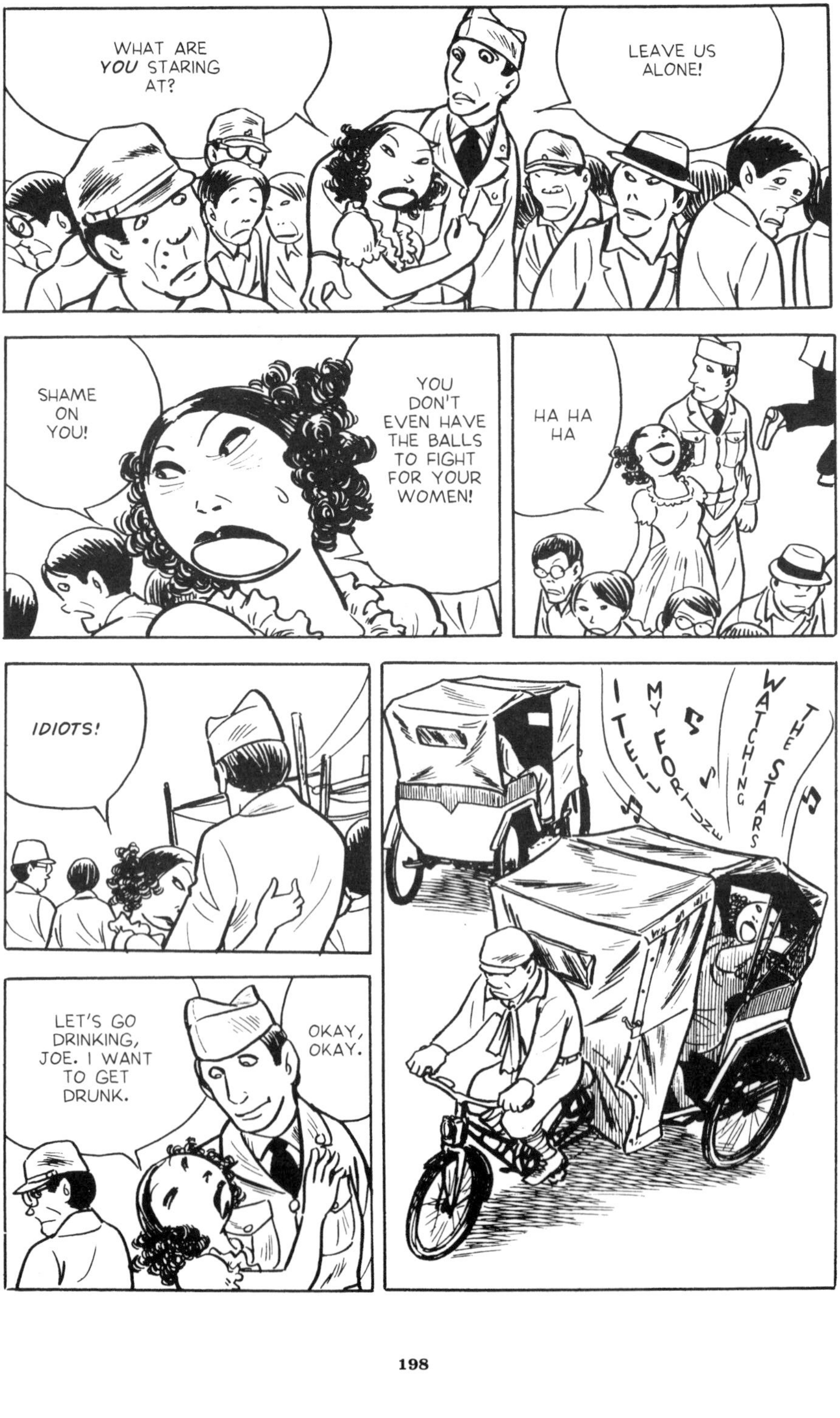
WHAT ARE *YOU* STARING AT?
LEAVE US ALONE!
SHAME ON YOU!
YOU DON'T EVEN HAVE THE BALLS TO FIGHT FOR YOUR WOMEN!
HA HA HA
IDIOTS!
LET'S GO DRINKING, JOE. I WANT TO GET DRUNK.
OKAY, OKAY.
I TELL MY FORTUNE WATCHING THE STARS

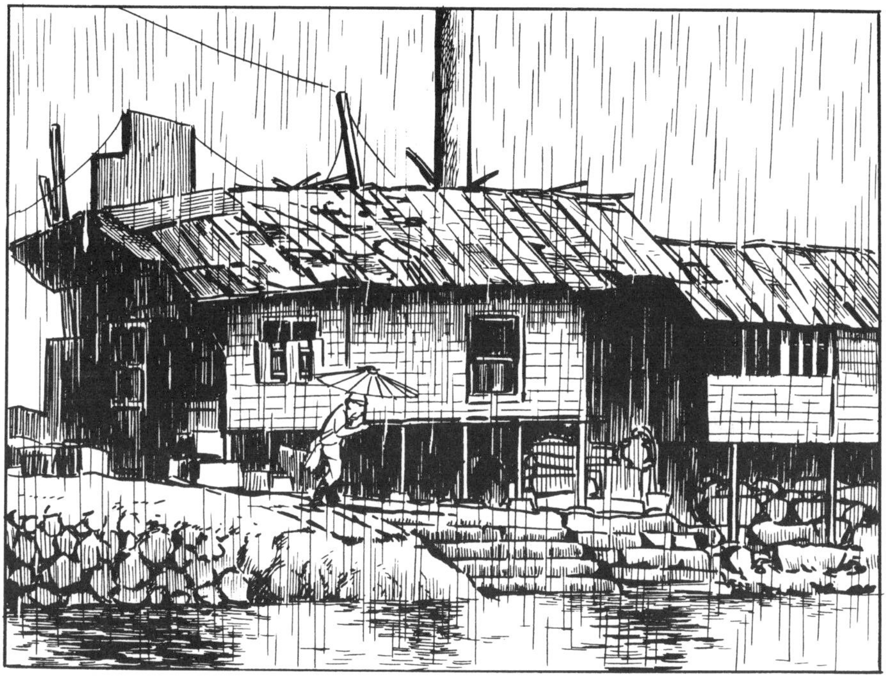

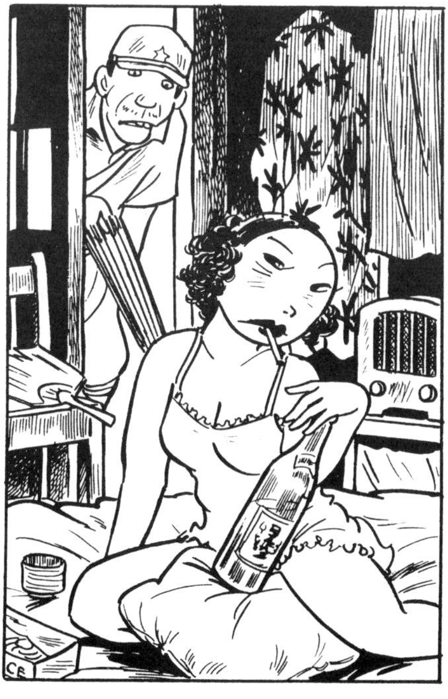

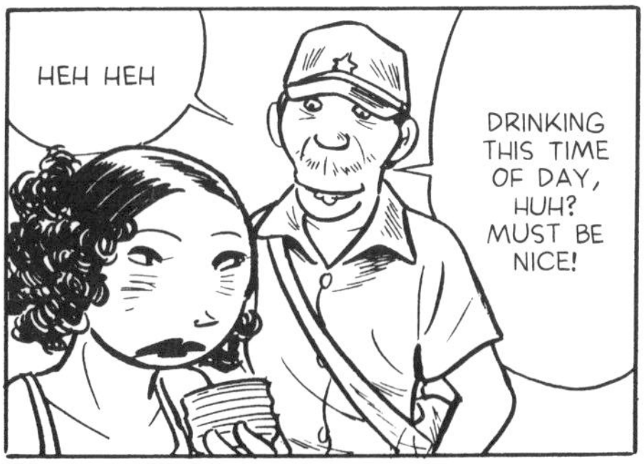
HEH HEH
DRINKING THIS TIME OF DAY, HUH? MUST BE NICE!

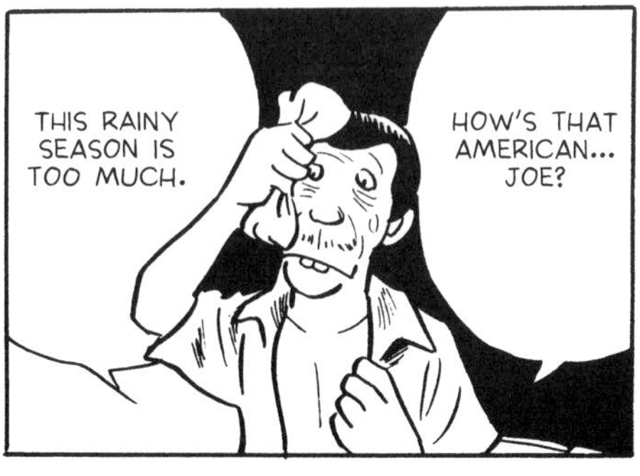
THIS RAINY SEASON IS TOO MUCH.
HOW'S THAT AMERICAN... JOE?

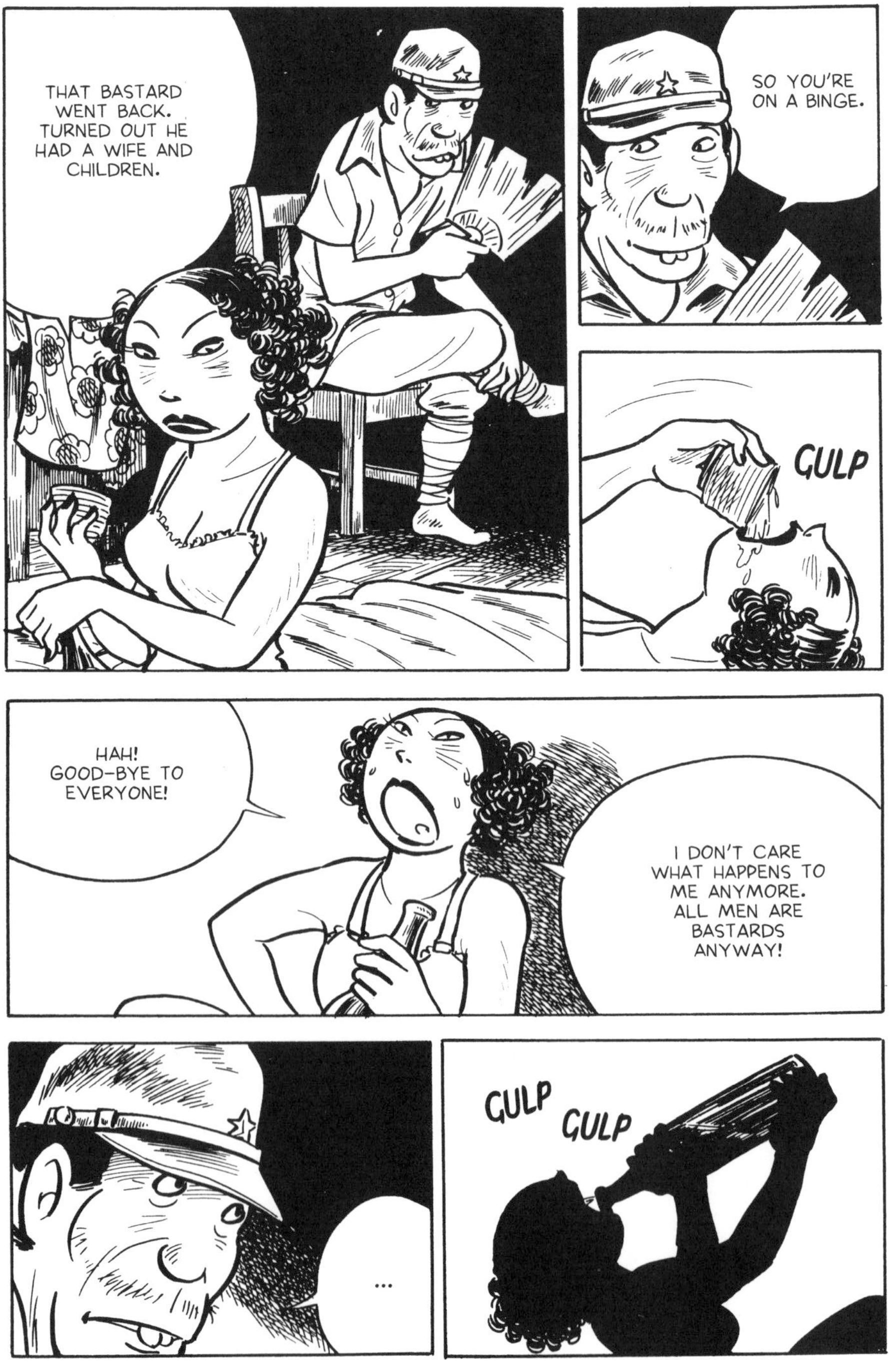
THAT BASTARD WENT BACK. TURNED OUT HE HAD A WIFE AND CHILDREN.
SO YOU'RE ON A BINGE.
GULP
HAH! GOOD-BYE TO EVERYONE!
I DON'T CARE WHAT HAPPENS TO ME ANYMORE. ALL MEN ARE BASTARDS ANYWAY!
...
GULP
GULP

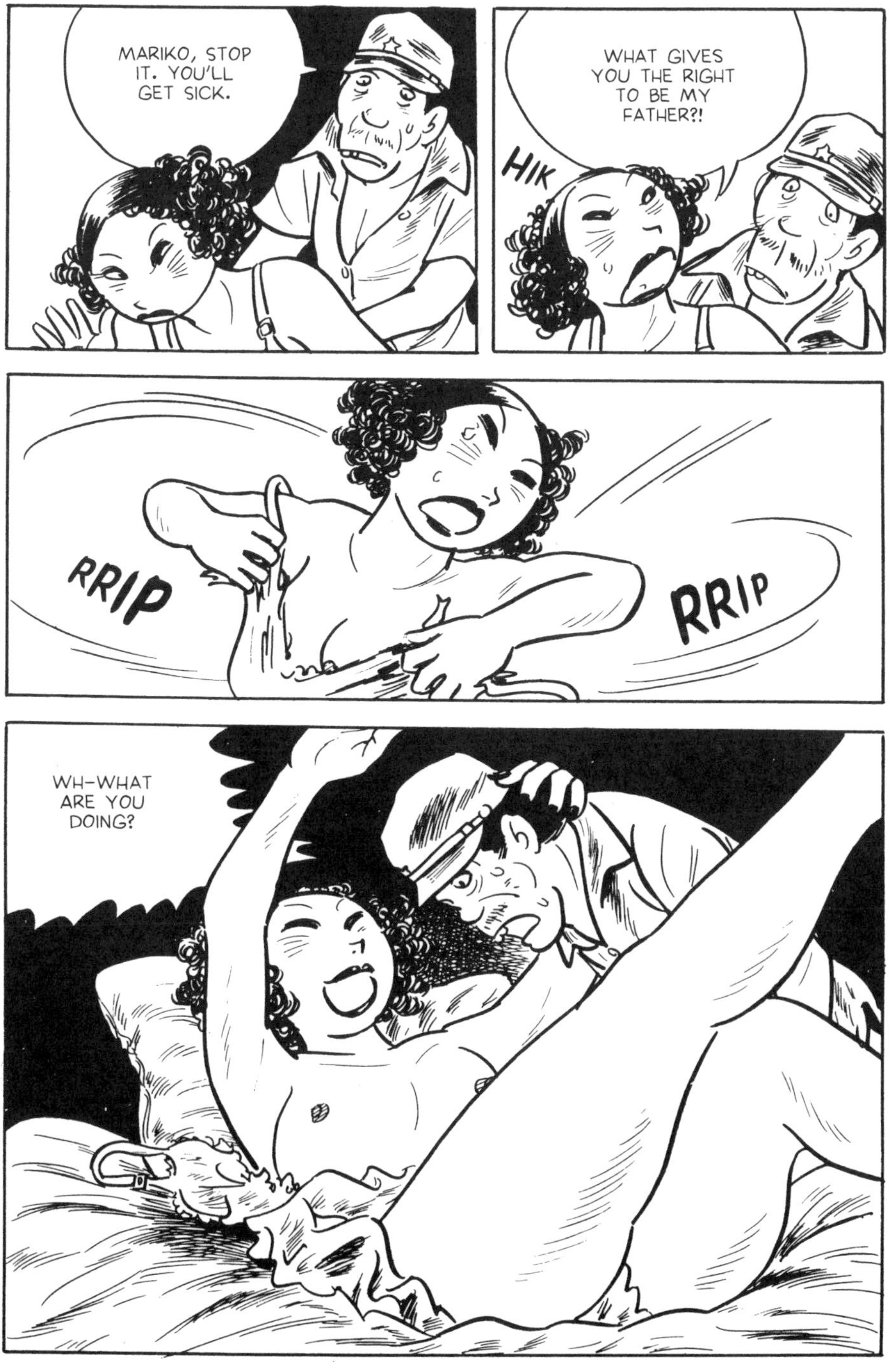
MARIKO, STOP IT. YOU'LL GET SICK.
WHAT GIVES YOU THE RIGHT TO BE MY FATHER?!
HIK
RRIP
RRIP
WH-WHAT ARE YOU DOING?

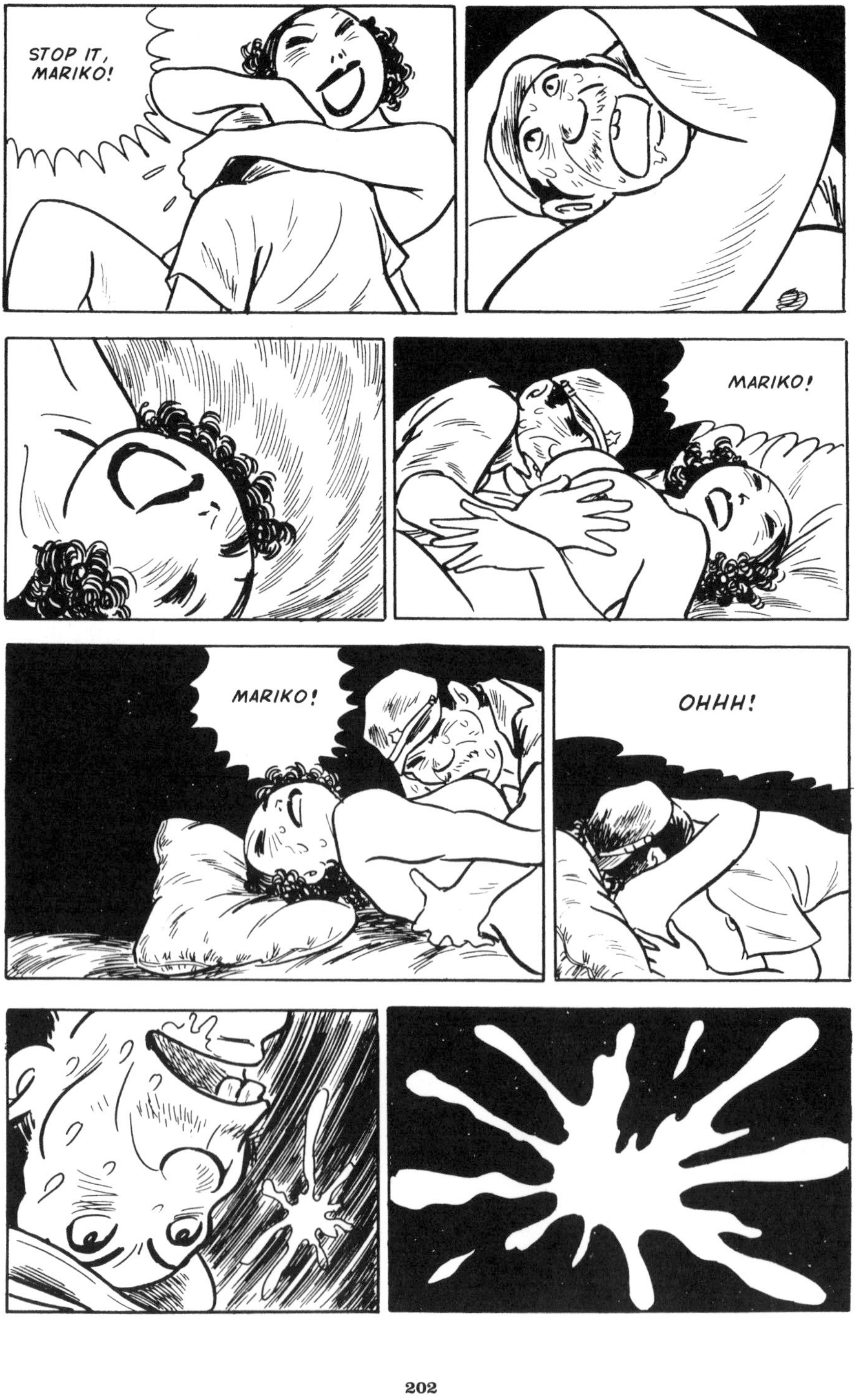
STOP IT, MARIKO!
MARIKO!
MARIKO!
OHHH!

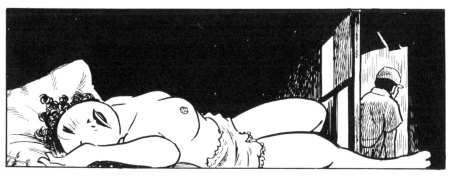

THIS IS HOW IT SHOULD BE. I DON'T WANT ANY FAMILY ANYMORE.

NOW HE'S JUST ANOTHER MAN...

GOOD-BYE, GOOD-BYE.

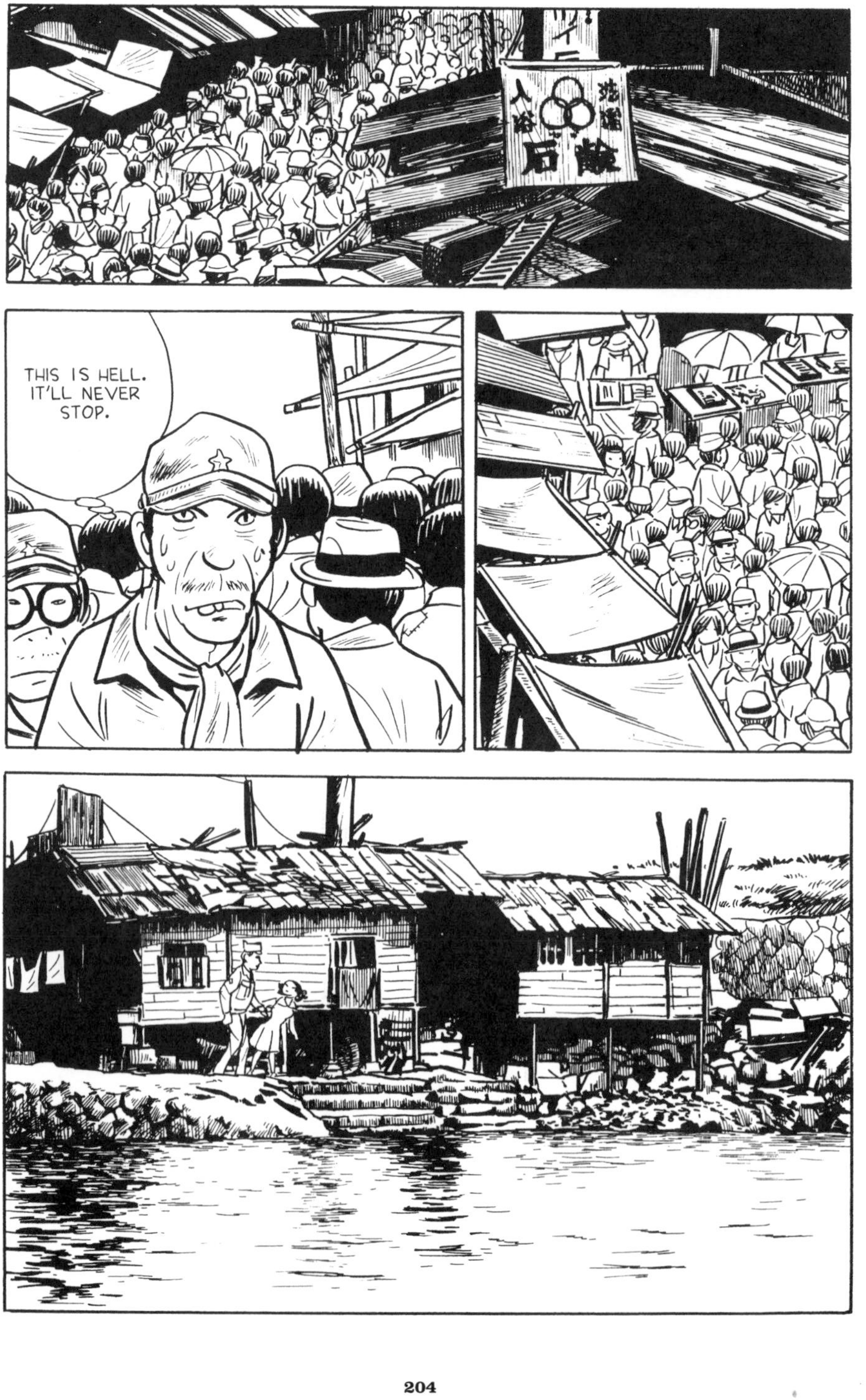
洗濯
入浴
石鹸
THIS IS HELL. IT'LL NEVER STOP.

Q & A with YOSHIHIRO TATSUMI

This written interview was conducted by series editor Adrian Tomine in December, 2007 with the
invaluable assistance of Mitsuhiro Asakawa, Beatrice Marechal, and Yuji Oniki.

ADRIAN TOMINE: *This book collects stories that you produced between the years 1971 and 1972. What was your life like at that time?*
YOSHIHIRO TATSUMI: My fifteen-year stint in rental comics[1] was coming to an end, and I was finally starting to get my work published in magazines. In Japan, we have the saying: "The ship arrives for every journey." It means that good fortune comes when you're in trouble or in a rut. The transition from rental comics to monthly magazines was smooth for me. What really surprised me, though, was the money: magazines paid over ten times what I got in the rental publishing. But the bank managed my income, so I only received a monthly stipend. You see, in the '60s, I published rental comics which sold very poorly, and I ended up owing the bank a lot of money. So in spite of being published in magazines, I was just as poor as I was back then.

AT: *Could you please describe your work environment and the various art supplies you use? (This can pertain to both the time at which the stories in this book were drawn, and the present, if there are differences.)*
YT: I didn't have any assistants for these stories, so I had to do everything from drawing the panel lines to filling in the black backgrounds myself.

Some of them took two days, while others took over a month. The type of paper didn't really matter. I used various kinds of paper. The original art was done on B5 paper (approximately 7" x 10"), smaller than the usual size for *manga* artists. I used a very firm Stein pen, and carbon ink that's used for Japanese calligraphy. Presently, in addition to drawing *manga*, I also publish a catalogue of second-hand *manga* as a hobby. So now piles of used *manga* crowd out my working desk.

AT: *I'm curious about the fate of the original artwork for these stories. Was it always returned to you, or did the publishers retain it? And if it was returned to you, have you held onto the thousands of pages you've drawn over the years?*
YT: The original art I did in rental publishing was never returned to me. Reprinting was inconceivable back then, not only to publishers, but artists as well, so the fact that our art wasn't returned was hardly surprising. A lot of original art for rental comics was just tossed out. So to answer your question, I don't have a single sheet of the original art I did when I worked in rental publishing. Even after my work was published in magazines, I didn't value my original art much. Getting my artwork back didn't seem very important to

---

[1]Rental comics were produced exclusively for *manga* lending shops, which operated similarly to today's video rental stores: the customer borrowed comics in exchange for a small fee. This industry enjoyed its greatest popularity in the 1950s and '60s, and was significant in the development of "alternative" comics in Japan.

me, so I lost over two–thirds of the material. That's how unreliable publishers were. I still have approximately 6,000 pages of artwork, though.

AT: *I believe that at least some of these stories were originally published in* Garo. *Can you explain a little bit about what* Garo *was, and what its impact was on Japanese comics?*

YT: The *manga* artist Sanpei Shirato founded the monthly magazine *Garo* in 1964 in order to publish his historical epic *Kamui Den (The Legend of Kamui)*. He put up the money and Katsuichi Nagai became the publisher. After the serialization of *Kamui Den* was completed, Nagai turned the magazine into an outlet for promising, ambitious *manga* artists. The print runs were low so the pay was the same as it was in rental comics, but artists admired it as "Sanpei Shirato's magazine" and wrote some really wonderful works. Many artists, including Yu Takida, Yoshiharu Tsuge, Shigeru Mizuki, Shinichi Abe, and Seiichi Hayashi, really blossomed as contributors to *Garo*.

AT: *Please correct me if I'm wrong, but I get the impression that your work prior to 1971 was not explicitly political, focusing more on the details of daily life, and with the stories in this book, we see something of a change in direction. Was it a conscious choice on your part to address topics like the war and America's nuclear attacks on Japan more directly? And if so, what prompted this shift?*

YT: I was still heavily influenced by the rental comics style until around 1970. As my work appeared in magazines, I started to tackle social themes. I don't know if it was because of my extensive work in rental publishing, but the magazine editors gave me complete creative freedom. It was the Nixon era, the Vietnam War was turning into a mess, and as the U.S., France, and the Soviet Union competed to launch satellites into space, the future seemed very ominous. Nuclear war seemed inevitable since the Kennedy era. But everyone in Japan was so taken with the rapid economic growth, greeting it as if they were part of some new era. As an alienated *manga* artist working away in a cramped room, I couldn't help but feel disconsolate. I'm sure this feeling permeates my work from this period.

AT: *In the story "Hell," your rendering of Prime Minister Sato seems to suggest that at least some of this story is grounded in factual events. Is the central image of the story (the silhouetted figures) and the emotionally–charged response to it based on real events? Or more broadly, can you talk a little bit about how you came to write this story?*

YT: "Hell" was published in the Japanese edition of *Playboy*. As I said, I was given creative freedom so I chose the topic of Hiroshima; it was something I'd wanted to tackle. I came up with the idea when I came across a famous photo of a shadow burnt into the wall from the radiation heat of the nuclear bomb. The "No More Hiroshima" anti–nuclear protests were very prominent back then. The problem was that most of them only revolved around publicizing gruesome photos of the burn victims with their skin peeling off or charred water bottles. I wanted to create an "anti–nuclear" *manga* that worked as a story. But most of the readers of *Playboy* were primarily interested in the young nude women, so they didn't really respond to it. When "Hell" was published in France, I brought the story with me when I met with an anti–nuclear organization. I was looking for a particular post–bombing photo of Hiroshima, but the woman I met with found the story so offensive she refused to lend me the photo, insisting no one would have murdered a parent in the aftermath of Hiroshima. I ended up purchasing the photo through the Associated Press or United Press International.

AT: *I think "Good–Bye" might be one of your most clearly political stories, at least in terms of depicting the thoughts and attitudes of a variety of people in the aftermath of the war. For the first time (that I'm aware of),* *you seem to make an explicit correlation between current events and the characters' behavior. You've also mentioned this story in one of our previous conversations when the subject of autobiography came up. Can you talk about how you arrived at this story?*

YT: "Good–Bye" was a short story published in a major magazine called *Big Comic*. I grew up in Osaka near a military air base called Itami Airfield. American B–29 bomber planes attacked the area relentlessly every night during the war, and many civilians were killed. I was in the fourth grade when the war ended. I'll never forget how the bombings suddenly came to a halt. The clear blue sky and the ruins shining under the blinding sun. It was so quiet you could only hear the cicadas chirping away. The soldiers from the American occupation came to our town immediately thereafter. During the war, the government had brainwashed us into believing American soldiers were demons, but when they showed up, we thought the "enemy" soldiers were very dashing and kind. That's how they first appeared to me as a fourth grader. But once I saw how these gentlemanly soldiers hugged and kissed young Japanese women in public, I was shocked and disappointed. How could they be so casual and coarse with women?! I was also very upset at the way Japanese adults pretended to be blind to all of this. Before or after school, my friends and I often saw American soldiers having intercourse with Japanese women in the bushes. I'm sure these experiences affected the way I wrote "Good–Bye." In "Good–Bye," the kid who bumps into Mary's father on page four is me. I think that if I had ended up being a writer, I still would have written a story like "Good–Bye." The story didn't really get much response. My editor told me he really liked it when we met at a bar.

AT: *What kind of reaction did you receive to the stories in this book, particularly "Hell" and "Good–Bye"? Has the reaction changed over time, as the stories have been re–printed and translated into other languages?*

YT: As I stated, I didn't get much feedback regarding those stories. A French translation appeared in 1983, twelve years after their original publication. That was the first time I felt I got any kind of response. A young producer from Hollywood actually flew over to Japan to purchase the rights to "Hell." The concept of the Hiroshima shadow still had currency in literature, but "Hell" has yet to be made into a film.

AT: *In the summer of 2006, you traveled to America in conjunction with the publication of* Abandon The Old in Tokyo. *Can you talk a bit about that experience?*

YT: I visited with my wife. Those six days in Los Angeles and San Diego were unforgettably wonderful for both of us. I couldn't believe how popular the convention was. I was so fortunate to receive such a warm welcome from D&Q publicist Peggy Burns and the rest of the staff. What a hectic schedule though! Television and press interviews, not to mention talk shows. Each interviewer had ten minutes. Sometimes the camera staff would barely get around measuring the light and it would be over. I really enjoyed the book signing I did with Adrian at the D&Q booth. I was worried that this book, which was Adrian's project, would sell poorly. So I'm relieved the first printing sold out. I couldn't imagine a more wonderful first visit to America.

AT: *The next work of yours that Drawn & Quarterly intends to publish is* A Drifting Life. *Can you please describe this book?*

YT: *A Drifting Life* is an 820–page autobiographical work set during the tumultuous postwar period in Japan. An untalented boy discovers and pursues the art of *manga*. Amidst the onslaught of American culture flooding the nation after the war, he gets involved in the world of "rental publishing," and develops as an artist. It's also an exploration of the *manga* genre called *gekiga*, and its development beginning in 1958. I hope that the story will reach a wide audience.

Yoshihiro Tatsumi, circa 1972

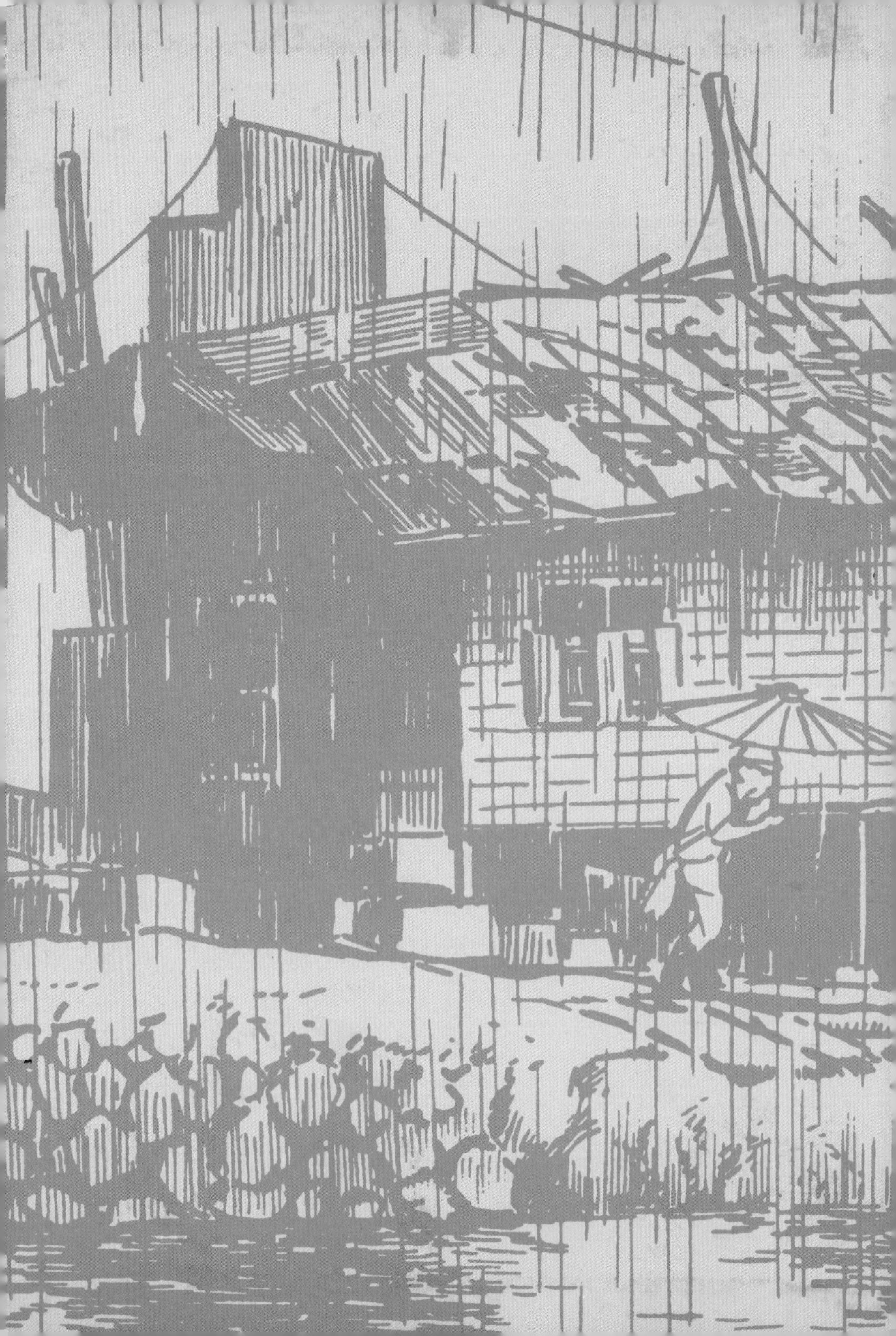